Legal Empowerment in Informal Settlements

This book investigates grassroots, community-led justice strategies — known as legal empowerment — being used to promote the human rights of people living in informal settlements in the Global South.

Residents of informal settlements, also known as slums or *favelas*, encounter a complex array of human rights violations; from systemic discrimination by public officials, to threats to physical security from forced evictions, or arbitrary arrests, to a lack of access to basic services such as housing, water, sanitation and education. This book shows how grassroots justice organizations around the world are working with residents to defend their rights and secure more dignified living conditions. Drawing on original empirical research across 10 countries in Africa, Asia and Latin America, the book demonstrates how legal empowerment can put residents at the centre of holistic approaches to urban development and confront exclusionary and undemocratic systems of governance. The book encompasses practical recommendations and strategies such as rights-based approaches to informality, participation, community mobilization and litigation.

Bridging the gaps between the law on the books and the harsh realities of informality on the ground, this book will be an important read for researchers, practitioners and policymakers, working in realms of social and economic rights, access to justice and urban poverty and development.

Adrian Di Giovanni is the Team Leader for Democratic and Inclusive Governance at Canada's International Development Research Centre (IDRC), where he has worked since 2011. In his prior role at IDRC, he spearheaded a stream of research on law and development, focusing on public law, human rights and legal empowerment. Past roles have included Counsel for the Department of Justice Canada's Human Rights Law Section, and the World Bank's Legal Vice-Presidency. Adrian holds an LLM in international law from New York University and a JD from the University of Toronto. He occasionally teaches at Carleton University's Norman Paterson School of International Affairs and has worked previously in Uganda and Tanzania. A proud dad of two boys who, on occasion, liked to sit on his lap at the computer well past their bedtimes while he worked away on contributions to this volume.

Luciana Bercovich is a human rights lawyer and activist from Argentina; she has been working on access to justice and social rights for more than 20 years. Currently, she is leading the agenda of the Grassroots Justice Network (convened by Namati) in Latin America. Previously, she was Co-Director of ACIJ — Civil Association for Equality and Justice in Argentina. She has a Law degree from Universidad de Buenos Aires, a master's degree in Urban and Regional Development from Universitat Politecnica de Catalunya (UPC), and an MS in International Affairs and Development from the New School. She has authored books, papers and op-eds about social rights, housing and access to justice.

Legal Empowerment in Informal Settlements

Grassroots Experiences in the Global South

Edited by
Adrian Di Giovanni and Luciana Bercovich

Routledge
Taylor & Francis Group
LONDON AND NEW YORK

IDRC · CRDI
International Development Research Centre
Centre de recherches pour le développement international
Canada

Grassroots Justice Network

Designed cover image: Pablo Vitale, 2023

First published 2025
by Routledge
4 Park Square, Milton Park, Abingdon, Oxon OX14 4RN

and by Routledge
605 Third Avenue, New York, NY 10158

Routledge is an imprint of the Taylor & Francis Group, an informa business

This work was carried out with the aid of a grant from the International Development Research Centre, Ottawa, Canada. The views expressed herein do not necessarily represent those of IDRC or its Board of Governors.

British Library Cataloguing-in-Publication Data
A catalogue record for this book is available from the British Library

ISBN: 978-1-032-88637-4 (hbk)
ISBN: 978-1-032-88628-2 (pbk)
ISBN: 978-1-003-53880-6 (ebk)

DOI: 10.4324/9781003538806

Typeset in Times New Roman
by Taylor & Francis Books

Contents

Illustrations

Figures

Tables

Contributors

Prince Aboagye Anokye, a Senior Lecturer in Planning, joined the Department of Planning in 2006. He studied Planning at Kwame Nkrumah University of Science and Technology, Kumasi, Planning, Growth and Regeneration at the University of Cambridge, UK, and Land Management at Erasmus University in Rotterdam. He has over 16 years of experience in teaching, consultancy and research. His research areas include urban planning, administration, and management, with a bias for urban finance, sustainability and governance. He is a member of the Ghana Institute of Planners (MGIP), a member of the International Research Group on Law and Urban Space (IRGLUS), a chartered member of the Chartered Institute of Housing (CMCIH) in the UK, a fellow of the Cambridge Commonwealth Society (FCCS) and an alumnus of the Rockefeller Centre, Bellagio. His research and consultancy have brought him in contact with local and international organisations such as Ministries, Departments and Agencies and Metropolitan, Municipal and District Assemblies in Ghana and Sierra Leone, USAID, ILO, UNDP, UN-Habitat, UNCDF, EU, VNG International, and the World Bank.

Nausheen Anwar is the Founder and Director of the Karachi Urban Lab (KUL) and Professor of City & Regional Planning in the Department of Social Sciences & Liberal Arts (SSLA) at the Institute of Business Administration (IBA). Her research is situated at the intersections of urban planning, critical urban studies, critical geography, anthropology and political ecology. She received her PhD from the Graduate School of Architecture, Planning and Preservation (GSAPP), Columbia University, and has held postdoctoral positions at Harvard University and the Asia Research Institute, National University Singapore.

Aakanksha Badkur is a lawyer, activist and researcher working with marginalized communities in India towards increasing their access to justice. She has worked in collaboration with organizations like Nazdeek, the National Campaign on Dalit Human Rights (NCDHR) and Indian Institute for Human Settlements (IIHS). Her work focuses on capacity-building for community-based activists and supporting them in developing and implementing advocacy strategies for better human rights protections. She has a background in constitutional and public law, human rights, and environmental law, and has represented Dalit communities before the Delhi High Court and the Supreme Court of India in cases pertaining to socio-economic rights and violations. Aakanksha is passionate about community-led research and action to make systems more inclusive and intersectional. Since 2023, Aakanksha has served as the Asia-South Pacific representative in the Steering Committee for the Strategic Litigation Working Group at ESCR-Net.

Rita Corrêa Brandão has served as Director of the Brazilian Institute for Social and Economic Analysis (Ibase) since 2017, becoming the first Black woman to hold this position at the institution. Prior to her directorship, she was a researcher and programmatic line coordinator at Ibase for 12 years. She has a degree in Social Work (UFRJ) and a master's degree in Social Work, Social Policies and Labor (UERJ). At Ibase, she is director of reference and coordinator of research, which has included overseeing the creation of Citizenship Indicators applied to territories and *favelas*, and projects on Local Development, affirmative action, gender and youth. She is also responsible for Ibase's actions and representations linked to human rights. Rita Corrêa Brandão also represents the institution in the Dhesca Brazil Platform, making up the Executive Secretariat, is a Councillor for Rio de Janeiro in the National Human Rights Movement (MNDH), and participates in the Universal Periodic Review Collective — Brazil (RPU) and the Articulation for Human Rights in Brazil.

Priya Ahsan Chowdhury is a Barrister, an Advocate at the Supreme Court of Bangladesh, and an Associate at Dr. Kamal Hossain and Associates. She was called to the Bar of England and Wales from Lincoln's Inn. Priya's main areas of practice are constitutional and administrative law, public interest, human rights and family law. She has provided legal research, drafting, opinions and assisted on litigation on issues related to freedom of expression and, in a pro bono role, on public interest litigation cases related to children's rights and sexual abuse, data protection, citizenship, disability rights, gender discrimination, workplace safety, and illegal eviction of slum dwellers. She has published articles on online speech and freedom of expression, modern-day slavery and the death penalty. Priya was Senior Article Editor for *The City Law Review*, London (2020–2022), and has also been involved with BLAST's Platform for Cyber Violence Against Women and Children. She holds an LLB (Hons.), a Postgraduate Certificate in Media and Communications, and a Post Graduate Diploma in Law from the City University of London, United Kingdom.

Maria Silvia Emanuelli has a law degree from the Statale University of Milan (Italy), and the title of lawyer from the National Forensic Council of Italy. She has a master's degree in Latin American Studies with honourable mention from the National Autonomous University of Mexico (UNAM).

Since 2003 she has worked at the Habitat International Coalition, Office for Latin America (HIC-AL), based in Mexico City, where she currently serves as the coordinator. In 2024, she founded the first clinic for the right to housing in the country together with the Ibero-American University of Mexico City. She is a member of the Advisory Group of the Cultural Space of the Institute of the National Housing Fund for Workers (INFONAVIT) and the Advisory Council of the Head of Government of Mexico City. In her 20 years of work, she has given presentations and courses in Europe, the United States and Latin America on housing, including informal settlements and displacements, land, and urban policies, and has contributed to more than 30 publications.

Sara Hossain is a Senior Advocate at the Supreme Court of Bangladesh, and a partner at the law firm of Dr. Kamal Hossain and Associates. She serves pro bono as the Honorary Executive Director of the Bangladesh Legal Aid and Services Trust (BLAST). She is also currently a Professor of Practice at SOAS, University of London, a member of the United Nations University International Institute of Global Health's High-Level Advisory Committee, and an Overseas Bencher of the Middle Temple. She currently chairs the Independent International Fact Finding Mission on Iran, appointed by the President of the UN Human Rights Council. Sara has been involved in landmark cases on forced eviction and the right to house, equality and discrimination, freedom from torture, and freedom of expression, among others. She writes and speaks on issues of women's rights, equality and non-discrimination, freedom of expression, access to justice and public interest litigation. Sara was educated at Wadham College, Oxford, and called to the Bar from Middle Temple.

Efadul Huq is an Assistant Professor of Environmental Science & Policy and Urban Studies at Smith College, where his work intersects city planning, environmental justice, and feminist geography. With a PhD in Urban and Regional Planning from the University of Illinois at Urbana-Champaign, Huq's research explores the politics of urban space and nature, particularly how informal settlement dwellers navigate and resist oppressive urbanization processes. Huq's scholarship is deeply informed by decolonial and feminist thought, focusing on insurgent planning practices. He is committed to advancing social justice and equitable urban futures through engaged pedagogy and community-centred research.

Mark Kakraba-Ampeh is the Executive Director of Land Resource Management Centre. He is a Land Economist by profession, a Fellow of the Ghana Institution of Surveyors and member of the International Federation of Surveyors (FIG). Mark started his professional practice in the field of Property Valuation, Land Administration and Estate Management in 1990. He served as a Special Assistant to the Minister for Lands and Forestry on land matters in 1998, and in July 1998 he was appointed the Regional Stool Lands Officer for the Western Region of Ghana with the rank of Principal Stool Lands Officer. Mark Kakraba-Ampeh was appointed National Facilitator in October 2007 to oversee the implementation of the component of the Ghana Land Administration Project directed towards Strengthening Customary Land Administration in Ghana. Since 2011, he has undertaken a number of collaborative action research projects with IIED, IDRC, IED Afrique of Senegal, GESDA of Mali and International Institute for Environment of Cameroon.

Soha Macktoom is an Associate Director at the Karachi Urban Lab at the Institute of Business Administration (IBA), Karachi, and Lecturer at the Social Sciences and Liberal Arts Department (SSLA) at IBA. She is an architect and urban planner, with her work looking at the physical transformations of the built environment and how architecture, design and history are tools for understanding the city's informal settlements, urbanization trends, infrastructure and climate.

Catalina Marino is an Argentinean political scientist specialising in urban development planning. She has professional experience in various access to justice and development-related roles. She currently coordinates the Right to the City Program in the Civil Association for Equality and Justice (ACIJ). Previously, she managed a local government upgrading program in one of Buenos Aires's largest slums. She also worked for the Ombudsman Office. She has over 10 years of management, advocacy and research experience in urban development, housing, and slum-upgrading projects, with a strong focus on community participation and gender justice.

Thato Masiangoako is a researcher at the Socio-Economic Rights Institute of South Africa (SERI). She holds a Master of Arts in Politics from the University of the Witwatersrand, a Master of Science in African Politics from the School of Oriental and African Studies (SOAS), University of London and a Bachelor of Arts Joint Honours degree in Politics and International Relations from the University of the Witwatersrand. Her research explores the place of the law in society, policing, protests and other forms of public participation.

Larissa de Souza Ferreira de Morais has a law degree from the Federal University of Rio de Janeiro (UFRJ) and a master's degree in Ethnic-Racial Relations from the Celso Suckow da Fonseca Federal Center for Technological Education (CEFET/RJ). A lawyer and conflict mediator, she is also a researcher at the Brazilian Institute for Social and Economic Analysis (Ibase) and is a member of the Racial Equality Commission of the OAB-RJ (Barra da Tijuca).

Patrick Njoroge, with over a decade of experience, works at Akiba Mashinani Trust. He manages programs in Kenya's informal settlements, emphasizing community-led advocacy, accountability and solution creation. His work focuses on improving basic services, securing land tenure and promoting policies for the inclusion of informal settlements in urban planning and development.

Robson de Aguiar Oliveira is studying for a master's degree in Social Work at the Federal University of Rio de Janeiro (UFRJ). As a researcher, he works on local development studies and projects and on defending the human rights of victims of state violence.

Smith Ouma is a Research Fellow at the Global Development Institute. With a background in Law, his research is inherently interdisciplinary, spanning legal geography, urban politics, urban health and development studies. His primary focus lies in understanding the political economy of informal settlements and systems failings in cities, particularly in Africa. Additionally, he has strong research and professional interest in the field of land law.

Kanza Rizvi is a practicing corporate lawyer in the Pakistan jurisdiction. She is also a dedicated researcher with the Karachi Urban Lab established at the Institute of Business Administration, Karachi, where her research focuses on analyzing the legal landscape of Pakistan in relation to the issue of land displacement in urban Pakistan.

Tanya Renee F. Rosales was a former Program Coordinator and eventually Chief Technical Officer of the Philippine government's P50 Billion Housing Program for informal settler families living in danger areas. She joined SALIGAN as a lawyer in 2022 and is currently a court attorney at the Philippine Court of Tax Appeals. She is also a senior lecturer at the University of the Philippines — College of Law.

Lauren Royston has a deep commitment to social justice and people-centered development. In her professional practice, for over 30 years, she has worked with public interest social justice organisations, urban and rural development NGOs, civic organisations, the public sector and the private sector. Her organisational home is the Socio-Economic Rights Institute of South Africa (SERI), with which she has been associated since its establishment, and currently serves as its Director of Research and Advocacy. Her fields of expertise are land and housing, land governance, development planning, community participation and anti-evictions work, with an emphasis on urban tenure security. She holds a Bachelor of Arts degree in Political Studies and English Literature, a Master of Science in Development Planning and a Master of Arts in Creative Writing, all from the University of the Witwatersrand.

Muhammad Arsam Saleem is a Senior Research Associate at the Karachi Urban Lab (KUL), a multidisciplinary research institute based in Karachi, Pakistan. He completed his master's in City and Regional Planning from Georgia Institute of Technology, USA through a Fulbright Fellowship, and is a current PhD Student in the Environmental Sciences Department at York University.

Jayshree Satpute, recognised by UK's *The Guardian* as one of the "World's Top 100 Inspiring Women", is a human rights lawyer and co-founder of Nazdeek. She started her career in 2006 as a trial court lawyer and advisor on refugee laws, juvenile justice and gender justice. She has litigated Constitutional and Civil matters, with a specialization in Right to Adequate Housing and Access to Health, Environmental and Labor Laws. Extensively experienced in pro-bono lawyering, she has been appointed as Amicus Curiae in several public interest cases. Jayshree has secured positive judgments on cases on Right to Safe Motherhood; Right to Adequate Housing; Rights of Persons with Disability; Prevention of Sexual Harassment of Workplace; Right to Privacy and Press; Minimum Wages of Textile and Garment Workers; and International Law on Diplomatic Immunity. Jayshree has been instrumental in developing and designing Nazdeek's Legal Empowerment Methodology and has authored and published various articles and books. She received her LLB from Dr. Babasaheb Ambedkar University College of Law, Nagpur in 2004 and her LLM from City University London in 2005.

Tauan da Silva Satyro has a degree in Social Work from the Fluminense Federal University (UFF), a master's degree in Public Policies in Human Rights from the Federal University of Rio de Janeiro (UFRJ) and is studying for a PhD in Comparative History at UFRJ. As a researcher at the Brazilian Institute of Social and Economic Analysis, he works on projects and studies related to the defense of human rights and affirmative action.

Nerishka Singh is the Gender Equity Analyst at the Socio-Economic Rights Institute of South Africa (SERI). She holds a Bachelor of Arts in Political Studies and a Bachelor of Law degree from the University of the Witwatersrand. Nerishka's interests include politics, legal transformation and current affairs which touch on the socio-economic realities of different groups in South Africa.

Juan Carlo P. Tejano is an alternative lawyer working with urban poor groups and non-government organizations advocating for community-led housing and the right to the city in the Philippines. He joined SALIGAN in 2019 after working in the public sector and briefly as a lawyer for persons deprived of liberty during the drug war. He is a lecturer at Ateneo de Manila University and De La Salle University Tañada-Diokno School of Law.

Pablo Vitale is the Co-Director of the Civil Association for Equality and Justice (ACIJ), has an undergraduate and postgraduate in Political Science and Social Policies and is a PhD candidate in Social Sciences at the University of Buenos Aires. In this academic unit, he is a member of the Urban Studies Area (IIGG, FSOC-UBA) and the Photography Studies Area (CCom, FSOC-UBA). He teaches undergraduate and graduate public policy, urbanism and photography courses at national and regional universities.

Jane Weru, a lawyer by profession, has over 30 years' experience in facilitating multistakeholder partnerships to address the needs of marginalized urban communities. She has contributed to numerous public interest litigations to stop forceful evictions and violent demolitions and has influenced policy processes to safeguard the land tenure rights of people living in informal settlements. Since August 2018, Jane has served as Project Leader of the Mukuru Special Planning Area, a project of the Nairobi County Government, aimed at developing an integrated development plan to improve the lives of the 100,000 households that presently occupy over 600 acres of land within the city. Jane is an Ashoka Fellow and served as a member of the National Task Force for the preparation of the Community Land Bill and the Evictions and Resettlement Bill. Jane holds a master's degree in NGO Management from the London School of Economics.

Acknowledgements

A note of thanks and deep gratitude to all the chapter authors for their trust in embarking on this journey with us, first in breathing life into the vision for this book and then generously sharing their experiences and reflections. We acknowledge the efforts and dedication of the authors to find time amidst many urgent and competing demands, and their determination in working through rounds of feedback and revision — as well as patience and understanding in bearing with all hiccups while working virtually.

This book would not have been possible without the ongoing help, big and small, along the way from colleagues in our respective organizations. A special note of appreciation, from Namati and the Grassroots Justice Network team to Marta Almela, Poorvi Chitalkar and Erin Kitchell, especially for hands-on assistance with an in-person workshop in Nairobi in March 2023, and from the International Development Research Centre to Ana De Oliveira, Tanya Bandula-Irwin, Anne-Lise Bloch, Laura Griffin and, in the final weeks, to Maggie Piper who jumped in with agility and skill to help with final fine-tuning and formatting of references. Maggie Piper prepared the Alt Text to accompany images in the book, for readers enjoying this book through use of a screen reader. We are deeply grateful to Mary O'Neill for her magical touch in editing the chapters to make all our words shine. Thank you also to Helena Hurd and Katerina Lade at Routledge for their patience and able guidance through the publishing process.

The book was finalized during a period in which we have seen many of the ideals that we have long championed, as well as long-time friends and collaborators, come increasingly under threat. Our hope is that the courage and determination of the informal settlement communities and the grassroots justice organizations featured in this book — and their tireless struggles for change against all odds — will offer some hope and inspiration, however small, as we continue to navigate choppy waters. We dedicate this book to them and the communities who continue to fight for justice around the world.

1 Legal empowerment in informal settlements

Grassroots experiences in the Global South[1]

Adrian Di Giovanni and Luciana Bercovich

Introduction[2]

In a Report to the United Nations (UN) General Assembly, Leilani Farha, at the time the UN Special Rapporteur on the Right to Adequate Housing, reflected on the realities of informal settlements in the following terms:

> Informal settlements are often an incredible accomplishment, a profound expression of individuals, families and communities claiming their place and their right to housing. They are "habitats made by people", who are creating homes, culture and community life in the most adverse circumstances.
>
> (Farha, 2018, p. 13)

Implicit in that passage is an attempt to overturn the dominant narrative of informal settlements — to see beyond the stigma and deplorable conditions residents face, and rather cast a light on their agency, rights and dignity. That framing is presented to start this book, as a beacon that shines across the analyses and experiences of informal settlement communities in the chapters that follow.

In the Global South, informal settlements (e.g. slums, *favelas*) are a persistent development challenge, as countries continue to face population growth and rapid urbanization. The number of people living in informal settlements is at an all-time high — over one billion people, or about a quarter of the world's urban population — accounting for over half of the population in some cities in the Global South (Reckford & Aki-Sawyerr, 2023).[3] With homelessness, forced evictions and urban expansion on the rise in virtually every country, urban poverty and exclusion stand to increase in the future. The development challenges posed by informal settlements and conditions of poverty and vulnerability in urban centres around the world are complex and structural in nature. Solving them requires addressing several problems at once, such as ensuring access to affordable housing and tenure security, and to health services, potable water[4] and sanitation, which often link to larger environmental injustices. It requires offering livelihood and educational opportunities and providing public financing for infrastructure and services,

DOI: 10.4324/9781003538806-1

like electricity (Asociación Civil por la Igualdad y la Justicia [ACIJ], 2010, p. 11). There are also perennial debates over how best to plan the world's ever-growing cities, with the intensifying pressures of migration from rural areas and neighbouring countries, and how best to ensure equitable access to urban space to accommodate a diversity of social, cultural and economic ways of life.

This book captures the experiences of informal settlement communities in 10 countries of Latin America, Africa and Asia, told from the perspective of organizations that have worked with residents to improve living conditions and guarantee their rights and dignity. While each is distinct, the communities share characteristics typically associated with living in informality. Consistent with UN-Habitat's (2015) definition of informal settlements, residents lack "security of tenure vis-à-vis the land or dwellings". This can range from "squatting to informal rental housing"; lacking or being "cut off from basic services and city infrastructure"; and, for the most part, non-compliance "with current planning and building regulations" in settlements that are "often situated in geographically and environmentally hazardous areas" (p. 1). Poor access to water stands out as a challenge shared across contexts, with access to toilets and proper sanitation being particularly scarce in the African contexts. Women and girls face a heightened risk of sexual violence, especially at night when needing to access services outside the home, which reflects the deep gender discrimination within each society. Communities also live with environmental hazards and a lack of public waste collection. Finally, across research contexts, residents generally lack an awareness of the rights and mechanisms that would ostensibly protect them from the challenges in the settlements.

Many of these conditions are summed up as the consequence of the wider public and institutional discrimination and stigmatization that residents suffer. The content and application of laws and policies, as well as the acts, decisions and omissions of public authorities, consequently perpetuate the denial of a host of civil and political rights for the urban poor, including rights related to democratic citizenship (UNGA, 2011). For instance, residents may face forced relocation or eviction, unlawful arrest or abuse by police, and are often driven to take up low paid, precarious or exploitative work in the informal sector. In this sense, informal settlements often represent, by their very existence, an interrelated set of human rights violations, which can generally be referred to as socio-spatial segregation (Vitale et al., 2020).[5]

The coronavirus pandemic and related lockdown measures foregrounded the segregated realities of informal settlements with painful clarity, especially their overcrowding, lack of basic public services[6] and rampant reduction of income and food insecurity, along with increased gender inequality, gender-based violence and forced evictions (Okem et al., 2022). According to UN-Habitat (n.d.), physical distancing, self-quarantine, self-isolation or community-wide lockdowns were often practically impossible in informal settlements, which exposed their populations to a higher risk of contracting the virus.

In the face of these deep challenges, grassroots organizations across the Global South, working hand-in-hand with communities, have deployed great resourcefulness, creativity and often courage. This book provides the first collection of studies of grassroots, community-led justice strategies — known as legal empowerment — in informal settlements. The organizations supporting those strategies describe, in their own words, ground-level empirical data and lessons from a mix of recent promising efforts, working with informal settlement communities to protect, promote and fulfil their rights in cities. Drawing on first-hand experiences in Buenos Aires, Rio de Janeiro, the State of Morelos in Mexico, Accra, the outskirts of Durban, Nairobi, Karachi, Delhi, Dhaka and Manila, the chapters capture the methods and processes, the successes and potential limitations of using the law and human rights to confront urban poverty and exclusion as part of a broader multidisciplinary and community-led approach to urban development. The authors are a mix of lawyers, activists, technical experts and researchers who all, in one way or another, have supported informal settlement communities and their use of legal empowerment strategies, such as rights-based approaches to participation, community mobilization and litigation. Several chapters describe results of participatory action-research projects that the authors led on legal empowerment in informal settlements; in other chapters, the authors reflect on several years or decades of support to informal settlement communities or social movements.

The book process

The objective of this book first and foremost is to provide a stage for the chapter authors to capture and share their grassroots experiences with a larger global audience of academics and practitioners. Most authors draw on years of support to the communities, which brings a unique and rich contribution to their analysis. This was enriched by a drafting process that included peer-to-peer exchanges at various points, to enable authors to share their experiences and lessons with one another. Most exchanges were conducted virtually, beginning during pandemic lockdown periods. Most authors convened in Nairobi, Kenya in March 2023 for an in-person workshop to present their draft chapters and exchange lessons collectively through structured discussion of a common set of questions (Grassroots Justice Network, 2023). Those questions in turn drew on the conceptual framework and priority themes from an earlier study on legal empowerment in informal settlements.[7] During this workshop and subsequently, authors also had the chance to peer-review each other's working drafts. Drawing on a wider range of country experiences, the in-person discussions provided an opportunity to update, expand and scrutinize the original conceptual framework, which underpins the comparative analysis in this introduction. That analysis similarly follows the methodology from the earlier study. It consists of a qualitative analysis of the chapters' case studies, which "took the form of a learning review rather than a more hypothesis-driven research", seeking to "capture, analyze, and distill" a common set of lessons from the primary findings of the participatory action-research projects (Lyall et al., 2013, pp. 63–64).

Taken together, the collection of chapters answers the call for deeper, systematic and comparative evidence and lesson-sharing on legal empowerment, including for the more specialized themes and problem-areas, such as urban informal settlements (Domingo & O'Neil, 2014; Goodwin & Maru, 2017; Waldorf, 2019). The lessons that emerge from the collection also help to articulate a distinct place for legal empowerment as a field of legal study, by situating legal empowerment efforts within existing debates on law and social change, law and development, community-based lawyering and public interest law advocacy — from the perspective of frontline legal empowerment leaders. This introductory chapter seeks to make this case in more detail. Briefly, from a legal perspective, existing analysis of the law in relation to various urban development challenges tends to focus on: the shortcomings of existing legal frameworks (e.g., planning laws, building standards and property rights); the law as a tool to enable financing and investment; or the use of legal frameworks to overcome informality in its different forms (Fernandes & Varley, 1998; Glasser & Berrisford, 2015; McAuslan, 2003). Relatively little analysis exists, however, on the strategies settlement residents have deployed to achieve access to justice and ensure that legal protections, for human rights or otherwise, respond to their needs and realities. Finally, in relation to urban development, the collection of chapters proposes an additional set of lessons and strategies to tackle socio-spatial segregation in informal settlements as part of a larger body of participatory, community-driven and human rights-based approaches.[8]

With those aims in mind, this introduction plays two complementary roles: first, to introduce the grassroots organizations, informal settlement communities and legal empowerment strategies that are the protagonists of each chapter; and second, to provide a comparative analysis of their experiences. The basic argument that underpins the chapters is that a holistic legal empowerment approach can contribute in unique ways to addressing socio-spatial segregation in informal settlements. To set the stage, this introduction first explains the concept of legal empowerment and its distinct features in informal settlements. To contextualize the range of legal empowerment strategies highlighted in subsequent chapters, it presents the informal settlement contexts, the residents and the organizations supporting them, following the sequence of chapters in the book.

Central to the conception of legal empowerment that emerges across the chapters is how it deploys the law — especially constitutional and human rights — to confront collective and structural challenges in the face of uncertain and complex institutional pathways. Informality, unsurprisingly, plays a defining role in efforts to use legal empowerment to bridge the gap between the laws as they exist on the books and the harsh realities in informal settlements — and thus bears a deeper discussion in its own right. The comparative analysis then focuses on some core elements that are part of the holistic approach that emerges from the chapters: rights-based approaches to participation; litigation as a strategy for mobilization; community-led, participatory upgrading; and the search for justice in closed spaces. This chapter concludes with some final reflections on recent and emerging crises like the COVID-19 pandemic and climate emergency, and mixed prospects and hope for positive change in the face of closing civic space across regions.

The chapters, organizations and their legal empowerment experiences

This book follows a broad arc, moving from comparative analysis of multiple contexts and experiences in the first two chapters to individual accounts of the legal empowerment struggles of urban communities and advocates in 10 countries on three continents.

Following this introduction, Chapter 2 presents an analytical lens to understand the experiences of women, and then applies it to the experiences in three of the chapter contexts: Delhi (Chapter 6), Durban (Chapter 9) and Buenos Aires (Chapter 8). The latter also draws on the Chapter 2 author's direct experiences with the Asociación Civil por la Igualdad y la Justicia (ACIJ, a civil society organization). Through comparative analysis, the author demonstrates how, even without adopting a gender lens, legal empowerment campaigns can achieve improved material conditions for women. Much more explicit efforts are needed, however, to advance gender equality, without which, deeper transformative changes — like strengthening women's awareness of their rights, or women's participation in key public decision-making spaces — will prove elusive. So too will the larger goal of redressing power imbalances, which is central to the conception of legal empowerment underpinning this book.

Following the comparative analyses provided by this introduction and Chapter 2, the first two case study chapters then describe experiences from action research projects that experimented with legal empowerment strategies for participation in informal settlements in Rio de Janeiro, Brazil and Accra, Ghana. While these two contexts and sets of interventions differ in important ways, the use of legal empowerment strategies was new to these communities and the organizations that supported them. In Rio de Janeiro, the civil society organization iBase worked alongside *favela* communities to defend their social and economic rights during a politically charged period in Brazil. Chapter 3 presents the positive lessons and shifts in perspective that iBase gained when they combined an existing participatory methodology based on citizenship indicators and ongoing social justice activism with grassroots legal advocacy strategies. In Accra, Ghana, a consortium of organizations — Kwame Nkrumah University of Science and Technology, the Land Resource Management Centre (a non-governmental organization), and the People's Dialogue on Human Settlements (a community-based organization) — piloted Community Governance Committees in three informal settlements. The experiences of these committees over three years, which are depicted in Chapter 4, demonstrate several successes but also limitations of legal empowerment participation strategies.

On a similar theme, Chapter 5 documents an innovative, large-scale participatory process developed by Akiba Mashinani Trust, a community-based organization, to secure access to water and sanitation for the residents of Mukuru, the largest informal settlement in Nairobi, Kenya. The chapter depicts the holistic approach taken in this participatory process, as part of a wider effort to implement Mukuru's designation as a special planning area (SPA), a path-breaking government action that aims to redevelop the settlement through community-led initiatives. These experiences are echoed in Chapter 6 which delves into the ongoing journey of Nazdeek, a women-led legal empowerment organization, to support women paralegals in Ambedkar Camp in Delhi, India. A holistic approach is similarly seen with Nazdeek's initial efforts to strengthen participatory decision-making and legal awareness within the community. Subsequent efforts to move beyond crisis-oriented responses to evictions by securing incremental improvements have, in recent years, culminated in a community-led participatory planning exercise to create a plan for *in situ* upgrading of the settlement. In the Philippines, Sentro ng Alternatibong Lingap Panlegal (SALIGAN), a legal resource non-governmental organization, has similarly promoted a community-led, participatory model for redevelopment of informal settlements — in this case through "people's plans". Chapter 7 offers reflections on SALIGAN's holistic efforts — analysed through a "right to the city" lens — to push for the incorporation of people's plans in national housing policy and legislation while also supporting two informal settler communities in Metro Manila in their effort to develop and achieve government buy-in of their plans.

The next two chapters zoom out to examine the longer-term cycles of legal and political mobilization of residents and community-led organizations, working with legal allies, over two decades or more in Argentina and South Africa. Chapter 8 traces the arc of legal empowerment strategies ACIJ has deployed in supporting residents of Villa 31 in Buenos Aires — spanning from their first efforts at the turn of the century to quell threats of mass eviction, up to the redevelopment of the neighbourhood in recent years under an urbanization law. Litigation and community-led advocacy appear as key strategies within broader efforts to achieve formal recognition of the settlement and expand residents' rights. Similarly, Chapter 9 analyses how the Socio-Economic Rights Institute of South Africa (SERI), a human rights civil society organization, has supported the use of litigation by South Africa's largest shack-dwellers social movement, Abahlali baseMjondolo, as part of a holistic and long-lasting accompaniment. Court cases to defend land occupations and address landlessness are pursued hand-in-hand with a broader set of strategies to push for structural change, build informal settlement residents' power and enjoin the government at different levels to uphold the rights of residents enshrined in South Africa's transformational Constitution.

The path to success, however, is by no means guaranteed, and often fraught with contradictory or unpredictable results. In Mexico, a litigation case that emerged from a broader social mobilization of several informal neighbourhoods resulted in the country's first-ever recognition of the violation of the human right to water. In Chapter 10, one of the lawyers who supported the litigation, from Habitat International Coalition America Latina (HIC-AL, the Latin America chapter of a global right to housing network), reflects on the legacy of that landmark judgment in the 10 years since. To this day, the women who brought the case enjoy access to water, albeit precariously, but the supply was never extended to the rest of the neighbourhood. Deeper challenges of structural discrimination and exclusion of poor populations — seemingly unaltered by litigation — persist. These are also front and centre in the final two case study chapters. In Chapter 11, drawing on findings from an action research project, a team from the Karachi Urban Lab (KUL) at the Institute of Business Administration (IBA University) analyse the results of using litigation to resist two large infrastructure projects in Karachi. Far from helping resist eviction and protect the rights of the informal settlement communities, the cases arguably served to perpetuate and reinforce longstanding discrimination and power imbalances against urban poor communities — due to the judiciary's tendency to uphold government interests, seemingly unquestioned. To conclude, Chapter 12 describes the efforts of the Bangladesh Legal Aid and Services Trust (BLAST) in supporting three ongoing public interest litigation cases in Dhaka, Bangladesh. The analysis of those cases demonstrates the positive impacts of litigation — whether tangibly, in stopping evictions, or more intangibly, in shifting officials' perceptions about settlement residents. It further recounts how litigation, even at the Supreme Court level, was combined with other strategies of community education, participation and mobilization. The authors also reflect on the impacts of climate change on informal settlements in Bangladesh and the challenges they face in the near future.

Finally, the exchanges that fed this volume also benefited greatly from the active participation and experiences of the Justice and Empowerment Initiatives (JEI), a grassroots legal empowerment organization in Nigeria that has supported an intercity network of paralegals, working hand-in-hand with the country's largest social movement of the urban poor — the Nigerian Slum / Informal Settlement Federation. Their experiences are referenced at various points in this chapter's comparative analysis. In recent years, setbacks have come to overshadow earlier hard-fought victories to expand communities' rights and resist violence and government abuse and unlawful evictions. These setbacks include government-sponsored brute force against settlements, in defiance of court orders. The very hope needed to sustain legal empowerment efforts now hangs in the balance, echoing challenges of shrinking democratic spaces globally — and across chapters. The compounding challenges and setbacks facing informal settlements are taken up in the concluding reflections below. More practically, the constant cycle of responding to emergencies thwarted multiple efforts by JEI to put pen to paper and tell their story in a planned chapter.

The distinctive features of legal empowerment in informal settlements

Legal empowerment is a relatively new and flexible concept that continues to evolve and be redefined with breakthroughs in its implementation in practice. The language of legal empowerment first appeared towards the start of the 21st century to capture "the use of legal services and related development activities to increase disadvantaged populations' control over their lives" (Golub, 2003, p. 5).[9] Central to legal empowerment are efforts to support "the poor and excluded" to lead the "process of systemic change through which [they] become able to use the law, the legal system, and legal services to protect and advance their rights and interests as citizens and economic actors" (Commission on Legal Empowerment of the Poor & United Nations Development Programme [UNDP], 2008, p. 3). Beyond the resolution of an individual or set of disputes, legal empowerment's use of the law and legal strategies ultimately seeks to shift the power imbalances that drive the denial of the rights of affected groups and the larger injustices they face in society.

Over time, a range of definitions has emerged which casts legal empowerment's goals and methods in broader or narrower terms. The tighter definitions tend to emphasize supporting the agency and capacity of individuals to claim rights on a more case-by-case level, reflecting legal empowerment's community legal aid roots.[10] A broader conception of legal empowerment is oriented towards systemic change, and links efforts to addressing structural injustices, socio-economic barriers and shifting power dynamics.[11] Based on experiences across the chapters in this book, we adopt a broader conception of legal empowerment. This conception entails a less circumscribed set of activities, but nonetheless delineates a distinctive boundary between legal empowerment and the complementary social and political efforts to tackle structural problems — again, rooted in power imbalances — like poverty and urban segregation (Sage et al., 2009). Similarly, this conception embraces what Satterthwaite (2022) terms "critical legal empowerment" which emphasizes "community-based efforts to engage the legal system in strategies to shift power downward" and how those efforts use human rights "as a means [to] fundamentally alter unjust systems" (p. 7).

There are several common elements distinctive to legal empowerment in informal settlement contexts. The first element, already alluded to, is legal empowerment's immediate targeting of collective and structural issues, notably the array of human rights violations suffered by informal settlement residents. The challenge at the structural level is to promote stronger social and urban integration, to improve residents' quality of life, and to overcome the visible markers that drive current narratives of stigmatization and prevent residents from exercising their citizenship and participating in society (Klaufus, 2012, p. 695). For instance, public policy responses aimed at providing access to services such as sanitation, electricity or water usually encompass all or part of a settlement by their nature and are not as effectively addressed through individual claims. From a practical standpoint, a basic insight guiding several of the case study efforts is that "achieving justice and legal solutions requires multidisciplinary research (lawyers, urban planners, finance specialists, and community organizers) and a mix of legal and nonlegal interventions" (Weru et al., 2015, p. 235). Conversely, the experiences in some of the chapters point to the limits of legal strategies and thus serve as a caution against relying too heavily on litigation or legal remedies, for instance. The emphasis on collective struggles in informal settlements also shares strong affinities to community lawyering, which sees the need to move beyond atomized, depoliticized or overly individualistic approaches to legal support as essential to achieving systemic change (Elsesser, 2013, p. 376). Communities are at the centre of these approaches: they are best positioned to understand the realities and injustices they face, and should therefore take the lead in any legal action and in defining their own political objectives. A difference with traditional legal advocacy is that community lawyering mainly prioritizes helping to build the capacity, leadership and power of communities more broadly, as opposed to achieving results or legal victories (Cruz, 1999, pp. 240–241; Diamond, 2015, p. 397; Healy & Taylor, 2016, p. 2). This mix of goals will re-emerge in the discussion of litigation below.

A main set of challenges in pursuing structural change in informal settlements relates to how residents access public institutions, including justice institutions. Residents tend to live physically close to local governments, state agencies and services providers' offices, yet nonetheless feel a symbolic distance or barrier. On one level, this distance arises because of the institutional complexity in urban settings. Municipal or local governments have gained an ever-larger set of roles and responsibilities in past decades (Joseph, 2019, pp. 77–79). At the same time, a range of powers and responsibilities tend to be spread across multiple layers of overlapping or competing provincial or state jurisdictions, institutions and related regulatory frameworks.[12] Policy approaches to urban poverty and planning have in some cases resulted in contradictory legal frameworks. For example, constitutional or international regulatory frameworks might oblige the state to guarantee the human rights of settlement residents on the one hand, yet criminal and administrative legal frameworks frequently treat settlements and many of their residents' activities as illegal on the other. This tension between applicable legal frameworks is particularly clear in eviction and relocation processes (Amigo, 2009, p. 21; Carman & Yacovino, 2007, p. 31). As a result, the pathway to seeking accountability is elusive and requires coordinating efforts across a complex network of institutional powers and capacities (Farha, 2014, para. 23). Even when the legal protections are clear, a few of the chapters capture how stubbornly entrenched discriminatory and anti-poor government practices can be — with governments seemingly impervious to the illegality of their own practices. Additionally, sweeping changes in policy approaches are common, particularly with changes in government, which can hinder the long-term coherence needed for structural change — and wipe out hard-fought victories, as seen in more than one chapter.

From a tactical standpoint, in the face of this symbolic distance, legal empowerment efforts take advantage of the physical closeness between residents and public officials and institutions in urban contexts and combine an arguably broader and more flexible range of strategies. One set of strategies could be described in terms of political or social advocacy, with communities and residents mobilizing collective action and using their physical presence to exert pressure at institutions' offices and front doors through demonstrations and sit-ins, for example. Similarly, in advocating for change, groups recognize the need for larger coalitions, i.e., "strength in numbers" strategies, to achieve a larger and effective voice by and on behalf of informal settlement residents (such as by linking with the media, non-governmental organizations, independent public institutions and other pressure groups). To illustrate, the team from Nairobi (Chapter 5) describes a petition-drive followed by a public demonstration by thousands of women from Mukuru, who marched to the Ministry of Health to demand improved sanitation in the settlement. Physical closeness is also used as a tool to raise societal awareness of the disparities in living conditions of informal settlement residents vis-à-vis residents of the "formal" city, with whom they often live side-by-side. In Karachi (Chapter 11), the authors describe how a series of efforts by communities in the past, like sit-ins, letter-writing, social media and traditional media campaigns helped raise public awareness enough to compel the state to offer compensation to residents for some evictions or forestall others before they occurred.

How human rights shape legal empowerment strategies

Unsurprisingly, the legal frameworks in the case study countries and cities play an important role in shaping the opportunities or obstacles for informal settlement populations and, in turn, the legal empowerment strategies that organizations identify as most relevant at a given moment. In the absence of supportive legislation, organizations have appealed to human rights to advocate for the legitimacy and legality of existing "illegal" settlement realities, or to underpin advocacy to improve existing legal protections, especially in contexts where public officials view the reality of the settlements in a simplified and binary way (i.e., formality–informality or legality–illegality). Constitutional protections, especially in guaranteeing social and economic rights — which include the right to housing — play a crucial role, where they exist. The experiences across chapters suggest that as human rights are more firmly entrenched in a country's constitution and legislation, the more likely those will be the first point of reference to ground residents' claims. In their absence, organizations sometimes look to international or regional human rights protections that their countries adhere to. For instance, within both Latin America and Africa there has been regional recognition of the right to housing with respect to informal settlements, which buttresses the national level protections, for instance, through the Inter-American Commission on Human Rights and the African Court on Human Rights. The normative value of human rights in those instances derives from the international responsibility of the state which, in some contexts, can contribute to tipping the scale towards the inhabitants' rights, or creating the basis for grounding a claim where none other exists. In a complementary way, organizations have taken inspiration, and even relied on, jurisprudence in other countries, notably South Africa, with trailblazing cases such as *Grootboom, Port Elizabeth*, and further afield in India, the *Olga Tellis*, and subsequent cases.

Lastly, using a human rights narrative to frame the situation of informal settlements can also have symbolic effects and contribute to generating greater support and sympathy in society. The deeper role of human rights in providing a normative framework, arguably, is to complexify positions about informality across contexts. As a set of standards or guidelines to integrate informal settlements into the formal "city with rights", human rights are conditioned on respecting the identity and preferences of the community and guaranteeing their active participation in the urban integration process. As Pablo Vitale, author of Chapter 8 (on Buenos Aires) notes, informality has two faces: the solidarity and efforts of communities to auto-construct housing and urban spaces, but also the grave urban inequalities that urban spaces too often represent and perpetuate.

More generally, the uses and framing of human rights in the chapters echo accounts in recent years, from academic research, of how social justice movements in "many parts of the world" are sharing "ideas and practices developed in one locality" across different countries — that is to say, "transnationally" (Merry, 2006, p. 38) — and transforming human rights "into tools that *become* relevant to everyday struggles of marginalised peoples" (Chase, 2016, p. 703). The uses of human rights by the communities and organizations across chapters gives further expression to the shift in roles for human rights advocates that Satterthwaite envisages as central to critical legal empowerment — in part to move beyond critiques of human rights as being overly centred on legalism. That shift entails legal empowerment advocates acting as "reliable partners" or "allies" of "movements led by the communities experiencing grave rights deprivations" as part of broader "efforts to shift power toward those most directly affected" (Satterthwaite, 2022, p. 3). In this sense, the chapters demonstrate the transformative potential of legal empowerment, whereby communities and social movements widely appropriate the human rights framework, changing narratives and discourses, while deploying approaches that then contribute to shifting planning policies and other efforts to address socio-urban segregation.

The emphasis on human rights, in that light, reflects the approaches that residents and legal empowerment organizations have pursued, as depicted across the chapters, and how they frame the challenges in informal settlements. Moreover, to echo legal scholar Daniel Brinks (2019), the challenge is not simply one of access to institutions and rights, but of the ability to shape those institutions and rights and contest outcomes, once residents manage to lower the barriers to access (pp. 348–349). In other words, the role of human rights stretches beyond doctrine to questions of how residents can shape the content and application of laws. Those questions, in turn, are fundamentally about state–society relationships and the power dynamics that govern them. The stronger constitutional guarantees in some contexts reflect a pre-existing shift in those relationships, premised on ensuring greater political, social and economic inclusion for citizens — especially those who have not previously benefited from ameliorative public policies. Constitutional protections, in this sense, contribute to the foundational ideal of human rights of "leveling the playing field" by mediating power dynamics and shaping inclusive terms of engagement. From that perspective, the crucial role of legal empowerment strategies in informal settlements is in how they contribute to confronting and shifting the power imbalances that drive the exclusion or segregation from public life that residents experience.[13] These strategies are essential for residents to give life on the ground to the transformative capacities of rights (Vitale et al., 2020, p. 11). The experiences across this volume suggest that the effectiveness of such strategies lies in their ability to move constantly in and out of the formal and informal spheres, and to mediate various inherent tensions between them.

The level of constitutional recognition of the right to housing and related human rights, across the chapter country contexts, roughly breaks down into three categories. In Argentina (especially under Buenos Aires' city constitution), Brazil, India, Kenya, South Africa and the Philippines, a stronger constitutional recognition arguably reflects a pre-existing, often transformative shift in those state–society relationships. This shift was realized through hard-fought constitutional reforms or, as in India, progressive expansion of rights under the constitution to align with widespread realities of poverty and exclusion in society. Interestingly, in those chapters, human rights could appear muted on the surface because informal settlement residents' strategies to claim their rights have moved beyond foundational questions of recognition. Those efforts, in other words, jump more quickly to finer-tuned questions of design and implementation of public policies; they have moved beyond a prior stage, to cite the Buenos Aires chapter, when "simple statements appealing to basic rights suffice". By contrast, organizations are more likely to rely on international human rights protections and mechanisms to drive prior efforts to open space for initial recognition of residents' rights (as in Mexico, with the right to water). The larger reflection is that legal empowerment organizations are strategic in mobilizing human rights in the dance between spheres. To be sure, even in the contexts where rights are more firmly established, their transformative capacity to neutralize power imbalances is by no means a given. The experiences in South Africa illustrate an enduring (and even violent) gap between the promise to level the playing field and the fulfillment on the ground of the country's transformative post-Apartheid constitution. In similar ways, drastic shifts in political power provide a backdrop to the Philippines and Brazil chapters. The former experienced a backsliding from earlier positive gains in rights, while the latter endured a more volatile pendulum swing between polar opposites.

The second category involves contexts that saw an initial incremental recognition and protection of rights. In Bangladesh, there is no legal or constitutional recognition of the right to housing, yet judicial interventions have been successful in securing interim protection orders — which government authorities then respected, sometimes for years, while cases worked their ways through the courts. A "nascent housing jurisprudence" (Chapter 12) is even emerging from the few cases that were decided. In Ghana, a case study community was able to take preventative action through the courts to thwart an eviction, at a time when the Supreme Court tentatively opened the door, on unrelated issues, to social and economic rights being justiciable under the country's constitution (*Ghana Lotto Operators Association and others v National Lottery Authority*, 2007–2008). In Mexico, as already described, a landmark judgment recognized the right to water for the first time under that country's constitution. The experiences in those three countries suggest some positive shifts to enable residents to claim their rights, but fewer signs of a deeper or more transformational political or legal shift needed to redress the widespread exclusion and inequalities in the informal settlements. Indeed, reflecting on the experiences in Dhaka, the team from BLAST is quite explicit on the need for deeper engagement with city officials and political actors to ensure housing justice, among other goals.

The experiences in Karachi, Pakistan involve a third category of contexts where the recognition of rights — whether in formal legislation or by the courts — is faltering or outright elusive. The power imbalances in those cases appear so deeply rooted that political officials enjoy nearly complete deference and alignment in views from the judiciary. The reality encountered in Lagos, Nigeria is perhaps more extreme, where public officials have defied the courts' orders to protect residents with seeming impunity (Grassroots Justice Network, 2023). In addition, the courts have repeatedly denied attempts to invoke international human rights treaties, in efforts to assert residents' rights domestically. As a result, the teams in Nigeria essentially face the double challenge of gaining a foothold for rights claims and taking the subsequent step of upholding those rights. Absent more supportive language in domestic law, the team appealed to foundational concepts of human rights, with mixed success in marshaling creative legal arguments to secure court orders to protect residents. This last category of contexts, in sum, tests the limits of legal empowerment and human rights in helping confront and shift power imbalances, suggesting the need for a broader set of social and political strategies — and likely longer-term processes — to push for transformative change.

Finally, the "right to the city" emerges from this analysis as an umbrella concept that helps capture the various approaches and goals of legal empowerment efforts in informal settlements. Although it remains an emerging, contested and largely political concept, the right to the city makes explicit the interdependence of rights that underpin the realities and complexities of urban life — political, civil, economic, social, cultural and environmental rights — and as a collective right, it "invokes by necessity the need for collective action, solidarity, and new forms of alliances between different stakeholder groups within society" (Global Platform for the Right to the City, 2015, p. 138). It calls for a multidisciplinary, holistic and integrated approach grounded in firm legal guarantees on the one hand, but serves to articulate large collective and democratic aspirations on the other. Social movements and urban poor organizations have embraced and mobilized this right to the city in support of a robust range of advocacy strategies as a normative standard for public policy. The chapter from the Philippines echoes this view and draws on the right to the city to demonstrate the "paradigm shift in Philippine policies" needed to make the promise of the holistic people's plan approach a reality. More than the right to housing, the authors argue that the right to the city upholds crucial guarantees of the political agency of residents, as key protagonists in decision-making and planning processes about where they live — including redevelopment of their settlements.

Confronting informality as power imbalances

The lack of voice of settlement residents in decision-making processes and institutions captures the symbolic way they experience informality in cities. This image of an urban space divided into two separate cities — the formal city, or the city "with rights", and the informal city, lying outside but next to a recognized legal, institutional and regulatory sphere — further defines how residents experience informality. Urban planning has long grappled with this spatial notion of informality, but it arguably remains under-examined from a legal or human rights perspective. Attention to informality in the legal empowerment field has generally centred on legal pluralism, largely in rural and post-colonial contexts. The focus from that vantage point has largely been to understand how Indigenous or other local populations can access justice using their own customary or informal legal rules and mechanisms (Tamanaha, 2007). In urban contexts, however, a common geographic space in the city is more often the decisive element shared by diverse populations (rather than a common ethnic identity or customary justice system).[14]

Informality has traditionally been conceived in binary terms, as the image of two urban spheres evokes. From that perspective, law and legal empowerment play a key role in bridging the two spheres, to enable secure or "legal" recognition and integration of informal settlements, their residents and residents' various rights within the formal city, while also respecting the collective cultural and social identity of those neighbourhoods. The bridging approach to informality arises in several ways, such as when appealing to constitutional rights to housing or other legal and regulatory guarantees in a protective function — to prevent evictions, gain longer-term recognition of settlements or compel governments to provide better access to services like sanitation and health. In reality, the neat separation between spheres quickly collapses. From a legal perspective, the clear and orderly hierarchy of laws needed to resolve competing claims is often not easy to identify. Emphasizing the bridging function in this sense risks an inherent bias towards the formal as the ideal state of affairs to achieve (Banks et al., 2019, p. 225).[15] This bias is witnessed in urban policy approaches that treat the informal sphere as "unplannable" or a "nuisance" and is at the root of much of the stigma against residents living in "poverty" or squalor (McAuslan, 2003, p. 143; Roy, 2005). The use of laws, including criminal sanctions, and the language of "beautification" or "decongestion" accompanying policies to address (or essentially eliminate) urban informality typifies such a bias.[16] From the case studies, that bias may be seen in Accra, Dhaka, Karachi, Manila and South Africa and in the failure to include informal settlements in the Nairobi Master Urban Plan (Weru et al., 2015, p. 235). Fernandes and Varley (1998) caution that holding too closely to the formal is more the norm than the exception, but it risks mistakenly viewing "the state as a neutral agent in charge of protecting the public good and social welfare" and failing to understand the "social reality" that by design or incapacity "deviat[es] from official law perspective" (p. 9). Other authors observe that the law should not by default be viewed as neutral (McAuslan, 2003, p. 139; Van Gelder, 2013, p. 496), and may in fact be exclusionary (Farha, 2018, para. 6) which could cause residents, in turn, to be "victims" of the law (Goodfellow, 2020, p. 290; Holston, 1991, p. 722).

The Manila and Karachi chapters illustrate those concerns when problematizing how courts have upheld and deferred to governments' application of public interest provisions — which on the surface are neutral — in the face of settlement populations' competing rights claims. In both contexts, the authors explain how the governments' application of the laws in the name of larger goals — respectively, the environment and development — was not accompanied by commensurate concern for the direct, exclusionary impacts of planning decisions on the settlement populations in question. Conversely, the Dhaka chapter, reflecting on experiences before the courts, describes how successful judgments rejected the government's pejorative characterization of informal settlement dwellers as "trespassers", "encroachers" or "criminals", but rather recognized those communities' "critical role" in the economic life of city. The relationship between the formal and informal spheres is thus more appropriately described as intertwined.

The different ways in which legal empowerment organizations engage with informality across chapters go beyond simply "bridging" to illustrate this deeply intertwined relationship between formal and informal spheres.[17] The most common situations that arise are efforts to improve the security of residents' housing by pushing governments to officially recognize settlements and fulfil obligations to provide essential services and infrastructure. Instances of "squatters" are instructive in that respect, and most chapters include situations where residents and communities initially occupied private or public lands to which they formally did not have any claim. A tension in those situations is that, despite their ostensibly irregular status and initial act of "illegality" or violation of property rights under the formal system, residents generally seek security of tenure and formalized recognition of their status on the lands (Van Gelder, 2010, p. 254, 2013, p. 496). Court orders to prevent evictions or displacement — as seen in Nairobi, Accra, Buenos Aires, South Africa, Karachi, Manila and Dhaka — alongside efforts to gain formal recognition of settlements under municipal law, are some of the incremental steps groups have pursued to assert claims, generally relying on constitutional or human rights to housing. In some cases, court orders to secure access to services like water (as in Mexico and Buenos Aires) can be a step towards regularizing land recognition. The additional tension in those instances is that efforts to uphold the rights of residents could be characterized as efforts to strengthen the rule of law. On the other hand, regularizing or legitimizing the status of residents on the settlement lands, in one form or another, could be seen as undermining respect for the rule of law, since the original encroachments were, formally speaking, illegal (Van Gelder, 2013, pp. 494–495). A related tension in some contexts arises within the formal system with competing claims to public-oriented rights like housing, and to constitutional protections of private property rights.[18]

A similar dynamic of seeking to formalize what are initially non-conforming conditions arises within local urban laws and their planning and building standards. The challenge posed in these situations is that bringing existing buildings and services into conformity with formal standards might not be immediately practical or affordable. At the same time, advocating for recognition of standards that fall below existing standards could entrench a two-tiered system, where poorer communities can only expect less than ideal conditions, which could pose challenges for tenants. Further still, bringing conditions up to standard could carry the risk of displacing residents by gentrifying or increasing the desirability of settlements and pricing residents out of the market (Vitale et al., 2020, p. 92).[19] Experiences in Villa Inflammable in Buenos Aires — another settlement the authors at ACIJ have been supporting — capture this tension starkly. Residents living on environmentally condemned lands have faced the choice of accepting state-sponsored relocation or advocating to continue living in pollution while seeking to compel a lengthy and expensive government clean-up through the courts (Echegoyemberry & Pilo, 2020).[20] As various authors have noted, "there are degrees of illegality" or informality, and "some forms… tend to be more accepted and/or tolerated than others, by both the state and public opinion" (Fernandes & Varley, 1998, p. 4).[21] Which manifestations of informality are allowed to persist is often highly dependent on political will and discretion, however legitimate they might be (Roy, 2005, p. 149; Van Gelder, 2010, p. 256). For instance, officials often turn a blind eye to parallel, "informal" markets within settlements (e.g., for service provision, rent and "purchase" of land or housing) that tend to be controlled by and benefit political and economic elites, particularly in the cases of Accra and Nairobi. In Buenos Aires, informal rental markets in the *villas* were found to reproduce or mimic rules of the formal market, which owners imposed on tenants in an effort to exploit and maintain existing power disparities (Rodriguez et al., 2018, p. 146). This dynamic illustrates how, far from a manifestation of poverty, informality might be perpetuated by powerful interests — again, blurring the neat distinction between who inhabits formal or informal spheres (Fernandes & Varley, 1998, p. 5; Roy, 2005, p. 153). The impacts on residents who fall prey to informal markets — suffering what the Nairobi team dubbed the "poverty penalty" — are far clearer: these residents pay far higher rates for substandard and even unsanitary services like water, electricity and housing.

Reflecting on these realities, various authors frame the relationship between informality and formality as a continuum or spectrum, containing varying degrees of legality and legitimacy (Goodfellow, 2020, p. 281; Land Resource Management Centre [LRMC] et al., 2018, p. 22; McAuslan, 2003, p. 8; Roy, 2005, p. 149). Ideas used to capture the dynamics of actors simultaneously working inside and outside the formal legal system include an "a-formal" space (Goodfellow, 2020, p. 281), the "suspension" of the formal (Roy, 2005, p. 149), and the invocation of the law as an "aspirational" assertion of rights (Parnell & Pieterse, 2010, p. 147).[22] Inasmuch as groups are working "outside", they nonetheless formulate their efforts in legal terms, while also invoking a broader set of social and political justifications to legitimate their claims. In this way, the law "can be used as a handle in the struggle for a more human or reasonable government" (McAuslan, 2003, p. 145). Those efforts, to echo Bonaventura de Sousa Santos's (1995) earlier insights, however, "must always be articulated with a political defense, so that both defenses are mutually reinforced" (p. 386). In this way, legal empowerment efforts are embedded in a broader social and political context (Fernandes & Varley, 1998, p. 10; Roy, 2005, p. 150). To the extent that a set of strategies could be framed as more legal or socio-political will differ by context, depending on a range of factors like which legal frameworks are in place and how receptive public officials are to legal or political claims. In some cases, actors knowingly rely on weaker legal arguments to obtain other strategic advantages using legal processes or "complications", notably, "to bring conflict into the legal arena as a way to keep it unresolved but contained, controlling it in a residual sense until the political will is found" (Holston, 1991, pp. 705–709). The larger reflection is that states of a-formality, although effective in describing the interplay between formal and informal spheres, pose great risk, uncertainty and insecurity for residents.

Legal empowerment efforts to confront informality, while not accepting existing formal structures as a necessary endpoint, are nonetheless oriented towards greater integration into the formal system. That stance embodies a conception of human rights premised on governments delivering on formal legal obligations. Moreover, as the urban planning scholar Ananya Roy (2005) notes, focusing too heavily on self-help or empowerment of the urban poor alone risks devolving "responsibility for poverty to the poor themselves", because it "obscures the role of the state and even renders it unnecessary" (p. 148).[23] The Buenos Aires chapter, in this connection, captures how the informal settlement community is often the first mover in establishing service-provision (of electricity or sewage, for example), with the municipal government subsequently taking over these bottom-up efforts. Governments must articulate stronger public responsibilities and actions that are sensitive to "informality" and guarantee residents' participation in defining the contours of the "formal" and integrating their realities into the urban fabric (Banks et al., 2019, pp. 232–233). Legal empowerment does not abandon, but rather reaffirms, a disciplinary commitment to the institutions, norms and processes underlying human rights and the rule of law. That commitment, however, remains agnostic to the appropriate balance between the formal and informal, in the abstract. As urban poverty and development scholars Banks, Lombard and Mitlin (2019) observe, "[i]ncorporating the 'informal' may require bringing it into the formal in ways that reflect the nature of informal processes in terms of flexibility, and its incremental and context-specific nature" (p. 233).[24] This open-ended concept, of not holding too closely to a specific set of institutional forms, reflects an experimental approach.[25]

The experiences of implementation seen with the SPA in Mukuru, Nairobi, with the urbanization law in Villa 31 in Buenos Aires, and with participatory *in situ* upgrading in Ambedkar Camp, Delhi embody this approach of ongoing, iterative testing and identifying ways to incrementally improve living conditions and gain recognition of tenure security. The SPA and urbanization law models — which have echoes in the people's plans in the Philippines — formally "suspend" the state of informality to give residents a chance to articulate an integrated set of solutions, tailored to context and premised on community participation. They are an attempt to recognize "incrementalism" without it becoming "a generalized condition where those unable to afford formal housing are condemned to a set of second-tier standards and codes" (Roy, 2005, p. 153). The experiences in Buenos Aires and Manila illustrate additional risks of incremental approaches. The pace of implementing the community-led plans in both cases was slow which, over multiple years, made them susceptible to shifts in political contexts, and even to government backtracking on earlier support for the plans. The extent to which such path-breaking attempts to merge formal and informal spheres in an incremental and adaptive manner will live up to their promise could ultimately hinge on the political openness to accept these more step-by-step standards. Looming larger is the need to sustain the political buy-in to see through the processes underway to ameliorate conditions, so as to avoid incomplete implementation or different "tiers" of standards (Roy, 2005, p. 153).

Indeed, these case study experiences demonstrate how much hinges on the political will of public officials, whether they are open to engage with or outright hostile towards informality. Concern for power imbalances re-emerges in this question of political will, which can be capricious by nature. Recent political economy understandings of informality have recognized such power imbalances as a central concern, and frame the relationship between the formal and informal in terms of who is able to define what counts as formal or informal. Viewing informality in this way brings into focus the winners and losers in urban development, and the processes by which advantage and disadvantage are conferred. Formality offers state resources and social status, and hence power. A focus on informality highlights those disadvantaged by their inability to be "formal", but also those who gain advantage from their ability to be selectively "informal" (Banks et al., 2019, pp. 223–224).

Overcoming informality again becomes a question of "leveling the playing field", which helps to capture the empowering dimension of legal empowerment in the face of informality. More pointedly, as a recent study on informal settlements in seven African cities underscored, public authorities are now keen to demonstrate commitment to improving conditions for settlement residents, as evidenced by a range of progressive policies and programs. Yet many of these go unimplemented, pointing to persistent or systemic failures that are yet to be overcome (Ouma et al., 2024). At the root of the legal empowerment efforts in informal settlements are efforts to confront a similar lack of political will, whether to initiate needed policies and programs, or implement them once in place.[26] Legal solutions on this framing become instrumentalized in support of a larger set of development or socio-political goals, while nonetheless providing a normative underpinning to other technical interventions. The following sections describe more concretely how the author teams featured in this volume have attempted to "level the playing field", using legal empowerment strategies centred on participation and litigation.

Participation, voice and empowerment grounded in legal rights

A priority across the case studies featured in these chapters has been to support structures to improve the participation and voice of residents. These efforts respond to perceived failures of different levels of government — municipal, provincial, national — to include community members and their concerns in efforts to address urban poverty. This lack of inclusion takes various shapes, ranging from degrees of general disregard seen in many of the chapters, to efforts to eliminate or criminalize settlements and activities within them (e.g., Pakistan, Nigeria). In other cases, groups have articulated the concern that existing state-led interventions to improve settlement conditions have tended to be overly technical or top-down in nature, ostensibly for the benefit of settlement communities but without residents' meaningful input in shaping and implementing the interventions (Ghana, India, Kenya, Philippines). The participation strategies pursued by legal empowerment advocates in these cases generally pursue multiple goals at the same time: targeting public processes of legislative and policy reform and decision-making, and zeroing in on the responsibilities of government actors. Such strategies aim to build awareness, capacity and empowerment of residents, while also targeting more instrumental and immediate goals, like advocating for improved settlement conditions.[27] The efforts at promoting participation tend to be oriented towards either the executive level, or the day-to-day exercise of public power (e.g., the implementation of programs and policies). The main strategies employed across these case studies include raising awareness and bolstering residents' legal literacy on their rights (including to participate), accompanying residents to public meetings or participating on their behalf, and taking legal action, such as seeking administrative review of decisions to challenge the lack of opportunities for public participation or information. A shorter-term goal has been to secure community recognition and input in planning processes, including those related to relocation. Longer-term, efforts have aimed to shift from a reactive to a more holistic mode of engagement, both at the settlement level and with respect to city-wide or national policies on urban poverty and planning (Global Platform for the Right to the City, 2015, p. 138; Parnell & Pieterse, 2010, p. 158).

Significant commentary and donor funds have been devoted to participatory approaches to development over the past several decades, both in urban settings and further afield.[28] A lack of "participation in decision-making and in civil, social, and cultural life is thus recognized… as a defining feature and cause of poverty, rather than just its consequence" (Sepúlveda Carmona, 2013, para. 14). By corollary, improving participation is seen as key to reducing poverty, by strengthening the cohesion and empowerment of communities, along with public and private sector accountability and responsiveness (Mansuri & Rao, 2013, pp. 15–16). In informal settlements, two dominant modes of participation are at play: decentralization and community-driven approaches. Decentralization is premised on making government institutions more accountable and responsive by bringing them closer to citizens, who are then better able to make demands and participate in governance processes (pp. 16–17).[29] Community-driven approaches focus on processes, to build the capacity and agency of community members to shape the development processes that implicate them. Over time, authors have developed a range of frameworks to describe the objectives, forms and functions that participation aims to promote by design or in practice. To illustrate, Sarah C. White (1996), a scholar of the sociology of international development, thus classifies various forms of participation from weakest to strongest: (1) nominal forms (perfunctory or tokenistic) used to legitimate interventions; (2) instrumental, aimed at improving interventions' efficacy and cost-effectiveness; (3) representative, which "allow the local people a voice" in shaping interventions; and (4) transformative, where participation itself builds empowerment — the consciousness and confidence of groups "in their ability to make a difference" (pp. 145–146).[30] Following the lead of Gaventa (2004), a well-known international development thinker, different strands of participation should be brought together under larger conceptions of citizenship and participation as a right (pp. 28–29).

Analysis across the chapters indicates that groups have supported an "integrated approach" to community participation, which combines multiple objectives and features across the spectrum, with more distinct legal empowerment elements (Joshi, 2017, pp. 163–164).[31] More generally, underlying the experiences of the legal empowerment groups is their appreciation of the fundamental lesson that participation is a social and political process that is not to be treated in a cursory or technocratic manner.[32] The groups thus recognize their status as "external" actors (as civil society advocates and experts), and that responding effectively to community concerns requires a deep understanding of settlement contexts, and the diverse and often competing interests within communities. The groups emphasize the need to work through existing community structures, whether formal or informal, to ensure the sustainability and legitimacy of efforts.[33] At the same time, they acknowledge a risk of entrenching poor participation and exclusion, or reinforcing weak accountability of leaders and other powerful actors, where those structures are not representative or prone to capture by powerful interests (Mitlin, 2001, pp. 384–385; Sepúlveda Carmona, 2013, para. 47).

Anecdotally, community structures are often male-dominated, but are generally more inclusive and responsive to the common good of residents when women play a stronger leadership role. As a result, in some instances, the groups profess to engage in frank discussions with community leaders about the need for greater inclusion in community structures.[34] More pointedly, the feminist analysis in Chapter 2 provides a deeper examination of the conditions needed to achieve empowerment and leadership of women in informal settlement communities. Transformative participation from a gender-differentiated perspective, in other words, requires an intentional set of strategies that address structural barriers to equality — whether internally, to create "collective spaces for discussion" that "help women to voice gender inequalities related to power structures within their communities and households", or externally, to expand "women's effective participation in public decisions" (Chapter 2). The experiences of Nazdeek in supporting women paralegals in Delhi stand out as efforts to build and sustain women's participation and empowerment both internally and externally. Promoting participation in this way often hinges on residents' own prior efforts to "self-build" the neighbourhood, or community cohesion, structures and democratic culture later needed to engage with the state or other external actors.[35] For communities to begin to recognize themselves as communities takes time, which the authors from Nairobi (Chapter 5) noted was the case with the Mukuru settlement (Grassroots Justice Network, 2023). The need for community readiness is further illustrated by the three case study communities, in Accra, where the team attempted to establish new governance committees, as a tool to promote greater participation and voice (Chapter 4). In two of the settlements, those efforts generated promising results and arguably helped to strengthen internal organization. By contrast, efforts to launch a committee in the third community failed twice despite working with existing community associations, due to social, ethnic and political divisions.

Legal empowerment approaches to participation arguably depart from purely community-based or political conceptions by viewing participation, in its essence, as a right. From a legal perspective, this framing is somewhat axiomatic since participation is a basic guarantee in public or administrative law frameworks to ensure procedural fairness. The maxim "*audi alteram partem*" (hear the other side), as legal scholar Liebenberg (2018) is quick to note, "recognizes that an essential element of fair administrative decision-making is for people to be given "an opportunity to participate in the decisions that will affect them, and — crucially — a chance of influencing the outcome of those decisions" (p. 623). The case study teams have proven resourceful in deploying guarantees under national legislation to open new or dormant spaces for participation or to resist the closing of existing ones. A salient feature of legal framings of human rights, to participation or otherwise, is that rights have "teeth" — namely, that they are backed by state obligations and the tacit threat of legal redress in the event of a government failure to meet them (Joshi, 2017, p. 163).[36] As the South Africa team notes, residents have turned to litigation to compel government action, after initial strategies to engage state-based processes fail.

The experiences in Rio de Janeiro illustrate the potential positive impacts of introducing rights-based strategies, in a legal "teeth" sense, alongside a pre-existing citizenship indicators methodology that fosters participation in a more political or social justice sense (Chapter 3). That methodology involves both a series of community meetings and collection of residents' perceptions on settlement conditions. Those efforts have contributed to building community cohesion and a shared understanding of challenges in the *favelas* as human rights issues. As a next step, the community develops various advocacy strategies to engage with public authorities; these strategies mostly relied on negotiation with authorities in the executive branch. As the team reflects, however, the introduction of legal strategies expanded the range of tools and avenues for engagement with the state (e.g., through the courts, public prosecutors, ombuds offices, the legislators). The result was to revitalize and strengthen civic engagement and long-standing struggles, such as those around the right to water and the right to education. A broader reflection from such experiences is that participation as a legal right promotes a more deliberative, rights-based conception of government authority and decision-making while also staying true to legal notions of redress and accountability. The teams in Buenos Aires and Nairobi describe how they actively negotiate two sides of this equation when engaging with public officials through participatory channels. To bolster their position, or when sensing that a process might not be proceeding in a fully participatory manner, they will stress to the officials their mutual interest in avoiding court.[37] The rights-based approach to participation, in short, is aptly described in terms of "optimistic" conflict or contestation (Gaventa, 2004, p. 28; Mansuri & Rao, 2013, p. 91; White, 1996, p. 15).

In the notion of participation as a right, which is oriented towards ensuring that "the voiceless gain a voice", the same concepts of "leveling the playing field" and shifting power imbalances resurface. Viewed this way, participation is not a purely procedural or instrumental goal — in service of other rights or development goals — but is inextricably linked to empowerment as an end in itself, "which is a key human rights goal and principle" (Sepúlveda Carmona, 2013, para. 22).[38] In this light, the legal empowerment approaches to participation as a right should be situated within conceptions of administrative and public law that view procedural justice as essentially about larger social and political aspirations, namely, ensuring dignity, personal autonomy and a larger culture or system of democratic citizenship (Dyzenhaus, 2012, p. 111).[39] More simply, to capture a point expressed by some of the authors, participation is about more than involving communities in a planning process, but ensuring that planning reflects the communities' vision (Grassroots Justice Network, 2023). Yet the challenge that co-author Bercovich notes is that promoting improved participation requires a cultural shift on the part of public authorities, to see themselves as accountable to citizens (Bercovich et al., 2010, p. 237; Gaventa, 2004, p. 27; Mansuri & Rao, 2013). This shift is akin to the one described previously, where engagement between settlement communities and authorities, starting from a position of confrontation or distrust, becomes increasingly collaborative. The team from Dhaka, in that connection, talks about broad advocacy efforts to create participatory spaces where settlement dwellers could push for systemic change and, in other words, "move beyond issue-specific engagement, to build a broader consensus around housing rights" when engaging with public authorities (Chapter 12). More profoundly, the shift or leveling of the playing field here thus comes when public officials cede greater power to communities to determine the future of their settlements. For that reason, some authors invoke the more encompassing language of the right to self-determination, over and above participation, to capture what is truly at stake (Grassroots Justice Network, 2023): this appears explicitly in the Karachi chapter. In a similar light, the team from South Africa evokes the idea of "invented spaces of participation" to capture a series of community-driven, creative strategies that communities turn to — like "protest, litigation and self-supply" — when the more formal state-based "invited" processes for democratic participation — "like meeting with local ward councilors, writing letters, submitting petitions, and participating in various community forums" — fail and leave residents simply ignored (Chapter 9).

Questions of participation and informality come together in these instances because, as described above, many of the participation efforts have built on existing community structures which later took on a more external or rights-claiming orientation. Those structures tend to be informal, in the sense of not having an officially recognized status within local governance structures or with respect to consultative requirements under various administrative law statutes. A dynamic witnessed over time, however, is that public authorities come to recognize the structure, formally or informally, depending on the case, as the legitimate representative structure for community members — the putative shift above. Reflecting on their experiences with the World Bank's Justice for the Poor program, Sage et al. (2009) refer to these setups that bridge between formal and informal spaces as "iterative, interim institutions" which could also be described as hybrid institutions (p. 9). On a practical level, a distinct challenge in informal settlement contexts is that the pathways for creating new openings for participation run through the dense web of, at times dysfunctional or unresponsive, administrative institutions and regulatory frameworks. The awareness of how and when their guarantees to participation "on the books" can live up to their empowering or transformative promise in practice often proves elusive. The success of legal empowerment groups is thus largely due to their ability to move, at strategic moments, between these institutional layers and, simultaneously, between the formal and informal spheres. Being able to navigate that institutional web is significant, given the tendency for public officials to hide behind the complexity of social problems as a convenient justification for inaction, claiming that "these problems are too difficult for us to solve" (Weru et al., 2015, p. 241).

This lack of knowledge, which presents itself as a technical problem, is often symptomatic of a larger lack of political will, and of clashes over more inclusive or pro-poor redistribution of public resources.[40] At a bureaucratic level, the negative political will takes shape, for instance, through a failure to collect official data on settlement populations and conditions. The authors in Chapter 3 describe a more extreme "official data blackout" in Brazil — which was part of a larger, deliberately anti-poor political strategy. On top of challenges of incomplete or poor official data on settlements seen elsewhere, in Pakistan, residents face an additional obstacle — that mapping community boundaries has to go through official channels: residents mapping their own communities is illegal (due to the history of contested international boundaries between Pakistan and India). The authors thus found resonance in the concept of "data empowerment", alongside or as part of larger legal empowerment approaches (Grassroots Justice Network, 2023). More concretely, across several chapters, communities were involved in data collection efforts that represent a form of participation and empowerment for their role in building residents' understanding of their community — namely, building their "ability to connect the marginalization that they encounter with violation of their rights" (Chapter 5), while generating data that more closely reflects their perspectives and experiences (Rio, Delhi, Nairobi, Accra, Buenos Aires).[41] Those efforts to fill gaps in data and knowledge have further served to strengthen participation, by building residents' confidence and credibility in their engagement with public officials, as seen when groups were able to demonstrate the rigour of their data and dispel officials' skepticism. To illustrate, efforts in Nairobi to diagnose the poverty penalty were critical in building buy-in and momentum of municipal officials to push for a special planning area declaration in Mukuru, with subsequent data helping underpin decisions taken later to implement redevelopment of the settlement (Chapter 5).

Asserting participation rights alongside a broader range of human rights and legal guarantees is by no means a foregone conclusion. As the lead author from Buenos Aires (Chapter 8) notes, participation is a widely used concept but, even in the best of circumstances, moving beyond providing information and engaging official consultation processes is very complex (Grassroots Justice Network, 2023). The groups' efforts across the various chapters could at best be described as a process of ongoing trial and error to shift both the attitudes of public officials and the application of legal standards. Experiences in Buenos Aires are some of the most far-reaching, where there is a local law that requires community representatives' participation in developing public policies regarding informal settlements. The government did not fulfil this law and, in the *Villa Elections* case, the court ordered elections in all settlements in the city for members of community-level committees, which were formally recognized as the main representatives of settlement residents in the urban plans — arguably adding a bureaucratic hurdle to participation in an already complex system. A salient aspect of this process is that the first step to achieving formal recognition, integration and land titles is the formalization of participation structures (Baldiviezo & Maranzana, 2013, p. 441).[42]

Participation plays an especially critical role where residents take on redevelopment of their settlements. In the case of Nairobi, the implementation of the SPA created a powerful new space for participation. The team seized that historical opportunity, working across multiple large consortiums, and developed a consultative process that extended participation across thousands of households to co-generate redevelopment plans. Chapter 5's account of the water and sanitation planning process demonstrates the intricacy and early successes of the efforts, which further entailed bridging between residents, an array of service providers and technical experts who devised water and sanitation solutions to give life to the needs and desire of residents. The experiences in Delhi paint a similar picture of deep community-led participatory processes through which residents co-designed upgrading of the settlement, working closely with multidisciplinary teams of technical experts, accompanied by uncertain and long processes of engagement to secure public officials' buy-in to implement the community's plans. The experiences with the people's plans in the Philippines (Chapter 7) provide a sobering counterpoint. On one level, the authors detail a series of technical challenges, bureaucratic delays and budgetary shortages that residents encountered in efforts to implement their community-led plans. On another level, the status of the people's plans, permitted in policy only, left them vulnerable to shifting political winds (even at advanced stages of implementation). Perhaps recognizing those potential limits, the political coalitions advocating for informal settlement residents' rights have long pushed for the people's plans to receive stronger legal protections (or "teeth"): those efforts continue as of the time of writing.

Finally, the experiences in the above contexts point to a larger question — which is more posed than answered here — about the added value of participation as a legal right. The ability of participation to shift power dynamics or promote empowerment arguably reflects broader levels of democratic citizenship and cultures of the rule of law. Successes in participation, in other words, may ultimately depend on broader recognition and respect for a vibrant civic space in countries and the ability meaningfully to seek legal redress when participation is denied. From that perspective, the positive experiences with participation in countries like Kenya, Ghana and Argentina (up until recently) could be said to reinforce and emerge from pre-existing positive shifts in democratic governance. Likewise, the obstacles that communities face in feeding decision-making or holding governments to account when they are excluded (Philippines, Brazil, South Africa, Mexico, India) mirror the vacillations or backsliding of democratic governance, which various authors point to in their chapters. The challenges of democratic backsliding are further touched on in the conclusion to this chapter.

Embedding litigation within wider political and social change strategies

> Whether legal mobilization and court action is perceived as a viable site of political and social contestation depends on particular political and social histories. Law is only one part of the story of political settlements, and its relative weight is intimately linked to whether national, local, or transnational elites agree through calculated consent or coercion to be bound by law in practice.
>
> (Domingo & O'Neil, 2014, p. 10)

The uses of litigation in this book present a complex and sophisticated vision of how legal strategies and the communities come together. Litigation is not depicted as the central or primary strategy for advancing justice or social change. Rather, it is portrayed as a tool employed for diverse purposes, yielding a variety of outcomes. This approach is embedded within a holistic, community-led framework of legal empowerment, emphasizing long-term engagement and partnership between communities and legal empowerment organizations. Stated differently, the approach affirms the broader vision of critical legal empowerment introduced above, while seeking to avoid the dynamic whereby legal professionals (most often lawyers) assume the roles of knowledge-bearers and protagonists of judicial proceedings, effectively sidelining or even disarming the community and their leadership in the process. The use of litigation to address poverty and inequality has been much debated among academics and practitioners — particularly, how success is defined, what impact those strategies have and what challenges impede real changes in people's lives. In an obvious sense, success is the recognition, even incremental, of claimants' rights, especially through judgments ordering ameliorative action by the government.

Litigation's value is also framed in "non-material" or symbolic terms, such as the changing power dynamics, the behaviour of public officials, the "social meanings and understandings" (or narratives) of issues, and the affected groups' sense of empowerment, dignity and self-understanding (Albiston, 2010, p. 62).[43] As described above in the discussion of informality, the court cases in Bangladesh contributed to shifting social meanings, when the courts rejected the government's pejorative portrayal of settlement residents in favour of their recognition as full citizens. In the case of Mexico, the litigation improved material conditions (access to water) for a small group of residents, but the case's larger significance was arguably its symbolic and legal effects, when the Supreme Court recognized the human right to water for the first time. Litigation can also produce a range of strategic results, such as attracting media attention and financial resources, which can serve as a rallying cry "to organize a movement" around or draw in new participants, as well as in bolstering a movement's standing "in informal negotiations" or by naming-and-shaming "opponents into capitulation" (Albiston, 2010, p. 63). Chapter 10 deftly describes how South Africa's Abahlali baseMjondolo social movement has used court cases to expand its membership and strengthen the notoriety of residents' struggles, which play out both before the court and in the streets. In some cases, moreover, going to court might be the only viable option when weighed against other alternatives (Dugard et al., 2014, p. 32).

Experiences with litigation appear in virtually every chapter, albeit sometimes largely in the background. Despite the unique contexts and objectives, there are several common elements that cut across how the various communities and legal groups approach litigation, namely: (1) communities adopt a central role in the decision-making process; (2) litigation is one tool within a larger set of legal empowerment and political strategies; and (3) it is pursued to advance outcomes or socio-political changes that stretch beyond a zero-sum, or win/lose process (Mesel et al., 2018, p. 279). Indeed, a striking element that cuts across many of the uses of litigation is the length and depth of partnership between the communities or social movements and civil society organizations or a coalition of several stakeholders. In chapters where litigation experiences are more central (Argentina, South Africa, Mexico and Bangladesh) the relationships portrayed in the chapters span at least a decade or two. Similarly, the experiences in contexts like India, Kenya and Philippines, which could be roughly said to flow from dissatisfaction with the outcomes of litigation, reflect around 20 years of direct engagement between the legal empowerment groups and communities. Longstanding relationships likewise underpinned the more recent introduction of judicial recourse in Brazil.

In an earlier study, the Buenos Aires team identified four categories of cases to frame the purposes and results of the use of litigation over time: to defend or protect; to ensure citizen participation in public processes; to provide compensation in the face of violations; and to address larger structural problems (Mesel et al., 2018). Most communities across the chapters have turned to the courts with defensive or protective aims, and in an effort to secure judgments recognizing residents' rights — such as to forestall evictions or relocations (Ghana, Kenya, South Africa, Pakistan, Philippines, Bangladesh, Argentina) or secure access to services (Mexico and Brazil, among others). The *Villa Elections* case in Buenos Aires, as described above, provides a deep example of litigation to secure guarantees of political participation and democratic representation in the development and implementation of public policies in the settlements; this was part of a larger wave of collective rights litigation that has focused on improving living conditions in the *villas* since 2004. Many of the uses of litigation, moreover, can be situated within efforts to address larger structural problems. These uses of litigation tend to go in two main directions.

A first set has aimed to solve the "meanwhile" and address urgent matters while a neighbourhood becomes more fully integrated into the city. For instance, residents fought for access to potable water in Villa 31 bis in Buenos Aires. In Dhaka, the team describes how they turned more to the political process, once interim orders were secured to prevent evictions, to push for electoral commitments and introduction of more progressive housing policies. In Nairobi, the special planning area in Mukuru likewise emerged after a first injunction was secured and while awaiting the substantive case to be heard by the court. To paraphrase one of the authors, they used litigation to buy time to do other things (Grassroots Justice Network, 2023). These types of outcomes are notable not only for generating positive recognition of rights claims, but also for opening dialogue channels for communities centred on their participation. This again underscores how the recognition and enforcement of rights can contribute to shifting power dynamics and leveling the playing field (Vitale et al., 2019, p. 21).

The second set of cases targets the far-reaching structural change and urban integration needed to fulfil the right to housing and right to the city. To be sure, across the chapters more focused on litigation — South Africa, Bangladesh, Argentina, Mexico — the limits of relying solely on the courts for structural change is echoed as a general conclusion. So is the need to combine use of the courts with a series of complementary strategies — to "work hand-in-hand with organization, mobilization, popular education and political conscientization" (Chapter 9). The Buenos Aires chapter provides a detailed account of challenges encountered in turning to the courts to regulate or oversee a whole range of technical urban planning and implementation questions. Such experiences, also seen in Delhi, Dhaka and Nairobi, point to a broader conclusion regarding structural litigation: it demands interdisciplinary knowledge and teams (comprised of community organizers and non-legal, technical experts such as urban planners and economists, in addition to lawyers), especially to develop an evidentiary basis to support rights-violation claims and to identify a feasible and persuasive range of remedies to assert (Open Society Justice Initiative [OSJI], 2018, p. 42). This broader conclusion, moreover, speaks to extensive debates that have emerged with the increasing use of social and economic rights litigation about the role and limits of judicial power in issuing orders to resolve complex policy challenges.[44]

The uncertain outcomes in structural cases are a reminder that litigation carries risks for communities, even in the most far-reaching and progressive cases. The teams reported being alive to litigation's risks, or the "distorting effects of the law" (Mesel et al., 2018, p. 279). At a practical level, these risks include the financial costs, time and emotional stress associated with cases. The chapter in Argentina also cites the challenges of sustaining community members' motivation throughout the duration of cases, and of creating outsized expectations about the potential positive impacts of a court decision on people's lives. In that regard, if litigation becomes mystified and groups place too much trust in it as the solution to their struggle, it can sap such movements to the detriment of building broader political efforts. The experiences in Villa 31 in Buenos Aires and in Mexico further validate concerns that litigation has a tendency to "atomize collective grievances" and unduly restrict the scope of claimants' human rights, especially when tailoring grievances to fit the legal remedy that has the most viable chance to succeed (Albiston, 2010, p. 63). In both contexts, the legal action did not include the entire community — a "segmenting effect", to cite Chapter 8. Chapter 10 describes how the case in Mexico ultimately landed "halfway between an ordinary litigation and a strategic one". It began as a strategic collaboration between community organizations but, over the course of the legal action, the wider collective struggle was atomized by procedural rules and reduced to a few individual court cases. As a result, only a few households ultimately benefited from the landmark precedent, which forestalled a collective outcome. The deeper structural challenges of discrimination faced by economically poor populations beyond the settlements persist in the background.

Such results point to the more profound limitations that litigation can face when confronting complex or politically contentious social challenges, such as socio-spatial segregation, that define informal settlements. For this reason, legal empowerment, as described above, frames litigation as a "lever for social change" within a broader set of socio-political strategies defined and led by the community. As the Open Society Justice Initiative (2018) underscores, "litigation operates in a complicated relationship with these other tools" or "other problem-solving approaches" (p. 33). More evocatively, in analyzing the impacts of the ground-breaking *Grootboom* right-to-housing case in South Africa, Dugard (2014) describes litigation as being "more of a background variable" and "not the foreground on which particular achievements were fought for and established" (p. 204). In contrast to public interest law's overriding focus on identifying strategies needed for a lawsuit to succeed, legal empowerment casts litigation as part of broader efforts to shift power dynamics and generate structural improvements in peoples' lives. The chapter on South Africa portrays some of the blunt responses to efforts to challenge entrenched power imbalances. Even when communities and social movements secure favorable court judgments, they find themselves pushing back against institutional reflexes to evict or demolish informal settlements, essentially in defiance of the judgments. Those reflexes, combined with corruption and brutal tactics of law enforcement, mean that the physical safety and even lives of community members and leaders are under direct threat.

Perhaps the most far-reaching risks of litigation, in that connection, are that unsuccessful claims and regressive or unenforced judgments discourage litigant groups, which can disempower or demobilize social and political movements. Some critics further question whether litigation produces any real change for disadvantaged groups due to the government's failure to "implement fully the court orders made in a number of socio-economic rights cases" (Mbazira, 2008, p. 2).[45] At a deeper level, some critics see human rights litigation as reinforcing entrenched power, class, racial or other negative structures in the legal system, which have traditionally protected elite interests and perpetuated the discrimination and exclusion of different groups (Dugard et al., 2014, p. 27; OSJI, 2018, p. 18). The outcomes of the litigation cases in Karachi (Chapter 12) vividly illustrate some of these concerns. There, litigation is seen as a last gasp attempt to avoid evictions and displacement, recognizing that the case will likely help perpetuate the Court's stamp of approval of the government's (exclusionary) stances. The general lack of awareness or empathy — and overt prejudice — of public officials concerning the plight of informal settlement residents often extends to judicial officials (Grassroots Justice Network, 2023).

Tackling structural challenges, to be sure, is a tall order. Undaunted by the limitations of litigation, the response of the organizations and communities featured in this volume, for the most part, reaffirms the need for a holistic approach. Their ability to combine diverse legal empowerment strategies, on multiple fronts at the same time, in taking on structural challenges is testament to their courage, determination, creativity and resourcefulness.

Conclusion

Informal settlements, and the underlying urban poverty and exclusion that perpetuate them, represent major challenges for governments in the Global South. The complexity of socio-spatial segregation requires policies to address how societies organize themselves at their very core, not only their physical dimensions (housing and access to services), but also their human relations (political, social and economic).

Settlement residents understand and experience urban segregation as multidimensional. In light of this reality, community-led political and legal strategies to achieve urban inclusion are not compartmentalized by disciplines or sectors. Urban poor communities the world over have been some of the most organized and politically active. It tends to be the professionals who support these residents who divide such strategies along sectoral lines: lawyers, for example, pursue litigation or other legal actions, while urban planners draw up participatory designs to reimagine urban spaces, and economists analyse models to finance urban integration. The experiences analysed in this volume reveal that a diverse and holistic set of strategies is more successful and critical to achieving urban inclusion. While the analysis in this introduction has covered tools and actions related to informality, participation and litigation in an ordered sequence, in reality, residents are simultaneously pursuing those strategies in mutually reinforcing, though often unpredictable, ways.

Achieving systemic and structural changes in the physical and social living conditions of informal settlements is a long-term and non-linear process. Residents stand a greater chance of achieving political change and the fulfilment of their rights when they act collectively, through community-led processes with the support of networks of institutions, organizations and professionals. Court-based, administrative or other purely legal actions are more likely to contribute to structural change when situated within a broader social and political strategy and struggle, which takes the power, risks and limitations of the law seriously. In this sense, legal empowerment provides an important set of tools to help mobilize the law to redress power imbalances underlying the exclusion of the urban poor — imbalances which in some cases might be inherent in formal legal structures. The human rights framework also provides a crucial source of norms and legal protections to orient the legal empowerment experiences in the following chapters. It serves to underpin legal actions at multiple levels while helping to frame political advocacy and narratives beyond strictly legal actions. Moreover, the contrasting range of experiences described in the volume — from legal victories to improved participation to ongoing discrimination and outright threats faced by settlement residents and leaders — reaffirms the indivisibility and interdependence of civil, political, social and economic rights.

The emerging "right to the city" concept offers a framework that encapsulates the broader political demands for structural change to redress the inequalities and power imbalances underlying socio-spatial segregation in the urban context. For one thing, the "city" as a concept and rights claim implies that informal settlements cannot be taken as a challenge in isolation; rather, it requires a shift in how cities are designed and how rights are distributed among inhabitants. At the same time, the right to the city frames those structural demands and struggles in a rights-based language that brings together the full range of interdependent social, economic, political, cultural and environmental rights at stake. Moreover, the use of the term "city" as an object of law and politics brings the corresponding obligations and responsibilities of local authorities and municipalities to the fore. The modest contribution that this volume sets out to make is to provide an initial portrait of the types of holistic strategies that could ground efforts to claim and fulfil a right to the city. What longer-term, tangible effects this holistic conceptualization of urban demands can generate — whether in terms of more democratic and inclusive public policies and local governance in urban settings; improved living conditions for informal settlement communities; or fostering residents' ability to shape a broader collective vision of the urban spaces they inhabit — is a question yet to be answered. It echoes and stands to feed broader ones currently pursued by a legal empowerment learning agenda that the authors are both supporting in different ways (Di Giovanni & Chitalkar, 2022). Efforts like those, and this book, are crucial steps in building bridges to academic spaces and debates, to ensure that research on larger questions — whether in the fields of human rights, access to justice, participatory development or urban planning — is centred on the voices and experiences of informal settlement communities and the grassroots justice activists supporting them.

Answers to such questions will invariably be tricky to pin down given the unpredictable and even cataclysmic societal shifts that can occur, at any moment, in informal settlement contexts. Such moments of profound change can serve to jumpstart or drastically reverse progress. They affect but are likely beyond the control of large portions of a national population, informal settlement residents included. Three such society-wide challenges played out in important if distinct ways during the preparation of this volume. The first was the COVID-19 pandemic, which thrust informal settlement residents into an even more precarious and life-threatening position, with severe impacts on their employment and livelihoods. Preparations for this volume began while the world was largely still in lockdown: its chapters describe the multiple responses, good and bad, that the pandemic spurred. In Kenya, the confinement of residents to squalid conditions in informal settlements finally pushed the government to implement redevelopment plans in Mukuru, under the SPA designation. In Delhi, it led residents in Ambedkar Camp to envision, plan and advocate for redevelopment of their community. In contrast, in both the Philippines and South Africa, government-sponsored evictions resumed during pandemic lockdowns, despite the health emergency. When the pandemic first hit, the team in Rio took on a largely humanitarian and public health role, as social advocacy was put on hold. As of the time of writing, the world has largely "moved on" from the pandemic, in the sense that it no longer represents a global health emergency. Nonetheless, its economic aftershocks continue to be felt across the Global South, with earlier successful efforts to reduce poverty globally now stalled, if not in reverse (Aguilar et al., 2024). Governments are grappling with deteriorating economic conditions and increased fiscal constraint (e.g., rising debt levels) which in turn impede their ability to meet the social and economic needs and fulfil the rights of their populations, urban poor or otherwise. Informal settlements thus risk being swept under by the currents of economic hardship — with deteriorating conditions and growing ranks — as more and more people are left with nowhere else to turn for affordable housing.

The full social and political impacts of post-pandemic economic hardships remain to be seen in coming years. This speaks to the second major series of societal shifts experienced in the contexts depicted in this volume: political upheaval. For better or worse, these countries experienced wide-scale and even polarized shifts in government. As this volume was being finalized, Kenya was experiencing widespread and prolonged youth-led protests, which began in reaction to a government proposal to raise taxes and spread to broader disillusionment with a lack of economic and employment opportunities, spurring calls for better governance. The protests were met with violent government crackdowns, resulting in dozens of deaths, which in turn had significant political fallout (Muia, 2024). At the same moment, weeks of student-led protests in Bangladesh culminated in the overthrow of the authoritarian government. This took place just as the authors were finalizing their chapter, meaning some of their conclusions about future prospects for informal settlement residents in Dhaka may be upended in the hopeful, if as yet uncertain, weeks and months ahead (Rabbee, 2024). A larger political trend observed across the chapters, however, is one of growing political polarization and fears of democratic backsliding, arguably echoing larger global trends of decline (Economist Intelligence, 2024). The authors in Argentina have also been coming to grips with a new president, a self-identified "anarcho-capitalist" who came to power in part on a platform of anti-poor rhetoric, and has shown a willing disregard for civil liberties and freedom of expression in pursuit of economic "shock therapy". The government aims to reduce the role of the state in both market regulation and public policies as much as possible; this makes it difficult to be optimistic in the near future about continued state support for socio-urban integration policies and upgrading of informal settlements in Argentina. The Rio de Janeiro chapter follows the arc of political polarization from one extreme to the other, beginning with the rollback of civic rights and pro-poor policies under the Bolsanaro government, through the polarization of the 2022 election, to the progress achieved with advocacy efforts under the new government. Finally, the South Africa and Mexico chapters both end with a slightly pessimistic outlook about the current state of human rights defense, because of crackdowns and the deaths of community leaders — which in Mexico is situated within larger threats to environmentalists.

The third monumental shift facing informal settlements, which is touched on predominantly in the Dhaka chapter, is the climate emergency. Climate change clearly risks compounding stresses on settlements, which are often constructed in environmentally precarious areas (such as flood plains, to take an example from Manila). Settlements are thus vulnerable to extremes such as more severe flooding or heat, while lacking sanitation or any protective refuge. As noted in the Karachi chapter, climate risk mitigation strategies may also pose an added risk by spurring a rise of new evictions (e.g., to clear flood plains or other vulnerable locales). Another main challenge posed by climate change, underscored in Dhaka, is that economically disadvantaged populations will be increasingly driven to urban settings, when survival is no longer viable in their home regions due to severe climate impacts (e.g., crop failure due to desertification, flooding or recurrent extreme weather events). The authors of the Dhaka chapter strike a note of optimism with the progressive features they describe of climate adaptation policies that recognize the need to address rural-to-urban migration, and recommend *in situ* upgrading and collective tenure rights for settlement residents.

The future is uncertain, and in the face of these new and existing challenges, legal empowerment efforts being put into practice, like those analysed here, offer some modest promise. They unveil the law as something that is alive and that defies traditional and conservative conceptions of the lawyer and legal practice. Legal empowerment offers a vital set of tools and methodologies for serving marginalized and vulnerable communities, as part of wider efforts to shift power imbalances, address inequalities and generate meaningful change in their living conditions. The main takeaway is that legal empowerment should be used more frequently and should become a part of conversations about urban poverty and development because it can help articulate solutions and respond to communities' demands. The tireless efforts of those community members and organizations portrayed across the following chapters merit gratitude and recognition for informing these conversations.

Notes

1 This work was carried out with the aid of a grant from the International Development Research Centre, Ottawa, Canada. The views expressed herein do not necessarily represent those of IDRC or its Board of Governors.
2 Portions of this chapter are reproduced from A. Di Giovanni & L. Bercovich (2021) "Legal empowerment in informal settlements: Lessons on using the law to overcome urban exclusion and poverty in the Global South", *NYU JILP*, 54(1), 93–151, with a note of thanks to the editors for their earlier assistance.
3 See Reckford and Aki-Sawyerr (2023) and UN Population Division (2019) estimating that 55 percent of the world's population lives in urban areas, which is expected to increase to 68 percent by 2050 (roughly 2.5 billion people) with close to 90 percent of this increase taking place in Asia and Africa. Globally, there was a reduction from 28 to 23 percent of urban populations living in informal settlements, from 2000 to 2014. The large majority, 80 percent, are located in the Global South: East and South-East Asia (370 million), sub-Saharan Africa (238 million), and Central and South Asia (227 million) (UN Population Division, 2019, p. 4).
4 See generally Muzondi (2014).
5 Vitale et al. (2020) define socio-spatial or socio-urban segregation, in brief, as the expression of an unequal social order that results in — and is the consequence of — structural inequality. Yet as Susan Parnell and Edgar Pieterse (2010) argue, urban governance reforms have focused too much on political rights and representation and not enough on corresponding socio-economic rights.
6 See generally Wilkinson (2020).
7 Di Giovanni and Bercovich (2021) article which undertook a qualitative analysis of six case studies, three of which appear in this book (Nairobi, Accra and Buenos Aires).
8 In contrast to more purely self-help models, see Parnell and Pieterse (2010, pp. 149–150).
9 Language which a United Nations General Assembly resolution, *Legal empowerment of the poor and eradication of poverty,* G.A. Res. 64/215 (2009), later adopted when endorsing a report by the United Nations Secretary-General: *Legal empowerment of the poor and eradication of poverty: Report of the Secretary-General*, UN Doc A/64/133, para. 3 (2009).
10 For a critique of narrower definitions, see, e.g., Sepúlveda Carmona and Donald (2015) who see the Commission on Legal Empowerment's definition as overprioritizing certain private rights (property, labour and business) while failing to engage directly with structural issues and power asymmetries.
11 In following this conception, we view as overstated a recent critique that broader conceptions blur the "boundary between what is and is not legal empowerment" and treat "legal empowerment as any activity that functions to support disadvantaged populations" (Gisselquist, 2019, p. 336). In short, efforts to link legal empowerment strategies to, or embed them within, a larger set of change processes need not be mistaken for a blurring or subsuming of those latter efforts.
12 For instance, on issues such as urban and land use planning, zoning, environmental regulation, public health or budgetary responsibilities, as well as public utilities, parastatal, private or public–private service-providers.
13 For broad definitions emphasizing power dynamics, see Domingo and O'Neil (2014, p. 8) and Golub (2003, p. 29).
14 These distinctions are not strict. In Ghana, the team cites instances where land tenure status was traditionally derived from customary or indigenous authority, which has later created insecurity of tenure over time as the city expanded — literally engulfing what were rural villages or settlements (McAuslan, 2003, p. 7).

15 Zárate (2016) notes how the term "informal" fails to capture a range and diversity of settlements, conditions of exclusion in them and their relevance and location within cities, resulting in a tendency to be uncritical of formal spaces.

16 To be sure, international development tends to emphasize "formal institutions as the crucial factor in development success, with informal rules and practices playing at best a secondary and often anti-developmental role", which betrays a "cookie-cutter" or one-size-fits-all mindset to institutional reform (Goodfellow, 2020, p. 281). See Andrews et al. (2017, pp. 4–5).

17 A systematic discussion of different notions of informality, which "as a generic concept has been defined in innumerable ways over the past five decades" (Goodfellow, 2020, p. 3), is beyond the scope of this paper. Based on a review of literature, conceptions that better represent how informality appears in different legal empowerment efforts are relied on, without presuming to resolve larger debates within urban studies on how best to characterize it.

18 These property rights carry police and court powers to ensure enforcement. A distinctive element in the Mukuru settlement, which is almost entirely on private lands, is that private property owners potentially have an obligation to the residents under a somewhat novel horizontal application of rights in Kenya's Constitution. See Weru et al. (2015, p. 235), for additional analysis.

19 This point is echoed by McAuslan (2003) who describes how reforms based on raising standards can fail to properly account for local conditions and exacerbate existing issues (pp. 35–36) and by Watson (2009) who reviews urban planning approaches but rejects ready-made solutions for southern urban contexts. Roy (2005) further cautions against the challenges of "formalization" which "can displace the most vulnerable residents of an informal settlement" and "be a moment when inequality is deepened" (p. 153).

20 This is the case for residents in Villa Inflammable who live by the Mantanza-Richuelo River, which has been a source of legal controversy and environmental challenges for decades (Duacastella Arbizu, 2018, p. 194).

21 See also Cueva (1987, p. 524).

22 See also Banks et al. (2019, pp. 227–228); Cueva (1987, p. 524).

23 See generally De Soto (2000).

24 See also McAuslan (2003, pp. 43–44).

25 Again, this has been the tendency with urban planning laws. See Sepúlveda Carmona and Donald (2015).

26 Those legal empowerment efforts also seek to overcome similar dynamics that advantage powerful private actors in the informal sphere (such as exploitive cartels and gangs) (Holston, 1991, p. 708).

27 Further, as White (1996) observes, external actors are more likely to identify empowerment as "the key issue", while residents might focus on "more immediate and tangible interests and goals" initially, with a greater appreciation for and focus on empowerment emerging later (pp. 146–147). Indeed, in settlement communities, concern with living conditions is often front of mind. In Accra, for instance, first efforts focused on water access and cleanup of garbage in the settlements (Bercovich et al., 2010, pp. 110–111).

28 The aim, again, is not to rehash longstanding debates but to describe a few salient features from the case studies that affirm or build on existing commentary and lessons. See generally Hickey and Mohan (2004); Mansuri and Rao (2013).

29 In the informal settlement contexts, the focus has indeed been on new and existing municipal levels, though by interacting with a complex mix of public institutions.

30 The team in Ghana lists four forms of participation: "information sharing; consultation; decision-making and initiating action" (LRMC et al., 2018, p. 124).

31 See also Maru (2010); Domingo and O'Neil (2014, pp. 41–42).

32 These lessons are adapted from International Development Research Centre Partners (2018). See White (1996, pp. 143–144); Beall (2001, p. 368).

33 Structures include community mobilization groups, savings cooperatives or traditional leaders.

34 Such discussions would link to questions of external actors building legitimacy and trust, in terms of the nature of participation they are seeking to promote and what support they can offer to settlement residents and leaders. The groups recognize the importance of ensuring clear expectations, alignment in goals and that residents are themselves defining and driving efforts. Participatory approaches, including in urban settings, are littered with examples of clashes in goals and external actors monopolizing funding and power and dictating terms of engagement (Hickey & Mohan, 2004, p. 17; Mitlin, 2001, pp. 382–383; Sepúlveda Carmona, 2013, p. 77; White, 1996, pp. 143–144).

35 To be clear, in the case study communities, efforts to achieve greater cohesion are reflective of a larger history of engagement of the groups within these and other communities predating research efforts.

36 Joshi (2017) evokes the notion of "teeth" in contrast to social accountability approaches, noting that, "while redress and justice is at the heart of legal empowerment approaches, it is the weakest part of social accountability, which for the most part lacks 'teeth'" (p. 163). As Joshi notes, legal empowerment approaches — inasmuch as they are underpinned by human rights considerations of equality and non-discrimination — tend to be better attuned to questions of exclusion and marginalization and more inclusive as a result. See also Weru et al. (2015, p. 252).

37 Witnessed firsthand by the authors in Nairobi (Di Giovanni), and evoked previously in Buenos Aires by team members, including one of the authors (Bercovich), who notes that ACIJ is one of the most frequent litigators on social rights against the Buenos Aires municipal authority.

38 See also White (1996, p. 146); Hickey and Mohan (2004, p. 13); Gaventa (2004, p. 29).

39 On procedural guarantees contributing to day-to-day, deliberative democracy, see Akech (2017, pp. 20–21) (on Kenya), and Liston et al. (2013, pp. 49–50).

40 Brinks and Gauri (2008), describing how "political elites… hide the true cost of fulfilling universalistic commitments so that public expenditures can continue to be used for narrow partisan or sectarian agendas" (p. 348).

41 See, e.g., Cities Alliance (2017).

42 Villa 31 is the informal settlement of Buenos Aires in which the participation of both organized neighbours and technical organizations has been more discussed and legally regulated. In 2018, a new law, Law No. 6.129, Dec. 13, 2018, B.O.C.B.A. 5537 (Arg.), explicitly recognized the involvement of various actors in the process of urban integration of Villa 31, including ACIJ (Mesel, 2019, p. 1).

43 See also OSJI (2018) and Liebenberg (2018, p. 631), as cited in Sabel and Simon (2004).

44 Again, the goal is not to wade into wider debates about separation of powers or courts' democratic legitimacy. See Yepes (2006) and Mehta (2007).

45 See also Langford (2014, p. 204); Rodríguez-Garavito and Kauffman (2014, p. 7); OSJI (2018, p. 8).

References

Aguilar, R. A. C., Diaz-Bonilla, C., Fujs, T., Lakner, C., Cong Nguyen, M., Viveros, M., & Baah, S. K. T. (2024, March 26). March 2024 global poverty update from the World Bank: First estimates of global poverty until 2022 from survey data. *World Bank Blogs.* https://blogs.worldbank.org/en/opendata/march-2024-global-poverty-update-from-the-world-bank–first-esti.

Akech, M. (2017). *Administrative law*. Strathmore University Press.

Albiston, C. (2010). The dark side of litigation as a social movement strategy. *Iowa Law Review Bulletin*, 96, 61.

Amigo, A. (2009). Derecho a la vivienda y desalojos forzosos: Legislación, discriminación y discursos en tensión [Housing Rights and Forced Evictions: Legislation, Discrimination and Discourses in Tension]. *Congreso Internacional de Investigación y Práctica Profesional En Psicología XVI Jornadas de Investigación Quinto Encuentro de Investigadores En Psicología Del MERCOSUR*. https://perma.cc/3MP9-6VUF.

Andrews, M., Pritchett, L., & Woolcock, M. (2017). *Building state capability: Evidence, analysis, action*. Oxford Academic.

Asociación Civil por la Igualdad y la Justicia (ACIJ). (2010). *A la luz de las desigualdades. Informe sobre la prestación discriminatoria del servicio de energía eléctrica en las villas de la ciudad* [*In the light of inequalities. Report on the discriminatory provision of electricity services in the city's slums*]. https://acij.org.ar/wp-content/uploads/informe_de_electricidad.pdf.

Baldiviezo, J. E., & Maranzana, A. (2013). El poder judicial en las villas de la ciudad: Vitalizando la democracia participativa [The judiciary in the slums of the city: Vitalising participatory democracy]. In L. Bercovich & G. Maurino (Eds.), *Los derechos sociales en la Gran Buenos Aires* (pp. 441–457). Eudeba.

Banks, N., Lombard, M., & Mitlin, D. (2019). Urban informality as a site of critical analysis. *The Journal of Development Studies*, 56(2), 223–238. doi:10.1080/00220388.2019.1577384.

Beall, J. (2001). Valuing social resources or capitalizing on them? Limits to pro-poor urban governance in nine cities of the south. *International Planning Studies*, 6(4), 357–375.

Bercovich, L., Acosta, M., Chellillo, M., & Giraudy, C. (2010). Desde el barrio hasta el juicio [From the neighborhood to the trial]. In *El derecho de la vivienda en la ciudad de Buenos Aires* (pp. 99–120). Asesoría General Tutelar de la Ciudad de Buenos Aires.

Brinks, D. M. (2019). Access to what? Legal agency and access to justice for Indigenous peoples in Latin America. *The Journal of Development Studies*, 55(3), 348–365. doi:10.1080/00220388.2018.1451632.

Brinks, D. M., & Gauri, V. (2008). A new policy landscape: Legalizing social and economic rights in the developing world. In V. Gauri and D. M. Brings (Eds.), *Courting social justice* (pp. 303–352). Cambridge University Press.

Carman, M., & Yacovino, M. P. (2007). Transgrediendo el derecho de los que nos vulneran: Espacios ocupados y recuperados en la Ciudad de Buenos Aires [Transgressing the rights of those who violate us: Occupied and recovered spaces in the City of Buenos Aires]. *Revista Argentina De Sociología*, 8, 26–48.

Chase, A. (2016). Human rights contestations: Sexual orientation and gender identity. *The International Journal of Human Rights*, 20(6), 703–723. doi:10.1080/13642987.2016.1147432.

Cities Alliance. (2017). *How data empowers women to drive change in informal urban settlements*. https://perma.cc/D3E8-CGDV.

Commission on Legal Empowerment of the Poor & United Nations Development Programme. (2008). *Making the law work for everyone: Report of the Commission on Legal Empowerment of the Poor*. https://perma.cc/9D3J-J7TW.

Cruz, C. Z. (1999). [On the] road back in: Community lawyering in Indigenous communities. *American Indian Law Review*, 24(1), 229–273.

Cueva, A. A. de la. (1987). Low income settlements and the law in Mexico City. *International Journal of Urban and Regional Research*, 11(4), 522–542. doi:10.1111/j.1468-2427.1987.tb00065.x.

De Soto, H. (2000). *The mystery of capital: Why capitalism triumphs in the west and fails everywhere else*. Black Swan.

Di Giovanni, A., & Bercovich, L. (2021). Legal Empowerment in informal settlements: Lessons on using the law to overcome urban exclusion and poverty in the Global South. *NYU Journal of International Law and Politics*, 54(93), 93–151.

Di Giovanni, A., & Chitalkar, P. (2022, November 10). Grassroots justice organizations are deploying research to stem the tide of injustice. *Open Global Rights*. www.openglobalrights.org/Grassroots-justice-organizations-research-combatting-injustice/.

Diamond, M. R. (2015). Community lawyering: Introductory thoughts on theory and practice. *Georgetown Journal on Poverty Law & Policy*, 22, 395.

Domingo, P., & O'Neil, T. (2014). The politics of legal empowerment: Legal mobilisation strategies and implications for development. *ODI*. https://perma.cc/YU7N-JUHV.

Duacastella Arbizu, L. E. (2018). Del saneamiento a la justicia ambiental: Conflictos en torno a la ejecución del litigio estructural en el caso "Mendoza" sobre la contaminación del Riachuelo [From clean-up to environmental justice: Conflicts surrounding the enforcement of structural litigation in the "Mendoza" case on the contamination of the Riachuelo]. *Revista Institucional De La Defensa Pública De La Ciudad Autónoma De Buenos Aires*, 8, 193.

Dugard, J. (2014). Urban basic services: Rights, reality, and resistance. In M. Langford, B. Cousins, J. Dugard, & T. Madlingozi (Eds.), *Socio-economic rights in South Africa: Symbols or substance?*Cambridge University Press.

Dugard, J., Madlingozi, T., & Tissington, K. (2014). Rights-compromised or rights-savvy? The use of rights-based strategies to advance socio-economic struggles by Abahlali baseMjondolo, the South African shack-dwellers' movement. In H. Alviar García, K. Klare, & L. A. Williams (Eds.), *Social and economic rights in theory and practice* (pp. 23–42). Routledge.

Dyzenhaus, D. (2012). Dignity in administrative law: Judicial deference in a culture of justification. *Review of Constitutional Studies*, 17, 87–114.

Echegoyemberry, N., & Pilo, S. (2020). Estudio de caso de vivienda y tierras [Housing and land case study]. *ACIJ*. https://occa.cejamericas.org/wp-content/uploads/2020/10/EstudioCaso_ViviendayTierras_Argentina.pdf.

Economist Intelligence. (2024, February 15). *Democracy index: Conflict and polarisation drive a new low for global democracy*. www.eiu.com/n/democracy-index-conflict-and-polarisation-drive-a-new-low-for-global-democracy/.

Elsesser, C. (2013). Community lawyering: The role of lawyers in the social justice movement. *Loyola Journal of Public Interest Law*, 14, 375.

Farha, L. (2014, December 22). *Report of the Special Rapporteur on adequate housing as a component of the right to an adequate standard of living, and on the right to non-discrimination in this context*. UN Doc. A/HRC/28/62.

Farha, L. (2018, September 19). *Report of the Special Rapporteur on adequate housing as a component of the right to an adequate standard of living, and on the right to non-discrimination in this context: Note by the Secretary-General*. UN Doc. A/73/310/Rev.1.

Fernandes, E., & Varley, A. (Eds.). (1998). *Illegal cities: Law and urban change in developing countries*. Zed Books.

Gaventa, J. (2004). Towards participatory local governance: Assessing the transformative possibilities. In S. Hickey & G. Mohan (Eds.), *Participation: From tyranny to transformation; exploring new approaches to participation in development* (pp. 25–41). Zed Books.

Ghana Lotto Operators Association and Others v National Lottery Authority [2007–2008] 2 SCGLR 1088. (The Supreme Court of Ghana 2008).

Gisselquist, R. M. (2019). Legal empowerment and group-based inequality. *The Journal of Development Studies*, 55(3), 333–347. doi:10.1080/00220388.2018.1451636.

Glasser, M., & Berrisford, S. (2015). Urban law: A key to accountable urban government and effective urban service delivery. *The World Bank Legal Review*, 6, 211.

Global Platform for the Right to the City. (2015). *Moving toward the implementation of the Right to the City in Latin America and Internationally*. Author.

Golub, S. (2003). *Beyond rule of law orthodoxy* (Working Paper 41). Carnegie Endowment for International Peace. www.jstor.org/stable/resrep12751.

Goodfellow, T. (2020). Political informality: Deals, trust networks, and the negotiation of value in the urban realm. *The Journal of Development Studies*, 56(2), 278–294. doi:10.1080/00220388.2019.1577385.

Goodwin, L., & Maru, V. (2017). What do we know about legal empowerment? Mapping the evidence. *Hague Journal on the Rule of Law*, 9, 157–194. doi:10.1007/s40803-016-0047-5.

Grassroots Justice Network. (2023). *Legal empowerment in informal settlements writeshop* [Unpublished document].

Healy, T., & Taylor, A. G. (2016). Making the case for community lawyering. *Clearinghouse Article*. https://perma.cc/U5AY-H8DS.

Hickey, S., & Mohan, G. (2004). Towards participation as transformation: Critical themes and challenges for a post-tyranny agenda. In *Participation: From tyranny to transformation; exploring new approaches to participation in development* (pp. 3–24). Zed Books.

Holston, J. (1991). The misrule of law: Land and usurpation in Brazil. *Comparative Studies in Society and History*, 33(4), 695–725. www.jstor.org/stable/179087.

International Development Research Centre. (2018). *Promoting legal empowerment in informal settlements: Recommendations & lessons learned*. https://perma.cc/JN5B-YZEZ.

Joseph, S.-L. (2019). Activating citizen engagement through the State of South African Cities People's Guide. In *A better world* (Vol. 5, p. 77). Tudor Rose.

Joshi, A. (2017). Legal empowerment and social accountability: Complementary strategies toward rights-based development in health? *World Development*, 99, 160–172. doi:10.1016/j.worlddev.2017.07.008.

Klaufus, C. (2012). The symbolic dimension of mobility: Architecture and social status in Ecuadorian informal settlements. *International Journal of Urban and Regional Research*, 36(4), 689–705. doi:10.1111/j.1468-2427.2012.01122.x.

Land Resource Management Centre, Kwame Nkrumah University of Science and Technology & Kumasi and People's Dialogue/Slum Dwellers International. (2018). *Improving governance, voice and access to justice in Ghana's informal settlements* [Unpublished document].

Langford, M. (2014). Housing rights litigation: Grootboom and beyond. In M. Langford, B. Cousins, J. Dugard & T. Madlingozi (Eds.), *Socio-economic rights in South Africa: Symbols or substance?* (pp. 187–225). Cambridge University Press.

Liebenberg, S. (2018). Participatory justice in social rights adjudication. *Human Rights Law Review*, 18(4), 623–649.
Liston, M. (2013). Governments in miniature: The rule of law in the administrative state. In C. Flood, & L. Sossin (Eds.), *Administrative Law in Context* (2nd ed., p. 39). Emond-Montgomery Publishing.
Lyall, C., Bruce, A., Marsden, W., & Meagher, L. (2013). The role of funding agencies in creating interdisciplinary knowledge. *Science and Public Policy*, 40(1), 62–71.
Mansuri, G., & Rao, V. (2013). *Localizing development: Does participation work?* International Bank for Reconstruction and Development / The World Bank.
Maru, V. (2010). Allies unknown: Social accountability and legal empowerment. *Health and Human Rights*, 12(1), 83–93.
Mbazira, C. (2008). Non-implementation of court orders in socio-economic rights litigation in South Africa? Is the cancer here to stay? *ESR Review*, 9(4), 2–7.
McAuslan, P. (2003). *Bringing the law back in: Essays in land, law and development*. Routledge.
Mehta, P. B. (2007). India's unlikely democracy: The rise of judicial sovereignty. *Journal of Democracy*, 18(2), 70–83.
Merry, S. E. (2006). Transnational human rights and local activism: Mapping the middle. *American Anthropologist*, 108(1), 38–51.
Mesel, F. (2019). ¿Como se encuentra garantizada la seguridad en la tenencia en la Villa 31? [How is security of tenure guaranteed in Villa 31?]. *Revista Hábitat Inclusivo*, 13.
Mesel, F., Vitale, P., & Valentini, M. (2018). El derecho y sus usos en el hábitat informal de la Ciudad de Buenos Aire. In A. R. Patiño & A. F. C. Cárdenas (Eds.), *Desarrollo Territorial, Reasentamiento Y Desplazamiento De Población Realidad, Política Pública Y Derechos En La Ciudad Latinoamericana Del Siglo XXI* (pp. 248–285). Centro de Publicaciones Universidad Nacional de Colombia, sede Medellín.
Mitlin, D. (2001). The formal and informal worlds of state and civil society: What do they offer to the urban poor? *International Planning Studies*, 6(4), 377–392. doi:10.1080/13563470120092386.
Muia, W. (2024, August 8). Kenya police tear-gas protesters as cabinet sworn in. *BBC*. www.bbc.com/news/articles/cdx69d41y2zo.
Muzondi, L. (2014). Urban development planning for sustainability: Urbanization and informal settlements in a democratic South Africa. *Mediterranean Journal of Social Sciences*, 5(14), 641–648. doi:10.5901/mjss.2014.v5n14p641.
Okem, A. E., Makanishe, T. B., Myeni, S. L., Roberts, D. C., & Zungu, S. (2022). A scoping review of COVID-19 in the context of informal settlements. *Urbanisation*, 7 (2), 147–162. doi:10.1177/24557471221129058.
Open Society Justice Initiative (OSJI). (2018). *Strategic litigation impacts: Insights from global experience*. Author.
Ouma, S., Beltrame, D. C., Mitlin, D., & Chitekwe-Biti, B. (2024). *Informal settlements: Domain report* (ACRC Working Paper 2024–2009). African Cities Research Consortium, The University of Manchester. www.african-cities.org/.
Parnell, S., & Pieterse, E. (2010). The "right to the city": Institutional imperatives of a developmental state. *International Journal of Urban and Regional Research*, 34(1), 146–162. doi:10.1111/j.1468-2427.2010.00954.x.
Rabbee, S. (2024, August 10). After Hasina: Cautious optimism for Bangladesh's future. *Aljazeera*. www.aljazeera.com/opinions/2024/8/10/after-hasina-cautious-optimism-for-bangladeshs-future#:~:text=The%20overthrow%20of%20Sheikh%20Ha

sina,However%2C%20many%20challenges%20lie%20ahead.&text=By%20all%20quantifiable%20measures%2C%20Bangladesh%27s,had%20seen%20since%20its%20independence.

Reckford, J. T. M., & Aki-Sawyerr, Y. (2023, August 22). Informal settlements are growing worldwide — Here's what we need to do. *World Economic Forum*. www.weforum.org/agenda/2023/08/informal-settlements-are-growing-heres-how-we-provide-everyone-a/.

Rodriguez, M. C., Rodriguez, M. F., & Zapata, M. C. (2018). Mercantilización y expansión de la inquilinización informal en villas de Buenos Aires, Argentina [Commodification and expansion of informal tenancy in the slums of Buenos Aires, Argentina]. *Revista Invi*, 34(93), 125.

Rodríguez-Garavito, C., & Kauffman, C. (2014). *Making social rights real: Implementation strategies for courts, decision makers and civil society* [Dejusticia Working Paper No. 2]. https://perma.cc/ZT3A-XQ7Q.

Roy, A. (2005). Urban informality: Toward an epistemology of planning. *Journal of the American Planning Association*, 71(2), 147–158. doi:10.1080/01944360508976689.

Sabel, C., & Simon, W. (2004). Destabilization rights: How public law litigation succeeds. *Harvard Law Review*, 117, 1016.

Sage, C., Menzies, N., & Woolcock, M. (2009). *Taking the rules of the game seriously: Mainstreaming justice in development — The World Bank's Justice for the Poor program* (Working Paper 51845). The World Bank. https://perma.cc/XK5D-GFH8.

Santos, B. de S. (1995). *Toward a new common sense: Law, science, and politics in the paradigmatic transition*. Routledge.

Satterthwaite, M. (2022). Critical legal empowerment for human rights. In G. de Búrca (Ed.), *Legal Mobilization for Human Rights*. Oxford Academic. www.law.nyu.edu/sites/default/files/SatterthwaiteCriticalLEforHR_EXCERPTED%20-ia%20remediated.pdf.

Sepúlveda Carmona, M. (2013, March 11). *Report of the Special Rapporteur on extreme poverty and human rights*. U.N. Doc. A/HRC/23/36.

Sepúlveda Carmona, M., & Donald, K. (2015). Beyond legal empowerment: Improving access to justice from the human rights perspective. *The International Journal of Human Rights*, 19(3), 242–259. doi:10.1080/13642987.2015.1029340.

Tamanaha, B. Z. (2007). Understanding legal pluralism: Past to present, local to global. *Sydney Law Review*, 29. https://ssrn.com/abstract=1010105.

UN-Habitat. (n.d.). *Key messages on COVID-19 and informal settlements*. https://unhabitat.org/key-messages-on-covid-19-and-informal-settlements.

UN-Habitat. (2015). *Habitat III issue papers: 22 — Informal settlements*. https://perma.cc/7TTC-QQEL.

United Nations General Assembly. (2009). *Legal empowerment of the poor and eradication of poverty*. G.A. Res. 64/215.

United Nations General Assembly. (2011). *Extreme poverty and human rights*. U.N. Doc. A/66/265.

United Nations Population Division. (2019). *World urbanization prospects: The 2018 revision*. U.N. Doc. ST/ESA/SER.A/420; Population Studies. https://digitallibrary.un.org/record/3833745?ln=en&v=pdf.

United Nations Secretary-General. (2009). *Legal empowerment of the poor and eradication of poverty: Report of the Secretary-General*. UN Doc A/64/133.

Van Gelder, J.-L. (2010). Tales of deviance and control: On space, rules, and law in squatter settlements. *Law & Society Review*, 44(2), 239–268. doi:10.1111/j.1540-5893.2010.00406.x.

Van Gelder, J.-L. (2013). Paradoxes of urban housing informality in the developing world. *Law & Society Review*, 473, 493–522. www.jstor.org/stable/43670344.

Vitale, P., Echegoyemberry, M. N., Mesel, F., & Valentini, M. (2019). Prácticas de empoderamiento jurídico y abogacía comunitaria en América Latina: Asentamientos y pobreza urbana [Legal empowerment practices and community advocacy in Latin America: Settlements and urban poverty]. In N. Echegoyemberry, S. Pilo, L. Bercovich & M. Almela (Eds.), *Empoderamiento Jurídico Y Abogacía Comunitaria En Latinoamérica* (p. 14). Asociación Civil por la Igualdad y la Justicia.

Vitale, P., Mesel, F., & Echegoyemberry, M. N. (2020). *Desafiando a la segregación socio — Espacial en grandes ciudades Latinoamericanas: Empoderamiento legal comunitario y acceso a la justicia* [*Dismantling Socio-Spatial Segregation in Large Latin American Cities: Community Legal Empowerment and Access to Justice — Final Technical Report*]. http://hdl.handle.net/10625/60673.

Waldorf, L. (2019). Legal empowerment and horizontal inequalities after conflict. *The Journal of Development Studies*, 55(3), 437–455. doi:10.1080/00220388.2018.1451635.

Watson, V. (2009). "The planned city sweeps the poor away…": Urban planning and 21st century urbanisation. *Progress in Planning*, 72(3), 151–193. doi:10.1016/j.progress.2009.06.002.

Weru, J., Wanyoike, W., & Di Giovanni, A. (2015). Confronting complexity: Using action-research to build voice, accountability, and justice in Nairobi's Mukuru informal settlements. *The World Bank Legal Review*, 6, 265.

White, S. C. (1996). Depoliticising development: The uses and abuses of participation. *Development in Practice*, 6(1), 142–155. doi:10.1080/0961452961000157564.

Wilkinson, A. (2020). Local response in health emergencies: Key considerations for addressing the COVID-19 pandemic in informal urban settlements. *Environment and Urbanization*, 32(2), 503–522. doi:10.1177/0956247820922843.

Yepes, R. U. (2006, October 11). Should courts enforce social rights? The experience of the Colombian Constitutional Court. *Dejusticia*. https://docs.google.com/document/d/1AVli6v8DbuVvufivHM2On-PHuj9iWi4a/edit.

Zárate, L. (2016). They are not "informal settlements" — They are habitats made by people. *The Nature of Cities*. https://perma.cc/RQ7E-CGE4.

2 Legal empowerment approaches to gender equality in informal settlements

Catalina Marino

Introduction

Gender inequalities remain deeply entrenched in today's cities, where gender gaps in income, assets, health, education, representation and vulnerability to violence are still the norm (Chant & McIlwaine, 2015; Jarvis et al., 2009). However, a substantial urban heterogeneity makes gender inequality trends most noticeable in marginalized communities, particularly in urban slums (Tacoli, 2012; Tacoli & Satterthwaite, 2013). Slum dwellers are exposed to multiple social, material and political exclusions reinforced by a discriminatory built environment (Jarvis et al., 2009). Nevertheless, female slum residents face unique challenges that make them more vulnerable to these inequalities.

Due to the "gendered division of labour" (Moser, 1993, p. 28) that has feminized child care and household duties, the burden of unpaid work falls disproportionately on women. Limited access to infrastructure and public services only exacerbates this trend (Jarvis et al., 2009). In addition to domestic and care duties within their homes, women living in slums often volunteer to provide water or other shared services (Tacoli, 2012). Consequently, additional time burdens from community-management roles further limit women's access to income-generating work and participation in other social and political spheres (Bradshaw et al., 2018; Chant, 2003, 2008). Poor street lighting, narrow corridors and limited security patrols also leave female slum residents more exposed to insecurity and violence (Chant & McIlwaine, 2015).

Access to housing is essential for "promoting women's autonomy in all spheres of life and for making other human rights effective" (Rolnik, 2012, p. 5). It is well established that housing rights contribute to women's bargaining power inside and outside their households and can enhance their agency over life choices (Datta, 2006; Kabeer, 2003; Miraftab, 2001; Moser, 2016). In domestic violence cases, not having access to secure housing at a safe remove from their aggressors can be fatal for women (Rolnik, 2012). In low-income contexts, the house also provides space for women to develop income-generating and community-building activities (Chant & McIlwaine, 2015). Consequently, housing is linked to women's daily wellbeing and is essential for promoting their independence, integrity and economic security, especially in urban slums.

DOI: 10.4324/9781003538806-2

This volume describes and reflects on various challenges faced by marginalized groups that are partially explained by the intersection of gender, ethnicity, religion, socio-economic status and nationality, among other social and economic factors. Without ignoring these intersectionalities, this article argues that adopting a gender lens is essential to identify challenges and opportunities for advocacy and legal empowerment approaches to secure the rights of marginalized communities, particularly women.

The role of women in identifying and advocating for essential community resources is explicitly addressed in several chapters that follow. In Mexico (Chapter 10), four female community leaders spearheaded court action to demand access to water connections in the settlement of Ampliación Tres de Mayo. In the Mukuru informal settlements within Nairobi, Kenya (Chapter 5), women led demands and demonstrations for access to water and sanitation services before government authorities. In Brazil (Chapter 3), women in a *favela* of Rio de Janeiro identified the reopening and access to a local preschool centre as an essential need, given women's unacknowledged caregiving role. In Ambedkar Nagar Camp in Delhi, India (Chapter 6), trained female paralegals were instrumental in catalyzing local participation in designing community upgrades to address gaps in water access, health, sanitation and food security. Finally, experiences from informal settlements on the outskirts of Durban, South Africa (Chapter 9) and Karachi, Pakistan (Chapter 11) also allow us to observe how eviction processes and access to land ownership produce certain differentiated impacts on women.

One of the central premises of this book is that legal empowerment is a fundamental tool to dispute power imbalances and guarantee the rights of marginalized communities (Di Giovanni & Bercovich, 2021). Using law and human rights as a strategy to confront urban and social segregation is common to all the cases analysed here. In turn, this chapter aims to understand how these strategies can promote advances in gender justice. Through a comparative analysis of the various community experiences in using legal empowerment in cities of the Global South described in this book, it highlights some strategies that seem more successful in advancing gender equality. The analysis is organized as follows:

- The following section reviews discussions of gender equality and proposes an analytical framework for assessing the impact of community legal empowerment on women slum-dwellers.
- The next section presents three selected cases, following the experiences reported by partner organizations: the experience of the Civil Association for Equality and Justice (ACIJ) in Villa 31, Buenos Aires, Argentina; the diverse interventions of the Socio-Economic Rights Institute (SERI) in South Africa, and Nazdeek's legal empowerment workshops in Delhi's Ambedkar Nagar Camp.
- Finally, the conclusion suggests some lessons to enhance the gender equality outcomes of future legal empowerment efforts.

Gender equality debates and a framework for analysis

Over the decades, different debates have dominated the conceptualization of gender equality. In the early 1970s, development policies and practice were chiefly concerned with the economic aspects of gender inequalities (Kabeer, 2003; Moser, 2014). However, by the early 1980s, it was clear to many activists that, beyond ensuring women's access to resources, the gender relations that allowed those restrictions to arise in the first place needed to be challenged (Razavi & Miller, 1995). Poverty-alleviation policies alone would not effectively promote gender equality, essentially because women's subordination was not caused by poverty (Jackson, 1996). As it was possible to improve women's condition without challenging their social position (Johnson, 2005), inequality necessarily had to be understood in terms of power (Razavi & Miller, 1995).

Feminists have historically argued that gender differences respond less to biological characteristics of the sexes than to culturally and socially constructed representations and the power relations between them (Whitehead, 1979). As there is nothing "natural" about women's subordination (Cornwall & Rivas, 2015), expressions of gender inequality involve various context-specific dynamics of power. However, the "gendered division of labour" is usually identified as one of the primary roots of gender inequality (Moser, 1993).

Many authors argue that this division of labour is fundamentally explained by the conflation of "biological reproduction" with the "reproduction of labour power" (Levy, 2009, pp. iv–v). This misconception makes women's reproductive role not limited to childbearing but extending to care duties and household organization (Levy, 2009). As women are expected to develop these responsibilities as part of their "natural" role, their work is often invisible, unpaid and unvalued (Chant & McIlwaine, 2015; Moser, 1993). In contexts where the state fails to provide basic infrastructure, women's reproductive role also extends to the community, making their active involvement essential for the maintenance and distribution of collective services (Chant & McIlwaine, 2015; Htun & Weldon, 2010; Jarvis et al., 2009; Tacoli, 2012; Tacoli & Satterthwaite, 2013). Consequently, women in urban slums usually develop a "triple role", that encompasses reproductive, productive and community management work (Moser, 1993, pp. 28–34).

Acknowledging the existence of this extended gendered division of labour and women's unequal control over power and resources has crucial implications for gender equality. Essentially, it leads to the understanding that different gender roles imply different gender needs (Moser, 1993). When urban, legal and public policy approaches overlook women's multiple and active roles in the family and the community, they tend to be unresponsive to their needs — or even reproduce inequalities.

The literature provides a variety of answers to the question of how to identify actions, policies and projects that contribute to gender equality. However, for this chapter's purposes, two valuable threads of discussion are especially useful to review: on women's gender needs and empowerment frameworks.

According to some scholars, actions can promote gender equality if they are rooted in women's "prioritised concerns" (Molyneux, 1985). Identifying women's needs is essential for any strategy that aims to bring about change. However, to identify wholly transformative actions, it is often helpful to first understand what kind of gender needs these actions are helping to meet. In this quest, it is helpful to borrow from Molyneux and Moser in distinguishing between practical and strategic gender needs.

Moser (1993) defines practical gender needs as the ones that "women identify in their socially accepted roles in society" (p. 40). These needs respond to an "immediate perceived necessity, identified within a specific context… [often] concerned with inadequacies in living conditions" (p. 40). In this case, the concerns arise from women's subordinate positions in society without challenging them. Addressing practical gender needs means to improve the conditions derived from women's placement within the gendered division of labour structure.

In contrast, strategic gender needs are those "women identify because of their subordinate position to men in their society" (Moser, 1993, p. 39). These are intimately related to claims to transform gendered divisions of labour and enhance women's position, power and control. Actions designed to meet strategic gender needs challenge existing power structures and help to promote gender equality. Strategic gender needs, then, are intrinsically political and transformative.

While achieving strategic gender needs is essential for gender equality, their identification and promotion imply a significant level of consciousness (Molyneux, 1998). Challenging the gender division of labour requires critical reflection, where "common sources of exclusion, exploitation and oppression are acknowledged" (Levy, 2009, p. viii). However, as Molyneux (1998) has noted, women's strategic gender needs are not necessarily clear or unanimously shared because women's political, economic and social subordination is not only the product of gender relations. Sometimes, gender identities can intersect and conflict with other identities related to class, caste, religion, ethnicity, sexuality, age or ability (Mohanty, 2003; Sweetman, 2013; Ward & Mouyly, 2013). Consequently, building consciousness around women's commonality of interests derived from their gender subordination becomes critical to enhancing their solidarity and collaboration (Moser, 1993).

The emphasis on building awareness around power inequalities appears as a crucial component in other discussions of the literature focused on the definitions and scope of women's empowerment. Although the contributions of this debate to the literature on gender equality are abundant, Naila Kabeer's reflections have focused on three concepts that are especially useful for this analysis.

The first dimension of empowerment refers precisely to individual and collective awareness. Empowerment is a process that cannot be "bestowed by others" (Cornwall & Rivas, 2015, p. 404). It requires both individual consciousness around power inequalities and collective action to promote change.

As institutional and cultural biases can prevent some choices or deny the injustices in power inequalities, true agency entails subjectivity and consciousness. This empowerment aspect implies the perception, awareness and challenge of previously unquestioned gender power relations (Kabeer, 2012, p. 5).

Empowerment depends also on agency. This second aspect entails "the processes by which those who have been denied the ability to make choices acquire such an ability" (Kabeer, 2003, p. 170). The concrete exercise of choice is thus an essential aspect of agency. From this approach, choices can be expressed through participation in decision-making processes, protests or negotiations, but always requires the existence of alternatives, that is, "the ability to choose something different" (p. 170). In other words, participation in decision-making spaces *per se* does not guarantee true agency if there are no alternative choices.

Finally, empowerment also entails access to resources (Kabeer, 2003, p. 172), the medium through which power and choice are exercised. Agency allows people to increase control over various tangible or intangible resources, whether economic, social or human. The combination of resources and agency constitutes people's ability and potential to exercise choice (Kabeer, 2003). This third dimension of the women's empowerment framework revisits the economic aspect of gender relations and emphasizes the complex relationship between women's self-awareness and their access to and control over resources (Cornwall & Rivas, 2015). In this sense, the framework is connected to other debates that affirm that protecting women's rights to land, housing and security of tenure could promote greater gender equality (Jones et al., 2010; Miraftab, 2001; Rakodi, 2014; Rolnik, 2012; Varley, 2007; Whitehead & Tsikata, 2003)

This review of previous debates has shown that there is no univocal method to understand and evaluate actions contributing to gender equality. Based on the literature, this chapter uses a framework based on three fundamental dimensions to analyse the gender-differentiated outcomes of the community legal empowerment efforts explored in specific case studies from this collection:

1 **Fulfilment of women's practical and strategic needs.** As the literature shows, progress in addressing both everyday practical concerns and structural inequalities is especially relevant for gender equality. Access to resources is essential to women's strategic interests as it can enable a substantive and transformative change in their access to power.
2 **Collective consciousness.** Women's awareness of power imbalances is an inherent dimension of empowerment and a precondition for identifying strategic gender needs. This dimension is useful in capturing the extent to which there is a change in the collective understanding of gender structures.
3 **Participation (agency).** Following Kabeer's guidelines, to be considered an exercise of agency, women's participation in decision-making spaces must offer them real and alternative options.

Case studies of advancing gender equality through legal empowerment

This section presents an analysis of three cases of legal empowerment included in this collection, using the dimensions outlined above to examine their role in advancing gender equality. These three cases — one from Latin America, one from Africa, and one from South Asia — differ considerably in the degree to which they integrated gender perspectives and pursued objectives for women's empowerment. In Argentina, there were no specific goals for gender equality or integration of gender perspectives. In South Africa, there was some analysis of how women are differentially affected by inadequate housing and tenure insecurity, but no specific objectives for women's empowerment. In contrast, the Indian case study was substantively led by women with an explicit goal of empowering women. Nonetheless, by design or incidentally, each can be seen to have advanced gender equality to some degree, given the important role that housing plays in meeting women's practical needs.

These cases were selected based on the expressed interest of their proponents in contributing to further gender analysis of their outcomes. In addition to drawing on the chapters that follow in this book, the author of this present chapter conducted further interviews and discussion with the researchers and advocates who supported the efforts in Argentina, South Africa and India. This gender analysis also draws on additional case material not found in the following chapters. It is thus complementary to their primary focus on broader community legal empowerment. In the first case study analysed, in Buenos Aires, Argentina, the author also draws on additional insights from her work with ACIJ, which has worked for decades with the residents of Villa 31.

Villa 31 in Buenos Aires, Argentina

During the last decade, Argentine feminist movements have generated strong awareness on sexual violence, reproductive rights, and gender inequality in reproductive roles and wage gaps (OGyPP, 2021). This renewed feminist consciousness has strengthened women's leadership and their role in public policy design at all levels. However, the legal empowerment strategies specifically promoted in Villa 31, one of the largest informal settlements in Buenos Aires, largely predate this recent discourse. In this sense, the example allows us to see how, even without a specific gender focus, advances in gender equality can still be possible, at least in relation to meeting women's practical needs. However, as literature has repeatedly warned, strategic needs and empowerment issues are less accomplished without a specific strategy designed to target them.

The experience documented in Chapter 8 by ACIJ covers almost 20 years of history and diverse legal strategies slum residents have used to fight for their rights and improve their quality of life. Like most informal settlements in the city, Villa 31's inhabitants lack formal land tenure, which has left them at the mercy of eviction threats. Houses are often affected by infrastructure, lighting and ventilation problems, but unlike other regions, most have individual (informal) connections to water, sewage and electricity systems. However, as these infrastructure lines are, in most cases, installed by the residents themselves, neither the continuity nor the quality of the services is guaranteed. Likewise, the settlement's inaccessibility limits residents' access to public transportation, ambulance services and fire trucks, which in turn affect their health and education rights.

One of the Villa 31 community's first experiences in using legal strategies to access public services began in 2006 when, with ACIJ's legal sponsorship, a group of neighbours sued the local government for deficiencies in the water and sanitation service. The claims were successful in court, allowing for some improvements in service provision. However, they failed to elicit a comprehensive plan to ensure access to infrastructure for the entire community. Nonetheless, the experience was vital to enhancing neighbourhood organization, opening spaces for community action in the courts and generating new strategic actions.[1]

Partly as a result of these lessons, community leaders came together with social organizations, activists and legal promoters to create a community roundtable (*Mesa por la Urbanización*) to discuss, design and promote an urban-integration project for their neighbourhood. Thanks to community mobilization, lobbying and coordination with local legislators, community members achieved the sanction of Law 3343 in 2009, which ordered the urban integration of Villa 31, contemplating direct participatory procedures of its inhabitants.

However, it was only in 2016 that the local government started implementing a comprehensive slum-upgrading program for Villa 31. This project built upon part of previous neighbourhood struggles, including the provision of public service infrastructure, construction of 1254 new homes, improvements to existing housing stock, and the creation of participatory mechanisms and an oversight committee that involved community leaders. Likewise, the government has built educational, commercial and institutional facilities within the settlement, including a new building for the Ministry of Education. While still in progress, the provision of land deeds for new and existing houses is also planned, guaranteeing tenure security for all residents. This policy incorporated two gender-sensitive criteria for the allocation of land titles: (1) the joint ownership of new houses, to be registered in the name of both partners or spouses; (2) prioritizing the allocation of land titles to women in reported domestic violence cases.

The Villa 31 example clearly shows how legal actions and mobilization have been fundamental to achieving greater community rights, although not immediately. But to what extent have these actions translated into greater gender equality?

While it did not specifically target women's needs, our first dimension of analysis, changes achieved through legal empowerment fulfilled both their practical and strategic needs, to some extent. In terms of practical gender needs, substantive progress can be seen in outcomes of the case study. Because care is widely considered women's role and duty, the community's greater access to water, sanitation and electricity services and to educational and commercial centres primarily benefits women. The diminished time-burden of domestic chores due to improved access to services directly affects women's time availability. In terms of strategic gender needs, the housing deed policy guarantees women access to material resources, even though it does not specifically target them. By allowing women to become owners of their homes (either individually or with their partners), the policy removes one structural barrier to gender equality.

However, the impact of this example is weaker in the two other dimensions of analysis — collective consciousness and participation with agency. The use of legal tools and actions allowed greater community participation in public policy discussions, and strengthened community leadership, even within the judicial arena. However, this collective success did not specifically benefit women. In fact, in the beginning, community meetings were held weekly on Friday nights, at a time utterly incompatible with care duties assumed by most female leaders. These spaces were also strongly masculinized, with active women's participation being the exception. In the same way, concrete impacts regarding the symbolic dimension or women's collective consciousness are not documented in this case study.

The lack of gender-differentiated impacts in both collective consciousness and participatory dimensions is partly explained by the absence of gender perspective in the legal strategies promoted by the community. When the ACIJ intervention in Villa 31 started in 2006, gender inequalities and women's participation were not conceptualized as specific goals to be achieved. As a consequence, neither collective awareness nor female participation were explicitly addressed by the legal strategies deployed. The example illustrates how the gender dimension must be incorporated into the approach's design to have structurally transformative effects.

Informal settlements near Durban, South Africa

The second case of analysis is the effort spearheaded by the Socio-Economic Rights Institute (SERI) and the shack dwellers movement Abahlali base-Mjondolo (Abahlali) to use legal tools and litigation to resist eviction of the residents of informal settlements on the outskirts of Durban, South Africa. Although access to infrastructure varies across these settlements, housing is scarce, and essential service provision is generally informal, deficient and poorly maintained. Water is generally provided through water tanks or communal taps located on the outskirts of the settlements, and sanitation services take the form of chemical toilets or self-dug pit latrines shared amongst large numbers of households. Only 43 percent of slum households have formal access to electricity. Consequently, families rely on wood, candles and coal or self-installed connections to the electric grid, which increases the risks of fires.

Residents also lack formal tenure security, which is even more precarious for women, who by custom can be dispossessed by relatives in the case of divorce or the death of a spouse.

South Africa's informal settlements also carry a strong burden of racial and spatial segregation, developed under colonial rule and apartheid. Furthered by processes of migration and industrialization, the urban structure of informal settlements is informed by regulations that banned the Black majority from living in urban areas and deprived them of individual property ownership. While significant progress has been made to reverse racial segregation, it is only recently that state formal positions have shifted from slum eradication to *in situ* upgrades of these communities.

In this context, SERI provides free legal sponsorship to social and community organizations and promotes strategic litigation to address human rights violations. The organization has worked on multiple occasions with Abahlali, a non-partisan and democratic movement whose membership is 60 percent women. Together, they have successfully promoted legal actions that challenged regulations promoted by local governments. For example, their judicial challenge of the KwaZulu-Natal Slums Act — which aimed to facilitate slum clearances — succeeded in having the Act declared unconstitutional, preventing municipalities from carrying out massive evictions. In two other cases, they spearheaded legal action that challenged the municipal authority's efforts to circumvent legal protection for squatter communities. Their challenge resulted in a High Court decision that ordered the municipality to provide alternative accommodation to those evicted, increasing the cost of evictions and requiring compliance with due process.

To what extent have these legal successes helped to promote greater gender equality? Various studies show that preventing evictions directly improves community wellbeing, especially women's. The impacts of forced evictions are not gender-neutral but tend to leave women poorer and more vulnerable to violence than before (Centre on Housing Rights and Evictions, 2010). Indeed, in one South African settlement that took legal action after a series of unlawful evictions, nine of 14 applicants who had had their homes demolished by the municipality were women — all with children in their care.

This gender-differentiated impact can be explained by multiple factors. First, evictions often involve the material destruction of people's homes and belongings. Given that gender inequalities have a substantial economic component, impoverishment resulting from eviction has a more significant impact on women. Besides their worse employment rates and lower wages, female slum dwellers depend more on their houses to carry out their productive activities. Expulsion from their neighbourhoods also destroys community ties and networks, which are essential to family care tasks. Finally, becoming homeless leaves women more exposed to situations of gender violence and sexual abuse (Committee on Economic, Social and Cultural Rights, 1997).

The judicial actions that stopped evictions are especially relevant to avoid deepening gender inequalities. In this sense, the legal actions promoted significant progress related to women's practical needs. However, its effects do not impact other dimensions of gender equality, including promoting women's strategic gender needs, collective consciousness and participation in decision-making.

To promote interventions with a greater gender perspective, SERI has recently developed a second line of strategic action, focused on consultation and advocacy, to identify violations of women's constitutional rights on the ground. It seeks to generate a comprehensive diagnosis of female slum dwellers' legal needs through workshops and anonymous surveys, to identify potential advocacy actions to influence policy. As the consultation is still ongoing, no concrete impacts can be identified. However, the initiative is relevant to the other dimensions of women's empowerment.

First, the workshops and consultations were carefully designed to promote the broad participation of women in the community and encourage their active engagement. An effort was made to schedule meetings at times that did not interfere with women's daily activities at home. Female participation was highly promoted in open plenary discussions, but anonymous surveys were also used as an alternative way to capture opinions. Language accessibility was also taken into consideration in designing the workshops and questionnaires.

Workshops and meetings provided a space for collective discussion and exchange, allowing women to identify some common problems and build collective awareness about their roles in the community. In some cases, these discussions enabled the identification of practical challenges derived from their roles as caregivers. Access to water was considered the top priority, given the time burdens associated with their daily tasks. In other cases, threats related to security and physical or sexual violence were identified, sometimes deepened by a lack of public lighting or poor access to communal toilets.

Tenure insecurity was also mentioned as a priority. In this case, two sources of insecurity were identified: external threats, linked to governmental eviction orders, and internal threats, coming from claims of other family members. The identification of this second type of insecurity problematized cultural beliefs and family property norms that leave women unprotected regarding the ownership of their home, especially when their claims are contested by their male partners or other men in the family.

The South African example shows how some practical gender needs can be addressed even when legal empowerment objectives do not focus specifically on women. Suspension of evictions, even when benefiting the whole community, is especially relevant to protect women. However, these actions fail to promote more transformative elements of women's empowerment, participation and collective consciousness. These areas are being addressed, in turn, by the more recent legal empowerment strategies being developed by SERI. Community workshops effectively promote shared awareness of strategic gender needs and help to conceptualize them as priorities to be addressed. Women being able to identify patriarchal norms, gender violence and sexual abuse as critical problems demonstrates how collective spaces for discussion can help women to voice gender inequalities related to power structures within their communities and households.

Ambedkar Nagar Camp in Delhi, India

Delhi's informal settlements vary in population size but are characterized by precarious housing conditions, lack of access to infrastructure and sanitation services, insecurity in tenure and threats of eviction. In the case of Ambedkar Camp, most houses are built with temporary materials and have severe deficiencies in lighting and ventilation. Although some have individual water connections, most households depend on community connections, which supply water for just one or two hours a day. The settlement also lacks a sewage line: while some families have built individual or shared bathrooms, these are usually connected to wells dug under the houses, a dangerous and risky practice.

The legal empowerment program implemented in Ambedkar Nagar Camp by the women-led community justice and empowerment organization Nazdeek had two complementary objectives: to guarantee greater community access to the legal system and to strengthen women's leadership role in their community. To do this, context-specific needs and challenges were first identified in a participatory process with grassroots organizations. Then 10 local women — mostly homemakers, with varying literacy levels — were selected for training as community paralegals. Training workshops covered four broad areas: (1) rights, laws, programs and resources; (2) tools and mechanisms to access non-judicial grievance redress and remedial mechanisms; (3) platforms for recording and reporting rights violations — including community meetings, surveys, and advocacy with elected officials; and (4) strategic litigation. Throughout the program, these women were encouraged to organize community meetings to share their knowledge with their neighbours.

After the training, the paralegals became engaged with identifying, documenting and reporting rights violations in Ambedkar Camp. The use of administrative and legal tools earned them several successes, which improved some infrastructure and services in the settlement. In addition, this group of paralegals was instrumental in promoting a community-led project for the incremental *in situ* upgrading of the settlement. Using their experience in bringing demands to their local representatives and following the example of neighbouring settlements, this group of women organized the community to demand sewage works and housing improvements in their neighbourhood.

With its intentional focus on empowering women as community leaders, this project achieved advances in gender equality across several dimensions. Significant advances can be seen in addressing gender needs, the first dimension of analysis. Through their work in seeking grievance redressal and government accountability, the paralegals addressed a number of practical gender needs, such as by restoring ambulance service in the neighbourhood, improving the quality of food rations, and attaining more frequent water supply, and sanitation and cleaning services. These collective improvements are fundamental for the community as a whole, but especially for women in their gender-assigned role of caretakers. Even when these gender-ascribed roles remain unchallenged, improvements in community health services, food security, and water and sanitation infrastructure can reduce the daily burden of care on women.

The legal empowerment program also addressed some strategic gender needs. First, the training workshops helped disseminate information on available public benefits, pensions and entitlements, which benefited women in the community, especially widows. Although insufficient, these programs provide women access to resources (assets) that contribute to their economic freedom, stability and independence. Furthermore, having been successful in their claims to the authorities, paralegals' leadership roles within the community were strengthened. This had an impact on two levels: first, it positioned women in a role of power within the community; second, on an individual level, it strengthened women's self-confidence, both among their peers and in their households.

The Ambedkar Nagar Camp case also produced exciting results in the dimension of collective consciousness. First, the legal empowerment program designed by Nazdeek fully acknowledges women's diversity within the community, reflecting an understanding that gender needs are not uniform. The workshops were developed on the assumption that, in the first instance, they would only achieve the participation of dominant groups in the community. Consequently, they have a medium-term approach, aiming to eventually involve other vulnerable female groups. The meetings are also designed to mitigate existing power hierarchies among women, linked in part to the predominant caste system. To this end, in addition to plenary discussions, they include small-group meetings and individual consultations in participants' homes, to offset the tendency of some voices to dominate in larger gatherings.

The careful design of these workshops fostered a sense of cohesion among the paralegals. Through the program, collective discussions allowed them to identify common problems and challenges. In addition to those related to their practical gender needs (maternal health, food security, sanitation and housing), women also pointed to patriarchal norms, gender violence and sexual abuse as critical problems. In this sense, collective spaces allowed them to verbalize inequalities related to power structures within the community and the household. The program also enabled paralegals to engage with women from other communities and rehabilitation sites in Delhi. This experience was crucial for them to understand the challenges of state resettlement programs in providing access to infrastructure, services, employment and the maintenance of community networks. Hearing the life experiences of other women enabled paralegals to understand their best interests regarding state renewal programs. Eventually, this experience allowed them to co-create their own *in situ* community upgrading project.

Finally, the Ambedkar Nagar Camp example also produced results relevant to the effective participation of women at two different levels. First, enhancing women's participation in the community was a core goal of the project, and the legal empowerment approach was designed to ensure it.

Consequently, meetings were set during weekdays and in the morning hours so as not to interfere with typical household and care tasks. Meeting spaces were also carefully designed to generate an environment of exchange, which would allow participants to overcome feelings of fear or hesitation.

Second, women's effective participation in public decisions expanded as a result of the legal empowerment program. As paralegals, women actively promoted administrative and judicial actions and engaged in advocacy and lobby strategies with local decision-makers. The success of these strategies not only contributed to improving some practical aspects of daily life but also allowed them to strengthen their leadership role within the community. This experience enabled the community to promote a bottom-up slum-upgrading project, designed with women's best interests in mind.

In conclusion, the Ambedkar Nagar Camp experience shows positive outcomes for gender equality across all three dimensions. Through the project, women addressed practical and strategic gender needs, forged greater collective gender awareness, and strengthened their leadership roles and participation in community decision-making. However, as Nazdeek activists themselves point out, the time-intensive responsibilities linked to their role as paralegals add new activities to the long list of unpaid care work that women already perform in their community work roles. This aspect can become a challenge to address, not only to protect the continuity of paralegals' roles but to guarantee adequate progress in gender equality.

Conclusion

The review of experiences in this article has illustrated several phenomena regarding the strategic uses of law. First, it confirms that legal strategies are a fundamental tool to contest power and guarantee the rights of communities living in informal settlements. Implementing these tools has been fundamental to confronting social and urban segregation processes in all the cases analysed.

Second, this comparative analysis also highlights some lessons learned about the potential use of legal strategies in promoting gender equality. In particular, this chapter suggests that embedding a gender perspective within the design of legal strategies is necessary to guarantee truly transformative changes that challenge gender power structures. This was apparent from the analysis of the three cases according to the gender equality dimensions that underpinned this chapter: women's practical and strategic needs, collective consciousness and participation.

Regarding the first dimension, all three cases show that legal empowerment strategies addressed at least some of women's practical gender needs without having been specifically designed to do so. Looking beyond these three cases to others explored in this book, suspending eviction processes (as in South Africa and Pakistan), improving the provision of public services, infrastructure or housing (as in Argentina, India and Mexico), or guaranteeing preschool education (as in Brazil) are immediate and urgent needs, which disproportionately affect women due to their gender-ascribed care roles. Making progress in these areas and directly improving women's daily well-being is urgent. However, these strategies alone will not help to break dominant power structures or end women's subordination.

Truly transformative actions challenge the gender division of labour that determines women's unequal access to power and resources. Attaining such a transformation can hardly be achieved as a "side effect" of broader collective strategies. On the contrary, achieving these goals requires spaces for exchange and discussion, which allow the emergence of a collective consciousness regarding strategic needs and enable the sources of exploitation and oppression to be disputed.

Regarding women's strategic gender needs, only two of the cases analysed above explicitly show progress in this area. In the case of Villa 31, community interventions managed to promote regulations that protected women's access to housing and land by recognizing them as beneficiaries of property titles (alone or with their partners). Likewise, in Delhi, women's access to public benefits and pensions was improved. In both cases, legal protection and improved material conditions can potentially pave the way for greater access to assets and influence (within and beyond the household). However, in South Africa, improvements in women's practical gender needs did not result in a rearrangement of gender structures, questioning of care tasks, or broader areas of gender empowerment.

Identifying women's strategic gender needs is not obvious, because they are not necessarily clear or unanimously shared by all women (Molyneux, 1985). There are thus no unique recipes for achieving this goal. However, promoting safe spaces for exchange and discussion where women can freely reflect and exchange opinions seems to be one of the enabling factors. In the South African case, women's collective (and private) interactions allowed them to identify certain common needs, both practical and strategic, usually linked to their caregiving roles. However, the case of Delhi's Ambedkar Camp stands out, as power structures within the community and households were discussed and revisited in women's spaces specifically designed for this purpose. In this sense, the case study suggests that collective consciousness can be achieved when it is framed as a concrete goal, and promoted within collective structures that enable it.

This same lesson applies to the participation dimension. Most chapters in this volume show that women have an active role to play in identifying and promoting community demands, either before government authorities or the courts. They illustrate that there is some agreement around the need to include historically marginalized groups in collective discussions. In this context, legal and community strategies can promote women's participation in collective spaces, even without explicitly intending to do so. However, such participation does not always translate into leadership or enable greater decision-making power. At its worst, women participation could become tokenistic, but even when it is not, it can have time-consuming effects that compete with other women's goals or needs. As the experience in Delhi shows, participation in collective spaces can become another duty that women must perform as part of their community responsibilities. In this sense, being able to identify the nuances of gender impacts becomes essential.

This chapter has shown that, to effectively promote greater gender equality, legal strategies must be specifically designed with a gender lens. To avoid creating additional time burdens and costs for women, awareness of gender-ascribed roles and responsibilities is essential when defining legal empowerment tools and activities. Being fully aware of the effects of these actions is key to alleviating adverse effects. However, legal empowerment experiences at the service of gender justice can become powerful examples. The experiences captured in this book show that there is ample room to promote greater socio-environmental justice through a widespread set of legal and community empowerment tools. This analysis has attempted to show how these successes can be extended and replicated for gender justice.

Note

1 In 2010, ACIJ sponsored another emblematic case to guarantee the educational rights of Villa 31 children, which sued the government to provide free school buses. The court recognized that children were forced to attend primary school far away, as there were no institutions nearby, and ordered the government to comply with the demand. Although, at the time, the case was not seen in terms of gender justice, it responded directly to one of women's practical needs, given their responsibility to ensure the safe transport of their children to school.

References

Bradshaw, S., Chant, S., & Linneker, B. (2018). Challenges and changes in gendered poverty: The feminization, de-feminization, and re-feminization of poverty in Latin America. *Feminist Economics*, 25(1), 119–144. doi:10.1080/13545701.2018.1529417.

Centre on Housing Rights and Evictions. (2010). The impact of forced evictions on women (p. 12) [Briefing Paper]. https://issuu.com/cohre/docs/cohre_briefpaper_impactforcedevicti.

Chant, S. (2003). *New contributions to the analysis of poverty: Methodological and conceptual challenges to understanding poverty from a gender perspective.* NU. CEPAL. Unidad Mujer y Desarrollo.

Chant, S. (2008). The "feminisation of poverty" and the "feminisation" of anti-poverty programmes: Room for revision? *The Journal of Development Studies*, 44(2), 165–197. doi:10.1080/00220380701789810.

Chant, S., & McIlwaine, C. (2015). *Cities, slums and gender in the Global South.* Routledge. doi:10.4324/9781315862996.

Committee on Economic, Social and Cultural Rights. (1997). *General comment No. 7: The right to adequate housing (Art.11.1): Forced evictions.* E/1998/22.

Cornwall, A., & Rivas, A.-M. (2015). From "gender equality and women's empowerment" to global justice: Reclaiming a transformative agenda for gender and development. *Third World Quarterly*, 36(2), 396–415. doi:10.1080/01436597.2015.1013341.

Datta, N. (2006). Joint titling — a win-win policy? Gender and property rights in urban informal settlements in Chandigarh, India. *Feminist Economics*, 12(1–2), 271–298. doi:10.1080/13545700500508569.

Di Giovanni, A., & Bercovich, L. (2021). Legal empowerment in informal settlements: Lessons on using the law to overcome urban exclusion and poverty in the Global South. *New York University Journal of International Law & Politics*, 54(1), 93–15.

Htun, M., & Weldon, S. L. (2010). When do governments promote women's rights? A framework for the comparative analysis of sex equality policy. *Perspectives on Politics*, 8(1), 207–216. doi:10.1017/S1537592709992787.

Jackson, C. (1996). Rescuing gender from the poverty trap. *World Development*, 24(3), 489–504.

Jarvis, H., Cloke, J., & Kantor, P. (2009). *Cities and gender*. Routledge. doi:10.4324/9780203878064.

Johnson, R. (2005). Not a sufficient condition: The limited relevance of the gender MDG to women's progress. *Gender & Development*, 13(1), 56–66. doi:10.1080/13552070512331332277.

Jones, N., Harper, C., Watson, C., Espey, J., Wadugodapitiya, D., Page, E., Stavropoulou, M., Presler-Marshall, E., & Clench, B. (2010). Stemming girls' chronic poverty: Catalysing development change by building just social institutions. *SSRN Electronic Journal*. doi:10.2139/ssrn.1719613.

Kabeer, N. (2003). *Gender mainstreaming in poverty eradication and the Millennium Development Goals*. OECD Publishing. doi:10.14217/9781848598133-en.

Kabeer, N. (2012). *Women's economic empowerment and inclusive growth: Labour markets and enterprise development*. Discussion Paper No. 29. Centre for Development Policy & Research, School of Oriental & African Studies, University of London, 65.

Levy, C. (2009). Viewpoint: Gender justice in a diversity approach to development?: The challenges for development planning. *International Development Planning Review*, 31 (4), i–xi. doi:10.3828/idpr.2009.6.

Miraftab, F. (2001). Risks and opportunities in gender gaps to access shelter: A platform for intervention. *International Journal of Politics, Culture and Society*, 15(1), 143–160.

Mohanty, C. T. (2003). "Under Western Eyes" revisited: Feminist solidarity through anticapitalist struggles. *Signs: Journal of Women in Culture and Society*, 28(2), 499–535. doi:10.1086/342914.

Molyneux, M. (1985). Mobilization without emancipation? Women's interests, the State, and revolution in Nicaragua. *Feminist Studies*, 11(2), 227. doi:10.2307/3177922.

Molyneux, M. (1998). Analysing women's movements. *Development and Change*, 29 (2), 219–245. doi:10.1111/1467-7660.00077.

Moser, C. (1993). Practical and strategic gender needs and the role of the state. In *Gender planning and development: Theory, practice and training* (pp. 37–54). Routledge. doi:10.4324/9780203411940.

Moser, C. (2014). Gender planning and development: Revisiting, deconstructing and reflecting. *DPU Working Paper Series*, 165, 1–28.

Moser, C. (2016). Introduction. Towards a nexus linking gender, assets, and transformational pathways to just cities. In C. Moser (Ed.), *Gender, asset accumulation and just cities: Pathways to transformation?* (pp. 1–20). Routledge.

Observatorio de Géneros y Políticas Públicas (OGyPP). (2021). *Ciudad desigual. Un análisis feminista de la situación social en los barrios populares de la Ciudad de*

Buenos Aires [*Unequal city. A feminist analysis of the social situation in the popular neighborhoods of the City of Buenos Aires*]. Observatorio de Género y Políticas Públicas. https://c015f97f-ebd0-4de8-be6f-104721f4c01f.usrfiles.com/ugd/c015f9_b4faee17dbe546f292f2d771ab2a476a.pdf.

Rakodi, C. (2014). *Expanding women's access to land and housing in urban areas* (Women's Voice and Agency Research Series, p. 56). https://openknowledge.worldbank.org/handle/10986/21030.

Razavi, S., & Miller, C. (1995). *From WID to GAD: Conceptual shifts in the women and development discourse* (pp. 1–51) (Occasional paper). United Nations Research Institute for Social Development United Nations Development Programme.

Rolnik, R. (2012). *How to make women's right to housing effective* (pp. 1–31). United Nations Special Rapporteur on the Right to Adequate Housing. www.ohchr.org/sites/default/files/Documents/Issues/Housing/GuideWomenandHousingEN.pdf.

Sweetman, C. (2013). Introduction, feminist solidarity and collective action. *Gender & Development*, 21(2), 217–229. doi:10.1080/13552074.2013.819176.

Tacoli, C. (2012). Urbanization, gender and urban poverty: Paid work and unpaid carework in the city. *Urbanization and Emerging Population Issues*. https://pubs.iied.org/10614iied.

Tacoli, C., & Satterthwaite, D. (2013). Gender and urban change. *Environment and Urbanization*, 25(1), 3–8. doi:10.1177/0956247813479086.

Varley, A. (2007). Gender and property formalization: Conventional and alternative approaches. *World Development*, 35(10), 1739–1753. doi:10.1016/j.worlddev.2007.06.005.

Ward, K., & Mouyly, V. (2013). The importance of being connected: Urban poor women's experience of self-help discourse in Cambodia. *Gender & Development*, 21(2), 313–326. doi:10.1080/13552074.2013.802482.

Whitehead, A. (1979). Some preliminary notes on the subordination of women. *The IDS Bulletin*, 10(3), 10–13. doi:10.1111/j.1759-5436.1979.mp10003003.x.

Whitehead, A., & Tsikata, D. (2003). Policy discourses on women's land rights in sub-Saharan Africa: The implications of the re-turn to the customary. *Journal of Agrarian Change*, 3(1–2), 67–112. doi:10.1111/1471-0366.00051.

3 Active citizenship and access to justice

Embedding citizenship indicators within access-to-justice strategies in Rio's *favelas*

Rita Corrêa Brandão, Larissa de Souza Ferreira de Morais, Robson de Aguiar Oliveira and Tauan da Silva Satyro

Introduction: Citizenship rights in Brazil's recent political context[1]

During its four years under the leadership of President Jair Bolsonaro (2019–2022), Brazil experienced relentless attacks on its democracy and constitutionally backed citizenship rights. The Bolsonaro administration decreased the state's ability to implement public policies that ensure these rights and dismantled the social framework protecting the most vulnerable population segments, including initiatives to fight hunger and poverty. It also reduced civic spaces by suspending mechanisms for social participation and control, while increasing unemployment and the number of Brazilians working informally.

With social investments frozen since 2016, strategic policies and programs intended to promote access to social justice have experienced gradual budget losses. As a result, several areas — including education, health care, social assistance, housing, basic sanitation, the environment and science and technology, among others — faced increasing cuts, which created even greater inequality in Brazil. The dismantling of public policies that had supported a minimum income and food and nutritional security constituted a setback in the fight against hunger in Brazil. This was marked by the return of Brazil to the FAO Hunger Map, which it had been removed from in 2014.

An aversion to political activism took root, expanding the legal and criminal toolkit waged against activists, with harsh legislation classifying demonstrations as terrorist acts. The criminalization of social movements and violence against human rights advocates increased.

Under the leadership of Governor Wilson Witzel (2019–2021), the State of Rio de Janeiro implemented a security policy based on the "war on drug trafficking", which advocated the summary execution of criminals without recourse to the law. This approach justified the death of civilians as part of the "burden of war". In just the first year of Witzel's administration, deaths caused by public authorities increased by 18 percent.

In the second half of 2022, tensions increased due to the political polarization that characterized the elections in Brazil. Experts have stated that the

DOI: 10.4324/9781003538806-3

political and social tensions were the fiercest seen since the country's return to democracy (Barbosa, 2022; Cerqueira & Moliterno, 2022; Da Silva, 2022). The 2022 presidential elections had the highest voter turnout in the 90 years of existence of Brazil's electoral court system (Statista, 2024). Backed by a wide coalition, President Luiz Inácio Lula da Silva was elected in the second round with a slim majority of 50.8 percent — a little over 60 million votes.

The newly elected president implemented the Social Participation System, under the direct scope of federal administration, which aimed at structuring relations with various civil society segments in the application of public policies. This led to closer alignment with an agenda of rights and social inclusion, which signalled to other segments of society the dawn of a new political order. A wider call to action was made among civil society in general, but especially for local active citizenship.

It is important to stress that, while there was no change in Rio de Janeiro's security policy — Governor Witzel's successor has retained the same approach regarding the "war on drug trafficking" — the entry of rights-focused legislators from the democratic camp into Rio de Janeiro's legislative assembly strengthened the possibility of wider political dialogue with the populace.

Against this background, at the end of 2019, the Brazilian Institute of Social and Economic Analysis (Ibase) launched a project called Active Citizenship and Access to Justice (CAAJ) in two locations within the Metropolitan Region of Rio de Janeiro: the Jardim Gramacho district in Duque de Caxias, on the outskirts of metropolitan Rio de Janeiro; and a group of four *favelas* (informal settlements) located within Tijuca district in northern Rio de Janeiro. Supported by the International Development Research Centre, the project ended in August 2023. Over its duration, planning and implementation were constantly adapted to the socio-political changes taking place in Brazil.

The initiative aimed to expand the possibility of fighting for the implementation of human rights for various social groups in these areas. With its unique action research methodology, Ibase sought to expand knowledge about individual and collective rights by collecting data and information, and developing indicators that could confirm the issues that territorial groups wished to change. Such data and indicators could then be used to underpin key arguments for political action, expanding the tools and strategies used in the struggle for justice.

In this time when dialogue was suppressed, Ibase piloted a combination of its existing action research methodology and drive for political action — widely used in other earlier contexts — with a process of strengthening the legal empowerment of territorial groups. This aimed to facilitate collective understanding of the tools available for accessing justice and their use as a pathway for implementing rights. For the first time, Ibase wedded an access-to-justice and legal empowerment approach to the participatory production of citizenship indicators.

In Brazil, fundamental rights are guaranteed by the 1988 Federal Constitution, also known as the Citizen Constitution, as it enshrined "citizenship" as an essential and fundamental principle. Civil and political rights (including access to justice),[2] social, economic and cultural rights (such as the right to housing, health care, education and culture), and collective rights (such as the right to the environment) are included in it.

The state is responsible for ensuring that all Brazilian citizens and foreigners residing in the country may claim their rights. Any Brazilian who feels their rights are threatened or violated may request an assessment by the judicial branch. The judicial branch decides whether or not a case deserves judicial relief, which consists of effective protection of the right, to be provided by the state.

We know, however, that rights do not take effect just because a legal system is in place. Several obstacles prevent access to justice, such as people's lack of familiarity with their rights, excessive red tape and the long timeframe needed for legal action. The use of language that is not widely understood often makes access to justice a class privilege, limited to those who can afford good legal representation. This has the effect of widening inequality, instead of legal action being an instrument to redress it. As a result, impoverished people face greater difficulty in understanding justice as an instrument to protect or restore violated rights.

The CAAJ project functioned sometimes as a link between the population and the courts, and between different governmental bodies, in seeking the realization of rights. It worked from the notion that active citizenship is key to promoting progress towards greater social justice. Those residing in the *favelas* and in the city outskirts, which are also areas of social exclusion, were seen as having important needs and a right to have their voices heard in the public arena.

In the authors' perspective, for justice to advance, it must be compelled to be more inclusive and comprehensive. It is through people's experience of lacking access to justice and their process of gaining awareness that pathways can be laid towards its realization, based on their demands for equity and justice. However, as Oliveira (2007) contends, the attempt to "impose an agenda does not necessarily mean success, or winning the argument; on the contrary, it means creating a specific field in which the adversary is obliged to move" (p. 15). Therefore, the struggle for more rights needs to be constant, and the mechanisms propelling the state and society to advance, through justice, need to be increasingly disseminated in the spaces where rights are violated.

The choice and characteristics of study sites

Ibase had previous partnerships within the two areas chosen for the Active Citizenship and Access to Justice project. In 2005, Ibase supported and promoted the creation of the Jardim Gramacho Community Forum and, over the first decade of this century, it organized and strengthened some organizations that were active in the *favelas* of Tijuca district. The choice of these sites was, however, not only due to the established environment of trust and exchange between Ibase and the local active citizenship: these are also areas of exclusion within the cities of Rio de Janeiro and Duque de Caxias, where people experience multidimensional and systemic violations of the human rights that are guaranteed for those residing in formal spaces of both cities.

Jardim Gramacho

Jardim Gramacho is a district located in the municipality of Duque de Caxias, in the Metropolitan Region of the State of Rio de Janeiro. A peripheral area of the state, its growth originated with the appearance of *favelas* and other types of irregular occupation of lands on the banks of Guanabara Bay. Large pockets of poverty characterize the site, which has approximately 20,000 residents.

One of Latin America's largest open-air garbage dumps was located there until 1996, when it was transformed into the Metropolitan Landfill of Jardim Gramacho. It operated as a controlled landfill up to 2012, when it was closed after the threat of soil cracking, which posed a serious environmental risk for Rio de Janeiro, given its proximity to Guanabara Bay.

The 36 years of operation of the dump and landfill generated a huge social and environmental liability for the district. A large group of people excluded from the formal labour market moved into the district, driven by job opportunities in collecting recyclable materials.[3] The district grew in a disorderly fashion, with no urban planning. Other issues, such as leachate ground contamination, river pollution flowing into Guanabara Bay, deforestation, silting and the contamination of mangrove swamp areas, reveal the serious socio-environmental problem that was exacerbated by the Metropolitan Landfill, which for many years was not addressed by public policy.

This district has an active and vibrant citizenry with several institutions, NGOs, sports associations, schools, community daycare centres, a strong Catholic grassroots movement, an Afro-Brazilian Black Movement, waste collectors' associations and activists promoting various rights. The Jardim Gramacho Community Forum, Ibase's partner, includes 35 local associations organized around six thematic work groups covering health care, education, labour and income, district living conditions, youth and the environment.

The group of favelas *in Tijuca*

This group consists of four *favelas*: Morro do Borel, Favela da Indiana, Morro da Chácara do Céu, and Morro Casa Branca. Located in the northern area of Rio de Janeiro, Tijuca is a middle-class district of great importance to the economic, cultural and social life of the city. The region hosts traditional samba schools, strongholds of Brazilian Funk music and large-scale commerce, along with all the services that typically guarantee rights, such as a wide network of public schools, healthcare centres and clinics, and an ample transportation network. It also hosts the Tijuca Massif, where Tijuca Forest — one of the world's largest urban forests — is located.[4]

Despite the abundance of public services, this group of *favelas* suffers serious violations of rights related to the absence of basic sanitation, education, health care and housing — exposing the region's social and economic inequality and its residents' frail exercise of the right to the city. Due to the area's high rainfall rate, landslides are also frequent and historic in scale, wrecking hillside houses and bringing death to their residents.

Currently, this group of *favelas* houses more than 20,000 residents, an overwhelmingly Black population with a large youth contingent. Residents suffer the repercussions of violence by drug dealers and by state police, preventing them from enjoying a decent life in accordance with their human rights.

In this group of Tijuca *favelas*, there is a history of organized and active citizenry, with some 20 local organizations. Here, Ibase partnered with the Brota na Laje Youth Collective, which brings together 20 fiery young activists.

The Incid methodology

As an institution that fights for human rights and the expansion of democracy, Ibase believes that to really know the living conditions of the population, indices such as the per capita gross domestic product (GDP) or the Human Development Index (HDI) are not enough. The importance of these indicators is undeniable, but political choices around the distribution of resources can't always ensure — even in a region with a high GDP — people's basic citizenship rights. While the HDI mixes income, longevity and education dimensions in a synthetic indicator, it leaves aside important aspects of social and economic development, such as access to health care, housing, public safety, working conditions, gender relations and how these dimensions promote or challenge the realization of rights.

On the other hand, the data from the state and federal institutions that comprise Brazil's Public Statistics Production and Dissemination System[5] are mostly management data that track progress in advancing public policies. These data do not reveal clearly how much still needs to be done, who is excluded and where they are located. The need to revisit the data produced about the population and their territories — to reveal the state of democracy and citizenship — has driven the creation of Incid, a citizenship indicator system.

The Incid System[6] favours different components in measuring the quality of life and the effectiveness of human rights, taking into account several aspects that are not cross-transferable to build a "menu" of indicators. The data is collected in such a way that it can be used to capture the state of rights within excluded settlements in three broad groupings —collective rights; economic, social and cultural rights; and civil and political rights) — and to analyse each of them according to four complementary dimensions. These dimensions include:

- Measured Citizenship — What do the official public data and statistics reveal about human rights within the territories? These indicators are built with secondary data produced and disclosed through Brazil's public data system.
- Guaranteed Citizenship — Which rights are guaranteed in the territories by public policies of the three government levels (local, state and federal) and by the judicial branch? These indicators are built with data provided by the various sectors of public administration.
- Perceived Citizenship — How do residents perceive the effectiveness or the violation of their rights? This is assessed based on primary data from surveys conducted directly with the population in the territory. A representative sample survey is carried out.
- Active Citizenship — How do people in the territories organize and exercise the right to social and political participation? These indicators are based on the registration of the territory's entire active citizenry (organizations, institutions, movements and individual activists).

Incid is an open system, meaning it allows new indicators to be created based on what is identified in terms of rights violations in each of the territories analysed. While its citizenship indicators need to be easy to understand, they must also be built with the utmost accuracy.

Incid is a methodology used by Ibase either in whole — with analysis of all four citizenship dimensions — or in part, using only some of the dimensions as applicable to each territory. As the result of a participatory process of a dialogue-based co-production with the territories analysed, in several instances, the indicators produced have been used as an important source of data to support informed action and momentum, strengthening communities' civic engagement in making their democratic demands, within their community, their city and the wider public arena.

The Incid methodology is based on a process where the priorities, interests and demands expressed by various local social actors are discussed. The production of indicators is entirely participatory, and the analysis and knowledge produced result from a progressive dialogue and exchange process between different subjects and types of knowledge, addressing various aspects of the problem. As a result, the data contribute to advocacy processes, providing tools that support local struggles.

Addressing new methodological challenges

The Active Citizenship and Access to Justice project was designed so that its stages unfolded in a participatory and systematic way, addressing four axes of research.

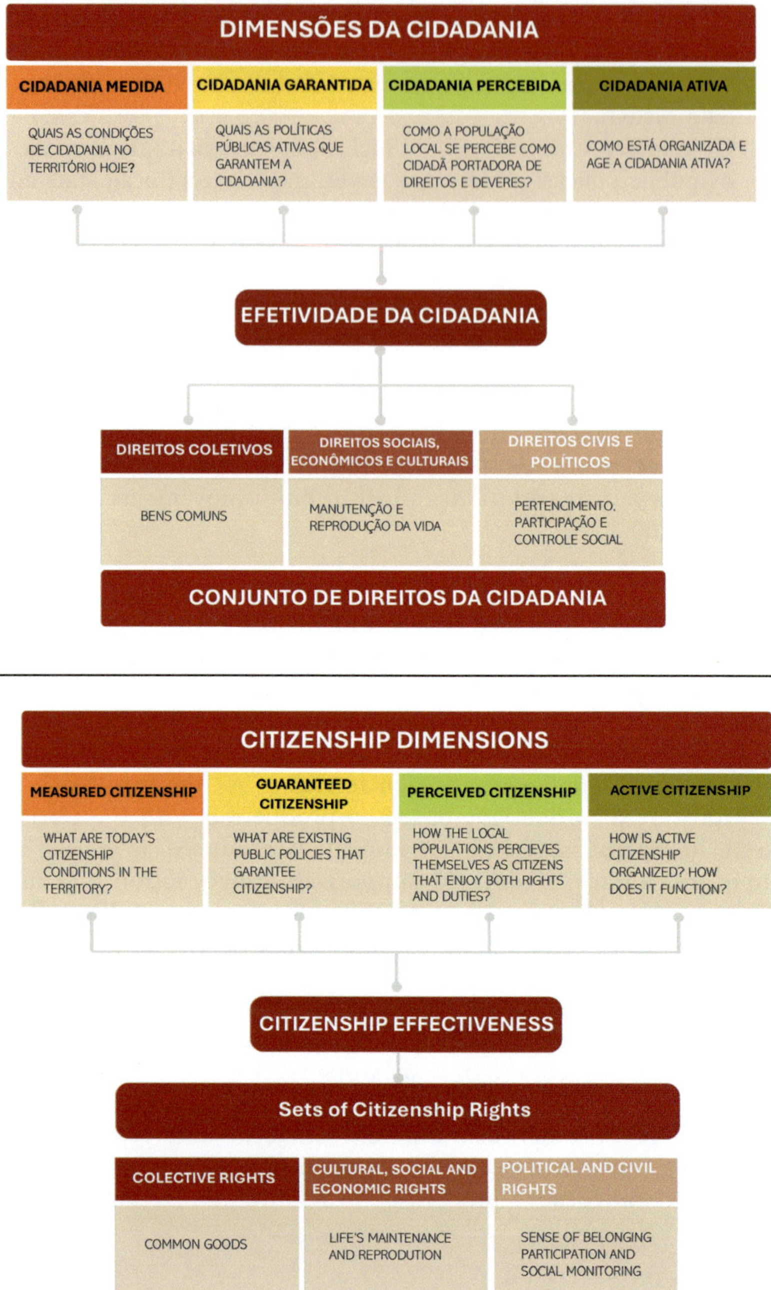

Figure 3.1 Incid's synthetic and integrative vision of citizenship dimensions and sets of citizenship rights

Source: Ibase/Incid Citizenship indicators (2011). Available at: Incid — Sistema de Indicadores.

- Axis 1: Application of the Incid methodology

This involved an extensive process of action research, and participatory production of data and indicators on living conditions and on the realization or violation of human rights.

- Axis 2: Participatory dialogue: building capacities and action strategies

Through participatory dialogue, the data collected was widely discussed and debated across the territory. Dialogue took the form of roundtables, meetings and seminars involving a progressively expanding audience. These gatherings aimed to apply the knowledge gained from the research process in the construction of demands. They identified various tools and possible forms of action, including complaint formulation, judicialization, civic action and advocacy strategies.

- Axis 3: Building capacity for human rights, civic engagement and access to justice

This entailed education and training on human rights, laws, regulatory frameworks and tools for accessing justice in Brazil and through international courts.

- Axis 4: Expanding and strengthening the project's technical and political capabilities through strategic dialogue

This axis brought civil society human rights organizations, Brazilian and international human rights promotion and protection networks, and representatives of the judicial branch — such as the Public Defender's Office, the Public Prosecutor's Office and human rights committees — together with parliamentarians who support human rights-related issues, and protect human rights advocates in exercising their right to participate.

In Ibase's previous experiences using the Incid methodology, tools for accessing justice could be included or not in discussions on building action agendas. The CAAJ project deliberately connected, for the first time, the participatory production of indicators and organization of political action plans with legal efforts to realize human rights in the study areas.

Four measures were adopted to enable this new approach:

1. Formation of a Technical-Scientific Reference Group that cooperated in training and decision-making processes and in structuring legal strategies
2. Continuous training on relevant themes, such as legal empowerment and gateways to Brazil's legal system
3. Constant dialogue with human rights movements in Brazil and abroad, and with advisors connected to popular advocacy, who provided guidance on how to effectively assert the demands raised

4 Dialogue with parliamentarians, such as councillors and state representatives (and the specific parliamentary committees related to each area of rights); public administration representatives (of municipal secretariats and other government bodies); and entities in the legal system (Public Defender's Office, Public Prosecutor's Office)

Ibase thus brought together a range of different social, legal and political tools and strategies. This was only possible after an extensive process of inquiry with experts, exchanges with other movements, and dialogue with parliamentarians and segments of the legal system in a continuous exchange of experience.

Using participatory methods to define community action priorities

The project began in December 2019. While it was in early stages of site scoping and implementation, in March 2020, the outbreak of the COVID-19 pandemic was officially declared in Brazil.

During the lockdown period, the activities within communities were suspended, and the project focused on continuous training initiatives. Meeting the demands of partner organizations (Brota na Lage Collective and Jardim Gramacho Community Forum) on the lack of information related to themes connected to the pandemic, the project organized a campaign called "It's your right". This had a humanitarian focus, pairing information on social distancing and the correct use of masks with awareness of pandemic-related rights and resources, such as Emergency Aid, rules on a reduced work day or the reduction of salaries, suspension of the employment contract, violence against women, and channels for victim support or for reporting violence against women. The campaign went viral in the communities studied, and the organizational representatives participating in the project were recognized as important players, including on the use of the legal system to address these issues.

Secondary data were collected to produce indicators of various dimensions of Measured Citizenship (Brazil's public data system) and Guaranteed Citizenship (data on public policy management) dimensions. But serious difficulties were encountered during this time, when Brazil went more than 10 years without a demographic census, and which became known as the "public data blackout period". The indicators of these citizenship dimensions were being built in online discussion processes with local active citizenship representatives; however, some of them had outdated data due to the gaps in public data disclosure.

In 2022, after progress in vaccinating the Brazilian population and the massive drop in COVID-19 infection rates, field activities fully resumed. Perceived Citizenship research could then be carried out, with the production of primary data. A representative sample survey was aimed at showing residents' perceptions on the effectiveness of human rights and on violations experienced. Data was collected directly from residents at key circulation points in the communities (such as transit nodes). A total of 2,715 questionnaires were completed in the *favelas* in Tijuca and 2,966 in Jardim Gramacho.

After data analysis, dialogue was established with the representatives of local organizations to discuss the creation of the Incid System for each area, with possible indicators for each citizenship dimension analysed. As a result, 118 indicators were created for the Tijuca *favelas* and 111 for Jardim Gramacho. These serve as a "menu" of relevant information on rights not yet realized in each area.

Gaps in the production and availability of public data in this period — both data related to public policy management (on education, health care and public security) and data from the demographic census (on population, income and housing characteristics) — meant the data from the representative sample survey was highly anticipated in the study areas. As a result of the official data blackout period, this would be the most recently produced valid information and the survey was welcomed with great enthusiasm by area representatives. It was deemed an important contribution to identifying the serious rights violations experienced and helped to articulate local demands in a clear and well-grounded way.

The process began with participatory dialogues. First, roundtables were held in the communities to verify the indicators produced. Then an action plan or advocacy agenda was constructed through a series of meetings with a wider set of local representatives. Ten roundtables were held in the two territories, designed so that all participants could discuss the entire set of information presented. At Jardim Gramacho, four roundtables were held, with 68 representatives of the local active citizenry participating. At the end of all these discussions, the indicators were validated with contributions made by all participants.

A series of wider stakeholder meetings held with area representatives focused on collectively defining action priorities for the short, medium and long term. These resulted in an action plan with the Jardim Gramacho Community and an advocacy agenda with the group of *favelas* at Tijuca.

Highlights of political action in the study areas

With the action plan and advocacy agenda in hand, priority rights violations were identified for the first political actions, and various strategies were designed. These combined: (1) clarification and information sharing; (2) denunciation of the rights violations (through campaigns or demonstrations); (3) advocacy initiatives through dialogue with councillors and state representatives, as well as with legislative assembly standing committees (such as those on public safety, women's rights, and anti-discrimination); and (4) access to justice through dialogue with public bodies promoting justice, such as the Public Prosecutor's Office and the Public Defender's Office (Rosa et al., 2023). When territories have knowledge about the law and are able to use and transform it, legal empowerment is built. This was, without a doubt, a success of this project.

Here, we analyse the political action — what Durham (1984) refers to as the set of different "collective forms of construction of citizenship" — achieved by the active citizenship in each territory.

In the two territories, the survey assessed a total of 14 rights, including the right to the city and to the environment, water supply, health, food, education, work, housing, social assistance, safety, information, participation, equality and diversity, and women's right to a safe life.

On this basis, the territories demanded: (1) the return of garbage collection programs within the *favelas*; (2) legalized transport with a guaranteed right to free access for groups protected by law, along with better transport services; and (3) engagement in civil actions involving wider audiences, beyond the limits of the territory, which in some cases even included engagement in the collective construction of complaints to be voiced at the international level. These are just a few examples of actions triggered by the project.

The project experience with the collective production of indicators was broad. As it helped to structure the struggle for rights deemed priorities by several movements, on a range of different action fronts, it cannot be described here in its entirety. The struggles to guarantee water supply in Jardim Gramacho and the right to education in the Chácara do Céu community serve as two examples. Among the rights chosen as priorities and as a starting point for action by local representatives, these two rights entailed processes that combined a wider number of local actions and engagement up to the end of the project.

The sections below illustrate the process, from the production of data and the discussions around it, to political organization, the implementation of actions and their outcomes.

Jardim Gramacho and the right to water supply

In Jardim Gramacho, the Incid Perception Indicator related to access to water showed that, in all areas of this district, a significant percentage of people do not have regular supply, demonstrating a violation of this fundamental right.[7]

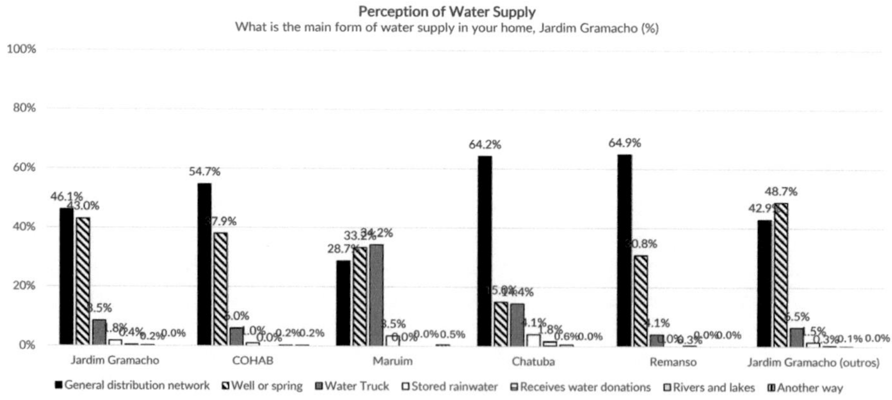

Figure 3.2 Perceptions on access to water in Jardim Gramacho
Source: Active Citizenship and Access to Justice project, Perceived Citizenship data set, 2022.

It also showed that, without service provided by the general water distribution network, residents needed to use other means to access this fundamental right. A great deal of Jardim Gramacho's water is obtained from wells or springs, in an area where local water tables are at high risk of contamination, given its long history as a landfill and ongoing illegal garbage dumping. Located near Guanabara Bay, the site is also crossed by rivers that traverse a wide stretch of the Baixada Fluminense,[8] into which the sewage of several municipalities is discharged. In Favela do Maruim, where the right to water is the most violated, 71.3 percent of residents have no access to treated water from the general supply grid.

Water supply in the State of Rio de Janeiro was provided by the Rio de Janeiro Water and Sewage State Company (Cedae), a public sector company that was privatized in 2021. The Águas do Rio firm then became the concessionaire in charge of water supply for this state. After privatization, there was an increase in water shortages, intermittent water supply, and charges applied in areas where water is not available, among other complaints.

At the project's wider stakeholder meetings, the demand for a continuous supply of quality water to be delivered to all houses in the district was chosen as the main priority.

To better prepare the people involved, the project organized training on the right to water, standards defined by the national constitution and internationally (through the UN system, treaties and agreements to which Brazil is a signatory), and civil society organizing to ensure that right. The event was attended by a university professor and a coordinator of the NGO FASE, both with proven experience on the topics and in political debates on the right to water.

The gateway for accessing justice was through contact with the State Public Defender's Office, which aimed to present the violation of this right and identify potential solutions. This dialogue revealed the existence of a larger number of complaints of rights violations by this concessionaire across the state.

As a result, the Jardim Gramacho Community Forum was invited to participate in a public hearing held at the Municipal Chamber of Duque de Caxias, for the presentation of an improvement plan by the Águas do Rio concessionaire for its service to the Duque de Caxias region. During the hearing, a company representative acknowledged the initial difficulties over its first 18 months of operation, and reported that Águas do Rio intended to make structural investments in the region.

Aware of the participation of district representatives, the company representative tried to explain that Águas do Rio had already implemented improvements in Jardim Gramacho, including updating some water consumption readers so that approximately two thousand residents would be fairly charged for their service. This speech was emphatically rejected by an area representative, who used the survey results to deny that improvements had been made in the supply, dependability or quality of the service. She demanded better service provision based on the human right to water.

A public defender from the Regional Collective Relief Centre of the Municipality of Duque de Caxias highlighted that the concession agreement is extremely favourable to Águas do Rio. The agreement requires the firm to charge a reduced social tariff to people who lack the means to pay the full price. In setting the reduced rate, however, the company is permitted to consider only whether paying the rate would put people's survival at risk and not whether they can afford to pay it. The Public Defender's Office also cited the indicators found in the project survey and concluded that the fact that district residents were being charged for a service that was either not offered or was provided in a precarious way, unsuitable for use, constituted a genuine violation of rights.

The second initiative using project tools for accessing justice was a meeting held with the External Ombudsman of the Public Defender's Office of the State of Rio de Janeiro. This ombudsman invited the local group to join its Minimum Water Requirement Public-Interest Civil Action (ACP, in Portuguese) and invited Ibase to join the action as an *amicus curiae* (friend of the court, or advisor).

The Jardim Gramacho Community Forum began to take part in the civil society network involved in the ACP and has attended meetings to define broad strategies that address specific violations of the right to water across the entire state. This network is comprised of several territorial movements, universities, NGOs and environmental activists, which shows their collective participation on a wider scale than their individual community-level action and focus. This brought local participants to recognize that some struggles need to be scaled up and voiced by more groups in society, by seeking partnerships with other movements involved in the same local struggle.

The meetings with the Minimum Water Requirement ACP Network defined a strategy that involved legal action through the courts; elaborating a mobilization campaign; and pressuring the state governor by requesting a decree setting forth a minimum water requirement to be supplied.

The project also worked with the Jardim Gramacho Community Forum to develop a partnership with Coordination for Monitoring Human Rights in Brazil — which is represented on the project's Technical-Scientific Reference Group — to prepare an international complaint on the violation of the district residents' right to water.

Tijuca's Chácara do Céu hilltop **favela** *and the right to education*

The data from Chácara do Céu on the right to education are alarming. In a survey that specifically targeted women, respondents were asked about the existence of places in the area where working mothers could leave their children, as related to children's right to education (in daycare centres and preschools). The result was negative for 28 percent of those surveyed.

Data also showed that the journey to schools in the surrounding area is an issue for those who want to study. Chácara do Céu is located atop a steep hill, which is very distant from the formal areas within Tijuca district. Discussions revealed that, due to the distance involved and the *favela*'s steep location, many mothers don't go down the hill to take their children to the school or leave them at daycare centres.

In roundtables organized in partnership with the Brota na Laje Youth Collective, residents complained about the fact that the Chácara do Céu Community Nursery School had closed down in February 2023, with 60 children enrolled. At the time of the survey, the nursery had been operating. So, the situation had worsened since the development of the advocacy agenda, which was based on data collected prior to the school's closure.

The school was closed on the eve of children's return to school, by a court order made without any prior notice to parents or guardians. The Public Prosecutor's Office of the State of Rio de Janeiro had lodged a public civil action at the First Children, Youth and Elders Court of the Judicial District of the Capital City, calling for closure of the community school due to irregularities in its infrastructure and its inadequate staffing levels. In addition to closing the nursery, the Public Prosecutor's Office requested the suspension of public funds transfers by the Municipality of Rio de Janeiro until the infrastructure and staffing issues could be addressed.

The project's technical team sought information on the ongoing process and found that the Municipal Government of Rio de Janeiro had filed an appeal asking for the judgment to be reversed, claiming that it had made the necessary adjustments and requesting that the nursery be reopened.

Based on the claims of the municipality, the Brota na Laje Youth Collective and other partner organizations, with the support from the project team, took steps to push for reopening. These included a local petition aimed at demonstrating to the Court the need to reopen the nursery. Area representatives, together with the project's technical team, also sought discussions with the

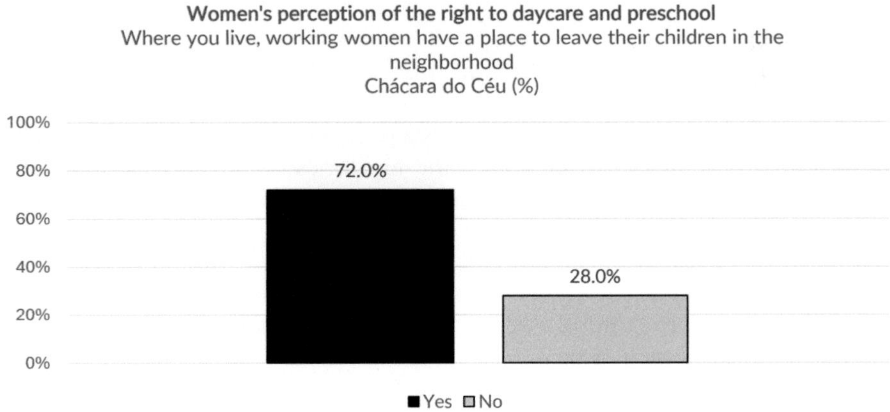

Figure 3.3 Access to daycare centres and preschools in Morro da Chácara do Céu
Source: Active Citizenship and Access to Justice Survey, Perceived Citizenship, 2022.

Municipal Education Committee of the City Council of Rio de Janeiro on the school closure, so they could present relevant survey data and discuss the lawsuit filed by the Public Prosecutor's Office and the municipality's claim that the issues that led to the closing had already been solved.

The councillor who coordinates the Education Committee agreed to ask the Public Prosecutor's Office to order the immediate reopening of the nursery. Facing this pressure, the Public Prosecutor's Office ordered a technical visit that concluded that the facility was in working condition and met all requirements. It then published the decision, which allowed the nursery to resume service, and restored the transfer of public funds.

Pressure was then put on the courts seeking a legal judgment authorizing the reopening. Local representatives delivered an appeal to the judge responsible for the lawsuit, attaching both the petition with 203 signatures and the judgment of the Public Prosecutor's Office. The technical and field team of the CAAJ project also visited the office of this judge, to show the urgent need to resume the nursery's activities. As a result, a judgment legally authorizing the centre to reopen was delivered, which it did at last in September 2023.

Conclusions

This case produced lessons, not only for local communities and their defence, but also for Ibase and its approaches.

Historically, the *favelas* and the city's outskirts have hosted different kinds of organizations that seek to respond to rights violations suffered by local people, with a range of tools available to each group, such as petitions, street demonstrations and public campaigns. In this instance, communities made use of information sets that helped to validate and expand their range of action. This stemmed from the data and indicators developed, and the training on relevant topics. The research and training processes were thus converted into tangible results. The project provided an expanded analytical understanding of the territory. Research data were used to support advocacy with parliamentarians who are human rights defenders and with judicial bodies.

By gaining a wider view of access to justice, seeing different parts of the three branches of government as gateways, the territories — which had previously only looked to the executive branch for redress — were able to expand their range of action and began to mobilize and pressure other branches. In this way, old tools gained a new dimension, new meaning and new uses. Including other branches in their advocacy agendas not only showed an expanded understanding of the functions of each branch of the state, but also enabled the formulation of strategies targeting each of them.

The innovative aspect in this case was thus the legal empowerment of the communities, based on knowledge of the tools for accessing justice. Where previously this access was made through negotiation between *favelas* and the government — particularly the executive branch — these territories could be seen pressuring other branches, creating new points of coordination with the legislative and judicial branches, in addition to the Public Prosecutor's Office.

The territories adopted new technique based on new tools introduced by the project, thanks in particular to the contributions of legal advisors and members of the Technical-Scientific Reference Group in the development of legal and political strategies. Each was adopted as a technique to be incorporated and used by the territories.

The project tangibly contributed to reversing rights violations and situations of exclusion. The political action that it propelled and validated gave rise to — and strengthened — processes of struggle that became irreversible for these communities, which are already demanding that parts of the government and judiciary get moving and take action. This represents a concrete change in the relationship between activists and their government, which is now objectively mediated by courts of justice, in a search to realize constitutional rights.

The project renewed civic engagement in study sites, such that it has reached a broader and stronger scale of action. The progress in each lawsuit filed revitalized the struggle and strengthened the engagement of those who had never stopped working to promote local improvements. Such lawsuits are, on their own, valuable outcomes of active citizenship in each of the locations studied and will certainly set precedents for other lawsuits.

Ibase is an established institution in the field of Brazilian NGOs, recognized for its initiative and engagement with important movements that fight for democracy and rights, and for providing social data and indicators. The fact that Ibase was an external agent driving the advocacy actions carried out by the territories certainly opened the doors to the dialogue achieved with the judiciary and the legislative branches in this short period of time. Ibase continues to accompany these communities, as an advisor in the processes of implementing the advocacy agenda and action plan, cooperating as a link to other social assets, such as other NGOs and wider movements, in these territorial struggles.

The project has also propelled innovation for Ibase. Its earlier methods of action did not have identifying gateways for accessing justice as a clear objective. In addition, legal empowerment was not necessarily included in the continuous training processes in its methodologies. Previously, tools for accessing justice to guarantee rights might or not be used, depending on the players with whom Ibase interacted in each instance. This experience changed Ibase's understandings and working methodology. Together with active citizenship, which it considers an important tool in reversing rights violations and exclusions, access to justice has been integrated within Ibase's core methodologies for working with communities.

Notes

1 This case study is a result of the Active Citizenship and Access to Justice project, which was conducted by Ibase in partnership with the Brota na Lage Youth Collective and the Jardim Gramacho Community Forum, with the support of the International Development Research Centre.

2 Article 5 of the 1988 Federal Constitution provides that: "All persons are equal before the law, without any distinction whatsoever, Brazilians and foreigners residing in the country being ensured of inviolability of the right to life, to liberty, to equality, to security and to property". Item XXXV provides that "the law shall not exclude any injury or threat to a right from the consideration of the Judicial Power".
3 See Brandão (2010).
4 See Cunha (2006).
5 The Brazilian Institute of Geography and Statistics, and the state statistical agencies, ministries and government secretariates are part of Brazil's Public Statistics Production and Dissemination System (Jannuzzi, 2002, p. 62).
6 See Ibase (2012).
7 In 2010, the United Nations recognized access to safe, potable water as an essential right for the full enjoyment of life and all remaining human rights, through its A/RES/64/292/2010 Resolution. The guarantee of drinkable water for all is also the UN's 6th Sustainable Development Goal (SDG) whose implementation by signatory countries, including Brazil, is expected to be concluded by 2030. SDG 6 aims to "ensure the availability and sustainable management of water and sanitation for all". Target 6.1 of this SDG is aimed at achieving "universal and equitable access to safe and affordable drinking water for all" by 2030.
8 A region comprising 13 municipalities that belong to the Metropolitan Region of Rio de Janeiro.

References

Barbosa, R. (2022). Eleição de 2022 é a mais polarizada desde a redemocratização [2022 election is the most polarized since redemocratization]. *Poder360*. www.poder360.com.br/eleicoes/eleicao-de-2022-e-a-mais-polarizada-desde-a-redemocratizacao/.

Brandão, R. C. (2010). *A Associação de Catadores do Aterro Metropolitano de Jardim Gramacho: ACAMJG e sua luta pelo direito ao trabalho* [*The Collectors Association of Landfill Metropolitan of Jardim Gramacho: ACAMJG and their struggle for the right to work*]. Universidade do Estado do Rio de Janeiro. www.bdtd.uerj.br/handle/1/16065.

Cerqueira, C., & Moliterno, D. (2022). Disputa entre Lula e Bolsonaro é a eleição para presidente mais acirrada da história [The race between Lula and Bolsonaro is the tightest presidential election in history]. *CNN Brasil*. www.cnnbrasil.com.br/politica/disputa-entre-lula-e-bolsonaro-e-a-eleicao-para-presidente-mais-acirrada-da-historia/.

Cunha, N. V. D. (2006). *Histórias de favelas da Grande Tijuca. Contadas por quem faz parte delas* [*History of the favelas of Greater Tijuca. Told by those who are part of them*]. IBASE.

Da Silva, C. (2022). Lula X Bolsonaro: Eleição de 2022 foi a mais disputada desde a redemocratização [Lula vs. Bolsonaro: The 2022 election was the most hotly contested since redemocratization]. *Carta Capital*. www.cartacapital.com.br/politica/lula-x-bolsonaro-eleicao-de-2022-foi-a-mais-disputada-desde-a-redemocratizacao/.

Durham, E. (1984). Movimentos socialism: A construção da cidadania [Social movements: Building citizenship]. *Novos Estudos, CEBRAP*, 10, 24–30.

Ibase. (2012). *Introdução ao Sistema Incid: Indicadores da Cidadania* [*Introduction to the Incid System: Citizenship Indicators*]. Author.

Jannuzzi, P. de M. (2002). Considerações sobre o uso, mau uso e abuso dos indicadores sociais na formulação e avaliação de políticas públicas municipais [Considerations on the use, misuse and abuse of social indicators in the formulation and evaluation of municipal public policies]. *Revista Brasileira de Administração Pública*, 36(1), 51–72.

Oliveira, F. de. (2007). Política numa era de indeterminação: Opacidade e reencantamento. In A. P. Castellani and J. A. Peschanski (Eds.), *A era da indeterminação* [*Politics in an age of indeterminacy: Opacity and re-enchantment. In The age of indeterminacy*] (pp. 15–48). Boitempo Editorial.

Rosa, B., Mentzingen, J., Chaves, M., & Sobral, P. (2023). ALERJ instala 21 comissões permanentes e define presidentes [ALERJ installs 21 standing committees and defines chairmen]. *Assembleia Legislativa do Estado do Rio de Janeiro (Alerj)*. www.alerj.rj.gov.br/Visualizar/Noticia/55312?AspxAutoDetectCookieSupport=1.

Statista. (2024). *Presidential elections in Brazil 2022 — Statistics & facts* [*dataset*]. Statista Research Department. www.statista.com/topics/9859/presidential-elections-in-brazil-2022/#topicOverview.

United Nations General Assembly. (2010). *The human right to water and sanitation.* GA Res 64/292, GAOR, 64th sess, Suppl. no. 49, UN Doc A/RES/64/292.

United Nations General Assembly. (2015). *The 2030 agenda and the Sustainable Development Goals.* UN GAOR, 70th sess, Agenda Item 15 & 116, UN Doc A/70/L.1.

4 Empowering informal settlement communities for recognition and inclusion in the urban development discourse

Lessons from Accra, Ghana

Mark Kakraba-Ampeh and Prince Aboagye Anokye

Background: The right to housing in Ghana[1]

Informal settlements are characterized by overcrowding, inadequate access to water and sanitation, tenure insecurity and the poor structural quality of housing. Despite their appalling and inhumane conditions, they are fast multiplying and expanding in the developing world, for a range of socio-economic, institutional, cultural, historical and political reasons. State actors and individuals with a private interest in urban land effectively criminalize the formation of these settlements, and the people who live in them, especially those without guaranteed security of tenure. Without legal protection, residents are vulnerable to brutal eviction. This threat could be curbed if informal settlement dwellers had a greater voice in urban governance systems and increased access to justice.

Ghana has been cited as a positive role model for its governance and democratic credentials (Armah-Attoh & Robertson, 2014). However, the country still faces the challenge of growing informal settlements, despite progress over the years. In 1990, about 65 percent of the urban population lived in slums. This percentage dropped to approximately 37.9 percent at the dawn of the millennium, partly due to the decline in poverty levels from 52 to 25 percent. Interventions by Ghana's government, development partners and civil society organizations have been crucial in achieving this progress. In 2014, an estimated 53 percent of Ghana's 27 million people lived in urban areas (World Bank, 2015). A significant portion, about 20 percent, are trapped in poorly planned, overcrowded, and unsanitary conditions, which could worsen without interventions.

Conditions in informal settlements, including slums, stem from urban poverty and inadequate recognition of residents' rights. Some sources suggest that informal settlements create weak land administration systems that cannot ensure secure tenure for settlers (De Soto, 2000). Insecure tenure in turn undermines people's desire to improve housing conditions. In 2008, the

DOI: 10.4324/9781003538806-4

United Nations Human Settlements Programme (UN-Habitat) revised its definition of informal settlements, highlighting their inadequate access to essential services like water, waste management, electricity and good roads. This lack of access may be due to direct neglect by city managers who fail to recognize informal settlements as integral parts of the city. Regardless of the underlying causes, informal settlements are characterized by poverty and social stigma, which fuels residents' exclusion from decision-making and prevents them from meaningfully enjoying their social, economic and cultural rights.

Ghana has committed to safeguarding fundamental human rights, including access to adequate housing, as a signatory to several international treaties and conventions. Under the Directive Principle of State Policy enshrined in Chapter Six of the 1992 National Constitution of Ghana, the state is mandated to "endeavour to secure and protect a social order founded on the ideals and principles of freedom, equality, justice…" while protecting and promoting all other forms of human rights and freedoms (Article XXXVII, §1). This commitment is primarily derived from international treaties and conventions but is not concretely anchored in legislation. Interventions to improve housing quality and safeguard economic, social and cultural rights therefore lack clear legal backing.

Recent policy interventions, such as the National Slum Upgrading Policy, the National Housing Policy and the National Housing Profile, have not been translated into an explicit legislative framework that offers protection for housing rights. In Ghana, a few interventions have been implemented to address the challenges faced by informal settlement households, focusing on both tangible and intangible aspects. Interventions such as the Participatory Slum Upgrading Programme and the Land, Services, and Citizenship Project aim to improve the conditions in slums by bridging the infrastructure gap. These interventions have focused on physical upgrades to avert forced evictions, rather than addressing a broader range of rights and entitlements such as the right to secure land rights, dignified living and participation in decision-making processes. These rights create legitimacy for slum dwellers and improve their access to essential services. This highlights the need for a more comprehensive approach to addressing the slum challenge in Ghana.

Achieving increased voice for slum residents also requires widening access to justice, a component of which is legal aid, to protect the rights of the most vulnerable. A justice system that delivers justice for all must be fair, transparent, adequate, non-discriminatory and accountable. Democratic constitutions prioritize access to justice as a fundamental principle, safeguarding human rights and enabling marginalized individuals to exercise their rights. However, for vulnerable and disadvantaged groups, particularly those living in illegal settlements, the lack of access to justice is widespread, according to the United Nations Office on Drugs and Crime (2013). Access to justice is a human rights issue involving legal representation and remedies for violations.

In Ghana, informal settlements face challenges such as pervasive fear, financial inaccessibility, a lack of lawyers and knowledge of rights and a weak justice system, especially for marginalized groups who often avoid formal courts. The action research described in this chapter found that only eight out of over 600 respondents had used the formal court system, highlighting the need for improved access to justice.

Chapters 5 and 6 of the Ghanaian Constitution (1992) protect human rights and economic, social and cultural rights. However, while the Constitution addresses socio-economic rights such as safe working conditions, equal pay and education, it lacks comprehensive provisions for economic, social and cultural rights. There is no explicit provision covering housing rights to enshrine Article 11 of the International Covenant on Economic, Social, and Cultural Rights, to which Ghana is a signatory. Thus, in its 2002 ruling on the *Issah Iddi Abass & 10 Others v. Accra Metropolitan Assembly & Anor* case, Ghana's High Court of Justice upheld that an eviction order against informal settlement dwellers was lawful based on their unlawful occupation of land in Sodom and Gomorrah, a slum community in Accra. The Court, in reference to the Constitution, stated that the ultimatum given by city authorities in respect of forced eviction did not infringe on residents' fundamental human rights. As a dualist country, Ghana must domesticate international laws, that is, by explicitly enacting them into domestic law, if they are to take effect. In its 2008 ruling on *Ghana Lotto Operators Association v. National Lottery Authority*, the Supreme Court upheld that the Constitution's economic objectives under Article 36 are legally binding and not just a matter of conscience for successive governments. If a government introduces legislation at odds with these objectives, the court therefore has jurisdiction to strike down the provisions. The rulings in these two cases highlight that, without clarity on the nature of rights guaranteed under the National Constitution, different courts may make subjective and contradictory decisions that may not ensure adequate protection of the rights of citizens.

Legal recognition of the housing rights of informal settlement residents is not enough in itself. Legally empowering the communities through structures for effective community mobilization is also essential. Legal empowerment is a strategy that extends legal provisions to those in poverty and encourages proactive claims of rights (Roseveare, 2013). Citizens actively shape the law through awareness-raising and legal education. Non-state dispute resolution mechanisms, such as those mediated by traditional authorities, faith-based organizations and prominent community members, can reduce state resource pressure. According to the UN Secretary-General:

> legal empowerment of the poor seeks to establish the rule of law, ensure equal and equitable access to justice, and tackle the root causes of exclusion, vulnerability and poverty. Legal empowerment is rooted in a human rights-based approach to development, recognizing that poverty results from disempowerment, exclusion, and discrimination. Thus, legal empowerment fosters development by strengthening the voices of individuals and communities, starting at the grassroots and from within.
>
> (United Nations General Assembly, 2009, p. 2)

Access to justice remains a critical constraint in Ghana's informal settlements. In addition to the non-incorporation of provisions of international charters and treaties within the national legislative framework, residents of informal settlements are challenged by their lack of knowledge regarding existing laws, institutions and channels for pursuing access to justice. The bureaucratic processes and associated costs for accessing the formal courts are not pro-poor and, therefore, not a preferred choice. The income levels of residents of these communities also force them to seek redress using mechanisms available in the community, irrespective of the nature of the dispute.

Project context and profiles of three informal settlements

In an effort to address these dynamics, the action research described in this chapter aimed to improve the socio-economic conditions of informal settlers in Ghana by strengthening their voice and improving their access to justice and essential services. This was pursued by applying public interest-oriented policy, legal, economic and planning tools. Following a review of relevant literature, researchers worked closely with communities to identify, develop and test gender-sensitive and pro-poor urban governance tools that offer practical solutions to the many challenges that fuel exclusion of informal settlers. This involved an iterative process focused on working closely with slum communities and maintaining dialogue with stakeholders. Emerging lessons and best practices from the project have also fed into ongoing discussions on informality through targeted and sustained advocacy and policy engagement at the local and national levels.

The literature review suggested that three key elements are essential for achieving sustainable solutions to informal settlement challenges: new laws to anchor international covenants on social, economic and cultural rights; a shift from viewing informal settlements solely through an infrastructure lens to considering both the tangible and intangible dimensions of informality; and taking a comprehensive approach to realizing citizens' rights. Working collaboratively with selected settlements and allied organizations — including Amnesty International, Peoples Dialogue on Human Settlements, the Ministry of Zongo Development and the Ministry of Gender, Children and Social Protection — the research effort aimed to enhance residents' recognition and voice and improve their ability to exercise their rights, while strengthening their access to basic infrastructure.

Field research was conducted in three slum communities in the national capital, Accra: Agbogbloshie, Chorkor-Chemuena (also known as Chorkor) and Madina Zongo (or simply Madina). The socio-economic conditions in the country, coupled with its inadequate yet expensive housing, have significantly contributed to the proliferation of informal settlements in Ghana. According to People's Dialogue on Human Settlements, an NGO that has done extensive work in Ghana, there are over 300 slums in Accra alone.

The roots of these settlements are diverse. Some slums emerged from squatters settling near existing formal settlements in the city. Others developed because of their proximity to the central business district (CBD), as people migrate from rural areas to cities in search of better economic opportunities. While all three settlements include migrants from various parts of the country, Chorkor-Chemuana has more indigenous residents than migrants, while Agbogbloshie and Madina Zongo both have more migrants. Madina Zongo and Chorkor originally developed around indigenous settlements, which degenerated into slums due to uncontrolled extensions and additions to existing structures, and unauthorized development of public open spaces and waterways. In Agbogbloshie and Madina, the existence of a market, industries and other sources of employment have attracted more of the urban poor who have erected shacks and other substandard accommodation to be close to employment sources.

Although not terrible, access to urban services in these three communities can be improved. Electricity coverage in all three communities is encouraging, but residents complain about how much they pay for available utilities. The availability of drains and sanitation facilities remains one of the key priorities in these communities.

Among other factors, the choice of the three study sites resulted from the intense pressure on informal settlements in Accra, and the diverse characteristics and experiences of these communities. These three sites offered the chance to explore the conditions and outcomes experienced by migrant and indigenous communities with varying stakes in land ownership, who have faced threats of eviction, and have experience with past and ongoing interventions aimed at improving their conditions.

Primary data for the research was obtained from household interviews and focus group discussions with key stakeholders such as landlords and landowners, migrant and indigenous tenants, youth groups, traders, community-based organizations, men's and women's groups, elected community representatives, and others.

The haphazard nature of housing meant that systematic sampling could not be used for the selection of heads of households for enumeration; instead, accidental sampling was used to select only one household head in each house visited by an enumerator. A total of 600 questionnaires were digitally administered in all three communities, with data checked for completeness, consistency and accuracy on a daily basis though post-field editing and debriefing. Following the field work, the data was collated, organized and analysed. Focus group discussions were subsequently held with all the stakeholders listed above to validate some of the preliminary findings and collect additional relevant data.

Data from the three slum communities revealed a need for increased awareness of rights, particularly political and social rights. It was also clear that financial constraints hindered residents' access to legal services and that communities needed to improve their knowledge on advocacy. In response to the findings on community needs, participatory interventions were then designed to strengthen community representation and governance, and raise awareness and knowledge of avenues for pursuing justice. These are further described in the section Tools and Strategies for Strengthening Community Voice and Access to Justice below.

Agbogbloshie

Agbogbloshie[2] is an informal settlement community near Agbogbloshie Market in the heart of Accra. Originally a typical indigenous community dominated by the Ga tribe of the Greater Accra region, its proximity to the CBD and the South Industrial Estate made it attractive to migrants. The population of the community was estimated at 79,684 in 2009 with a density of over 2,424 persons per hectare. About two-thirds are migrants from the northern regions of Ghana (Housing the Masses, 2010), many of whom have fled tribal wars. Some migrants have developed land belonging to the Railways Company and in public open spaces.

The community's poor environmental condition makes the residents susceptible to health risks; ponds of stagnant turbid water are visible reminders of the threat of water-borne diseases and an avenue for breeding insect vectors, particularly mosquitoes. In addition, respiratory problems are associated with settlements such as Agbogbloshie, where people live in small rooms of high density and with poor ventilation (COHRE, 2004). The settlement has experienced earlier attempts at eviction: in 1991, residents of Agbogbloshie

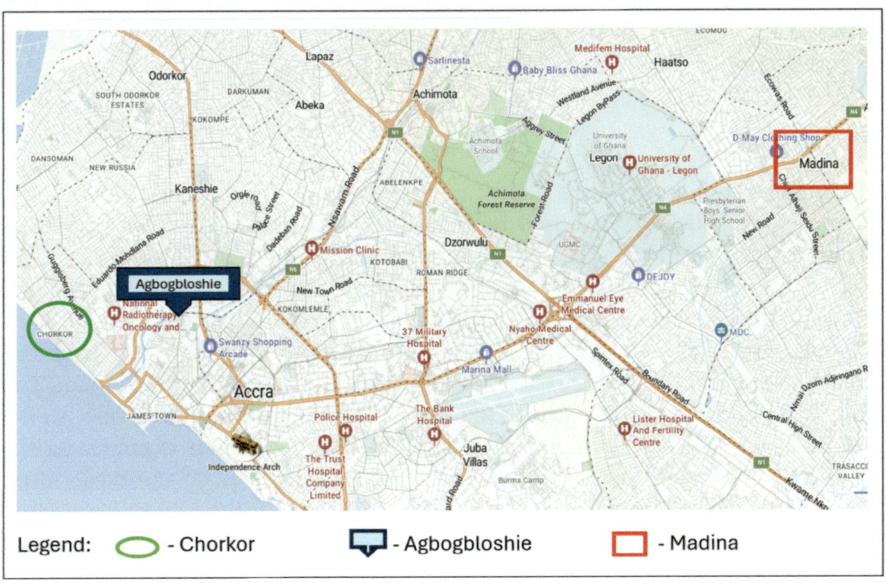

Figure 4.1 A section of Accra showing the locations of Agbogbloshie, Chorkor-Chemuena and Madina Zongo

Source: Authors, developed from Google Maps with project communities inserted.

brought an action against the Accra Metropolitan Assembly, which had threatened them with eviction, alleging they were squatters.

Chorkor-Chemuana

Chorkor is a poorly planned, overpopulated area southwest of Accra. The 2010 Population and Housing Census estimated the population of Chorkor at 344,627, with an average growth rate of 6 percent. Developments here are of brick- and mud-made houses, and basic infrastructure is lacking. Most residents are indigenous Gas, with most houses being family homes. As a fishing community, Chorkor attracts a large population of fisherfolk from the country's Western, Central and Volta regions and other parts of the Greater Accra region. These fisherfolk prefer to stay close to the beach, developing available space without planning. Here, land ownership is not such a challenge, and the threat of eviction is less. Even though residents may not have any land documents proving ownership, their tenure rights are not contested.

Chorkor's proximity to the CBD also attracts poor families who commute to the city centre to work as head porters and perform other menial jobs. The community faces poor transportation access as every available space is fully developed, especially in the coastal section. Compared to other settlements, residents have low education and high unemployment rates and live in crowded houses with poor living conditions. These conditions are exacerbated by a lack of proper sewage systems and drains, leading to open defecation along the beach and the Chemu Lagoon. Despite efforts to restore Accra's beaches, Chorkor beach remains polluted by garbage dumping and the lack of hygiene and sanitation.

Madina Zongo

Madina is a rapidly growing suburb in the Accra plains, located 16 kilometres northeast of Accra. Established in June 2012, it is part of the La Nkwantanang-Madina Municipality. With a population of 76,697, Madina has a diverse ethnic composition, including migrants from the northern regions, along with Ga-Adangmes, Ewes, Akans and non-Ghanaians from Cote d'Ivoire, Togo and Nigeria. It is a preferred destination for poor migrants seeking accommodation near the CBD. Christianity, Islam and African traditional religions are the main faiths among residents. Madina is one of several areas in Accra with high concentrations of migrants. It is characterized by poor transportation, unsanitary conditions, and a lack of the basic infrastructure needed to promote the economic and social wellbeing of residents.

Tenure insecurity and fear of eviction

These three communities have thrived for over a decade due to their proximity to the CBD, affordable rent, and the proliferation of informal economic activities. Most respondents have been in their current location for over 10 years, indicating their extensive community knowledge. This information benefits decision-making and governance involvement in these communities.

However, there is a strong correlation between land ownership and threat of eviction. According to UN-Habitat (2014), "lack of title and residency in informal settlements are often used as a justification for forced evictions". Most international human rights organizations do not support forced eviction because it violates, directly and indirectly, the civil, cultural, economic, political and social rights enshrined in international instruments. It also has enormous and catastrophic effects on informal settlers, especially people already living in poverty. Most residents living under threat of eviction will not invest in house construction or improvements nor take part fully in the development of their community.

In Agbogbloshie, only 33 percent of survey respondents own the land they occupy compared to 47.4 percent in Chorkor and 44.9 percent in Madina Zongo. Land ownership informs the kind of structures occupied by residents in the three project communities. Most buildings are made of cement blocks with iron sheet or thatch roofing. These are more prevalent in Madina Zongo and Chorkor. There are also several wooden structures with aluminium roofing sheets in the three communities but mostly in Agbogbloshie, where makeshift structures are prevalent and some respondents reside in structures made of mud, wood and aluminium sheet. The ad-hoc nature of these structures is one reason why residents of Agbogbloshie feel at greater risk of eviction than those in Madina and Chorkor.

The role of traditional authorities in land allocation is quite significant in all three communities. In Chorkor, 84 percent of property owners acquired their lands from traditional authorities compared to 43 percent in Madina Zongo and 29 percent in Agbogbloshie. These numbers suggest that most property owners at Agbogbloshie acquired their lands from sources other than traditional authorities, including from private individuals. However, it is not clear how legitimate private ownership of the lands allocated to developers in this community may be. Even though the issue of squatting is not pronounced in the three project communities, the number of people who responded that they had acquired land from "no one" at Madina Zongo (seven persons) far outnumbers those in the other two communities (four in Agbogbloshie and only one in Madina Zongo).

Most people living in settlements considered "illegal" or "irregular" by the authorities have little or no security of tenure. This makes them vulnerable to forced eviction and many other human rights violations (Amnesty International, 2011). Land tenure issues pose greater challenges in most developing countries, including Ghana, where about 80 percent of the land is in the hands of customary authorities. Over the years, there have been reports of people losing their properties and even their lives due to a lack clear ownership supported by appropriate land title documents. Ghanaian law requires that all owners of landed property acquire the right documentation to back their respective claims. This is crucial to avoid land disputes.

At Madina Zongo, 65 out of 107 landlords who obtained formal grants from traditional authorities claimed that they have documents which they described as title, lease or indenture. The remaining 42 indicated that they have tenancy agreements or allocation notes. However, during focus group discussions in the community, participants clarified that 80 percent of landlords only have written receipts issued to them by the traditional authority. They explained that the whole area had been given to one Chief Dagadu by the traditional chiefs of Labadi. Chief Dagadu in turn sold plots of land in the area to developers sometime in the 1970s; almost all these grants were backed only by handwritten receipts.

In Agbogbloshie, a smaller number indicated that they have documentary evidence to back their claims. Out of a sample population of 189, 64 landlords in Agbogbloshie claim to have documentary evidence to back their ownership. They described their land documents as tenancy agreements, titles or indentures. In Chorkor, about 87 residents (41.2 percent) reported having documentary evidence on the structures they occupy. Residents here describe their land documents as title deeds, allocation notes, tenancy agreements and indentures. Focus group participants in Chorkor clarified that about 60 percent of landlords in the community inherited their land from parents or other family members; these have land documents in the form of site plans and indentures given to them either by traditional authorities or individuals from whom they acquired the land. The remaining 40 percent of landlords acquired their lands by outright purchase from individuals and families.

The field evidence of this study shows that threat of eviction is very high in Agbogbloshie, with about 50.8 percent of survey respondents saying they face an eviction threat. This compared with only 15.4 percent of respondents in Madina Zongo and only 16.6 percent of respondents in Chorkor. Various reasons were given by residents for their fears regarding eviction. Besides a lack of tenure documentation, another major challenge is the threat of eviction from city authorities because their buildings do not have the required permit or were built at an illegal site. Residents in Madina Zongo noted that city authorities constantly demand monies for development permits that they cannot afford. In Chorkor, on the other hand, some residents fear they will be evicted by investors who want to use the land for commercial projects along the beach front. Others fear that elected or traditional community leaders are likely to transfer the land to some prospective investors. In Agbogbloshie, residents cite a mix of all these reasons. Most fear they may be evicted because of their lack of documented tenure, while many others think local authorities may evict them to ease congestion in the city.

A lack of voice in decision-making

Good governance is essential for a country's rule of law, democracy, and development, ensuring citizens' civil, political, economic and social rights (Alam & Hasina, 2014). It involves competent management of resources and affairs in an open, transparent, accountable, equitable and responsive manner. Urban growth and development face significant challenges, which require a multilevel governance approach. Herrle et al. (2006) and Jordan (2008) advocate for network-based governance, focusing on participatory planning, urban management and governance. UN-Habitat (2009) also emphasizes the importance of participatory urban planning, involving affected inhabitants and stakeholders, to address urbanization challenges and ensure effective decision-making.

Despite the enormous efforts that have been put into promoting good governance in the development field, less attention has been given to citizens' voice. Governance devoid of the voice of the poor and vulnerable defies the very tenets of good governance. Citizens need a compelling "voice" to convey their opinions and hold governments accountable, through complaints, protests, lobbying and other forms of advocacy. Sharma (2008) identifies empowerment and the individual's belief that they have rights that must be met by the state as components of voice. In informal settlements, a shared agenda and access to information are crucial if residents are to participate in decision-making processes. The state must be responsive to the needs and rights of these dwellers, moving beyond consultative exercises to affording them direct influence over policy and spending decisions. Initiatives to strengthen the voice of informal settlement residents should increase their participation in interventions to improve their situation. This will help them engage in decision-making processes that directly affect their lives (Sharma, 2008; Weru et al., 2015).

Regarding planning and development decision-making in Ghana, city authorities do not have any arrangements to involve slum communities — despite explicit legal provisions such as those found in section 16 of the Local Governance Act, 2016 (Act 936) and the Land Use and Spatial Planning Act, 2016 (Act 925). Decisions, including on eviction, are taken without consultation and involvement of the persons affected. There are no visible structures for community mobilization to give voice to slum residents and enable them to engage effectively with city authorities and other relevant duty-bearers. Although some NGOs and CSOs are trying to make an impact, almost half of the respondents in the communities say their efforts have not translated into tangible results for them (49 percent in Madina Zongo; 46 percent in Agbogbloshie; 47 percent in Chorkor). The exclusion and lack of voice results in several injustices meted out to slum dwellers, including threats of forced eviction and inadequate provision of municipal services and infrastructure, thereby deepening the poor environmental conditions of these slums.

To assess the level of voice and access to justice in the three settlements studied, the research team considered residents' awareness of rights, opportunities for participation in decision-making processes, gender dimensions of decision-making in the communities and avenues for dispute resolution.

Knowledge of one's constitutional rights is very important to the governance process. It enables citizens to seek justice whenever they feel that their rights are being infringed upon. Research found residents' knowledge of their rights, as enshrined in the Constitution, was very high in all three communities studied. Approximately 92 percent, 95 percent and 94 percent of respondents in Madina Zongo, Agbogbloshie and Chorkor, respectively, said they knew the Constitution of Ghana guaranteed them a number of rights as citizens. Almost all recognized that their right to vote was guaranteed by the Constitution. Roughly three-quarters or more of each community also knew of their right to justice under the Constitution. A high percentage of residents were also aware of their right to participate in development decision-making: 70.6 percent, 61.4 percent and 82.0 percent in Madina Zongo, Agbogbloshie and Chorkor, respectively. With the exception of those in Agbogbloshie, most residents were also aware that they had rights to demand urban services.

Participation in decision-making in all three communities was found to be very weak. Only 14 percent of Madina Zongo residents had ever been invited by city authorities to join in a discussion or decision-making on development. In Agbogbloshie and Chorkor, only 22 percent and 18 percent, respectively, had ever been involved in decision-making by city authorities.

Whenever a decision is to be made that concerns them, most residents in all three communities expect that the entire community would be consulted beforehand. Some described their involvement in decision-making as meaningful because their views could positively influence decisions concerning the community. This was expressed by 35.5 percent of residents in Madina Zongo, 36 percent in Agbogbloshie and 42.7 percent in Chorkor. In contrast, 33.2 percent of Madina Zongo residents, 30.7 percent of Agbogbloshie residents and 38.4 percent of Chorkor residents expressed the view that they may not have the opportunity to participate in the processes at all. In Madina Zongo especially, some said they would only listen without talking while more Agbogbloshie residents say they may share their views but are afraid that this may not influence the final decision. A solid majority of residents (nearly two-thirds in Madina Zongo and Agbogbloshie and 57.3 percent in Chorkor) felt they may not have the opportunity to participate in decision-making, and that even if they do, their views may not influence the decisions; others felt they may only participate but express no views.

As noted, community representatives can also be key to community involvement in decision-making. To achieve development objectives, city authorities need to establish a close working relationship with leaders of the communities over which they have oversight responsibilities. These leaders are better placed to articulate community needs and ensure they are reflected in the development agenda. In all three communities, most residents did not know if their leaders had ever been invited by city authorities for a joint discussion. Only a small number of residents (33 in Madina Zongo, 59 in Agbogbloshie and 26 in Chorkor) said their leaders have been involved in decision-making with city authorities in the past. It is possible that city authorities engaged more with community leaders in Agbogbloshie because of interactions relating to the frequent threats of eviction.

In terms of gender involvement in decision-making, an absolute majority in the three communities said men usually took part in key decision-making. However, women in all three communities have now become more aware of their rights in the community even without the support of the men. Almost half of respondents of each community expressed mixed feelings about the involvement of NGOs in empowering women. While some (51 percent in Madina Zongo, 54 percent in Agbogbloshie and 53 percent in Chorkor) said NGO/CSO involvement was high, others said they are not doing enough in terms of women empowerment. Most residents (71 percent in Madina Zongo, 75 percent in Agbogbloshie and 71 percent in Chorkor) also did not agree that the local government was doing much to empower women. Most also felt that religious bodies were doing little to empower women. Thus, while community participation in decision-making is generally weak, women's participation is even weaker and would require some level of affirmative action and support to address the grave challenges women face, particularly in slums where access to services remain a challenge.

Tools and strategies for strengthening community voice and access to justice

Through engagements with residents of the three settlements and key collaborators such as Amnesty International, the Ministry of Gender, Children and Social Protection, and Peoples Dialogue on Human Settlements, three tools were initially identified and proposed to address community challenges related to gaining voice and participation in governance processes, and access to justice.

1. Legal empowerment tools aimed at strengthening residents' awareness of available rights and increasing their knowledge about how to use those rights to access justice.
2. A land regularization tool aimed at promoting tenure security and abating the incidence of forced eviction. This tool was particularly relevant for the Agbogbloshie community, where threats of eviction are frequent.
3. Community mobilization and advocacy tools to strengthen the voice and inclusion of informal settlement residents in discussions on planning and development.

However, during community engagements focused on the development of these tools, it was clear that land issues were highly contentious. In Agbogbloshie and Madina Zongo, most residents were sceptical about discussions on land: they feared that opening discussions on land rights could trigger conflict between them and the government or customary owners of the lands they occupy. For this reason, land tools were dropped. Attention was therefore focused on developing and testing the legal empowerment and community mobilization tools across the three communities.

The communities were engaged in various ways in developing these tools. The engagement processes aimed to help the communities take the lead, to foster their ownership of the processes and outcomes. The identified tools were then redefined and shaped by the context and input of community representatives in two main ways. To increase community voice and participation, community structures were established to facilitate engagement with authorities on planning and development control, provision of services and improved environmental sanitation. To strengthen legal empowerment, capacity building was provided on rights and avenues for accessing justice, and partnerships with NGOs and human rights institutions were established and strengthened.

New structures to enhance voice and participation

The process of establishing community structures that would mobilize the community and engage with relevant institutions and agencies started with discussions with community representatives on their expectations of the role and composition of these groups. Community Governance Committees were thus formed through a participatory process involving representatives from various segments of society, taking gender, age and social status into account. Community participants were given suggested guidelines from which they developed criteria for selecting members of the proposed community structures. Some of the factors considered in selecting the Community Governance Committees are provided in Table 4.1.

The various communities formed their respective community governance structures based on the above criteria. Of a 12-member governance committee

Table 4.1 Criteria for the selection of Community Governance Committees members

Item	*Membership Criteria*	*Example*
1	Gender	Men, women, youth
2	Existing community leadership	Traditional authorities, elected community representatives such as assemblymen/women, unit committee members, etc.
3	Prominent members of the community	Local businessmen/women, religious leaders, teachers, civil servants, etc.
4	Community mobilization skill	Persons with charisma
5	Availability	Persons who are ready to serve and willing to sacrifice their time for the sake of the community's interest
6	Local knowledge	Persons who are well informed of issues concerning the community, including the history of the place, customs and traditions, etc.
7	Degree of permanence	Length of stay as a member of the community

Source: Authors construct.

for the Agbogbloshie community, one-third were female, with two-thirds men. In Chorkor, women comprised one-quarter of the governance structure, while in Madina Zongo, 22 percent of members were women and 78 percent were men.

The committees were then trained to build their capacity in legal empowerment and community mobilization, using a toolkit as described below. Facilitators worked with these committees to identify areas for improvement and organize workshops on action planning. A system for continuous monitoring was also instituted.

A tool for legal empowerment

To foster community legal empowerment, researchers worked with the communities on developing a toolkit that would build capacity in essential areas, addressing the nature of their rights as citizens (including the rights of residents of informal settlements); relevant legislation and policies that guarantee these rights; and channels and potential partners for accessing justice, among other topics. In developing this toolkit, it was also recognized that the community governance structures would need enhanced capacity for effective community mobilization. Furthermore, residents of informal settlements also needed to be aware of the responsibilities that go with their rights as citizens. To empower the established community governance structures to lead residents in addressing the challenges confronting them, a training manual entitled *Community Mobilization and Legal Empowerment Toolkit* was created. Along with citizen's rights, the upgrading of informal settlements and the laws governing eviction, it also addressed good governance and community mobilization, the responsibilities of citizens, and their role in the development permitting process.

Supported by this toolkit, community governance structures would be better able to represent their communities, and better equipped with knowledge on existing laws, institutions and channels for pursuing access to justice.

Alongside these new tools and structures, monitoring systems were put in place to track the resulting performance and transformation processes.

Outcomes observed in the three communities

Every six months, review meetings were held with the three governance committees in their respective communities. These meetings provided briefings on activities, milestones and stakeholder engagements within the last six months. They thus enabled both researchers and community representatives to reflect on the outcomes of the strategies pursued for legal empowerment and to increase community voice in decision-making. The most successful outcomes were seen in Agbogbloshie, where the community secured a high court order staving off an imminent eviction order, and in Chorkor, where the new Community Governance Committee achieved wide community respect and transformed its leadership. In Madina Zongo, unfortunately, efforts to strengthen community governance were undermined by political polarization and weak social capital in the settlement.

In Agbogbloshie: Engaging residents and resisting eviction

As noted, the Agbogbloshie community, a mix of indigenous and migrant households, has faced eviction threats for decades. Following legal empowerment training of Agbogbloshie's newly struck Community Governance Committee, the Accra Metropolitan Assembly attempted to demolish around 1,800 structures, putting 8,000 people at risk of homelessness. Residents of the informal settlement, led by the Committee, questioned the adequacy of notice given for such an exercise, and highlighted the need for better due process in eviction. The city authority's plan to demolish their structures was justified by the AMA's public relations officer, who claimed that the land was government property, and the city was thus mandated to determine its best use. They aimed to relocate tomato sellers from the deplorable Agbogbloshie Market to a new location.

Drawing on their knowledge of community mobilization, organized protest and litigation as tools for averting the imminent threat, residents worked in unison and with the leadership of their Community Governance Committee to contest the move by the AMA and prevent any attempt to demolish their structures. Educated in approaches to seeking legal redress and equipped with community mobilization skills, the Agbogbloshie Community Governance Committee successfully raised the legal fees needed from community members. The group reached out to Amnesty International, which facilitated advocacy and supported the community to engage the services of a legal practitioner to file an interlocutory injunction with the High Court of Justice, Land Division, Accra to stop the demolition.

As a result of their efforts, the community secured a court injunction that temporarily halted the evictions. Although the injunction was only for a short duration, the city authority did not pursue an order to carry out the eviction; nor did it attempt to evict the inhabitants again. With the threat of imminent eviction reduced, there has since been visible housing improvement in the settlement. In some instances, people are converting their wooden structures, using more permanent and durable materials. This suggests that, as long as informality is deemed criminal, leveraging private capital to improve these areas and service delivery in informal settlements of Ghana will continue to be challenging.

> It is hereby ordered that the Defendants/Respondents, either by themselves or their agents, servants, assigns are restrained from trespassing to carry out any intended demolition exercise at Agbogbloshie, the parcel of land in dispute, to avoid an immediate hardship and loss to the Plaintiffs for a period of ten (10) days.
>
> Injunction issued by Ellen Vivian Amoah, Justice of the High Court (Land Division) on September 20, 2018

The Agbogbloshie Community Governance Committee has since become the community's mouthpiece and serves as a gatekeeper that receives all stakeholders who come into the community. It also mobilizes the community to provide labour to clean the environment and educates residents on public health issues. This is vital, as poor sanitary conditions can pose a wider public health risk that could provide a justification for their removal. During the COVID-19 outbreak, committee members continued to play valuable roles as contact tracers and supported the distribution of relief support to needy households.

In Chorkor: Widening the governance circle and transforming leadership

As provided in section 16 of the Local Governance Act, 2016 (Act 936), the Chorkor community had an elected representative to liaise between them and the local government authority. However, this individual was notably out of touch with his constituents. For instance, he would not visit the community nor engage with his associates, even in times of crisis. In the community's view, the absentee leader could not effectively represent them at the local government level. Through their training, the Community Governance Committee had become more aware of an elected political representative's roles and responsibilities as provided by law. Meanwhile, their effectiveness as a committee earned them the respect and trust of the community. They educated community members on how they needed a voice in decision-making to somehow make up for their absentee political representative.

The community decided to back a member of the Community Governance Committee in the next local government elections; this individual won the seat with a landslide victory to unseat the incumbent. Using fundraising knowledge gained from the community mobilization training, residents mobilized resources to implement regular community clean-up exercises. Figure 4.2 shows some of the activities they carried out under the lead of the Community Governance Committee. The group also played a vital role in contact tracing and distributing household relief when the COVID-19 pandemic was at its peak. Additionally, to ensure a peaceful national election in December 2020, the Chorkor Community Governance Committee collaborated with the National Electoral Commission during voter registration and educated residents on voting procedures and the expected conduct of community members before, during and after the election.

Forming an inclusive Community Governance Committee also provided the community a vehicle for engaging with all stakeholders, including city authorities, municipal service providers and NGOs. The Committee collaborated with the National Health Insurance Scheme (NHIS) to raise awareness and register people who did not have national health insurance subscriptions. This campaign allowed community members to register right at their doorsteps, saving them time and sparing them the inconvenience of registering with the scheme at the NHIS district office, which was far from the community.

Having demonstrated leadership in protecting the community's interests, the Chorkor Committee forged a cordial working relationship with the

Figure 4.2 Periodic clean-up exercises organized by the Chorkor Community Governance Committee
Source: Land Resource Management Centre Project Team (Photos taken by project team).

District Police Command. This helped in curbing community disturbances, such as social events that blocked access roads, which on at least one occasion had resulted in the death of a patient being transported to hospital. As a result, the district police mandated and gave full backing to the Committee to take practical steps to remove any roadblocks mounted for social activities in the community.

In collaboration with the Ghana Water Ladies, a worker association within the Ghana Water Company, a 10-unit toilet facility, accessible to those with disabilities, has been built for the Chorkor community, which had been plagued by unsanitary conditions. A *durbar* (ceremony) to commission the facility was chaired by the head of the Chorkor Community Governance Committee, and attended by the Minister of Sanitation and Rural Development. As in the other communities, the Chorkor Committee played a key role in facilitating, consulting, organizing and mobilizing funding for this new community facility. The toilets have helped to reduce the indiscriminate open-air defecation that had been a major problem for the community.

In Madina Zongo: Governance undermined by political polarization and weak social capital

From an early stage in its implementation, it was apparent that the Community Governance Committee of Madina Zongo needed help. A first iteration of the Committee had dissolved due to a need for more cooperation among its members. The group was deeply divided by its diverse social and ethnic makeup and its members' partisan political affiliations. Actions and decisions taken by members were mostly construed as having political party connotations. This lack of trust and solidarity manifested in residents' inability to appoint champions who would advance their collective interest; this lack of cohesion ultimately led to the first committee's demise. When a second governance committee was formed, this new group faced the same challenges that had confronted the first group.

The Madina Zongo governance group received enormous support from the research team aimed at helping them overcome their challenges and learn valuable lessons as to why they were failing while other community committees were doing well. Just before the closure of the action research project, there were several engagements with the group that showed some positive developments. The governance group had reconstituted in a way that was less politically polarized, and members had developed a work plan they intended to follow in the ensuing months.

The experience with this governance committee runs counter to the notion that informal settlements tend to have high social capital. It also illustrates the corrosive effects of political polarization in undermining the solidarity, trust and mutual respect that characterize many informal settlements.

Conclusion: Lessons learned and their policy implications

The experiences observed in these three communities suggest that the inability of poor households in informal settlements to access justice stems at least in part from their low access to legal information and education. This aligns with observations from the literature and is corroborated by field data that showed less than 2 percent of all community respondents had ever used the formal legal system.

Through the action research effort described in this chapter, the hurdles to accessing justice were addressed by providing communities with fundamental legal knowledge and information, and identifying organizations that could support such efforts, such as Amnesty International. Any future intervention, drawing on the lessons learned from this research, must continuously deepen community engagements and expand the depth and breadth of community participation throughout the process. To sustain the gains made, an exit strategy needs to be embedded in the process, a step which unfortunately was not possible in this instance due to the constraints imposed by the COVID-19 pandemic.

Testing the law, as Agbogbloshie did when it obtained an interlocutory injunction, is important in order to clarify what constitutes due process in evictions in Ghana. Although there still needs to be a codified law on these issues, this decision adds to the existing case law. As the courts make further pronouncements in such cases, the justiciability of social, economic and cultural rights enshrined in the Constitution will be further grounded.

Legal empowerment strategies, such as those tested in Agbogbloshie, Chorkor and Madina Zongo, can embolden poor urban residents in informal settlements, giving them the dignity and voice to engage on issues that affect their rights. As seen in Agbogbloshie and Chorkor, these efforts are strengthened by having an institutionalized governance structure in place to drive such an agenda, a role performed by the Community Governance Committees in these settlements. Their continuous work with community members and their accountable stewardship ensured that they earned community trust in their leadership. Working with external actors, such as Amnesty, the Ghana Police Service, the water authority and CBOs, also ensured that they constantly applied newly acquired knowledge and skills, while sharing these with other community members.

These efforts also show that widening the urban governance circle to include the urban poor is possible, if the right approach and systems are instituted. As gleaned from the literature, the tenets of good governance include participation, transparency, responsiveness, equity, inclusiveness and accountability, among others. These tenets foster trust between leaders and those they lead. Through the training provided, the Community Governance Committees were helped to see the need to be transparent and accountable to residents. The participatory approach adopted by these committees, their responsiveness to residents' real needs and their accountability gave community members confidence in them — even to the extent that, in one instance, they were willing to back a committee member to run for election to represent them within local government. With one of their own in government, Chorkor residents are more likely to have their voices heard.

The Madina Zongo case tests the perception that high social capital inherently exists in informal settlements. It amply demonstrates that political polarization and a lack of mutual respect in some of these communities can undermine social cohesion. Among the essential lessons learned is the need to test the ground before selecting a community for legal empowerment programs. The early warning signs observed here included participants wearing political party paraphernalia to project meetings, people taking entrenched positions on matters that were inherently not political and the formation of cliques within a group. In this case, dissension started when the election to select leaders for community governance led to the creation of factions. Although the reconstituted group offers hope, they still need to meet expectations. The lessons here are clear: with unity of purpose, empowerment initiatives have the potential to deliver the results that communities expect; but political polarization leads to conflicting and adverse development outcomes. Initiatives aimed at improving the lives of residents of slums should first evaluate the level of social capital as part of their scoping activities and develop strategies to address this within their intervention planning.

Finally, the experience of these three settlements highlights the need to address both the tangible infrastructure and service needs of slum communities and their intangible need for information and abilities that can empower them. As learned from the results of this intervention, empowerment initiatives can prepare the community for action now and in the future, using legal avenues to advance and sustain their development.

Notes

1 Action research was conducted through the project "Improving Governance, Voice and Access to Justice in Ghana's Informal Settlements" (2017 to 2021) by the Land Resource Management Centre, in collaboration with Slum Dwellers International, People's Dialogue, and the faculties of Law and Built Environment of Kwame Nkrumah University of Science and Technology. This multidisciplinary team aimed to investigate the causes of exclusion in Ghana's informal settlements, identify gaps and opportunities for residents' voices, and improve access to essential services and justice. The project was funded by the International Development Research Centre.

2 For those familiar with Accra, this site is not to be confused with Old Fadama, an adjacent area that houses an e-waste site, and is also often referred to as Agbogbloshie, including in a considerable body of research literature (Caravanos et al., 2011; COHRE, 2004; Daum et al., 2017; Nartey et al., 2017).

References

Alam, M. A., & Hasina, N. (2014). Constitutional voice for good governance in Bangladesh. *Global Disclosure of Economics and Business*, 3(2), 149–156.

Amnesty International. (2011). *Amnesty International report 2011: The state of the world's human rights*. Amnesty International. www.amnesty.org/en/documents/POL10/001/2011/en/.

Armah-Attoh, D., & Robertson, A. (2014). *The practice of democracy in Ghana: beyond the formal framework* (Afrobarometer Briefing Paper No. 137). Afrobarometer.

Caravanos, J., Clark, E., Fuller, R., & Lambertson, C. (2011). Assessing worker and environmental chemical exposure risks at an e-waste recycling and disposal site in Accra, Ghana. *Journal of Health and Pollution*, 1(1), 16–25.

Centre on Housing Rights and Evictions (COHRE). (2004). *A precarious future: The informal settlement of Agbogbloshie, Accra, Ghana*. COHRE.

Daum, K., Stoler, J., & Grant, R. J. (2017). Toward a more sustainable trajectory for e-waste policy: a review of a decade of e-waste research in Accra, Ghana. *International Journal of Environmental Research and Public Health*, 14(2), 135.

De Soto, H. (2000). *The mystery of capital*. Basic Books.

Herrle, P., Jachnow, A., & Ley, A. (2006). *Die Metropolen des Südens: Labor für Innovationen? Mit neuen Allianzen zu besserem Stadtmanagement* [*The metropolitan areas of the South: a laboratory for innovation? New alliances for better urban management*] (Policy paper 25). Development and Peace Institute.

Housing the Masses. (2010). *Final report to people's dialogue on human settlements on community-led enumeration of old Fadama Community, Accra — Ghana*. Author, p. 2. Jordan, B. (2008). *Welfare and well-being: Social value in public policy*. Policy Press. doi:10.1332/policypress/9781847420800.001.0001.

Nartey, Y., Hill, P. C., Amo-Antwi, K., Nyarko, K. M., Yarney, J., & Cox, B. (2017). Cervical cancer in the Greater Accra and Ashanti regions of Ghana. *Journal of Global Oncology*, 3(6), 782–790.

Roseveare, C. (2013). *Rule of law and international development*. DFID.

Sharma, P. (2008). Commentary: Familiness: Capital stocks and flows between family and business. *Entrepreneurship Theory and Practice*, 32(6), 971–977. doi:10.1111/j.1540-6520.2008.00266.x.

UN General Assembly. (2009, July 13). *Legal empowerment of the poor and eradication of poverty: Report of the Secretary-General, A/64/133*. Author.

UN-Habitat. (2009). *Global report on human settlements: Planning sustainable cities*. Author.

UN-Habitat. (2014). *Forced evictions: Fact sheet no. 25/Rev. 1*. Author.

United Nations Office on Drugs and Crime (UNODC). (2013). *Accounting for security and justice in the post-2015 development agenda*. UNODC. www.unodc.org/documents/about-unodc/Post-2015-Development-Agenda/UNODC_-_Accounting_for_Security_and_Justice_in_the_Post-2015_Development_Agenda.pdf.

Weru, J., Wanyoike, W., & Di Giovanni, A. (2015). Confronting complexity: Using action-research to build voice, accountability, and justice in Nairobi's Mukuru informal settlements. In J. Wouters, A. Ninio, T. Doherty, & H. Cisse' (Eds.), *The World Bank legal review*, Volume 6: *Improving delivery in development: The role of voice, social contract, and accountability* (pp. 233–257). World Bank. doi:10.1596/978-1-4648-0378-9_ch10.

World Bank. (2015). *Rising through cities in Ghana; Ghana urbanisation review*. World Bank.

5 Innovating participation to expand water and sanitation access under a special planning area in Mukuru informal settlements, Nairobi

Smith Ouma, Patrick Njoroge and Jane Weru

Introduction

The Mukuru informal settlements of Nairobi, Kenya are densely populated, spanning 689 acres with an estimated population of some half-million people, in a city of 4.3 million (Weru et al., 2015, p. 233).[1] As with many informal settlements globally, the land tenure question in Mukuru is highly complex and problematic. This situation arises from the layered claims and resulting contestations among the various stakeholders within and outside the settlements. Mukuru also provides an important case study on the close interlinkages between security of tenure and access to basic services (p. 235). As a result of the contested tenure relationships, the Nairobi City County Government (NCCG) and other government utility providers supply next to no basic services and social amenities to residents (p. 236). Consequently, there are stark sanitation challenges within the settlements, with women and children largely bearing the brunt as a result.[2] A situational analysis conducted by a number of stakeholders in 2017 indicated that only 1 percent of Mukuru residents had access to a private or individual water source and access to a private, in-home toilet. Over 85 percent of electricity connections are informal and illegal and the settlements have almost no solid waste collection, leaving the work to be done by youth groups (University of California Berkeley et al., 2017). The inhabitants are often forced to access basic services from informal providers at costs that exceed ordinary rates. This imposes a poverty penalty on them (Mutinda & Otieno, 2015).

In August 2017, the NCCG declared the settlements to be a special planning area (SPA). This marked the first time in the history of planning in Nairobi that a local development plan was being formulated at scale and in a participatory manner at the local level for an informal settlement. Designation as a SPA was made pursuant to the Physical Planning Act and the Constitution, which both invest the planning authority with the power to prepare a physical development plan, in a participatory manner, for an area with unique development potential or problems. The declaration was the culmination, in large part, of years of advocacy by Muungano wa Wanavijiji — the main slum dwellers federation in Nairobi's settlements — working closely with its support organization, Akiba Mashinani Trust (AMT).

DOI: 10.4324/9781003538806-5

Working hand-in-hand with inhabitants, Muungano and AMT harnessed the participatory processes activated by the SPA to plan and implement water and sanitation projects for Mukuru. Significantly, those participatory approaches provided the inhabitants — whose knowledge and agency had historically been disqualified as inadequate in Nairobi planning processes — with visibility and a voice to articulate their claims. The inhabitants were empowered through rigorous community-led research to understand their sanitation needs and subsequently participate in the co-production of interventions to address these challenges.

This chapter analyses in more detail how participation was employed in the SPA as a force of empowerment. Its main argument is that these participation strategies allowed the historically marginalized residents of Mukuru to subvert the dominant and exclusionary spatial planning practices in Nairobi. The success of Mukuru inhabitants in expanding access to sanitation facilities, on one level, collapsed the traditional distinctions between experts and the subjects of planning and, on a deeper level, redesigned and reconstructed a more equitable form of urban citizenship. The chapter focuses on how participation as a tool for, and outcome of, legal empowerment enabled the inhabitants of Mukuru to identify the sanitation shortfalls within their neighbourhoods, co-produce interventions to remedy the identified gaps and then demand the establishment of critical infrastructure to address them. Participation also facilitated the adoption of relaxed standards of planning to respond to the unique circumstances within the settlements. For instance, the Water, Sanitation and Energy (WSE) consortium, together with the inhabitants, developed a simplified sewer system and pre-paid water dispensers that would facilitate the inhabitants' access to water and sanitation facilities.

After this introduction, the chapter briefly outlines the history of urban planning in Nairobi while highlighting the exclusionary logic that has featured in the dominant urban planning approaches adopted. It then discusses the mobilization efforts that fed into the initiatives to declare Mukuru a SPA. Subsequently, the concept of legal empowerment is unpacked, highlighting its role in supporting the development of communities' voice and agency. The chapter then evaluates how the participation model employed by the WSE consortium of the Mukuru SPA was largely shaped by the demands of beneficiary groups and the different ways in which that model contributed to community empowerment. The authors conclude with a few reflections on the lessons learned from the Mukuru SPA and how participation can be structured to realize transformative outcomes.

Impetus for a paradigm shift in urban planning in Nairobi

Urban planning approaches historically adopted in Kenya's capital city have exhibited glaring dissonance when it comes to understanding and prescribing solutions tailored to the urban realities of residents.[3] They have particularly failed to take as their principal focus the needs of the excluded urban majority and have instead acted to entrench exclusion (McAuslan, 1982, p. 549). What is manifest from these approaches is an ambivalent attitude by planning authorities towards certain urban enclaves. The existence or humanity of the inhabitants of these spaces has either been denied or called into question, with the resulting spatial plans developed for the city rendering these residents invisible (Kimari, 2016, p. 4).

The planning ideologies that have shaped the growth of Nairobi cannot be examined in isolation from the history of urbanization and colonialism in Kenya (Akatch, 1995, p. 39). This history has been imbued with controversy and contestation as a result of deprivation and discontent among various groups. Contestations have been particularly rife when it comes to access to and control of space in the city and with regard to whose voice is given recognition.[4] Urban planning in Nairobi has been approached from two ideological standpoints: a colonial segregationist approach, which later morphed into a scheme of social exclusion; and a functional planning model (Claire, 2006, p. 27). A functional approach to planning adopts an elitist and technical orientation (what Cornwall refers to as "closed spaces" of participation) (Cornwall, 2002). It foregrounds the experience of external experts while paying little to no attention to the lived realities of the intended beneficiaries of the planning processes. The result has been the development of spatial plans that rest on shaky foundations, making them non-responsive to local needs.

Urban planning approaches are also haunted by the intractable land policy problems bequeathed by an exclusionary British colonial rule. This colonial legacy in urban land policy is omnipresent in the cities of many African countries, like Nairobi in Kenya, Lusaka in Zambia and Lilongwe in Malawi (Chitonge & Mfune, 2015, p. 213; Myers, 2003, p. 2). The spatial dynamics that have emerged in these postcolonial cities are marked by a visible hierarchy of spatial order — in other words, with an evident segregation and exclusion of low-income groups from basic city life (Pieterse, 2008, p. 17). In this way, in Kenya, as in many other African countries, urban land policies, and consequently urban planning attitudes, fail to acknowledge the realities occasioned by the inequalities and injustices in the way land is distributed, accessed, owned and controlled (Chitonge & Mfune, 2015, p. 210).[5] Planning practices have been shaped by exclusionary logic, where space is constantly manipulated to exclude certain groups in the city and entrench feelings of non-belonging. Tenure insecurity has habitually been deployed in a well-calculated and deliberate scheme of social exclusion by state functionaries and political elites. The net effect has been to render the excluded ineligible to participate in formulating and implementing spatial plans.

The undemocratic nature of planning creates and sustains what Kimari refers to as "ecologies of exclusion", which have taken different forms since the colonial period (Kimari, 2018, p. 52). Planning practices adopted in Nairobi have denied certain groups a platform to assert their "right to the city", to benefit from its resources and opportunities, and to collectively participate in its betterment. Paradoxically, the so-called "global city" is built upon the labour and exclusion of these groups. In Nairobi, the glaring gaps in basic services in informal settlements like Mukuru are clear manifestations of the city's undemocratic and failed approaches to urban land use planning.

Laying the base for a special planning intervention in Mukuru

The experiences of Mukuru residents under the SPA are significant because of how they were able, at the same time, to overcome the failed, conventional planning approaches, while strengthening their ability to assert their rights and citizenship over many years. Quests by residents in Mukuru for expanded citizenship rights, along with their history of resistance, took inspiration from the efforts of residents in different locations across the city. Low-income groups in Nairobi have struggled to (re)assert their rights to belong by employing different strategies and tools. Blokland et al. have referred to such occurrences as "splintered acts of citizenship" (Blokland et al., 2015, p. 663). The focus of these struggles has been to conserve living spaces and assert their right to belong in the city (Rodriguez-Torres, 2006, p. 92).

Historically, residents' actions in Mukuru have also been sustained by alliances formed with a diverse range of civil society organizations (CSOs). The slum dwellers' federation Muungano wa Wanavijiji, working closely with AMT, has for over 20 years supported community action in Mukuru, with a focus on resistance to forced evictions. The federation was established in 1996 to unite informal settlement residents to address evictions and other challenges in their settlements.

The close partnerships that Muungano and AMT have fostered with local communities have seen Muungano's members navigate and gain access to state institutions that are critical for access to basic services. Women-led campaigns and protests emerged as the preferred strategy used to bring the state's attention to the dire health and sanitation situation in Mukuru. Groups of women that were part of Muungano federations led protests to deliver petitions to state agencies like the Ministry of Health. AMT and Muungano mobilized women in Mukuru to collect signatures from other residents in support of petitions that would also be delivered to the NCCG and the Ministry of Lands. Other campaigns have targeted school children. An essay-writing competition organized in 2013 invited school-going girls of ages 12 to 15 from 21 informal schools in Mukuru Kwa Njenga and Kwa Reuben to write reflective essays on their day-to-day experiences with accessing sanitation amenities at home and in school.

The support of organizations like AMT and Muungano has also enabled residents to take advantage of the legal and political openings presented by the Kenyan Constitution. The Constitution, in Article 56, elevates public participation to a national value and a justiciable right that can be claimed by marginalized groups. It also requires the state to put in place adequate measures to ensure the participation of marginalized groups in development processes. It is from this normative framework that inhabitants of Mukuru were able to ground their demands to be included in spatial planning processes. With the support of AMT and the Katiba Institute (an NGO based in Nairobi), Muungano has in the past led inhabitants in instituting legal claims against the state to demand provision of secure tenure, particularly in the period following the enactment of the Constitution. The use of litigation as a strategy for realizing rights succeeded in halting a trend of rampant evictions in Mukuru (through a 2012 injunction). The use of litigation alone was found to have its limitations, particularly due to its reactive nature — being an option only after rights have already been violated (Ouma, 2022). Yet the use of court orders marked a turning point for residents, precisely because it enabled a shift away from reactive strategies.

Crucially, Muungano and AMT were now able to mobilize evidence in support of their efforts. AMT, Slum Dwellers International-Kenya (SDI-Kenya), the University of Nairobi and Strathmore University conducted action research in Mukuru to establish the number of households, prevailing service and governance conditions, and tenure typologies. This study was funded by Canada's International Development Research Centre (IDRC). Findings were published in a situational analysis report. One of its findings highlighted that the residents of Mukuru suffer a staggering "poverty penalty", whereby households can only access more expensive yet lower-quality services than in Nairobi's formal estates. For instance, Mukuru households must pay 45 to 142 percent more for their monthly electricity bills than residents enjoying formal Kenya Power provision. For water, residents pay 172 percent more per cubic metre of water than rates paid by residents living in other parts of the city. Not only is Mukuru's water and shelter of extremely low quality, but households also bear the inequitable burden of higher per-unit costs than their wealthier neighbours. Researchers presented these and other findings to the NCCG.

With support from AMT, residents of Mukuru attempted to persuade the county to start a planning process to address the entrenched poverty, inequality and indignities that stem from paltry housing and services. After about two years of persistence, the NCCG agreed to declare Mukuru a SPA under the Physical Planning Act[6] in 2017. The declaration demonstrates a historical recognition that conventional planning tools are insufficient to address the realities within the Mukuru SPA.[7] It soon set in motion a co-production process aimed at formulating a physical development plan for the settlements. In other words, the inhabitants of Mukuru now had an opportunity to prepare these plans, together with external experts who were convened for the process. Plans were developed through eight thematic consortia which were constituted to align with the departments within the NCCG: Education, Youth Affairs and Culture; Health Services; Environment and Natural Resources; Housing, Infrastructure and Commerce; Land and Institutional Frameworks; Finance and Economic Planning; Water, Sanitation and Energy; and Coordination, Community Organization and Communication. Each consortium was chaired by the relevant NCCG department and supported by a lead partner organization.

The SPA process was then guided by a recognition that conventional planning approaches were insufficient in places like Mukuru, where contextual factors like settlement density would make it difficult to adopt rigid statutory standards (Ouma et al., 2023). Muungano and its partners understood the issues identified in the Mukuru SPA to be both technical and political in nature. Muungano then played the lead role in mobilizing residents to develop collective consciousness around the SPA. Muungano would also act as the link between the community and the technical planning team when the planning processes commenced. Community exchanges were facilitated by Muungano to expose Mukuru residents to projects in other informal settlements in Nairobi. The primary goal of these exchanges was to equip the community with the relevant skills needed to manage the SPA as a communal project. The technical aspects of the planning process would be led by the external actors that Muungano, AMT and SDI-Kenya had mobilized to participate in the SPA process. The technical teams were tasked with developing suitable technical models that would attend to the unique needs within the settlements and result in the least disruption possible for the inhabitants. Details of how the WSE consortium approached community participation are discussed later in this chapter. The following section first examines the important roles that a properly fashioned participation regime can play in fostering empowerment.

Realizing legal empowerment through participation

Participation in decision-making is widely accepted as the "most adequate means for the expression of agency" (Gould, 1989, p. 217).[8] It gives individuals opportunities to expand various capabilities and realize improved outcomes. It is a capability-building tool, in that it brings individuals together to express their agency and collectively pursue responses to local challenges they identify. Through their participation, individuals signal that they have a stake in local matters and the right to shape them. Participation can also play key empowerment roles, especially in arrangements that value community knowledge and work to dismantle hierarchical power relations. Participation is both a tool and an outcome of empowerment. As a tool for empowerment, participation can enable individuals and communities to understand their situation and increase their control over factors that affect their lives and ultimately enhance their wellbeing.[9] As an outcome of empowerment, participation signals that individuals understand that they have a stake in local matters and that they have the right to shape local affairs (Ouma, 2022). Empowerment aims at fostering ownership of programs while maintaining accountability to the beneficiaries of development projects. It also challenges the power imbalances between external experts and communities (p. 38).[10] As Corburn and Makau have noted, involving communities in generating knowledge to devise interventions that address their local conditions allows these groups to reclaim power over data interpretation and decision-making

(Corburn & Makau, 2016, p. 185). Participation as a form of empowerment should therefore be concerned with illuminating the internal power relations in decision-making processes and reorienting them to elevate voices that are often underrepresented or excluded (Frediani et al., 2019, pp. 101–124).

In this chapter, legal empowerment is understood as both a basis for, and outcome of, meaningful participation. The concept has attracted several definitions, both broad and narrow in their interpretation. In a report to the Commission on Legal Empowerment of the Poor, the United Nations General Assembly (UNGA) Secretary General understood legal empowerment as the "process of systemic change through which the poor are protected and enabled to use the law to advance their rights and their interests as citizens and economic actors" (United Nations General Assembly, 2008). Goodwin and Maru (2017), on the other hand, define civil society legal empowerment efforts as "those that seek to increase the capacity of people to understand and use the law" (p. 160). The UNGA Secretary General's view on legal empowerment is that it is both a means to an end and an end in itself. Under this definition, the objectives of legal empowerment are both broad (enabling the realization of systemic change) and narrow (elevating individuals' agency and capacity to effect change). Both objectives are important, especially when seeking change in contexts of historical marginalization and material deprivation. The Commission on Legal Empowerment of the Poor identifies four key conditions for legal empowerment of low-income groups: identity, information, voice and organization (Commission on Legal Empowerment of the Poor, 2008).

Legal empowerment can also be viewed as a tool that enables low-income groups to articulate the issues that affect them. Perspectives from low-income groups have historically been muted in arrangements that fail to recognize their capacity to shape decisions that affect their lives. Very little effort has been directed at learning how these groups perceive their rights, how they act on these meanings, and how these perceptions and actions are bounded by issues of knowledge and representation (Gaventa, 2002, p. 8). The concept of agency has therefore received considerable attention from those examining how individuals interact with political institutions and how those interactions inform the status and practice of their citizenship. Ruth Lister, for instance, refers to the concept when characterizing individuals as "autonomous, purposive actors, capable of choice" (Lister, 1997, p. 36). To her, equal agency means that no one group should have the right to exercise free choice and domination over another (p. 38). Like Susan James, Lister contends that the development of a conscious sense of agency arises from the development of individuals' self-esteem, which represents confidence that one can participate in political life (p. 39).[11] The political theorist Carol Gould views agency as an aid to self-development. She defines agency as "concretely becoming the person one chooses to be through carrying out those actions that express one's purposes and needs" (Gould, 1989, p. 47). In summary, agency is the ability of individuals to exert influence in processes that affect them.

Legal empowerment occupies an important place in equipping communities with the requisite skills and voice to confront the drivers of marginality within their spaces. In properly fashioned participation frameworks, vulnerable and marginalized groups can be equipped to connect their marginalization with violations of their rights. This exercise requires supporting these groups so that they know their legal rights (Knight, 2021, p. 3). This can be accomplished through partnerships with other stakeholders and engaging in the "politics of rights" to advance their claims and locate them in law (Scheingold, 2004). These groups must also be equipped with the ability to claim rights, enforce and protect them, and advocate for more equitable laws and policies (Knight, 2021). In this way, legally empowered individuals will be asserting agency through legal rights and strategies (Cotula, 2022). The following section examines how legal empowerment of Mukuru residents, facilitated by their participation in the WSE consortium, not only enabled an expanded understanding of their constitutional right to participation, but also facilitated the development of innovative ways to deliver water and sanitation solutions.

Participation in the Water, Sanitation and Energy consortium

To prepare Mukuru residents to participate in the SPA processes, the Community Mobilization and Coordination consortium — comprised of the NCCG, Muungano, AMT and SDI-Kenya — established a physical address system for all households in the settlements. Communities in Kwa Njenga, Kwa Reuben and Viwandani settlements were organized into 13 representative neighbourhood associations. A total of 270 community mobilizers from the three settlements were informed about the Mukuru SPA and taken through a rigorous training on settlement mapping, community household data collection and project monitoring and evaluation, among other topics. Design of the data collection tools was done together with the community to ensure their relevance. The mobilization consortium used various channels, including radio talk shows and elected and appointed representatives, to convey information on the SPA process to settlement residents. Reuben FM, a radio station dedicated to Mukuru, was instrumental in ensuring local dissemination of information on the SPA. Concerned residents would call in and ask questions relating to the SPA, which would then be addressed by station hosts.

Even before community consultations commenced, the WSE consortium had undertaken a situational analysis to assess existing challenges in Mukuru and the available opportunities for ensuring residents as wide access to water and sanitation as possible. The analysis aimed to establish the context of planning and provide crucial evidence to support informed decision-making during the planning process. It found deplorable water and sanitation challenges, with only 3,863 pit latrines serving 100,561 families. Significantly, the situational analysis relied on Mukuru residents to perform community mapping, detailing their neighbourhoods and the surrounding infrastructure and services. Through this co-productive process — whereby the WSE consortium relied on data generated by and with residents — the SPA process signalled its recognition of local expertise and its commitment to developing interventions grounded in residents' experiences. This co-production further enabled the consortium to organize participation in the SPA around grassroots unit levels such as the household, cell, sub-cluster and segment, as illustrated in Figure 5.1.

Settlement profiling, mapping and enumeration are key community-led processes used by WSE and other SPA consortia to generate evidence on the most pressing issues to be addressed by planning interventions. Enumeration entails having the beneficiary community lead information-gathering processes; this helps build residents' capacity to engage with formal actors, while acknowledging the community as a repository of local knowledge (Bradlow, 2011, p. 48). Profiling entails generating data on the resources available in a community, while giving visibility to community needs to be taken into account during planning and service delivery.[12] Through the enumeration process, individuals within the community provide external experts and government agencies with concrete data on local conditions and priority areas in need of intervention (Lines & Makau, 2018, p. 419).

The WSE consortium held 13 community pre-consultative and consultative meetings (*barazas*): these included two community mobilizer trainings, one community mobilizer feedback meeting and 10 community consultative meetings in Viwandani, Kwa Reuben and Kwa Njenga settlement. A total of 1,174 community members (458 were male; 716 were female) were engaged

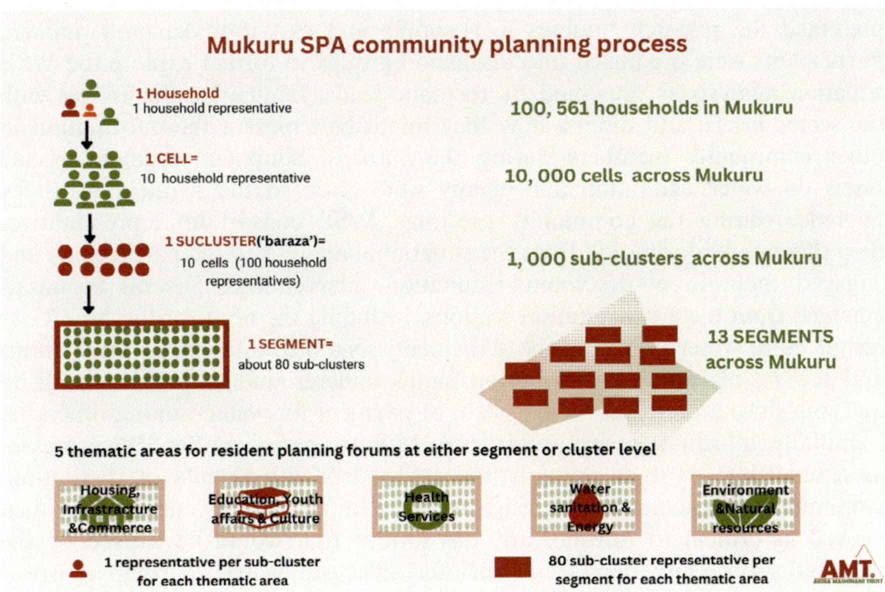

Figure 5.1 Mukuru SPA community planning process
Source: Akiba Mashinani Trust.

during community consultations held between August and November 2018. The makeup of community members attending the meetings was inclusive and represented all relevant groups — men, women, youth and people with disabilities. In attendance were WSE community mobilizers and consortium members; community representatives; and local administration representatives. Some of the key community stakeholders who participated were community water vendors, water technicians and plumbers, electricians, toilet owners, pit emptiers, landlords, structure owners and waste collectors.

In Mukuru, these processes have facilitated household-level data gathering on the social determinants of health and the distribution and quality of healthcare resources within the settlements (Wanavijiji, 2020, p. 20). Community preparation of these inventories also plays the important role of generating household situational analyses that can inform targeted interventions for each unique case.[13] Ultimately, community-led enumeration and profiling processes challenge the idea that the inhabitants of Mukuru are helpless actors, unable to articulate their needs or act upon them. This co-production of data also promotes local buy-in of participatory processes, which is essential for the sustainability and success of subsequent community interventions.

Designing the interventions

During the consultation sessions, community mobilizers and residents were given an overview of the SPA process and taken through the water, sanitation and energy situation in Mukuru. This was done using posters that visually presented the research findings in a simple and easy-to-understand manner. Participants were organized into discussion groups to further explore the WSE situation analysis as presented by thematic leads; familiarize themselves with the sector briefs; and discuss how they might best present the information to other community members during the *barazas.* Simplified segment-specific briefs on water, sanitation and energy were given to the segment leads for reference during the community meetings. WSE consortium representatives then presented information from the situational analysis to the participants and engaged them in co-developing sanitation interventions. Several proposals emerged from these consultation sessions, including the need for the NCCG to install more water points in the settlement; separate water pipes from drains and sewers; place water distribution mains underground to avoid vandalism; and introduce a pre-paid token system of payment for water, among others.

Initially, informal service providers in Mukuru perceived the SPA processes as a challenge to their domain and responded with threats of disruption. Community participation in designing the sanitation interventions was then viewed as critical to forestall any disruptions that would be caused by the informal service providers. Residents' and structure owners' participation was also seen as crucial to achieving higher household connection rates and fostering ownership of the interventions. This would later prove important during the development of the management frameworks for the systems that would ultimately be established. During the consultation meetings, the inhabitants were very vocal about the types of intervention that they deemed suitable for their neighbourhoods. They challenged conventional models such as public toilets that were proposed as an intervention by some of the technical experts. Instead, the majority felt that establishing a toilet and a water tap at the plot level, comprising 10–12 households in a courtyard, would be the most suitable way to approach sanitation issues in the short term, with permanent housing and an internal toilet for each housing unit being a longer-term solution.

The technical team was then responsible for identifying models that would align with the specifications presented by the inhabitants. AMT and SDI facilitated a learning exchange visit for the WSE consortium to Dar es Salaam, Tanzania. The exchange was meant to support learning on how sustainable decentralized sanitation systems have been operationalized by water utilities there, to increase consortium members' awareness of existing sanitation options in informal settlements. In addition, AMT and Muungano supported exchanges to Nairobi's Kahawa West and Mathare informal settlements, where Mukuru residents learned more about prepaid water dispensers (PPD) constructed by the local utility company.

Figure 5.2 shows the number of toilets in one of the three settlements during the SPA planning phase.

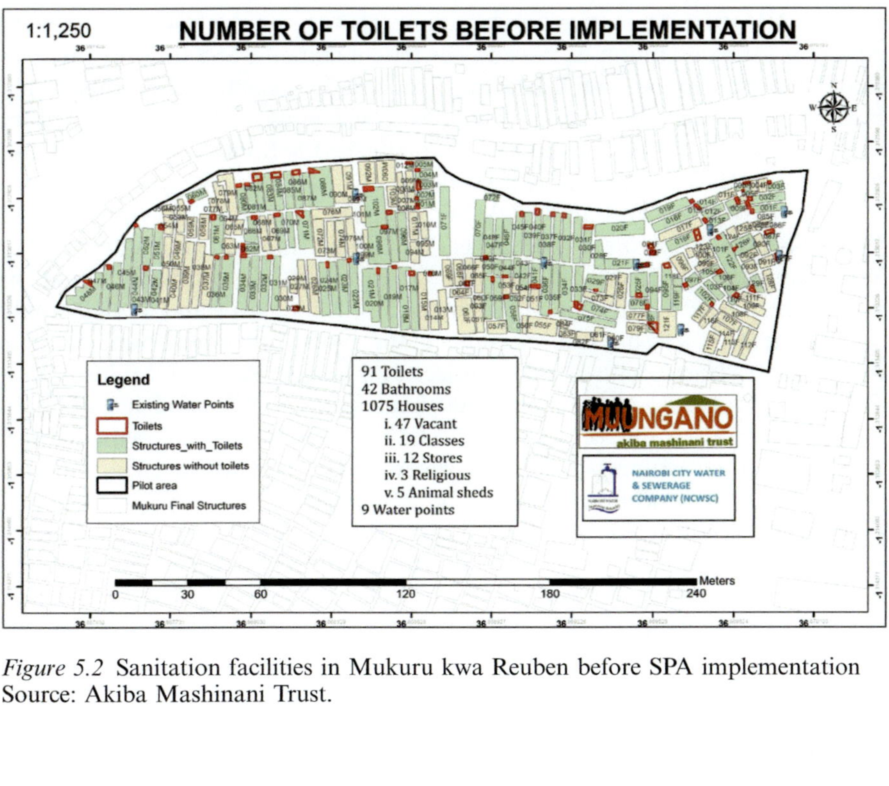

Figure 5.2 Sanitation facilities in Mukuru kwa Reuben before SPA implementation
Source: Akiba Mashinani Trust.

WSE also held a workshop with representatives from the Nairobi City Water and Sewerage Company (NCWSC) and other partners to deliberate on the practicality of adopting the technology required to roll out simplified sewer systems (SSS) in Mukuru and to identify the technical standards that would be needed to successfully implement the proposed interventions. The WSE consortium developed spatial and infrastructure designs to facilitate the establishment of SSS and PPDs. As discussed below, implementation of the WSE proposals by residents and structure owners in Mukuru signalled their strong willingness to be agents of change in their neighbourhoods. It also showed how collective deliberation can contribute to changes that ultimately improve settlement living conditions.

Implementing the water and sanitation proposals

WSE prioritized the creation of design plans that could offer flexibilities during the establishment of infrastructure, and could be scaled out across the settlements. PPDs and SSS emerged as the most suitable sanitation options for the Mukuru context. Simplified sewer systems are constructed using smaller diameter pipes laid at a shallower depth and at a flatter gradient than conventional sewers. Prepaid water dispensers, in contrast, could be structured around existing borehole systems in settlements that were established during the COVID-19 pandemic. This technological innovation allows consumers to purchase water through prepaid water tokens, dispensing with the need for billing. Adopting these two interventions also stemmed from the need to ensure as little disruption as possible for the inhabitants. SSS networks require shallow depths to be established and can usually accommodate other light infrastructure after installation. This meant that houses and other temporary structures could still be constructed on established SSS lines, which could also be moved to different locations if needed.

AMT partnered with the NCWSC, Nairobi Metropolitan Services and Water Sanitation for the Urban Poor (WSUP) for the implementation of the WSE consortium proposals. In this partnership, Government would be responsible for setting up the main sewer lines, while AMT and WSUP would set up lateral sewer lines connecting to the plots. Implementation of these interventions began with a pilot project at Mosque Road in Mukuru Kwa Ruben that targeted connecting 1,000 households to SSS and installing 10 PPDs to serve a total of 1,000 households. Community-led mapping and numbering of structures was done to generate data that was needed to design the SSS networks and install PPDs. The pilot project commenced in 2020 and successfully constructed 1.44 km of SSS network by August 2021 with 94 connections to 100 toilets that would benefit over 850 households. Additionally, 1.6 km of water network and 10 PPDs, each serving 100 households, were constructed. Initial connections to the SSS network would be at no cost to the residents, while connections made after the pilot would cost a one-time fee of KES5,000 (approximately USD35). This amount was still considered prohibitive by residents, which triggered the development of a financial product, in the form of a loan facility by AMT, which residents could access to establish connections and improve toilets at the plot level. The following diagram shows the SSS and PPD connections established in the pilot test area as of August 2021.

Experience with these interventions demonstrated the need for appropriate mechanisms to support governance of the amenities at the community level. There was a pressing need to instil users with a sense of responsibility, sustainability and ownership by assigning them duties. AMT then convened community meetings in Mukuru to formulate guidelines for managing the PPDs and SSS networks. Meetings were held at the plot and cluster levels. A total of 100 plots were targeted along Mosque Road, the location of the pilot project. Meetings at the plot level aimed to identify and create roles for representatives who would then be responsible for collecting and articulating concerns emerging within plots. The representatives would also be tasked with promoting household uptake of prepaid water token cards. The configuration of clusters adhered to the existing borehole locations within the settlements. During cluster meetings, it was agreed that frameworks would be established to assign roles and responsibilities to various stakeholders. Residents from Mukuru participated in exchange visits to informal settlements

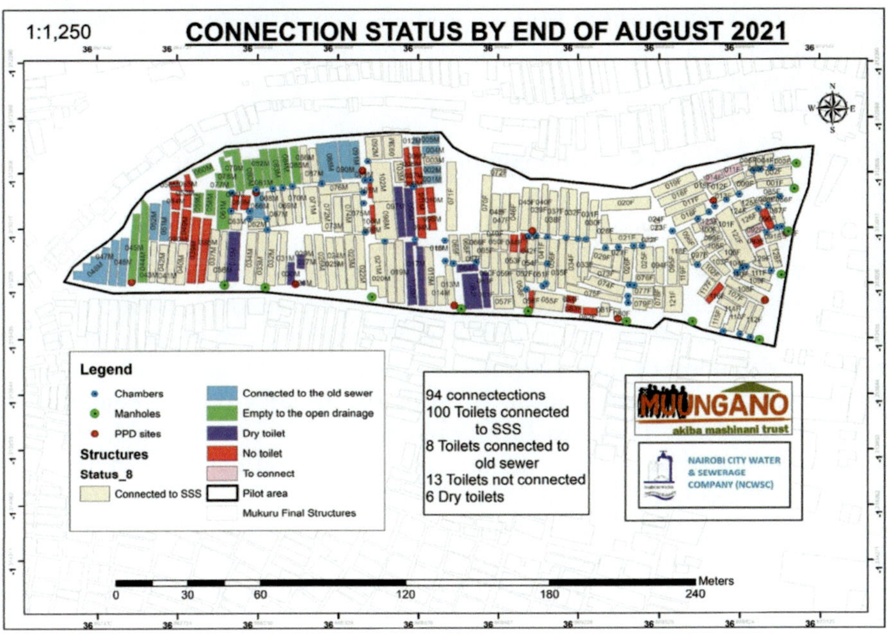

Figure 5.3 Sanitation facilities in Mukuru kwa Reuben after SSS and PPD implementation

Source: Akiba Mashinani Trust.

such as Kiambiu, Kibera and Kahawa Soweto, to learn from their experiences with the implementation of similar PPDs. Participants included plot representatives, cluster leaders and residents selected from the 10 clusters along Mosque Road.

Lessons from the exchanges, together with conclusions emerging from the cluster meetings, were consolidated and used to formulate draft SSS and PPD user guidelines. A draft was then presented to Mosque Road residents for their comments and input. Similarly, inputs were sought from the NCWSC, WSUP and other professionals involved in the WSE consortium. Validation meetings were then held with the cluster leaders and residents, who ultimately adopted the guidelines. The guidelines define different roles for tenants, structure owners, and plot and cluster representatives. A memorandum of understanding has also been developed by the NCCG with other stakeholders, including AMT. Under this framework, the NCCG has committed to support the extension of PPD and sewer networks in Mukuru. It will also support the establishment of at least 5,000 toilets at the plot level, which will serve approximately 50,000 households. Ultimately, there has been recognition of the pressing need for clear regulatory frameworks at the county level to guide the design, implementation and governance of decentralized water and sanitation interventions across informal settlements in Nairobi.

Following the successful implementation of the pilot, the work was expanded to other villages within Mukuru leading to construction of approximately 1,000 plot-level toilets that are connected to the sewer system, serving about 12,000 households.

Conclusion: SPA lessons on community empowerment for improved sanitation

The declaration of the Mukuru informal settlements as a SPA and the participatory processes that followed were aimed at rescaling spatial governance through community-led initiatives. Under the SPA, residents took ownership and situated themselves at the centre of collaborative processes — spanning from the definition of their problems to the formulation and implementation of interventions to resolve them. In Mukuru, the SPA process continues to empower residents. It equips them with relevant tools that enable them to tackle the underlying drivers of marginalization. Participation in the SPA facilitated the community's understanding of its situation and increased residents' control over water and sanitation services. This empowerment facilitated their entry into spaces of participation — such as the ones organized by the WSE consortium — and enabled the community to identify and co-produce innovative solutions.

Participation in the Mukuru SPA was approached both as a tool for empowerment and as an outcome of an empowered group of residents. As seen from the WSE consortium whose participation framework has been discussed above, participation led to material outcomes for the inhabitants of Mukuru, in the form of improved access to water and sanitation. SPA processes treated residents as custodians of knowledge that fed into solutions to existing challenges. These processes recognized the unique strengths and shared responsibilities that permeate partnerships between external experts and beneficiary communities.

The SPA participatory processes emphasized residents undertaking lead roles, as seen in the community-led mapping and enumeration processes, whereby residents spearheaded the identification of existing problems and opportunities within their localities. This approach represents a critical form of legal empowerment that allows beneficiary communities to take the lead, while external experts limit their roles to focus more on technical design. This, according to Satterthwaite, leaves the affected groups to be authors of their own empowerment as they directly engage with institutions that affect their lives and demand systems that are more accessible and responsive to their challenges (Satterthwaite, n.d.). The approach treats empowerment as a political project that aims to reorient urban power relations and redefine the conditions of urban citizenship. By leading deliberations within participatory spaces created under planning laws, residents are critically positioned to undo an entrenched regime of discriminatory spatial governance, selective planning and unequal citizenship.

In this chapter, citizen mobilization has been treated as a critical factor that facilitated the identification of practical opportunities to expand water and sanitation access in Mukuru. It has demonstrated how mobilized citizens can be equipped with the tools needed to identify their water and sanitation priorities and co-produce interventions to address gaps in access. The conducive legal frameworks in Kenya — which mandate citizen participation in governance processes, including spatial planning — facilitated the realization of these milestones. In Mukuru, the mobilization of residents sheds light on the meaning of the right to participation and to adequate sanitation. Kenya's Constitution provides these as justiciable rights, but their scope and content have remained untested in informal settlement contexts.

The adoption of flexible standards of sanitation in the form of SSS networks and PPDs, and the state's provision of financial resources and technical expertise to establish this infrastructure, is a positive step towards universal realization of water and sanitation rights by informal settlement residents. Residents' direct engagements with relevant state and non-state stakeholders during the SPA processes helped them advance and claim these rights "in their own idiom" (Satterthwaite, n.d., p. 5). In doing this, they gave meaning to these rights.

It is this rights-conscious orientation that makes the SPA's participatory arrangements transformative. Indeed, as Di Giovanni and Bercovich (2021) argue, statutory rights can have "teeth" when framed and approached in certain ways. In the Mukuru case, residents give their legally protected rights "teeth" by claiming them and testing their limits through the participatory SPA processes and in designing and implementing the interventions. They engage with external actors while retaining their autonomy, expressing their needs on their own terms, and crafting interventions tailored to their distinctive contexts. These interventions are all the more significant for being equitable and scalable. Indeed, the WSE consortium's current priority is to scale out the interventions already implemented in kwa Reuben to other villages in Mukuru and develop practical mechanisms to influence the policy frameworks at the local government level.

Those new efforts, if successful, point to the larger potential of the Mukuru SPA participation model to facilitate the entry of historically marginalized urban residents into spaces from which they can directly engage with institutional actors and redefine the meanings of participation. The success of this political project is premised on having an empowered group of residents equipped with the tools and legal protections to identify and co-produce solutions to the problems they identify. This underscores this chapter's conclusion that participation as adopted in the SPA acted both as a tool and an outcome of empowerment. It equipped residents with the ability to connect their marginalization with violation of their rights. They then located their claims for improved access to sanitation in positive law and engaged with institutional actors for the adoption of flexible standards. Empowerment here brings the inhabitants into spaces from which they define rights in their own idiom and confront systemic barriers to adequate sanitation.

Notes

1 See also Kenya National Bureau of Statistics (2019, p. 7).
2 See Anderson (2014).
3 This chapter uses "urban planning" interchangeably with the term "spatial planning". The latter is defined under the Physical and Land Use Planning Act (No. 13 of 2019) as "the methodology and approach used to influence the distribution of people and activities to achieve optimal utilization of physical, economic and sociocultural resources". Mazza, on the other hand, defines it as "the technical knowledge and professional know-how contributing to and supporting spatial governance choices". See Mazza (2016, p. 1). These two definitions essentially recognize the role played by various stakeholders, that is, professionals and the public or beneficiaries of spatial planning. Moreover, the Physical and Land Use Planning Act is guided by the national values and principles set out in Articles 10 and 232 of the Constitution which includes public participation.
4 Lonsdale argues that in order to understand urban life, historians need to pay close attention to three key issues: economic and political relations between town and country; the control of urban property; and the nature of work in town. See Lonsdale (2010, p. 7).
5 See also Weru et al., (2015, p. 6).
6 Act No. 6 of 1996 (revised 2012).
7 See Communication, Coordination, and Community Mobilization Consortium for the City County of Nairobi (2017, p. 1).
8 See also Lister (1998, p. 228).
9 Participation also increases the sense of ownership of programs by the communities and in effect enables their sustainability. See Gould (1989, p. 13).
10 See also Wallerstein (2002, p. 74).

11 See also James (1992, p. 60).
12 See Bryant (n.d.).
13 See Karanja (2010, pp. 217–239).

References

Akatch, S. (1995). Evaluative review of urban planning practice and experiences in the African region. In A. C. Mosha (Ed.), *A reappraisal of the urban planning process* (pp. 39–56). UN-Habitat.

Anderson, M. (2014). Nairobi's female slum dwellers march for sanitation and land rights. *The Guardian*. www.theguardian.com/global-development/2014/oct/29/nairobi-slum-dwellers-sanitation-land-rights.

Blokland, T., Hentschel, C., Holm, A., Lebuhn, H., & Margalit, T. (2015). Urban citizenship and the right to the city: The fragmentation of claims. *International Journal of Urban and Regional Research*, 39(4), 655–665.

Bradlow, B. (2011). Out of the Garden of Eden: Moving beyond the rights-based agenda in the urban sector. *Sustainable Development Law & Policy*, 11(1). https://digitalcommons.wcl.american.edu/sdlp/vol11/iss1/17/

Bryant, K. (n.d.). SDI rituals: Profiling and enumeration through the Vusi Ntsunthsha project. *SDI*. https://knowyourcity.info/2019/11/sdi-rituals-profiling-enumeration-vusi-ntsuntsha-project/.

Chitonge, H., & Mfune, O. (2015). The urban land question in Africa: The case of urban land conflicts in the city of Lusaka, 100 years after its founding. *Habitat International*, 48, 209–218.

Claire, M. (2006). City planning in Nairobi: The stakes, the people, the sidetracking. In H. Charton-Bigot & D. Rodriguez-Torres (Eds.), *Nairobi today: The paradox of a fragmented city* (pp. 25–60). Mkuki na Nyota Publishers.

Commission on Legal Empowerment of the Poor. (2008). *Making the law work for everyone* (Report of the Commission on Legal Empowerment of the Poor). Author.

Communication, Coordination, and Community Mobilization Consortium for the City County of Nairobi. (2017). *An integrated development plan: Mukuru SPA inception report* (Technical paper). Author.

Corburn, J., & Makau, J. (2016). Coproducing slum health in Nairobi, Kenya. In J. Corburn (Ed.), *Slum health: From the cell to the street* (pp. 149–188). University of California Press.

Cornwall, A. (2002). Locating citizen participation. *IDS Bulletin*, 33(2), i–x.

Cotula, L. (2022, January 11). Legal empowerment as action research. *IIED*. www.iied.org/legal-empowerment-action-research.

Di Giovanni, A., & Bercovich, L. (2021). Legal empowerment in informal settlements: Lessons on using the law to overcome urban exclusion and poverty in the Global South. *New York University Journal of International Law and Politics*, 54(1), 93–151.

Frediani, A. A., Peris, J., & Boni, A. (2019). Notions of empowerment and participation: Contributions from and to the capability approach. In D. A. Clark, M. Biggeri & A. Apsan Frediani (Eds.), *The capability approach, empowerment and participation* (pp. 101–124). Palgrave Macmillan.

Gaventa, J. (2002). Introduction: Exploring citizenship, participation and accountability. *IDS Bulletin*, 33(2). www.ids.ac.uk/download.php?file=files/dmfile/gaventa332.pdf

Goodwin, L., & Maru, V. (2017). What do we know about legal empowerment? Mapping the evidence. *Hague Journal on the Rule of Law*, 9, 157–194.

Gould, C. C. (1989). *Rethinking democracy: Freedom and social co-operation in politics, economy, and society.* Cambridge University Press.

James, S. (1992). The good-enough citizen: Citizenship and independence. In G. Bock & S. James (Eds.), *Beyond equality and difference* (1st ed.) (pp. 48–65). Routledge.

Karanja, I. (2010). An enumeration and mapping of informal settlements in Kisumu, Kenya, implemented by their inhabitants. *Environment & Urbanization*, 22(1), 217–239. doi:10.1177/0956247809362642.

Kenya National Bureau of Statistics. (2019). *2019 Kenya population and housing census*, Vol. 1. KNBS.

Kimari, W. (2016). "We do not want any more masters": Ruins, planning and the "messy labours" of the urban poor. *Mambo!*, XIV(5). https://hal.archives-ouvertes.fr/hal-01461496

Kimari, W. (2018). *'Nai-rob-me Nai-beg-me Nai-shanty: Historicizing space-subjectivity connections in Nairobi from its ruins.* York University.

Knight, R. (2021). *Legal empowerment to promote legitimate tenure rights* (Legal Brief 4). FAO.

Lines, K., & Makau, J. (2018). Taking the long view: 20 years of Muungano wa Wanavijiji, the Kenyan federation of slum dwellers. *Environment and Urbanization*, 30(2), 407–424. doi:10.1177/0956247818785327.

Lister, R. (1997). *Citizenship: Feminist perspectives* (J. Campling, Ed.). Red Globe Press.

Lister, R. (1998). Citizen in action: Citizenship and community development in a Northern Ireland context. *Community Development Journal*, 33(3), 226–235.

Lonsdale, J. (2010). Town life in colonial Kenya. In H. Charton-Bigot & D. Rodriguez-Torres (Eds.), *Nairobi today: The paradox of a fragmented city* (pp. 3–22). Mkuki na Nyota Publishers.

Mazza, L. (2016). *Planning and citizenship* (1st ed.). Routledge.

McAuslan, P. (1982). The urban land question. *Habitat International*, 6(5–6), 545–554. doi:10.1016/0197-3975(82)90021–90022.

Mutinda, M., & Otieno, S. (2015). Unlocking financing for slum redevelopment: The case of Mukuru. *Africa Policy Journal*, 11(44). www.researchgate.net/publication/348804913_Unlocking_Financing_for_Slum_Redevelopment_The_Case_of_Mukuru

Myers, G. A. (2003). *Verandahs of power: Colonialism and space in urban Africa.* Syracuse University Press.

Ouma, S. (2022). *Inclusive urban planning for improved health outcomes in informal settlements* [Unpublished PhD thesis, Cardiff University].

Ouma, S., Corburn, J., & Weru, J. (2023). Property rights, public health, and planning for informal settlements in Nairobi, Kenya. *Journal of Urban Affairs*, 45(3), 302–316.

Pieterse, E. A. (2008). *City futures: Confronting the crisis of urban development.* UCT Press.

Rodriguez-Torres, D. (2006). Public authorities and urban upgrading policies in Eastlands. In H. Charton-Bigot & D. Rodriguez-Torres (Eds.), *Nairobi today: The paradox of a fragmented city* (pp. 61–94). Mkuki na Nyota Publishers.

Satterthwaite, M. (n.d.). *Critical legal empowerment for human rights.* NYU School of Law. www.law.nyu.edu/sites/default/files/SatterthwaiteCriticalLEforHR_EXCERPTED%20-ia%20remediated.pdf.

Scheingold, S. A. (2004). *The politics of rights: Lawyers, public policy, and political change.* University of Michigan Press.

United Nations General Assembly. (2008). *Legal empowerment of the poor and eradication of poverty.* UN Doc A/64/133.

University of California Berkeley, Muungano Wa Wanavijiji, Slum Dwellers International, Akiba Mashinani Trust, University of Nairobi, Strathmore University, & Katiba Institute. (2017). *Makuru Nairobi, Kenya. 2017 situational analysis: Mukuru Kwa Njenga, Kwa Reuben & Viwandani*. Authors.

Wallerstein, N. (2002). Empowerment to reduce health disparities. *Scandinavian Journal of Public Health*, 59, 72–77.

Wanavijiji, M. wa. (2020). *Unlocking the poverty penalty and up-scaling the respect for rights in informal settlements in Kenya* (Final technical report). Akiba Mashinani Trust (AMT). https://idl-bnc-idrc.dspacedirect.org/bitstream/handle/10625/58604/IDL-58604.pdf?sequence=2.

Weru, J., Wanyoike, W., & Di Giovanni, A. (2015). Confronting complexity: Using action research to build voice, accountability and justice in Nairobi's Mukuru informal settlements. In J. Wouters, A. Ninio, T. Doherty, & H. Cisse' (Eds.), *Improving delivery in development: The role of voice, social contract, and accountability.* World Bank. doi:10.1596/978-1-4648-0378-9_ch10.

6 Staking a claim

A case study of women's ongoing campaign to ensure inclusive and safe housing in Delhi

Aakanksha Badkur and Jayshree Satpute

Introduction

In Delhi, with a population estimate of 32 million (World Population Review, 2024) and one of the highest population densities in the world, formal housing[1] remains largely unaffordable for the common person. Around 30 percent of the urban poor face acute housing poverty and struggle to access affordable, adequate and safe housing. The resulting settlements are informal in nature and lack adequate space and the basic services required to live a safe and dignified life. Spatial and legal inequalities are exacerbated by the informal nature of these settlements. The residents lack secure tenure and struggle to exercise their rights, further deepening their exclusion.

An additional 2.6 million new or upgraded housing units are required to meet New Delhi's housing deficit (Planning Department, Government of NCT of Delhi, 2023). Despite the large shortfall in housing, evictions in Delhi are rampant. Approximately 40 settlements were demolished in 2023 alone (The Missing Basti Project, n.d.). Evicted communities either find space to build other informal shelters or are rendered homeless. Due to exclusionary government policies and their arbitrary application, most evicted families are found ineligible for rehabilitation. Even the few evicted communities declared eligible after long-drawn-out legal battles are still waiting for rehabilitation a decade later.

Where *in situ* redevelopment has been attempted by governments, it has largely been considered unsuccessful (Banda et al., 2013; Raj, 2023). Implementation of this model of rehousing has been hampered by vague eligibility criteria, opaque administrative processes, prolonged delays, displacement into transit camps, lack of community participation, cost fluctuations and the profit motives of private developers. Residents are often left in a state of insecurity and struggle to exercise their housing rights.

Informal settlements in cities often emerge to accommodate the housing needs of the urban poor and migrant workers. The residents of these settlements are mostly Dalits,[2] Tribals[3] or members of other marginalized communities that have been historically discriminated against on the grounds of caste, class, religion or gender. Exclusion and chronically low wages further

DOI: 10.4324/9781003538806-6

perpetuate the cycle of poverty and prevent these groups from accessing opportunities for advancement. Such exclusion is not limited to their economic growth: it permeates other aspects of life, such as housing, health care and education.

In Delhi, one form of settlement is the *jhuggi jhopri* cluster (JJC), a group of small houses or shelters — usually made of mud, wood or metal — with thatched, tin or plastic sheet roofing. JJCs can take diverse forms and sizes, with settlements ranging from thousands of households to those hosting fewer than 50 families. They tend to emerge on public land and expand over the course of decades in an unplanned and *ad hoc* manner. The legal status of these settlements is tenuous, with residents under constant threat of eviction and demolition. Most contribute to the city's informal economy, providing necessary services to the affluent classes. These city makers provide services that range from domestic help and care work to construction, street vending, transport and sanitation, making their contributions to the city significant. Many of these families are either landless or rendered landless by way of state action for developmental projects, and have migrated from various states in India in search of livelihoods. They endeavour to integrate themselves into the city's service network systems for survival and security of tenure. There have been few efforts to bring such settlements under the purview of city planning and governance, with varying levels of success (Banda et al., 2013).

Women from these communities face additional forms of marginalization due to prevalent patriarchal norms and their limited economic and social agency. Gaps in social protection and basic infrastructure prevent the sharing of domestic work between men and women. Women are often restricted to their homes as they take on a larger share of household responsibilities than men. Women engaged in paid work are also responsible for the day-to-day functioning of their homes, placing an additional burden on them. Given the erratic availability of essential services in JJCs, tasks such as fetching water from community taps, washing or disposing of garbage require them to be at home and constantly alert. Despite their substantial household contributions, women rarely have decision-making power, either in their family or community. Their low status also determines the forms of documentation they possess, impacting their formal rights and claims on their homes.

In this context, the authors detail the inspiring story of women residing in a Delhi JJC called Ambedkar Nagar Camp (herein referred to as Ambedkar Camp), and their continuing journey to realize their right to adequate housing through legal empowerment strategies. The following sections provide context on the settlement and recount the emergence of a group of women paralegals through legal training, participatory decision-making and strategic action to bring about incremental but meaningful change in their community.

Through an initial set of victories that improved access to sanitation, health care and food rations in Ambedkar Camp, these paralegals first gained the trust of the wider community. The impacts of the COVID-19 pandemic and lockdown measures then catalysed a push for large-scale change. Women paralegals took leadership and facilitated a participatory exercise, supported by technical experts, to collaboratively create a plan to upgrade community-level services within the settlement. This exercise aimed to navigate the informal standing of JJCs and strengthen residents' rights through collective action. The paralegals were able to incorporate the lessons and impacts of long-term engagement with state agencies during the planning process.

This case demonstrates the power of legal empowerment strategies in supporting a community to overcome limited technical and legal knowledge. Using legal empowerment tools and methodologies, the community successfully participated in the process of planning *in situ* upgrading of their JJC and advocated to bring about its implementation. The methodology adopted in Ambedkar Camp has the potential to be replicated in other jurisdictions, encouraging people to engage actively in the planning and governance of their settlements. This can result in a transfer of decision-making power and agency as long-term sustainable outcomes.

Governance in Delhi and the framework for housing rights

In India, government policies regarding affordable housing are inconsistent, with progressively shrinking coverage. These inconsistencies exist between central and state government policies, in terms of eligibility, financial contributions and the nature of tenure rights conferred on residents. Delhi, as the capital, is governed by both the central and state stakeholders, making the implementation of these policies even more complex and time consuming. Post-independence, in 1947, Delhi had a state legislature; however, between 1956 and 1992, it was converted into a union territory and governed by the central government.[4] In 1992, the Government of National Capital Territory of Delhi (GNCTD) Act, 1991 came into force, creating Delhi as a state with a new state-level representative government. While the Legislative Assembly has the power to make laws for the whole or any part of the National Capital Territory of Delhi with respect to matters set out in the State List or in the Concurrent List of the Constitution, it does not have the power to make laws relating to police, public order or land; these areas remain the purview of the Parliament of India. This limitation extends to executive power: according to the Constitution of India, executive power is "co-extensive" with the legislative power of the Parliament of India. In other words, the GNCTD is not responsible for physical planning, development of land or law and order. "These functions are overseen by bodies that are directly accountable to the Government of India, leading to a governance structure that is often described as 'limited statehood'" (Cities of Delhi, 2015). Furthermore, recent years have seen a renewed power tussle between the state and central government over administrative control in the capital, leading to multiple long-drawn-out court battles, hindering administration and governance in Delhi.

After 1947, the management and upkeep of JJCs in Delhi was shuffled between various government departments. Initially governed by the state-level

Municipal Corporation of Delhi (MCD), control was later transferred to the central government's Delhi Development Authority (DDA). From 1967 to 2010, control of JJCs transferred back and forth between the MCD and DDA. Since 2010, the responsibility for provision of civic amenities and the resettlement of JJC residents has been with the Delhi Urban Shelter Improvement Board (DUSIB).

DUSIB was created after landmark judgments[5] expanding the scope of a citizen's right to adequate and safe housing.[6] The right to housing is protected under Parts III and IV of the Constitution of India, which deal respectively with fundamental rights and directive principles of state policy. Several important judgments have clearly established the relation between the right to housing and right to life as guaranteed by Article 21. The Supreme Court of India has held that the right to shelter or adequate housing is a fundamental human right emanating from this provision.[7] In principle, these Constitutional protections are complemented by a range of international human rights instruments to which India is a party, such as the International Covenant on Economic, Social and Cultural Rights, for example. However, governments have failed to give further effect in domestic law to India's international obligations to uphold the right to housing beyond the Constitution, resulting in rather vague standards for the universal right to housing. Consequently, India has witnessed a wide variety of approaches taken by states when addressing issues of housing and land, ranging from proactively providing residents with tenure documents to arbitrarily and illegally evicting residents from informal settlements.

Apart from the recognition and upkeep of JJCs in Delhi, DUSIB is also the nodal agency for facilitating collective community rehabilitation, relocation or *in situ* upgradation. This must be done in partnership with the land-owning agency, with a view to improving the environment and residents' living conditions. To some extent, the State of Delhi has a progressive statute to rehabilitate the urban poor who cannot afford basic shelter due to their financial constraints and the exclusionary nature of cities. The DUSIB Act and its Rehabilitation and Resettlement Policy of 2015 bars any eviction of notified JJC residents without following due legal process. It also mandates *in situ* upgradation and rehabilitation, either on the same land or within five kilometres; only in exceptional circumstances should rehousing exceed five kilometres.

However, in recent years, there have been many instances of communities being displaced and their houses being demolished in contravention of the law and procedure laid out by the state and judiciary (The Missing Basti Project, n.d.). These eviction and demolition drives — termed "anti-encroachment" drives for neighbourhood beautification and gentrification — are usually carried out with force. There have been reports of injuries, miscarriages and deaths during these demolition drives, along with other violations such as the destruction of documents and properties. Despite meeting the eligibility criteria set out by state policy, tens of thousands of families have been awaiting rehabilitation for more than a decade. The handful that have been relocated by the government have reported issues of poor and unsafe construction and a lack of basic amenities and public services such as transport, schools and health care. These rehabilitation sites often lie at the city periphery in contravention of the five-kilometre range, greatly limiting residents' livelihood opportunities. It is thus evident that the government has failed to deliver on its promise of safe and equitable housing for the urban poor, compelling residents to find other ways to secure housing tenure.

Ambedkar Camp: Composition and built form

Ambedkar Camp JJC is located in Dakshinpuri in South Delhi district, an area that has emerged as a commercial hub, with several markets and surrounding residential areas. The JJC was established more than three decades ago by a group of migrants from the neighbouring states of Uttar Pradesh, Haryana and Bihar. A compact triangle of just over half an acre, Ambedkar Camp is squeezed between a government hospital and public land occupied by government offices. Home to 112 households, it is one of the smallest JJCs in Delhi. Most residents are categorized as Other Backward Classes in the Indian government population classification system.[8] The community is largely Hindu, with a handful of Muslim families in the settlement. Residents are primarily engaged in daily or weekly labour in neighbouring businesses and enterprises, while some have contract jobs in the service sector.

As with most informal settlements, the overall condition of the housing structures in Ambedkar Camp is severely inadequate. An average family of five resides in a two-room shelter of less than 25 square metres. Initially, residents started by clearing unused public land to build *kutcha* houses, typically made from mud, straw, wood leaves, plastic and other temporary materials. Over time, these were consolidated and upgraded to more permanent *semi-pukka* and *pukka* structures made of durable materials such as stone, brick or cement. Currently, only a quarter of the houses are *pukka* construction. Most walls, however, are half-brick, which poses significant risks in the earthquake-prone city of Delhi. At the same time, the widespread use of temporary materials, such as tin or asbestos sheets, creates fire risks and has adverse health impacts. Most houses lack windows or ventilators, leading to dark, damp conditions that contribute to health issues over time.

Most basic services available to residents are substandard, as shown in Table 6.1. Currently, there is a government-supplied water line (provided by the Delhi Jal Board), and an old bore well. Only a handful of houses have a water connection, while around 100 households jointly depend on eight points within the community that supply water for only one or two hours a day. Notably, there is no sewage line in the settlement. Some households have constructed an individual or shared toilet with deep pits dug right under the housing to collect waste — a dangerous practice. The JJC has concrete

Table 6.1 Summary of public facilities near Ambedkar Camp

Public amenity	*Specifications and remarks*
Public toilet	• Open from 4 am to 11 pm, and for emergencies when the caretaker is available • Men's and women's sections each have 10 Indian-style toilets, 1 Western-style toilet, 3 bathing cubicles and 3 wash basins • Sewage pipe is connected to the Delhi Jal Board main sewer
Government-run *anganwadi* (childcare) centre	• Provides free pre-school education to children up to 6 years of age • Open from 10 am to 12 pm except on Sundays • Small facility with no toilet • 1 teacher and 1 helper for approximately 30 children
Government-run Mohalla Clinic for primary health care	• 1 doctor; 2 compounders; 1 nurse • Free consultations • Open from 8 am to 2 pm except on Sundays • Wait time of 30 to 60 minutes
Water purification plant	• 2 rupees for 5 litres of drinking water • Caretaker is a resident and available on request
Public park	• 112 m^2 (1200 ft^2) = 11 ft^2 per family • Open at all times • Used by the community for religious and cultural ceremonies • One corner used for garbage

Figure 6.1 Delhi map with pin showing location of Ambedkar Camp
Source: Maps of India (https://d-maps.com/carte.php?num_car=270165&lang=en).

Figures 6.2 Kutcha and pukka construction comparisons
Source: Nazdeek (www.nazdeek.org) and Pradhan Mantri Awas Yojana (Urban), Govt of India (https://twitter.com/pmayurban).

PMAY-U house of Sasikala V in Thiruvananthapuram, Kerala

Figure 6.3 Services and conditions in Ambedkar Camp, prior to upgrades
Source: Swastik Harish and Associates (https://swastikharish.com).

pathways and a wastewater and storm water drain. Most families have one or more forms of documentation showing their tenure in the settlement, and almost all households have an electricity connection.

Legal empowerment and Ambedkar Camp

The legal empowerment journey in Ambedkar Camp was guided by Nazdeek, a community justice and empowerment organization that was founded in 2011 by lawyers and researchers disillusioned by the ineffectiveness of legal battles when isolated from community participation, and disappointed by how rarely court victories translate into reality for impacted communities. Their work with Ambedkar Camp spans over eight years, from the first scoping visits in 2016 to the development of technical proposals and today's ongoing advocacy.

This section describes the participatory methods employed in Nazdeek's approach to legal empowerment. It then traces the journey of women paralegals in Ambedkar Camp who received training in rights-based approaches and played a crucial role in mobilizing and representing the community as it sought to define and realize its own vision for *in situ* upgrades.

Legal empowerment methodology and approach

Nazdeek is a women-led organization that advances community justice and legal empowerment through grants, strategic advice and research support across South Asia. In partnership with grassroots organisations, it aims to bring justice closer to marginalized communities. It envisions a just and equitable world, where everyone has an opportunity to lead a dignified life. To transfer agency and decision-making power back to communities, Nazdeek began implementing and refining its legal empowerment (LE) methodology through targeted interventions.

Nazdeek believes that legal empowerment is the process of understanding rights, with the ability to shape and assert them for a life of dignity. It strengthens the capacity of those facing injustices and enables them to pursue transformative improvements to laws and systems. By promoting accountability and transparency, legal empowerment helps communities gain greater access to justice so they can enjoy their rights. The LE methodology developed by Nazdeek takes a bottom-up approach that allows for community leadership, ownership and participation. The process focuses on increasing knowledge and creating behavioural change among participants, often through a long-term intervention requiring consistent engagement.

Multiple stakeholders engage in the implementation of Nazdeek's LE methodology. They can largely be mapped and categorised as follows:

a. *Target community*

   This refers to the wider community as well as specific subgroups within it, having a common characteristic and shared interests. This shared identity can be based on employment, residence or linguistic and cultural commonalities. Any successful LE intervention would benefit all sections of the target community, and may extend beyond it.

b. *Women and marginalized groups*

   Even within target communities, women and marginalized groups, such as those belonging to oppressed castes and gender minorities, face additional discrimination and exclusion. The LE methodology aims to promote the participation of these vulnerable groups within their own communities.

c. *Dominant actors within the target community*

Community leaders, workers' union members and residents who exercise political and social agency from within communities often emerge as dominant actors, and influence the trajectory of LE interventions. It is imperative to engage with these actors to mobilize the larger target community and promote solidarity.

d. *Government and elected officials and decision-makers*

State stakeholders and elected representatives have the power and ability to bring about systemic changes, and play a critical role in determining the success of any LE intervention. Issues identified for policy advocacy are highlighted to these stakeholders.

e. *Community-level service providers and frontline workers*

Issues of day-to-day service delivery within communities are resolved by service providers and frontline workers. They often belong to the same class of persons as the target communities and can also be residents of the same settlement. They form a crucial link between residents and state-level stakeholders.

f. *Local leaders and neighbouring communities*

Local political and community leaders and residents from neighbouring communities can often affect the course of various interventions, either through incidental support or opposition. It is important to map these actors to pre-empt and mitigate any unforeseen risks and barriers.

g. *LE practitioners and technical experts*

These external intervenors facilitate the implementation of the LE methodology in target communities. The role of the LE practitioner is primarily to support communities in strengthening their understanding of rights, laws and policies, and to guide them on grievance redressal, advocacy, community mobilization and strategic legal action.

The empowerment journey of Ambedkar Camp

The LE journey of Ambedkar Camp began in 2016. It followed the steps that Nazdeek typically undertakes when initiating a partnership with a community. During the initial scoping exercise, local civil society organizations working in and around the area approached Nazdeek with the desire to build legal capacity in the community. As the first step, Nazdeek and the local organizations[9] conducted a preliminary survey to understand Ambedkar Camp's demography, identify prevalent human rights issues, their scale and the need for intervention. Initial conversations with the community focused on their history, composition, and the state of services. LE practitioners also sought to gauge the degree of decision-making and mobility of women in the community, and the potential for long-term engagement. Considering the history of the settlement, it was determined that no immediate threat of displacement existed. This made it ideal for implementation of the LE model, as communities facing immediate eviction threats require a crisis-oriented approach, which is difficult in the early stages of LE engagements as many families relocate once evicted, and develop a distrust of state machinery. Engagement and strategies to help communities facing imminent eviction tend to be short term, while relatively secure tenure allows for more structured long-term engagement.

The 10 paralegals who volunteered for training were between the ages of 18 and 60 years, with varied literacy levels. Most of these women are homemakers, while some are engaged in part-time care and domestic work. The paralegals live with their families, including their husbands, children and grandchildren. Husbands and sons are mostly engaged in some degree of formal or semi-formal employment.

The first step in building the capacity of these paralegals was to train them in a rights-based approach to the issues, rooted in the legal and normative framework governing these rights (see Table 6.2). Training sessions were designed with a participatory lens, with fun activities designed to improve knowledge retention and sustain engagement. In terms of legal content, the sessions focused on specific laws governing each right and delved into their

Table 6.2 Capacity building and training topics for women paralegals

Issue-based training	• Good governance • Gender equity • Deconstructing patriarchy • Non-discrimination • Maternal and child health • Food security • Water, sanitation and hygiene • Adequate housing • Risk mitigation and safeguarding
Skill-based training	• Writing applications and grievances • Drafting and submitting representation to relevant officials • Accessing IT and communication channels • Accessing information • Data collection and analysis

administrative implementation. Training on rights and entitlements was followed by sessions on accessing systems for remedial action. These included building paralegals' skills around facilitating community meetings, conducting surveys and fact-findings, advocating with local authorities and writing complaints and representations. The training curriculum also sought to strengthen interpersonal skills such as public speaking and networking. As a result, the paralegals were equipped with a holistic understanding of their rights, and the skills needed to identify violations and articulate them within the rights framework.

Once paralegals learned to identify violations and measure their scale in the community, it became imperative to document and build evidence for strategic action. Several methods were tested, keeping in mind the specific contexts and needs of the paralegals. These included virtual case management systems, maintaining physical records of complaints and representations, photo documentation and individual case studies.[10] Additionally, women also used government helplines and online grievance redressal portals to report deficiencies in services and seek accountability. These concerted efforts towards evidence creation helped identify gaps in grievance redressal mechanisms, requiring changes at the policy level to address systemic challenges. During the pandemic, paralegals faced challenges in accessing redressal systems, which had shifted to the virtual sphere. Limited access to technology and low literacy levels required innovative approaches to build these additional skills of using the internet, navigating government websites and filing online complaints.

After each session, participants were encouraged to organize community meetings to pass on the knowledge they had acquired. This improved their confidence, while reviewing the training content also increased retention. The real boost in morale happened when the paralegals successfully employed LE tools to bring tangible change within their community. This also led to the emergence of paralegals as leaders. In cases where the available grievance mechanisms were ineffective or adversarial to the complainant, strategic advocacy and legal action were required. Through training and practical experience, paralegals further learned to identify appropriate avenues for advocacy. LE practitioners supported them in creating strategies based on emerging needs, enabling the paralegals to engage with the larger people's movements and technical experts. After nearly five years of continuous engagement, paralegals gradually began taking complete ownership of rights-based work, allowing the practitioners to transition to an advisory capacity. Paralegals now remain organized in ways that work for them as they continue to monitor community-level services.

Residents were able to reflect on how the state could better address their needs, based on interactions with other communities where women were participating in legal empowerment training. Exposure and cross-context learning sessions were facilitated every year for the last eight years, allowing the women to follow the LE journeys of other communities as well. Paralegals benefited greatly from engaging with women residing in government rehabilitation sites during their LE training. This allowed them to learn from the lived experiences of rehabilitated residents and understand the many challenges faced at these sites.

The outcomes of this legal empowerment journey can be seen in a number of short-term and long-term gains spearheaded by trained paralegals. They also include residents' growing awareness of the deficiencies in their living situation, and their collective participation in planning, designing and advocating for significant *in situ* upgrades, as discussed in the following sections.

Shift in residents' perspectives due to COVID-19

Through their initial engagement with government agencies and civil society organizations, paralegals in Ambedkar Camp were able to obtain several wins for their community. These included gaining significant improvements in the quality of existing public services and securing previously unavailable services.

For example, ambulance services were reinstated, the delivery of food rations (subsidized food grain) was improved, water supplies are now more regular and frequent in the JJC, and nearby parks and drains are regularly cleaned. One of the most notable victories for the community was the improvement in the functioning of public toilets. These toilets usually function during the day and close at night, despite government directives mandating round-the-clock access. The untimely closure of toilets disproportionately affects vulnerable groups, including pregnant and menstruating women, children, persons with disabilities and senior citizens. Training and community meetings helped generate awareness of the fundamental right to water, sanitation and hygiene and residents were able to connect the abstract concept of this right to the limited availability of their sanitation services. Paralegals also identified the government officials who were responsible for ensuring the regular functioning of the public toilets. All these improvements were brought about through regular filing of complaints and in-person advocacy with the relevant government officials over the course of many years.

The victories described to this point, while significant, were relatively small in scale, involving mostly incremental changes to the pre-existing squalid services and infrastructure. The COVID-19 pandemic, however, catalysed awareness and action by the community to push for settlement-wide upgradation of Ambedkar Camp, through paralegal support. At the onset of the pandemic, government resources were redirected towards large-scale emergency public health measures. The Government of India imposed a 21-day nationwide lockdown on March 24, 2020 and issued orders to prevent and limit the spread of COVID-19 in the country.

The impacts of the pandemic were deeply felt in two ways by the community. Firstly, government orders halted the movement of individuals and shut down all commercial, industrial and transport activity. Low-income families, like those in Ambedkar Camp, had no savings to fall back on during a prolonged crisis, and the sudden disruption resulted in lost livelihoods and wages at a time when the supply of essential goods was already disrupted, further exacerbating the effects of inflation and shortages. Secondly, the pandemic triggered a greater awareness of what adequate housing and dignified conditions meant, especially when faced with the wide gap between conditions in Ambedkar Camp and the public health standards required to prevent infection, such as distancing, personal hygiene and sanitation. The pandemic, and the attention it brought to public health conditions needed to prevent the spread of disease, made blindingly clear to residents the importance of improving sanitation in Ambedkar Camp. The increased emphasis on sanitation and cleanliness to limit transmission of the virus placed an additional stress on residents, who were already dealing with the risks associated with cramped living quarters and limited access to water.

The aggregated challenges of the pandemic and resulting lockdown deepened residents' understanding of adequate and safe housing. Recognizing the fundamental deficiencies in their current conditions compelled the community to band together and take concerted steps to improve their housing. Paralegals emerged as a key catalyst in mobilizing households in Ambedkar Camp that had not yet engaged with government officials (or otherwise participated in advocacy efforts). The community was further emboldened by the provision of sewerage infrastructure in neighbouring JJCs. This proved to be a key consideration when discussing the various alternatives available to them, creating a window of opportunity to envision and plan for the upgradation of their settlement with the support of the elected government through executive action.

Participatory planning exercise for *in situ* upgradation

With the support of civil society organizations, the paralegals were able to approach technical experts[11] and architects to collaboratively create a plan to upgrade community level services. One of the first choices made by the community was to focus on the incremental upgradation of their existing settlement through improved housing infrastructure. This approach is in sharp contrast with redevelopment and rehabilitation strategies proposed by various government housing schemes, which are premised largely on community relocation.

A strengths, weaknesses, opportunities and threats analysis was undertaken to explore the potential benefits and disadvantages associated with upgrading and redevelopment. Although redevelopment would have allowed for better planning, compliance and integration into city systems, upgradation emerged as a better approach for two main reasons: affordability, as it is more cost effective for both the government and residents; and greater inclusion of all residents. Furthermore, redevelopment causes massive disruption for the entire settlement, whereas upgradation allows for incremental changes without displacement, preventing school dropouts and unemployment. The potential for exclusion due to the inability to pay the beneficiary contribution associated with redevelopment is also high. Lastly, long-term tenants are also often excluded from benefits of such projects due to lack of documentation. Despite concerns around specific housing features that make it difficult to upgrade them, this solution would ultimately afford residents more autonomy over the financial and spatial planning.

In 2022, the mapping, planning and designing exercise was conducted with the support of technical experts over three phases. Phase 1 involved a physical survey of the JJC and its built structures using an innovative technology stack. The first step entailed drone mapping for estimating building lines and the use of augmented reality (AR) for accurate volumetric mapping and modelling of buildings through a phone-based application. Using an AR survey app, technical experts generated building information models (BIM) for each individual house and integrated these on a platform to generate the built form of the settlement and its context.[12] These digital three-dimensional models helped to overcome information asymmetry among stakeholders, including communities (who are usually not equipped to understand technical drawings); architects and engineers (who have limited capacity to communicate technical information to communities); and decision-makers and policymakers (who are more focused on outcomes rather than the process). This innovative use of technology also enhanced the speed and accuracy of the digital modelling of the settlement, saving time and resources.

Phase 2 included community consultations on the development options, where the primary objective was to socialize the model within the community to achieve a shared understanding of the different aspects and complexities of the upgradation process. The model was presented to the community in-person and online. Several rounds of presentation within the settlement — featuring a projected display of the model — enabled a sense of familiarity and comfort with the model among residents, who could pinpoint their own houses. Additionally, the BIM was uploaded to a 3D model-viewing website that allowed residents to view the model and raise questions or concerns with the technical support team at their convenience.

The last phase included finalizing design interventions based on the priorities set by the community and other stakeholders. The design interventions were finalized by the technical support team and detailed in terms of upgrading houses for: (1) decent living standards; (2) physical infrastructure upgrading for public health and maternal and child health outcomes; (3) social infrastructure upgrading for better living conditions in the neighbourhood; and (4) sustainability measures for climate change and disaster risk mitigation.

Given the diversity of house structures in the settlement, the project team developed housing typologies that covered all the different types of houses. This was done to generate design options and details, including the costing for improvements. Thereafter, the design and costing of the typologies were mapped on to all the houses, working out differentials based on size, number of floors already existing, and existing features such as toilets. The main purpose of developing typologies was to develop the framework and applicability of key interventions such as adding toilets, making houses *pukka* and adding floors.

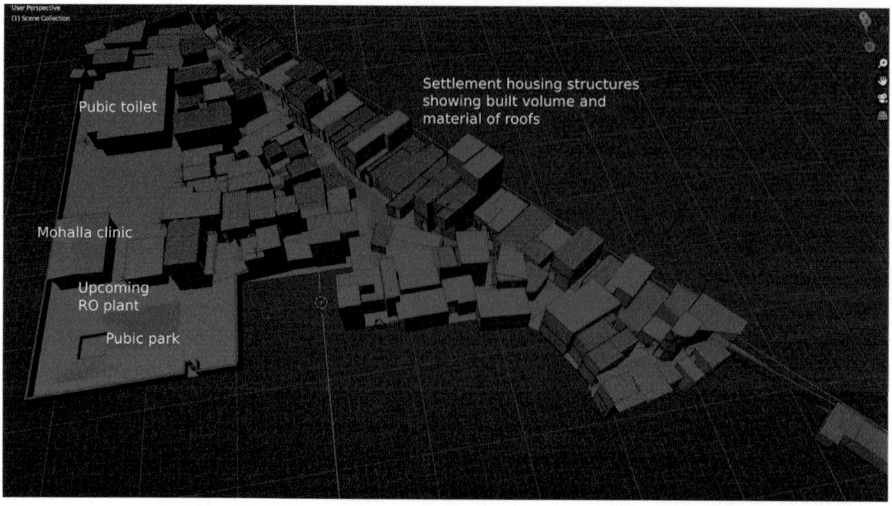

Figure 6.4 Three-dimensional information model of Ambedkar Camp, showing house structures and amenities

Source: Swastik Harish and Associates (https://swastikharish.com).

Advocacy for community upgrades

Once the proposal for upgradation was finalized by the community and technical team, the next step was to engage with relevant stakeholders and strategize for its implementation. The community collectively decided that the paralegals would lead the advocacy, through formal presentations and follow-up meetings. The technical team conducted multiple meetings with the paralegals to familiarize them with technical aspects of the proposal. They discussed the current state of the JJC, the methodology adopted for creating the proposal, the typology of houses that emerged as a result of the mapping, and the details of costing.

Civil society organizations and academics involved with the project were able to facilitate key connections to policymakers and bureaucrats to generate interest in the model. The advocacy strategy was designed with the objective of presenting the proposal to stakeholders in a way that would trigger settlement-wide upgrades first, enabling residents to make personalized incremental changes to their own housing at a later stage. The paralegals requested a meeting with their local elected official, the CEO of DUSIB, local Delhi Jal Board officials, and the Vice-Chair of the Dialogue and Development Commission of Delhi (the state government's policy think tank), to present the proposal. By addressing them together at the onset of their advocacy efforts, paralegals sought to ensure approval and coordination among the relevant officials to prevent bureaucratic delay.

During these initial meetings with stakeholders, paralegals introduced the vision for upgradation, and showed how it was developed through an innovative and time-efficient methodology while complying with existing policy and budgetary norms. To demonstrate community-wide consensus and support for the proposal, women carried representations endorsed by the community to each meeting. This strategy proved successful in ensuring the presence of all stakeholders during the formal presentation of the proposal.

After these presentations, stakeholders visited the community to assess the current state of housing and interventions required. One of their primary considerations was the financial implications of the proposal, and the availability of adequate funds within relevant budgetary allocations. This was addressed by providing a detailed breakdown of the expense for each component of the proposal, with an equitable division of financial responsibility between the relevant state and central government agencies. This aligned with existing policies to provide affordable housing and universal sanitation coverage, in addition to local area development funding, beneficiary contribution and potential corporate social responsibility sponsorship. The presentation by the paralegals was met with great enthusiasm and appreciation, and women's leadership during the process lent a great degree of credibility to the model itself. As a result of the multistakeholder meeting, stakeholders and residents jointly decided that DUSIB and the settlement's elected representative would initiate the process of implementing the proposal's first phase. This focused on the provision of sewerage infrastructure in the community, with support from the Delhi Jal Board and the Dialogue and Development Commission of Delhi.

Despite garnering wide-spread support for the proposal from all concerned stakeholders, the process of seeking implementation has been challenging and long drawn. Due to ongoing political differences and tensions between the state and central government, many key stakeholders were transferred or removed from their offices soon after the presentation of the model. This caused uncertainty amongst the paralegals and community regarding the timeline for implementation. Elections in neighbouring states also resulted in delays as most government officials and political party workers were deployed. Despite these challenges, the paralegals continued to pursue the proposal by writing emails to the state government and pursuing advocacy with independent stakeholders. It was critical that paralegals maintain constant communication with these stakeholders, and regularly follow up on any developments. The role of the local area representative was noteworthy during this entire process, as they promised constituency funds to kick start the process of providing sewerage infrastructure and coordinating with government agencies for requisite permissions. At the same time, paralegals also approached the newly appointed stakeholders to build rapport and garner support for the proposal.

The process of seeking implementation has been a slow one, rife with bureaucratic changes and challenges. However, the paralegals have proven steadfast, responsive to changes and unwavering in their commitment to the meaningful implementation of the community's vision. They have also been managing expectations of the wider community during this long delay. The attitude of the paralegals, their learning from over seven years of advocacy, and their belief in the proposal and its potential to improve their living conditions have sustained their engagement. Signs that this persistence is paying off came in October 2024, as this chapter was going to press. The upgradation process started in the community, with the first step being the provision of water lines in the basti, which will eventually enable sewerage access for the residents as well.

Lessons learned: Positive changes and obstacles

It is evident from Ambedkar Camp's example that legal empowerment strategies and interventions encourage citizen engagement with formal administrative and legal systems. Such long-term engagement can build critical competencies within the community, help meet their needs and drive sustainable and lasting systemic changes. LE practitioners can encourage participation and bolster resilience to sustain activism. Well-organized communities play an important role in driving democratic governance and promoting state accountability.

Moreover, the success of any intervention is determined by its scale, nature and desired impact. The mapping and planning exercise in Ambedkar Camp was preceded by more than six years of LE action and advocacy in a relatively small community. The process of developing the proposal sought to facilitate free, accessible and meaningful participation. For similar interventions to be planned in other locations and contexts, it will be essential to strengthen shared understanding amongst stakeholders and identify approaches that champion community agency, resilience and wellbeing.

It is imperative to honour the women paralegals in Ambedkar Camp while reflecting on the strategies that enabled their growth. Over the past seven years, there has been demonstrated improvement in the state of services in the JJC, and a shift in community perspectives. Women have reported an increase in knowledge and confidence, and greater responsiveness of local stakeholders as a result of their continued engagement. For the upgradation to be a meaningful success, however, several stakeholders from the community, state and central government will have to work in collaboration. The paralegals and community members continue to patiently wait for upgrading to begin, so they can celebrate the success of their efforts.

The journey of community participation through the LE methodology in Ambedkar Camp has not been without its challenges. At the onset of training, it was difficult for residents to identify a shared purpose and strategy to direct their energies and efforts. Despite the largely homogenous socio-economic composition of the community, caste, gender and power hierarchies nonetheless limit the participation and decision-making ability of certain groups. Participatory tools and exercises — such as issue mapping, issue prioritization and stakeholder mapping — helped to address uneven power dynamics among the residents. Women were able to discuss problems pertinent to them in their community and identify barriers they face in their socio-political context. This was supplemented by training aimed at improving residents' confidence in their right of grievance redressal, and by accompanying and supporting them during key advocacy meetings.

Women's families and neighbours initially found it difficult to deal with their new-found agency, which often resulted in women facing increased scrutiny and policing. Counselling by LE practitioners helped community members overcome these reservations, which subsided as the massive impact of the work the women undertook became apparent.

Another challenge was that residents feared backlash from government functionaries as a result of their complaints about gaps in administration. Renters Tenants were especially vulnerable to adverse reactions to their complaints, given the precarious nature of their tenure in an already informal settlement. Lease agreements are very rarely executed in favour of renters, and they are considered ineligible for rehabilitation as they do not have any claim over the housing units in such informal settlements. In the larger context, training and knowledge transfer alone proved insufficient as tools to prompt collective action. This was addressed through resilience and confidence building.

The time-intensive process of engaging with government officials with no guarantee of positive outcomes also weighed on the paralegals and the community. This tedious process can be physically and emotionally draining as it demands time, vigilance and resilience from people already stretched thin. LE practitioners' continuous support to the paralegals —through calls and messages or during community visits — helped mitigate these barriers and sustain interest. Building trust, adopting a participatory approach and assessing risk have proven highly effective in this context.

Ultimately, in cases where communities are typically at the losing end of political disagreements and executive inaction, collective advocacy and action offer a viable response strategy. As residents of informal settlements grapple with housing insecurity, either due to their absence of tenure or lack of options for rehabilitation, *in situ* upgradation is also an important strategy to consider. With the upgrading of a settlement, residents can continue to live where they are and collectively plan for structural and spatial improvements for a better quality of life. Adults can retain their employment, children's studies are not disturbed and families can continue to receive government entitlements where they have been registered.

Community-led experiences and efforts must feed into the larger conversation on the progressive expansion of rights protections and universal guarantees to citizens by the state. It is equally paramount to strengthen both substantive and procedural frameworks that protect fundamental economic and social rights to ensure their meaningful realization. Normative frameworks for housing need to reaffirm security of tenure and equal access to land to all, including women and those living in poverty.

Legislative and administrative reforms are required to enable this in practice, by weeding out bureaucratic delays and injecting adequate economic resources (UN, 2006).

Conclusion

With the world's largest population, India's ambition for development and a stronger economy is ever growing. Development and beautification projects mostly happen at the expense of the most marginalized, exacerbating income inequality and a rapidly increasing wealth gap. With the rise in population and shrinking access to public land, adequate and affordable housing is one of the biggest issues marginalized communities are grappling with. Housing is a fundamental need, with profound effects on psychological, physical and financial wellbeing. The suitability and habitability of informal housing is generally poor, adversely impacting residents' overall quality of life. These factors, along with the constant maintenance and upkeep required, drain the financial resources of the residents.

Residents' limited knowledge of their rights, a lack of effective redressal mechanisms, slow and complex bureaucracy and pervasive corruption often leave impacted communities with no viable solution. The few residents who despite all odds have managed to get favourable policies, government directives and court orders continue to struggle with their meaningful implementation.

From the perspective of legal empowerment, it is crucial for citizens to have knowledge of their rights and be active participants in their own governance. They should be able to seek accountability and redress without fear of retaliation. This is especially important for a healthy democracy, as it puts the ownership and leadership of laws and policies in the hands of people who are directly impacted by them. By promoting women's leadership, community ownership, sustainability and replicability, the LE model outlined in this case study provides a framework for inclusive and sustainable development that can help bridge the gap between the haves and have-nots. This democratic and participatory approach takes time and extraordinary effort but offers equitable solutions to the most complex issues.

The present case study highlights issues of democratic governance and the impact of bureaucratic delays on the day-to-day lives of constituents. It deepens our knowledge of how communities can organize themselves and work towards a shared understanding of their interests and proposed interventions. Lessons from women's LE engagement and their anchoring of the upgradation effort highlight issues that require examination in the wider pursuit of the right to adequate and safe housing.

The journey of the women of Ambedkar Camp — from trainees to paralegals to unwavering forces for positive change — has been inspiring. They not only broke barriers of formal education, patriarchy and caste- and class-based discrimination, but also developed the confidence to demand their rights. When the state failed to respond to their housing problems, women paralegals led the residents of Ambedkar Camp in taking ownership of solution-oriented interventions. They not only actively participated in designing their living spaces but are ardently pursuing the proposal's implementation. Their determination and resolve stems from their belief that tenure security and quality housing will allow their families to break the cycle of poverty.

Notes

1 Formal housing dwellers have defensible and documented rights (e.g., property registration documents). These are referred to as *de jure* rights. Informal housing dwellers, on the other hand, lack some or all the documentation and may contravene municipal development plans or land regulations. Therefore, they could be evicted, or their houses could be demolished. Informal housing includes a spectrum of housing, including: (1) unauthorized housing, where the residents have uncontested ownership of the land and tolerance by the government implying *de facto* rights to use and transfer their dwelling; (2) notified slums, where residents cannot be evicted without due process (i.e., they have some *de jure* rights); and (3) unidentified slums, where the residents have no property rights (Jain et al., 2016).

2 Dalits are officially referred to by Indian state authorities as Scheduled Castes, a group of people suffering from extreme social, educational and economic disadvantage because of the age-old practice of untouchability.

3 The term generally refers to territorial communities living in relative isolation in foothills and forests.

4 Constitution of India (Seventh Amendment) Act, which subsequently implemented the States Re-Organization Act, 1956.

5 Writ petitions were brought on behalf of residents of slum clusters whose huts had been demolished by government land development agencies to advance road development related to hosting the 2010 Commonwealth Games in New Delhi. In this case, the Court established procedures to be followed before and after slum demolitions. In particular, the Court held that the government agency can only clear land when it falls within the public purpose; a survey must be conducted to determine eligibility of relocation prior to demolition with "meaningful engagement" of the residents; and relocation options must be identified to all eligible beneficiaries prior to demolition.

6 *Sudama Singh v. Government of Delhi & Anr*, 2010.

7 *U.P. Avas Evam Vikas Parishad & Anr vs. Friends Coop. Housing Society ltd & Anr*, 1995; *Francis Coralie Mullin v. The Administrator, Union Territory of Delhi & Ors*, 1981; *Chameli Singh and others v. State of U.P. & Anr*, 1996.

8 Other Backward Classes refers to classes of citizens other than the Scheduled Castes and Scheduled Tribes as may be specified by the central government from time to time for purposes of making provision for the reservation of appointments or posts in favour of those classes of citizens which, in the opinion of that government, are not adequately represented in the services under the Government of India and any local or other authority within the territory of India or under the control of the Government of India.

9 Organizations include: National Campaign for Dalit Human Rights, Indian Institute for Human Settlements and ActionAid

10 See ICAAD Human Rights Innovation for more information on a partner collaboration for the collection of ground-level data necessary to improve access to basic needs and improve health outcomes for marginalized women (https://icaad.ngo/sms-for-justice/).

11 Swastik Harish and Associates, https://swastikharish.com/
12 Model is available on Sketchfab (https://sketchfab.com/3d-models/3d-model-906038b93dcb4efaa655e3d5a40eab47)

References

Banda, S., Vaidya, Y., & Adler, D. (2013). *The case of Kathputli Colony: Mapping Delhi's first in-situ slum rehabilitation project* (CPR Working Paper 3). Centre for Policy Research. https://cprindia.org/wp-content/uploads/2022/07/The-Case-of-Kathputli-Colony_CPRWorkingPaper.pdf.

Chameli Singh and others v. State of U.P. & Anr. (1996) 2 SCC 549

Cities of Delhi. (2015). *The intersection of governments in Delhi.* Centre for Policy Research. https://cprindia.org/wp-content/uploads/2021/12/The-Intersection-of-Governments-in-Delhi.pdf.

Francis Coralie Mullin v. The Administrator, Union Territory of Delhi & Ors (1981) 2 SCR 516.

Jain, V., Subhash, C., & Karamchandani, A. (2016). *Informal housing, inadequate property rights: Understanding the needs of India's informal housing dwellers.* FSG. www.citiesalliance.org/sites/default/files/Informal%20Housing,%20Inadequate%20Property%20Rights.pdf.

The Missing Basti Project. (n.d.). *The Missing Basti Project* [Dataset]. https://missingbasti.com/.

Planning Department, Government of NCT of Delhi. (2023). *Economic survey of Delhi 2022–2023.* https://delhiplanning.delhi.gov.in/sites/default/files/Planning/ch._14_housing_and_urban_development_0.pdf.

Raj, A. (2023, January 23). Not quite home sweet home: At DDA flats for slum dwellers, some problems. *The Indian Express.* https://indianexpress.com/article/cities/delhi/not-quite-home-sweet-home-at-dda-flats-for-slum-dwellers-some-problems-8398287/.

Sudama Singh v. Government of Delhi & Anr (February 11, 2010) Delhi High Court. https://indiankanoon.org/doc/39539866/.

United Nations. (2006). *The Habitat Agenda: Istanbul declaration on human settlements.* https://unhabitat.org/sites/default/files/2014/07/The-Habitat-Agenda-Istanbul-Declaration-on-Human-Settlements-20061.pdf.

U.P. Avas Evam Vikas Parishad & Anr vs. Friends Coop. Housing Society ltd & Anr (1995) Supp (3) S.C.C. 456

World Population Review. (2024). *Delhi population 2024* [Dataset]. https://worldpopulationreview.com/world-cities/delhi-population.

7 The right to the city and people's planning in the Philippines

Policies and prospects

Tanya Renee F. Rosales and Juan Carlo P. Tejano

SALIGAN, PHILIPPINES

Introduction

For decades, the Philippine policy on socialized housing centred on forcible relocation of informal settlers to government housing sites. Citing a lack of available and affordable land in cities (Ballesteros et al., 2022), most of these sites are constructed "off-city" or in distant peri-urban areas. However, off-city relocation is correlated with poor development outcomes and social exclusion,[1] including loss of livelihood, access to basic services, social networks and safety nets (Romero, 2019). It is unsurprising therefore that, as of 2022, more than 61,000 government housing units remained unoccupied (National Housing Association, 2022) despite the evident demand for socialized housing (Torres, 2022).

Metro Manila, the country's capital, is home to more than 550,000 informal settler families (UP Planning and Development Research Foundation, 2014). An estimated 104,219 of them reside in danger areas, such as riverbanks, railroad tracks, public roads and garbage dumps. Those living along waterways are particularly vulnerable to extreme weather events. When tropical storm *Ondoy* — known internationally as Ketsana — hit in 2009, a total of 464 people died (National Disaster Coordinating Council, 2009). This was followed by deadlier typhoons: *Sendong* (Washi) in 2011, *Pablo* (Bopha) in 2012 and *Yolanda* (Haiyan) in 2013, each claiming more than a thousand lives (De La Cruz, 2014).[2] Despite this, a 2014 census revealed that 11,731 families still resided within the three-metre easements of Metro Manila's eight major waterways.[3] About 79 percent of these families were aware of the risks associated with their dwellings, but 32 percent of them had no plans to relocate. The top reason was accessibility to their workplace, school and hospital (UP Planning and Development Research Foundation, 2014).

In 1992, the Philippine Congress passed the Urban Development and Housing Act (UDHA) (Republic Act No. 7279, 1992), a law that upholds the due process rights of informal settlers. A product of the lobbying efforts of the organized urban poor, UDHA mandates the conduct of adequate consultations with affected families in the implementation of socialized housing programs (§28). It permits eviction and demolition only in three specific

DOI: 10.4324/9781003538806-7

instances: (1) when the settlers occupy a danger area; (2) when government infrastructure projects with available funding are about to be implemented; or (3) when there is a court order.

Yet, evictions and demolitions remained rampant. From 1992 to 2014, the Urban Poor Associates monitored a total of 895 cases (Urban Poor Associates, 2014). The majority of these were illegal for lack of notice, consultation and certificate of compliance. At least 51 cases were reported to be violent. Even the COVID-19 pandemic did not stop the evictions. In 2020, nearly 300 informal settler families lost their dwellings to make way for expansion of the Philippine railway system (Garcia, 2020). This was amid the government's stay-at-home directive to control the pandemic (Reuters, 2020).

The state's approach is inconsistent with its international commitments to human rights, which include the right to adequate shelter.[4] In 2016, the Philippines took part in Habitat III and adopted the New Urban Agenda which formally recognized the "right to the city". Defined as "the right of all inhabitants present and future, to occupy, use and produce just, inclusive and sustainable cities", the right to the city has three pillars: (1) spatially just resource distribution; (2) political agency; and (3) social, economic and cultural diversity (United Nations, 2017). But while the Philippine Constitution expressly adopts a policy of making decent housing available to the homeless and underprivileged (art. VII, § 9), domestic legislation has yet to shift to a rights-based approach, much less a right-to-the-city approach. Key housing policies remain focused on the roles of government and the private sector to provide shelter, without reference to the role of beneficiaries as rights-holders. Their political agency stops at pre-decisional consultations, and even this finds no effective mechanism for enforcement.

This chapter presents the emergence of the "people's plan" approach from the political mobilization and strategic policy advocacy of informal settlements, its development as a government housing program, and its short-lived push-back against the history of forcible relocation in the Philippines. The next section provides the context in which the concept materialized and the struggles to incorporate it in housing policies. The following two sections draw from the experiences of two settlements to explore the potential of the approach to realize the right to the city as well as its limitations and shortcomings. We then analyse the reasons for these limitations, and propose a paradigm shift to address these reasons, noting current efforts at policy change. The final section concludes that, to build on the gains of people's plans, institutional reforms must be made towards the democratization of government processes.

Setting the stage for people's plans

In 2008, *Metropolitan Manila Development Authority v. Concerned Residents of Manila Bay* ("*MMDA*"), a landmark environmental case, directed the demolition of all structures within the three-metre easements of Metro Manila waterways. According to the Philippine Supreme Court: "[i]f there is one factor responsible for the pollution of the major river systems and the Manila Bay, these unauthorized structures would be on top of the list". Represented by SALIGAN,[5] civil society organizations such as the Urban Poor Associates sought clarification from the Court on whether it was giving the government blanket authority to summarily demolish informal settlements without due process. In response, the Court clarified that "the authority of the [government] to dismantle illegal structures was not given as a means to circumvent the [UDHA]" and that "the eviction of underprivileged and homeless persons must conform to the mandatory requirements found in [UDHA] on, among others, notice, consultation, and resettlement".

Still, the directive in the *MMDA* case, followed by *Ondoy* in 2009, lent legitimacy to the government's demolition drive. As resistance would have been "illegitimate", the urban poor had to adopt new strategies to survive. Fortunately, the next national elections were just around the corner. In March 2010, a coalition of urban poor groups presented their agenda to Benigno Aquino III and Manuel Roxas, then presidential and vice-presidential candidates, respectively, who were running under the platform of participatory governance and inclusive development. This culminated in the signing of the "Ten-Point Covenant with the Urban Poor", which included a commitment to ensure stakeholder participation in finding solutions to the housing problem.

When Aquino won and assumed office, he directed the creation of a technical working group composed of government agencies and civil society organizations (Republic of the Philippines, 2013). The group, chaired by Interior and Local Government Secretary Jesse Robredo, was tasked to create a flood-resilient permanent housing solution for informal settlers in Metro Manila's danger areas. An annual budget of PHP10 billion (about USD177 million) for a period of five years (2011–2015), or a total of PHP50 billion (about USD885 million), was earmarked for this purpose. Robredo, a known champion of the urban poor, actively engaged the sector as a partner rather than a passive beneficiary (Andrade, 2012). In all official functions of the technical working group, non-governmental and people's organizations were represented. According to the Urban Poor Associates, a cabinet-level meeting in early August 2012 had already "sealed the deal" for the in-city relocation of around 5,000 families along Manila's waterways. Unfortunately, while the operationalization documents were being finalized, Robredo died in a plane crash.

Manuel Roxas replaced Robredo and brought in Francisco Fernandez, a veteran community organizer, as undersecretary. In April 2013, the *Policy Guidelines on the Operationalization and Utilization of the P50 Billion Housing Fund for ISFs in the Danger Areas of the NCR* was finalized. For the first time, the concept of a people's plan was incorporated in a government policy document. Under the policy guidelines, relocation would be "on-site, near-city, and in-city, and in accordance with the People's Plan" while "[o]ff-sites shall only be resorted to in accordance with the People's Plans after adequate and genuine consultation, or when directly requested by the affected [informal settler families] themselves". The people's plan was defined as a "community development plan" formulated by people's organizations through a process of consultations, with or without the support of government agencies or non-governmental organizations.

Within one year, a total of 68 people's plans were submitted by various people's organizations for 31,111 informal settler families (ISF-PMO, 2014). However, turning them into reality had not been smooth sailing. Land constraints were a major obstacle. Aside from the high costs of urban land, many institutional and regulatory failures in the land market existed due to poor governance. Important land administration functions were performed by at least seven national government agencies and the courts, but land use planning and zoning were undertaken by local governments. Due to the lack of an integrated system, land records and classification data were incomplete or inconsistent (World Bank, 2016). Furthermore, transaction costs were restrictive. The process of registering property rights was complex, expensive and slow. According to private developers, it could take up to 18 months to secure all the requirements for new development.

The birth pains of the people's plans caused delays in relocation that the government could not risk in view of imminent calamities, especially after typhoon *Yolanda*. Thus, in 2014, funds allocated for the people's plans were diverted to temporary shelter assistance in the form of a one-time subsidy intended to cover rental expenses for six months. However, since most of the people's plans still could not be completed, many who availed of the subsidy just transferred to available off-city housing units of the National Housing Association (NHA).

To fast-track the implementation of people's plans, the national government began engaging local governments as direct implementers. In 2015, the local government department issued guidelines for micro- and medium-rise housing projects to be undertaken by local governments (hereinafter *MMRB Guidelines*) (Department of the Interior and Local Government, 2015). Recognizing their lack of financial and technical capacity, local governments were permitted to receive program funds on certain conditions, including the establishment of a local project management team, a strengthened local housing board with at least 50 percent of voting members coming from the proponents of the people's plans and their partner organizations, and "[w]illingness to facilitate or provide resources… for subsidies such as but not limited to land and land development".

But five years was too short for the people's plans to gain ground. By the end of Aquino's term in 2016, 34 approved people's plans covering 26,236 informal settler families were still being processed. Of the 104,219 families eligible for people's plans, 29,511 had already relocated to off-city housing sites. Meanwhile, 74,708 families remained along waterways and in danger areas, including those whose people's plans were still being processed (ISF-PMO, 2014).

Nonetheless, the adoption of the people's plan approach as a government strategy planted the seeds of institutional change. In 2019, after years of advocacy by urban poor groups, Congress passed a law creating the Philippine housing department. The law empowers the department to "[d]evelop mechanisms and implement programs… including the people's plan approach, while encouraging the participation therein of local government partnerships with civil society organizations, nongovernment organizations, private groups and communities" (Rep. Act No. 11201).

The case of Manggahan Residences[6]

The Alliance of People's Organizations Along Manggahan Floodway (APOAMF) was one of the organizations that benefitted from these policy developments. Their settlement was among those affected by the *MMDA* decision. Constructed in 1986 (Galuszka, 2020, p. 16), the Manggahan Floodway is a 10-kilometre waterway in Pasig City that diverts floodwater from a river to a lake before draining to Manila Bay (IHP Regional Steering Committee for Asia and the Pacific, 2004, p. 179). Over the years, families started building homes along the floodway's banks (Galuszka, 2020, pp. 16–17).

In 1994, President Fidel Ramos proclaimed the east and west banks of the Manggahan Floodway as lands reserved for socialized housing (Proc. No. 458, s. 1994). The ownership of the lands, with a combined area of 1,239,930 square metres, was transferred to the NHA for disposition. This encouraged more families to settle along the floodway, expecting the land to be distributed to settlers.

At the time, the local Eusebio dynasty had just started in Pasig City. For 27 years since 1992, the Eusebios served as mayors of Pasig City, beginning with Vicente Eusebio, followed by his wife, his son, and his son's wife. The dynasty accommodated the growing number of settlers along Manggahan Floodway as a political constituency. A number of people's organizations were formed among them, with leaders allying themselves with the Eusebios. They delivered votes for the dynasty; in exchange, the Eusebios promised that, as long as they were in power, their settlement would not be demolished.

In 2002, the national government engaged a private contractor for a project called "Home Along the Floodway", which was supposed to provide low-cost housing for government employees and informal settlers along Manggahan Floodway (The Philippine Star, 2002). Then, in 2006, President Gloria Macapagal Arroyo amended Ramos's earlier proclamation with a proclamation of her own, reserving 12-metre strips of berms on both sides of the floodway for the housing project (Proc. No. 1160, s. 2006). However, the project never materialized. This was partly due to the Supreme Court ruling in *MMDA*. As the settlers were also blamed for the extreme flooding brought by *Ondoy*, Arroyo issued an executive order revoking her own proclamation. Declaring the previous technical plan a geohazard, Arroyo described the settlers as obstructions to the flow of water and ordered their relocation (Exec. Order No. 854, s. 2009).

Soon after, eviction notices were posted on houses along the floodway. In exchange for voluntarily vacating their homes, the informal settlers were offered relocation units outside Metro Manila. The offer was coursed through the leaders of people's organizations allied with the Eusebios. They convinced some families, especially those who feared available units would run out in the proposed relocation site. The leaders themselves were among the first to relocate.

But not everyone agreed. Leaders of some people's organizations in partnership with Community Organizers Multiversity (COM), a non-governmental organization advocating for the empowerment of informal settlers, called for an assembly. Jenilyn David, former general secretary of APOAMF, described the widely attended assembly as a source of hope. Before it, she believed that compliance was their only option. But she realized that, "*kaming* urban poor *na tinatapon, kami ang* backbone *ng ekonomiya*" (We, the urban poor who were being thrown out, are the backbone of the economy) (M. Suarez & J. David, personal communication, April 20, 2023). The participants agreed to object to the planned eviction, demand consultations and support onsite development instead of the offer of off-city relocation.

With the assistance of COM, the organizations partnered with Technical Assistance Organization Pilipinas (TAO-Pilipinas), a women-led non-governmental organization of architects, to come up with housing design proposals for onsite development. TAO-Pilipinas proposed floating and stilt-type homes to accommodate the flood risks cited in Arroyo's executive order. These were presented during a stakeholders' forum that was attended by government representatives. After the forum, the government stopped serving eviction notices.

The organizations also lobbied for representation in the relocation process. They demanded a seat in the local inter-agency committee and joined the alliance of urban poor groups that secured the Ten-Point Covenant with Aquino and Roxas. The *Policy Guidelines* adopted by the Aquino government in 2013 secured them a seat in the local inter-agency committee. To formalize their representation, the organizations formed APOAMF and registered it as a non-stock corporation. Thus, APOAMF became the informal settlers' representative in the committee.

APOAMF sought alternatives to the government's plan. It held consultations at all levels of the organization and kept their members informed. As it developed its alternative, APOAMF called it the "people's plan" to distinguish it from the government's plan. The term was borrowed from COM, which played an important role in the long history of advocacy for people's plans among the urban poor.

Based on the consultations, APOAMF formed two internal committees — one to study the possibility of onsite development and another to look for nearby land for in-city relocation. However, the first committee faced two problems. First, the proposed housing designs developed by TAO-Pilipinas were flatly rejected by the government because they did not align with its models and standards for socialized housing. Second, the proposal was anchored on Arroyo's revoked proclamation, which was found to be unsupported by technical studies. Areas reserved by the proclamation for socialized housing could not be definitively located and probably covered existing roads.

The second committee found better prospects in in-city relocation. It studied Pasig City's land use plan and visited possible relocation sites. It was no easy task. The city government was not open to disclosing information about the lands within its jurisdiction. But the committee struck gold when it eventually found the Metropolitan Manila Development Authority (MMDA) Depot, a two-hectare parcel of land that was almost adjacent to the settlement but sufficiently distant "from the dreaded Floodway waters" (Mawis, 2018). Upon verification with government, the depot was found to be part of the lands originally proclaimed by Ramos for socialized housing. It was being used by the MMDA for its motor pool and as an impoundment lot. There was an office, but the land was mostly open without other structures.

With available land in the city, APOAMF conducted workshops and consultations among its members to develop a new proposal for the housing structures. The members agreed on a housing design consisting of residential units in multiple low-rise buildings with five stories each. Initially, the design had wraparound balconies on the upper floors to ensure ventilation and privacy. The NHA was not amenable to this as it would be expensive and would eat up limited space. It insisted on a condominium-like setup, with a common hallway on each floor, without balconies. APOAMF agreed, but not without some haggling. It bargained for wider hallways — 3 metres instead of 1.5 metres — so that units' doors would not face each other for better privacy, and for additional windows to enhance ventilation. The government acceded to these demands. Meanwhile, the interior of the residential units followed the NHA's standard design. They were studio-type 24-square metre units that had their own toilets and baths, sinks and laundry areas. Occupants were allowed to modify the interiors. They could create rooms by adding partition walls or convert the laundry area to other uses. They had to furnish the units on their own.

Overall, because the resulting design was a product of negotiations, it met both the community's needs and the government's requirements. APOAMF's leaders took on the task of studying these technical requirements. Although they had no prior expertise on these matters, the leaders knew that understanding them was necessary if they wanted to negotiate with the government's lawyers, engineers and architects. They also knew it was necessary if they wanted to take charge of estate management, which was one of their objectives.

With the benefit of hindsight, the leaders later realized that they could have also negotiated for other aspects of the relocation plan. At the time, with the pending threats of forced eviction, they had focused their attention and resources on the structural design of each low-rise building and did not initially bargain for facilities such as carparks and spaces for children to play. These have often been neglected in socialized housing projects. When the leaders later raised the need for these facilities, the government responded by saying that these were not part of the negotiations. A lack of attention to the site's sewerage system also later became a problem for APOAMF. To service 900 families, the site only had one sewage treatment plant, which was not even operational when the settlers moved in. It only became operational years later, in 2018. It was supposed to be built by the site's water distributor, but was built instead by a project subcontractor. Unfortunately, according to the distributor, the sewage treatment plant was substandard and did not meet the government's minimum requirements.

Building construction started in 2013. The project was called "Manggahan Residences". It consisted of three phases, each with progressively more buildings to be constructed. Phase 1 was for two low-rise buildings, Phase 2 was for five more buildings and Phase 3 was for the remaining eight buildings. There was one overall project contractor with different subcontractors for the different phases. APOAMF participated as an observer in the bidding process, although it was not privy to the project contracts.

The project cost of Phase 1 was PHP60.49 million (about USD1.07 million). To finance this, the NHA used its allocation from the government's PHP50 billion housing fund. Each residential unit was awarded to one informal settler family under an individual usufruct contract of 50 years. Under Philippine law, a usufruct gives a person the right to use and enjoy the property of another with the obligation of preserving it (Phil. Civil Code, art. 562). Thus, ownership of the land and the units remained with the state. APOAMF initially tried to negotiate for a special contract of community financing, but the NHA did not agree.

The contract prices, amortization and interest rate were also a result of negotiations. Units on lower-level floors were more expensive than those on higher-level floors, with the most expensive at PHP500,000 (about USD8,843) each and the cheapest at PHP400,000 (about USD7,074) each. The prices were payable in 30 years, with 3 percent interest per annum. Originally, the scheme imposed 6.5 percent annual interest on the first PHP50,000 (about USD884) and 4.5 percent annual interest on the remaining amounts. APOAMF lobbied for a lower interest rate through Albee Benitez, a legislator who advocated for informal settlers' rights. Benitez was able to negotiate for the lower interest rate of 3 percent.

Estate management was left to APOAMF. This meant that it oversaw the maintenance of community spaces and facilities, the security of the premises and the formulation and enforcement of community rules. For these, APOAMF has been collecting a monthly assessment fee of PHP300 (about USD5) from each household. After participating in an estate management workshop, APOAMF formulated its community rules together with the NHA. It also set up an internal grievance mechanism for dispute conciliation between members.

By August 2015, the first two low-rise buildings of Phase 1 were completed and inaugurated, with President Aquino himself attending. It was less than a year before the next presidential election. The construction of Phase 2 was also ongoing at the time. The NHA promised to inaugurate Phase 3 of the project before the end of Aquino's term. This did not happen.

In May 2016, Rodrigo Duterte was elected as the new president of the Philippines. Not only did Duterte launch a brutal drug war against the urban poor, he also resumed forcible evictions. In a year, eviction notices were again served by the government on the remaining settlers along Manggahan Floodway. Despite APOAMF's efforts to negotiate, the forced eviction pushed through in 2017. Thus, hundreds of families were forced to relocate to the unfinished buildings of Phase 2 of the Manggahan Residences. There were no toilets and sinks, the sewage treatment plant was not operational and the units had no access to electricity.

It took another change in administration to stop the forced evictions. In 2019, Victor Sotto was elected mayor of Pasig City, ending the 27-year rule of the Eusebio dynasty. APOAMF became hopeful again that the relocation process would be properly implemented. In February 2020, they gathered in front of the NHA office to demand construction of the remaining buildings and the necessary works on their sewage treatment plant.

Unfortunately, just a month later, the COVID-19 pandemic struck the Philippines. Construction of the remaining buildings was halted. Out of the 15 low-rise buildings, only 10 had been constructed. Of the remaining five, three were unfinished and two had not started construction. With the 10 finished buildings already fully occupied, hundreds of families on the west bank of Manggahan Floodway had not yet relocated.

The pandemic also affected APOAMF's members in another way. Duterte responded to the pandemic with one of the world's longest lockdowns (Balagtas See, 2021). Businesses were temporarily closed, public transportation was limited and vendors were not allowed on the streets. The economy plunged. Many of the urban poor were left without employment and livelihood. In July 2020, APOAMF, together with SALIGAN and other civil society organizations, called on the government to address the multiple crises faced by the urban poor — in health, the economy, housing, education, safety and human rights. They called the urban poor the "crisis epicentre" of the pandemic. They also asked for an extended moratorium on amortization payments amid the crises. Despite this, amortization collection continued in Manggahan Residences, and penalties were imposed on residents who were unable to pay on time.

APOAMF's members joined the presidential campaign in 2022 to support Vice President Maria Leonor Robredo, a lawyer who had a track record of working with the urban poor and other sectors.[7] They believed that, with Robredo as president, their relocation concerns would be addressed. But Robredo did not win. It was Ferdinand Marcos, Jr., son of the late dictator Ferdinand Marcos, Sr., who was elected president. People's plans were not among Marcos's priorities in the housing sector.

The case of People's Plan Ville[8]

Another community affected by the wave of eviction notices following *Ondoy* was that of Ugnayang Lakas ng mga Apektadong Pamilya sa Baybaying Ilog Pasig — Manila (ULAP-Manila). The association, composed of seven people's organizations representing more than a thousand informal settler families, was also part of the urban poor covenant in 2010. After the presidential elections, ULAP-Manila embarked on district-wide consultations in Binondo, Manila and started conceptualizing their own people's plan. The consultations provided an opportunity for the affected settlers to assess their situation, envision their ideal community, discuss site selection and explore financing options. ULAP-Manila was also assisted by COM and TAO-Pilipinas.

As with other people's plan proponents, land availability for in-city resettlement was a critical issue. ULAP-Manila identified nine target sites. To obtain copies of the land titles and other documents, ULAP-Manila's members pooled in funds and started a community savings scheme (*impukan*). The savings would also serve as a fund for future expenses of their people's plan. After a series of consultations and workshops with government agencies and non-governmental organizations, ULAP-Manila selected a parcel of land owned by the Government Service Insurance System (GSIS) as its project site. The 5,715-square-metre lot is located at De Dios Street, Santa Mesa, Manila, and is covered by an executive order declaring certain properties of the GSIS as socialized housing sites (Exec. Order No. 71, s. 2002). With TAO-Pilipinas, ULAP-Manila came up with a proposal for six low-rise buildings with five stories and 60 units each.

The local government department began facilitating negotiations for land acquisition in 2014. It signed an agreement with the city government of Manila for the transfer of PHP62.865 million (about USD1.11 million) for site development and construction of housing units for 359 informal settler families. The amount was chargeable against the national budget for micro- and medium-rise building projects.

Despite this, the people's plan did not materialize the following year. It faced three setbacks — legal, financial and technical. Under Philippine law, public funds that were unused within the year they were appropriated would revert to the national treasury. In ULAP-Manila's case, the funds could not be used to acquire the GSIS property because the appropriation law used the word "construction" only. In a clarificatory meeting, the state auditor stated that there would be consequences if any portion of the fund were utilized for land purchase.

Another major setback was the property's selling price. ULAP-Manila offered to buy the property at PHP11,000 (about USD195) per square metre, but the GSIS was only willing to sell it at its market value of PHP22,700 (about USD402) per square metre. Due to the standstill, the local government department restarted efforts to facilitate the acquisition of the property, this time by a government-owned corporation, the Social Housing Finance

Corporation (SHFC). The SHFC would retain ownership of the land, allowing beneficiaries to pay only for the cost of the building. The department informed GSIS of the proposed arrangement in August 2015. It noted that the executive order declaring the property as a socialized housing site provided that the acquisition price should be determined by an executive committee chaired by GSIS, with government agencies and a non-governmental organization as members. The department asked GSIS to convene this committee.

However, the third setback was that portions of the land were found to be covered by six other land titles. Before the property could be transferred, it was necessary to consolidate these with GSIS's title, conduct a new survey and segregate the proposed site. This was not possible within the fund's timeframe. Hence, the PHP62.865 budget for the people's plan lapsed in 2015.

These setbacks did not deter the community. ULAP-Manila continued its dialogues with government officials. In January 2016, their efforts paid off when the budget department approved the allocation of PHP129 million (about USD2.28 million) to the SHFC for purchase of the GSIS property. Around the same time, ULAP-Manila registered as a homeowners' association under the name People's Plan Ville Homeowners Association (PPVHOA).

But the year 2016 also marked the beginning of new challenges. The newly elected President Duterte appointed a new SHFC president, and the board composition also changed. Although PPVHOA was able to secure some commitments from the new board in October 2017, follow-ups on the purchase were ignored. The organization also lost direct access to SHFC officials. When PPVHOA leaders tried to meet with them, the leaders were prevented from entering SHFC's office and were met instead by SHFC employees outside.

Shifting their strategy, PPVHOA demanded a dialogue with the budget department. They secured copies of two special allotment release orders from September 2016 and December 2017, indicating SHFC's authority to disburse the total amount of PHP435 million (about USD7.69 million) for their people's plan. Armed with these documents, PPVHOA sent letters and position papers to the housing coordinating council and the presidential complaint centre.

The year 2019 showed some movement. SHFC facilitated the validation of beneficiaries, discussions on the housing specifications were reinitiated and technical workshops were again conducted. By 2020, PPVHOA had already finalized the housing design and selected a contractor. During this entire period, the issues regarding land acquisition were still pending.

A year later, however, SHFC issued a new policy requiring project contractors to have at least an 80 percent accomplishment rate. PPVHOA's chosen contractor did not meet this due to the COVID-19 pandemic. SHFC advised PPVHOA to change its contractor but, among SHFC's list of accredited contractors, none were responsive to PPVHOA's inquiries. It took PPVHOA another year to secure a new contractor.

Without any of the major issues being resolved, another challenge surfaced. The GSIS property had real property tax arrears amounting to around PHP40 million (about USD707,451) payable to Manila's city government.

GSIS insisted on the as-is-where-is clause in the deed of sale, which meant that PPVHOA would have to shoulder the taxes. This prompted PPVHOA to reach out to the city government. They met with Manila Vice Mayor Yul Servo who assured them that he would raise the possibility of condoning the tax arrears with the city council. Later, however, it was discovered that the property was actually exempt from these taxes. In September 2022, PPVHOA obtained a copy of the tax certificate confirming this.

With the tax arrears resolved, PPVHOA went back to SHFC only to face another stumbling block. With the change in national government in 2022, Marcos, the new president, had appointed another SHFC president. Again, negotiations came to a standstill. PPVHOA demanded a dialogue with the new SHFC president, but they were met instead by SHFC's vice president who said that the deed of sale would be finalized in January 2023.

Unfortunately, in January 2023, PPVHOA was informed that the new SHFC president was looking into the construction of a 21-story building instead of the original proposal of low-rise buildings to maximize the lot area of the project site. The counterproposal aligns with the new Marcos government's flagship housing program called the *Pambansang Pabahay para sa Pilipino* (National Housing for the Filipino) Program or 4PH (Exec. Order No. 34, s. 2023). The program aims to construct one million housing units every year for six years from 2023.

Ostensibly, 4PH seeks to provide in-city housing for informal settlers (Department of Human Settlements and Urban Development [DHSUD], 2023), maximizing available land in highly urbanized areas "by prioritizing vertical housing and mixed-use development" (DHSUD, 2002, §2.3). It bears noting, however, that the program's eligibility criteria do not explicitly limit beneficiaries to informal settlers or underprivileged and homeless citizens, unlike the eligibility criteria for socialized housing under the UDHA. In fact, 4PH prioritizes workers in the formal sector (DHSUD, 2023), even though many informal settlers work in the informal economy. Estimates from the housing department peg the monthly amortization for high-rise buildings under 4PH at around PHP2,400 (about USD42) (Malaya Business Insight, 2023). Meanwhile, a government survey on family incomes and expenditures reported in 2018 that the bottom 30 percent of Filipino families earned at most about PHP14,000 (about USD248) monthly and spent at most about PHP12,250 (about USD217) monthly. Thus, the estimated monthly amortization for 4PH would account for at least 19.6 percent of these families' expenditures, whereas in 2018 their spending for housing only accounted for 8.1 percent of their expenditures or less than PHP1,000 (about USD18) a month (Philippine Statistics Authority, 2020, pp. 26–28).

Ultimately, informal settlers can be crowded out of the flagship housing program that supposedly targets them. More fundamentally, 4PH was formulated without the participation of the target beneficiaries themselves, the informal settlers. SHFC's proposal of a 21-story building was a complete deviation from the people's plan of PPVHOA, which was the product of extensive consultations, feasibility studies and the settlers' collective vision of a livable community.

The end of people's plans?

The drastic turn of events following the assumption of the new Marcos government threatens the people's plan approach and the work informal settlers have put into their respective people's plans. While the priority it gives to in-city housing is a welcome departure from decades of off-city relocations, 4PH was developed with neither the needs nor the participation of directly affected stakeholders in mind. If left unchanged, the program might even crowd them out of available lands in cities. How could the people's plan approach be so short-lived as a housing strategy for informal settlements? Three factors may provide some explanation.

First, the Philippine policy on informal settlements remains a policy of marginalization. Laws mandate the demolition of informal settlements on public and private properties without sufficient standards on relocation. Onsite development is preferred under the UDHA "whenever possible", but this is considered impossible by the government in danger areas like waterways. To preserve urban resources, local governments have often resorted to off-city relocation, transferring informal settlers to peri-urban areas, literally at the margins of urbanity.

The problem is aggravated by the perceived urgency of evicting informal settlers in light of stronger typhoons and water pollution. Fifteen years since *MMDA*, the continuing directive for government agencies is to demolish informal settlements along the waterways connected to Manila Bay. Although it clarified that any such demolition must comply with the UDHA, the Supreme Court was silent on how and where affected families should be relocated. The initial response from the Arroyo government was to do what the government had always done: transfer the families to off-city sites. This changed when the Aquino government took over and implemented a program that was based on people's plans. However, without legislative enactment, Aquino's program was not binding on succeeding presidents. Today, Marcos's 4PH jeopardizes the people's plans that were developed during Aquino's term, as shown by PPVHOA's case. Thus, even informal settlements with existing people's plans are at risk of being marginalized from the in-city lands that they targeted.

Second, despite its formal recognition of people's plans, the legal framework for housing in the Philippines remains dominated by a supply-driven approach. The law tackles housing from the perspective of the government as the producer of housing units — not from the perspective of the community demanding adequate housing as a human right. This is antithetical to the people's plan approach. This supply-driven approach can be seen in how housing policies and programs characterize informal settlers as "beneficiaries" instead of rights-holders. It can also be observed in how the UDHA merely requires the government to consult affected families in cases of forced evictions, without recognizing that their communities can take the lead in their quest for secure tenure and decent homes. The law mentions affording a settlement the opportunity "to participate in the decision-making process on matters involving the protection and promotion of its legitimate collective interests", but no implementing mechanism exists to ensure this beyond consultations. It comes as no surprise then that 4PH centres only on housing production as the solution to the housing backlog, regardless of whether informal settlers would be able to afford the housing units produced or whether they would have a say in the process.

The UDHA also lacks clear and comprehensive standards for the conduct of "adequate consultations" or the inputs, results and outcomes expected from them. Whether the results of such consultations will ultimately matter is left entirely to government decision-makers. Decision-making on site selection, housing specifications and other major aspects of socialized housing and resettlement remains the exclusive function of government. Still, in many cases, consultations are not even statutorily required. Under the UDHA, any new structure built in a danger area after the law's enactment is declared illegal. It is subject to summary demolition by local governments without the need for consultations (DILG & HUDCC, n.d.). This covers many informal settlements, as there is no explicit definition of what constitutes a danger area. Instead, under the law, danger areas include "*esteros*, [9] railroad tracks, garbage dumps, riverbanks, shorelines, waterways, and other public places such as sidewalks, roads, parks, and playgrounds".

Third, patronage remains a pervasive theme in Philippine politics, including in the housing sector.[10] Powerful patrons provide favours and privileges to their dependent clientele in exchange for the latter's support and loyalty. Although it has been argued that this patron–client model no longer fully explains Philippine politics,[11] it was particularly evident in the experiences of APOAMF and PPVHOA. Prior to its downfall, the Eusebio dynasty relied on the electoral support of people's organizations along Manggahan Floodway in exchange for promises that there would be no demolition of their settlement. While it led to attempts to institutionalize the people's plan approach, President Aquino's urban poor covenant may be considered as another example. Today, without any covenant between President Marcos and the urban poor, the latter cannot rely on him to continue Aquino's housing program or at least honour any existing people's plans: hence, the radically different 4PH under Marcos.

The right to the city as a way forward

Institutionalizing the people's plan approach as the core housing strategy for informal settlements requires a paradigm shift in Philippine policies. This entails reframing solutions to the housing problem from *ad hoc* programs patronizing informal settlers as "beneficiaries" to permanent interventions with a rights-based approach. This new approach must be grounded in not only the right to adequate shelter but also the right to the city.

The right to adequate shelter is recognized in the Philippine Constitution, albeit expressed in terms of state obligations and limited to underprivileged and homeless citizens (Phil. Const. art. XIII, §9). In 2011, the Philippine Commission on Human Rights identified the following criteria for housing to be adequate: (1) security of tenure; (2) availability of adequate services and facilities; (3) affordability; (4) habitability; (5) accessibility for marginalized groups; (6) a location that must be safe and not cut off from employment opportunities and social services; and (7) cultural adequacy (CHR (IV) No. A2011–003). Statutorily adopting these criteria as demandable and enforceable rights can prevent problematic programs that will ultimately be rejected by informal settler families. The criterion on location provides a basis for prioritizing in-city over off-city resettlement. Moreover, the criterion on affordability can justify favouring less expensive options for the urban poor.

Meanwhile, the right to the city provides additional dimensions to housing for informal settlers, especially with respect to their role in planning, construction, financing and estate management. One of the pillars of the right to the city is political agency. Based on this principle, informal settlers themselves should have a say on the matter of their housing and resettlement, including how and where they should be relocated. This is the basic idea underlying the people's plan approach. APOAMF's story, while not a complete success, is an example of how political agency can be exercised by informal settlements given an enabling policy environment. If recognized as a demandable and enforceable right, whether in its entirety or in terms of its component pillars, the right to the city could revolutionize housing for informal settlements in the Philippines.

In 2016, SALIGAN consulted local governments, civil society organizations and children in informal settlements and relocation sites regarding the laws that governed the relocation of informal settlers (Lavitoria et al., 2017). Based on the recommendations gathered, SALIGAN drafted policy proposals that would, among other things: require the formulation and implementation of people's plans in any resettlement of informal settlers; provide clear standards for "genuine and adequate consultations"; prioritize in-city over off-city relocation; and set up accountability mechanisms for local governments.

These stipulations were incorporated in the proposed Least Displacement of Informal Settlers Act, which was filed as a bill by Senators Risa Hontiveros and Leila de Lima in 2021. In their explanatory note, the senators cited the right to the city as a basis for the measure. Specifically, the bill sought "to translate into domestic policy the right to the city of Filipino urban dwellers, especially the Filipino urban poor who have long been marginalized in decision-making processes on and the enjoyment of urban resource" (Senate Bill No. 2069). In 2022, the House of Representatives passed a similar version of the bill (Lalu, 2022). The Senate is now expected to deliberate on the bill.

Conclusion

The state-centred approach to informal settlements in the Philippines is not working. Its focus on forced evictions and off-city relocation has only led to violence against families and children, unoccupied housing projects and dismal outcomes for the urban poor. It requires fundamental change to overturn the current supply-driven, top-down approach that treats informal settlers as passive beneficiaries and replace it with a demand-driven, bottom-up approach that recognizes settlers as rights-holders. Instead of projects to be implemented, housing for the urban poor must be seen as a collective of rights, including the right to adequate shelter and the right to the city.

The successes of the people's plan approach in fulfilling these rights demonstrate its viability as an alternative worth considering. People's planning is the right to the city in practice. Through it, communities like that of APOAMF have been able to "'de-alienate' urban space" by appropriating it through "real and active participation" in a "living struggle" for control over their lives in the city.[12] In short, they collectively remade their city and, in the process, remade themselves.[13]

Although the people's plan approach has been gaining recognition in Philippine law, it remains at the margins of the national housing strategy. Permanent measures, such as the Least Displacement of Informal Settlers Act, must be adopted to bring the approach to the core of the Philippines' housing strategy. Of course, even when such measures have already been adopted, implementation becomes the next question. Not all the people's plans under Aquino's program succeeded. The program's shortfalls must be examined in terms of the capacity of the government to accommodate and support the participatory mechanisms required by the people's plan approach. Housing is a multifaceted issue that demands a holistic solution. Decades of experience have proven that current mechanisms fail to account for the rights, needs and aspirations of informal settlers. For people-driven solutions to work, further democratization of the entire government machinery involved in housing is necessary.

Notes

1 See Singh and Gadgil (2017, pp. 13–14).
2 These typhoons killed 1,439, 1,901 and 6,300 people, respectively.
3 San Juan River, Tullahan River, Estero Tripa de Gallina, Estero de Maypajo, Estero de Sunog Apog, Maricaban Creek, Pasig River and Manggahan Floodway.
4 Universal Declaration of Human Rights, art. 25(1); International Covenant on Economic, Social, and Cultural Rights, art. 11(1); International Covenant on Civil and Political Rights (ICCPR), art. 25(a).
5 Sentro ng Alternatibong Lingap Panlegal (SALIGAN) is a legal resource non-governmental organization working with the urban poor, labour unions, women, LGBTQIA+ persons, children and Indigenous peoples on sectoral and other issues, including the environment. SALIGAN engages in strategic litigation, paralegal training, policy advocacy and legal research in its work with the sectors. It has been in partnership with informal settlements and urban poor groups since the

fall of the Marcos dictatorship in the late 1980s. The authors are part of the SALIGAN legal team.

6 For this Part, the authors interviewed Madeline Suarez and Jenilyn David, President and Former General Secretary, respectively, of the Alliance of People's Organizations Along Manggahan Floodway.

7 Before her election as Vice President in 2016, Maria Leonor Robredo worked at SALIGAN and the Public Attorney's Office. During her term as Vice President, she chaired the government's housing coordinating council.

8 For this section, the authors interviewed Jonjon Elago, President of Ugnayang Lakas ng mga Apektadong Pamilya sa Baybaying Ilog Pasig — Manila.

9 Estuaries or estuarial creeks.

10 See, e.g. Villanueva and Salazar (2015).

11 See, e.g. Quimpo (2008).

12 See Purcell (2014, pp. 149–150).

13 See Harvey (2008).

References

Andrade, J. I. (2012, August 21). Urban poor on Robredo death: Why him? *INQUIRER.Net*. https://newsinfo.inquirer.net/255046/urban-poor-on-robredo-death-why-him.

Balagtas See, A. (2021). Rodrigo Duterte is using one of the world's longest COVID-19 lockdowns to strengthen his grip on the Philippines. *Time*. https://time.com/5945616/covid-philippines-pandemic-lockdown.

Ballesteros, M. M., Ramos, T. P., & Ancheta, J. A. (2022). *Measuring housing affordability in the Philippines* (PIDS Discussion Paper no. 2022–2022). Philippine Institute for Development Studies. https://pidswebs.pids.gov.ph/CDN/document/pidsdps2222.pdf.

De La Cruz, G. (2014, August 1). Worst natural disasters in the Philippines. *Rappler*. www.rappler.com/environment/disasters/64916-worst-natural-disasters-philippines/.

Department of Human Settlements and Urban Development. (2002). *Circ. No. 2022–2004*. Author.

Department of Human Settlements and Urban Development. (2023). *4PH operations manual: Requirements, processes, and guidelines for the implementation of the 4PH Program*. Author.

Department of the Interior and Local Government. (2015). *Mem. Circ. No. 2015–2056*. Author.

Department of the Interior and Local Government & Housing and Urban Development Coordinating Council. (n.d.). *Implementing rules and regulations governing summary eviction*. Author.

Exec. Order No. 71, s. (2002). www.officialgazette.gov.ph/2002/02/11/executive-order-no-71-s-2002/.

Exec. Order No. 854, s. (2009). www.officialgazette.gov.ph/2009/12/04/executive-order-no-854-s-2009/.

Exec. Order No. 34, s. (2023). www.officialgazette.gov.ph/2023/07/17/executive-order-no-34-s-2023/.

Galuszka, J. (2020). Adapting to informality: Multistory housing driven by a co-productive process and the People's Plans in Metro Manila, Philippines. *International Development Planning Review*, 43(1), 1–29.

Garcia, Ma. A. (2020, July 22). Nearly 300 families on PNR land lose homes in demolition. *GMA News Online*. www.gmanetwork.com/news/topstories/regions/748074/nearly-300-families-on-pnr-land-lose-homes-in-demolition/story/.

Harvey, D. (2008). The right to the city. *New Left Review*, 53. https://newleftreview.org/II/53/david-harvey-the-right-to-the-city

IHP Regional Steering Committee for Asia and the Pacific. (2004). *Catalogue of rivers for Southeast Asia and the Pacific*, Vol. V (Y. Tachikawa, J. Ross, K. Abdullah, & Mohd. N. bin Mohd. Desa, Eds.). UNESCO-IHP.

ISF Project Management Office (PMO), Office for the Urban Poor, Informal Settler Families (ISF) and Other Special Concerns. (2014). *Progress report 2014: 2nd terminal report*. Author.

Lalu, G. P. (2022, November 9). House bill on on-site relocation of informal settlers approved on 2nd reading. *INQUIRER.Net*. https://newsinfo.inquirer.net/1691353/bill-prioritizing-on-site-relocation-of-informal-settlers-approved-on-second-reading.

Lavitoria, M. H. E., Silva, J. K. B., Saura, III, R. A., & Deloso, O. P. (2017). *Child rights-centered assessment report of off-city relocation mechanism of informal settler families*. Sentro ng Alternatibong Lingap Panlegal.

Malaya Business Insight. (2023). House for P2,400/mo possible with 4PH. *Malaya Business Insight*. https://malaya.com.ph/news_business/house-for-p2400-mo-possible-with-4ph/.

Mawis, V. L. (2018, August 11). When God wills the people's plan. *Philippine Daily Inquirer*. https://business.inquirer.net/255474/god-wills-peoples-plan.

Metropolitan Manila Development Authority v. Concerned Residents of Manila Bay, G. R. No. 171947–171948 (December 18, 2008) Supreme Court.

National Housing Authority (NHA). (2022). *Performance scorecard*. https://icrs.gcg.gov.ph/files/kFPCjcyuLe63VEQUVHJU.pdf.

National Disaster Coordinating Council. (2009). *Situation report No. 48 on Tropical Storm "Ondoy" {Ketsana}*. Author.

The Philippine Star. (2002, January 13). Low-cost housing project to benefit 30,000 families. *The Philippine Star*. www.philstar.com/headlines/2002/01/13/146912/low-cost-housing-project-benefit-30000-families.

Philippine Statistics Authority. (2020). *2018 family income and expenditure survey*. Author.

Proc. No. 458, s. (1994). www.officialgazette.gov.ph/1994/08/29/proclamation-no-458-s-1994/.

Proc. No. 1160, s. (2006). www.officialgazette.gov.ph/2006/10/17/proclamation-no-1160-s-2006/.

Purcell, M. (2014). Possible worlds: Henri Lefebvre and the right to the city. *Journal of Urban Affairs*, 36(1), 141–154. doi:10.1111/juaf.12034.

Quimpo, N. G. (2008). *Contested democracy and the left in the Philippines after Marcos*. Yale University Southeast Asia Studies; Ateneo de Manila University Press.

Rep. Act No. 11201 (2019). www.officialgazette.gov.ph/2019/02/14/republic-act-no-11201/.

Rep. Act No. 7279 (1992). www.officialgazette.gov.ph/1992/03/24/republic-act-no-7279/.

Republic of the Philippines. (2013). *Joint mem. circ. on policy guidelines on the operationalization and utilization of the P.50 billion housing fund for ISFs in danger areas of the NCR*. Circ. No. 1, s. 2013. Author.

Reuters. (2020, March 12). Philippines' Duterte announces "lockdown" of Manila to fight coronavirus. *Reuters.* www.reuters.com/article/us-health-coronavirus-philippines-idUSKBN20Z22P.

Romero, S. (2019, August 5). Why in-city resettlement is best. *INQUIRER.Net*. https://opinion.inquirer.net/123065/why-in-city-resettlement-is-best.

Singh, G., & Gadgil, G. (2017). *Navigating informality: Perils and prospects in Metro Manila's slums.* International Bank for Reconstruction and Development / The World Bank. https://pubdocs.worldbank.org/en/564861506978931790/Navigating-Informality-Metro-Manila-7-26-17web.pdf.

Torres, S. A. (2022, October 21). Philippine housing backlog may reach 10 million by end of Marcos admin: DHSUD exec. *ABS-CBN News.* https://news.abs-cbn.com/news/10/21/22/ph-housing-backlog-may-hit-10m-in-by-end-of-marcos-admin-official.

United Nations. (2017). *The right to the city and cities for all* (Habitat III Policy Paper 1). Author.

UP Planning and Development Research Foundation. (2014). *Informal settler families (ISF) socio-economic profile* [Unpublished report]. Author.

Urban Poor Associates. (2014). *Eviction monitor: 2014 annual report*. Author.

Villanueva, P. A. G., & Salazar, J. N. P. (2015). Patronage politics and clientelism in housing welfare: The case of Gawad Kalinga (GK) villages in Parañaque City, the Philippines. *Indonesian Journal of Government and Politics*, 6(2), 170–185.

World Bank. (2016). *Closing the gap in affordable housing in the Philippines: Policy paper for the national housing summit on housing and urban development*. Author.

8 Past resistance, present challenges

The law's contribution to the urban integration of Villa 31

Pablo Vitale

Introduction[1]

In Buenos Aires, informal settlements known as *villas* are home to a relatively smaller portion of the population than in other Latin American capitals. However, their rapid growth, the stigma surrounding these neighbourhoods, and the stark divide between living conditions in the *villas* and the rest of the city make them particularly controversial places. Villa 31, today known as Barrio Carlos Mugica,[2] is unquestionably the city's most famous *villa* given its longevity, scale and central location. This strategic position has been a pivotal factor behind successive eviction attempts spearheaded by constitutional governments and dictatorships — both conservative and progressive — for nearly a century. In recent decades, this neighbourhood has emerged as a paradigmatic case study of the community's legal recourse in battles over urban space and the right to live in the city. Currently, after an intense struggle that involved the deployment of a wide range of legal, political and social tools, a comprehensive neighbourhood improvement process is now underway. Although fraught with enormous risks and challenges, it nonetheless stands as a remarkable achievement for the community, bolstered by a vast support network that included academic teams, civil society organizations and public advocacy agencies.

The developments of the past decade and a half reflect a pivotal shift in state policies, from outright neglect and the threat of eviction to regulatory recognition and the building of infrastructure, facilities and housing in the neighbourhood. To examine these transformative years, background context is provided, and three distinct stages of the community's struggle are identified. The link between legal and political mobilization will be analysed in each of these stages, while also introducing several distinctive aspects of the problems of the *villas* and their community organization. The following section thus covers background on Villa 31, its collective organization and relevant legislation up to the early 21st century. The next section covers the first stage (2006–2009) of community struggle, when it moved from defence to offense by using judicial strategies against eviction threats. In the second stage (2009–2015), a system of representation for the community is formalized, and

DOI: 10.4324/9781003538806-8

Law 3343 — covering the regularization and urban integration of the *villa* — is enacted, but not fulfilled. The third stage (2015 to the present) covers the ongoing progress and emerging challenges of urbanization.[3]

Through each of these stages, this chapter will attempt to retrace a process of tremendous legal, community and political productivity, interwoven with collective mobilization experiences that have had a decisive impact on the city's three branches of government. Moreover, in this case, significant strides have been made towards realizing the right to the city for Villa 31's populace, rippling outward to influence policies for other *villas* in Buenos Aires and the rest of the country.

Background, collective organization and legislation

Founded in the 1930s, Villa 31 was Buenos Aires' first *villa* and has since received successive waves of migrants. It is located in the Retiro neighbourhood, which hosts the city's largest port terminal as well as three major train stations, the intercity bus terminal and a concentration of international hotels, offices and upscale housing. Within this environment, Villa 31 is tucked between railway grids and the Puerto Nuevo (New Port), making it centrally located yet marginal.

Due to this strategic location, the fate of the *villa* and its residents has been mired in controversy and disputes from the start. The resistance of residents and neighbourhood organizations has been shaped by the constantly looming threat of eviction, combined with unfulfilled promises of legalization and urban integration.

The *villa* experienced its largest population influxes in the mid-1970s and in recent years, while the most intense and far-reaching eviction attempt occurred during the last military dictatorship (1976–1982). Of the approximately 40,000 residents who were living in Villa 31 in 1976, only 38 families managed to remain, resisting eradication through various means, including legal action (Blaustein, 2001; Oszlak, 1991).[4] This history of the community's legal recourse is deeply ingrained in accounts from its longstanding leaders.

Although it represents a single region under one regulatory framework, the Barrio Mugica is currently divided into two large sectors: Villa 31 proper[5] and Villa 31 bis,[6] which began to grow in 1996 after the eviction of a strip of houses for the construction of the Presidente Illia highway — which, incidentally, serves as a border between the two sections.[7]

For a better understanding of the community framework that underpins legal empowerment processes, it is helpful to examine several of the most widespread forms of territorial organization and their links with state structures.

Collective organization: Self-management and public services

Community organization in the *villas* is deeply linked to the state's underperformance when it comes to providing services and infrastructure. Residents must resort to diverse forms of community self-management and collective action to get their needs addressed. More than just sporadic, reactive responses, neighbourhood organization, protests and appeals have been the bedrock for a significant portion of the public policies and infrastructure developed in the *villas*. For instance, residents often install electricity or sewage lines themselves, which are subsequently maintained by public bodies, while soup kitchens[8] created to respond to food scarcity crises have evolved into community dining hall programs. Likewise, various state institutions and services that operate in the *villas* have roots in self-managed community initiatives, ranging from kindergartens to educational and recreational spaces to health centres (see Vitale, 2016, among others).

This dynamic of bottom-up organization, shifting from emergency response to the management of infrastructure and facilities, and from there to demands for structural interventions, is replicated across all *villas* but is particularly pronounced in Villa 31. This is largely the result of its exclusion from the few *villa* urbanization programs implemented in recent decades. This failure to act by different governments stems from the interest of real estate developers in the land on which the *villa* is located, and the complex networks of state influence exerted over it by the city and national governments.[9] Community practices in response to state neglect and threats constitute a genuine exercise in the management of public services within the neighbourhood. These practices, in turn, are critical precursors for the community demand for structural responses to the substandard living conditions in the *villas* and for community participation in neighbourhood improvement processes involving state intervention.

These conflictive — and sometimes collaborative or co-productive — arrangements with the state and its agencies lay the foundations for a dynamic link between community leaders, organizations and public power. These relations are far removed from notions of a *lack of state presence* or a *mere informality*. The state's presence in the *villas* is welfare-based, deficient, threatening — even repressive — but it also involves a set of interlocutors who, depending on the public agency, forge ties of familiarity or hostility with the community.

These complex connections with the state provide the cornerstones for building legal resources into the repertoire of community actions. This legal facet manifests itself, on the one hand, in the growing regulatory recognition of the right of *villa* residents to remain in their neighbourhoods and the subsequent obligation of the state to match their housing standards with those of the rest of the city. On the other hand, the state's failure to implement these regulations resulted in an intense campaign to the judiciary to demand action, which led to rulings that confirmed the recognition of the rights of *villa* residents, as discussed below.

The connection between these previously informal communities with the three branches of the state was reshaped and developed on the basis of a regulatory framework that was constructed between the mid-1990s and early 2000s, in step with the constant threat of eviction from Villa 31.

Regulatory framework: Constitutional and legal recognition (1994–2006)

In 1994, modifications to the national constitution had two significant implications for the *villas*. The City of Buenos Aires was granted autonomy, and international agreements recognizing the right to decent housing in urban areas were given constitutional recognition.[10]

Since the country's return to democracy in 1983, public authorities had been promoting, at least on paper, the relocation and integration of the *villas*. However, in 1996, a section of Villa 31 was forcibly evicted to clear the way for construction of a highway. That same year, the Constitution of the Autonomous City of Buenos Aires (CCABA, 1996) reaffirmed the right to housing and shelter, specifically geared towards giving "priority to people in sectors of critical poverty and with special low-income needs" (art. XXXI).[11]

In 1998, the city legislature passed Law 148 (1998), giving "priority attention to the social and housing problems in the *villas*". This law established a five-year implementation period, regular reporting of progress and the execution of all necessary measures to ensure that its objectives were met. It also created a Participatory Coordinating Commission "for the diagnosis, proposal, planning and monitoring of the execution of social housing policies developed under the framework of the law" (Law 148, 1998, art III). This commission included members of the local executive and legislative branches, as well as representatives from the *villas* and transitional housing units. However, there was once again a mismatch between the legislatively declared intentions and reality on the ground.

It would take another three years before the Program for the Settlement, Integration and Transformation of Villas (PRIT) was launched as the first concrete initiative under the Law, which had highlighted

> the need to implement a program that specifically provides a comprehensive solution to the social, housing and urban problem in the *villas* of the City of Buenos Aires, subject to principles of social integration and participation of the affected sectors.
>
> (Decreto nº 206/GCABA/01, 2001)

Despite exciting initial momentum, the PRIT was gradually underfunded, so its reach proved to be more limited than its objectives (The Center for Housing Rights Against Evictions [COHRE] & Asociación Civil por la Igualdad y la Justicia [ACIJ], 2008).

Reflections on legislation and collective organization in the *villas*

The extensive legislation sanctioning the state's duty to ensure adequate housing conditions in the *villas* represented a pivotal shift, effectively revoking the illegality previously ascribed to these neighbourhoods and their residents. The failure to enforce constitutional provisions and local laws meant the state itself became the transgressor, with its actions (and inaction) rendering it liable in local courts. Initial lawsuits aimed to shed light on the city government's discriminatory practices while seeking remediation measures, but progressively evolved into structural demands for urbanization.

With this shift, compliance with the law went from a threat (evicting squatters) to formal recognition of longstanding demands (settlement and urbanization) — profoundly impacting the dynamic between public institutions and *villa* leaders and residents.

However, the change ushered in by the new regulatory framework's recognition of rights has been gradual and non-linear. At first, residents collaborated with organizations and legal activists to pursue legal recognition of their right to access specific public services. These initial steps cultivated a rights-based narrative that would, years later, catalyse into the executive branch's push for structural policies for the reurbanization[12] of the *villas.*

Stage 1: From defence to offense (2006–2009)

The continual violation of rights in the *villas*, the widening chasm between regulations and their enforcement following the integration of *villa* urbanization laws, and burgeoning legal and community activism converged in a process of judicial recognition of rights that started in Buenos Aires in the mid-2000s. This process was marked by unprecedented and intense social and legal interactions between community representatives, legal actors and a remarkably receptive judiciary.[13]

Water and health risk in Villa 31 bis

One of the first collective litigation efforts seeking better social and housing conditions in Villa 31 was a lawsuit filed jointly by a group of residents from blocks 11, 12, 13 and 14 of the recently occupied Villa 31 bis[14] and the Asociación Civil por la Igualdad y la Justicia (ACIJ) in the years following Argentina's 2001 political crisis.[15] The goal was to secure recognition of the human right to clean, safe and uninterrupted drinking water.

In a city with near-total coverage of sewage and drinking water networks, the local government at the time provided water to the affected sector by tanker trucks. However, in June 2006, it suspended even this service, impacting 304 families and prompting the filing of an *acción de amparo* — an appeal for the protection of constitutional rights (Mesel et al., 2018). The court issued an injunction ordering the city to restore the water supply, and in November 2006, ruled in favour of the lawsuit, a decision subsequently upheld by the Court of Appeals in July 2007.

Just a month after initiating the drinking water appeal in July 2006, a group of Villa 31 bis residents and ACIJ filed an additional lawsuit against the city government due to the lack of adequate pavement and sewage and storm water networks, for the purpose of preventing serious health risks.[16]

These two lawsuits sparked nascent collective organization within the affected blocks. This was one of the most significant impacts of these legal actions as they focused on the *villa*'s most disadvantaged and least organized areas. A *villa*'s most recently formed sectors are often physically and symbolically marginalized; time and concerted efforts are needed to establish a connection with the broader territorial organizational structure.

Throughout these legal processes, hearings and fines imposed on officials became crucial tools for involving affected residents and pressuring the government to comply with rulings. Interestingly, several residents from sectors adjacent to the blocks included in the lawsuit felt "left out" and complained that the sentences in their favour fell short of addressing their needs. This "segmentation effect" can be seen when people affected by the same rights violations are divided based on whether they can access a legal solution, even in collective cases. While these neighbourhood tensions were resolved through conflict resolution and community organization, they reveal some of the challenges in the legal interpretation of social demands.

Board for Urbanization: From attempted eviction to legal battle

In those same years between 2006 and 2007, local organizations opened avenues for dialogue with national state agencies, which began to give shape to the representation of Villa 31. These interactions were at times contentious, with the head of one national agency having voiced earlier support for evictions.[17] A broad coalition, comprising several neighbours, human rights organizations, legal activist NGOs (ACIJ and COHRE), professionals and teams from national universities, was the precursor of the Board for the Urbanization of Villa 31–31 bis established a few months later.

The expectations generated by this dialogue with national bodies were bolstered by the climate of uncertainty that emerged during the 2007 election campaign for Chief of Government of Buenos Aires, when the relocation of Villa 31 was once again suggested. Although these avenues of negotiation ultimately fell through,[18] the foundations of a space for neighbourhood coordination, with technical backing from organizations and academic institutions, were now laid.

The *villas* played a significant role during this 2007 election, particularly as one of the central themes for the centre-right candidate: Mauricio Macri, who was elected, had stated his intention to evict Villa 31–31 bis, at least partially, on several occasions.

After several inconclusive hostile announcements (such as the proposed measure of fencing off the neighbourhood and restrictions on the entry of people and construction material), the city government filed a legal appeal to stop work on the houses in the *villa*, alleging that there was a risk that they would collapse. In response to both this appeal and the city's failure to take action to maintain the already precarious services, in late 2008, the Board staged a blockade of the highway that runs through Villa 31, a major route into the city. For eight hours, they held protests to demand an open dialogue with the city government to find solutions to urgent needs and to demand the urbanization of the neighbourhood (Videla, 2008). The residents and their supporting organizations brought the case to court that same day, asking to appear in front of the authorities and demanding urbanization and compliance with the laws that recognize their rights.[19]

The local government's initial public response was confrontational,[20] but it shifted a few weeks later towards opening a space for negotiation with neighbourhood representatives of Villa 31–31 bis. These opportunities for dialogue came within the context of a redistribution of state responsibilities for the *villas*, to address the dispersion of authority across a range of different agencies (and which was driving the multiple deficits experienced in the *villas*).[21] The government's drastic change in strategy reflected in part an understanding that eviction was unfeasible.

Alongside the Board's territorial and negotiation efforts, the chair of the Legislature's Housing Commission began to advance a proposal for a law on the urbanization of the *villa*. [22] During those intense early years of the Board, the involvement of legal professionals from organizations like ACIJ and COHRE, coupled with defensive and offensive interactions with the courts and legislators, became formative experiences that legally empowered the engaged community of Villa 31 and its representatives. Although more structured legal training courses were also held, it was the authentic exchange of knowledge occurring within the Board's meetings and actions that substantively enhanced neighbourhood activists' comprehension and application of the law.

Considerations on legal strategies and neighbourhood organization

In this stage, new forms of community organization were backed by expert support (legal, urban planning, etc.). This contributed to a qualitative leap in action, from defensive claims to comprehensive demands. The role of the judiciary, in this sense, bolstered the community's position by validating their complaints about discriminatory treatment in service provision by the local government. However, it also had a fragmenting effect on both the responses by public authorities and the areas impacted. In this respect, there was also a disconnect between the high expectations raised by legal provisions, the judiciary's intervention in this regard, and the material effects they produced (laws and rulings alike). Translating community claims into legal language can lead to an overly narrow focus on specific thematic and spatial issues, because of the need to frame lawsuits in terms that the courts can legally entertain. Likewise, both the slow and lengthy nature of judicial responses and the executive branch's reluctance to enforce rulings further undermined the urgency of a need to uphold the violated rights in question.

However, alongside the formal rebuffs from the judiciary or non-compliance with the law in all its terms, specific improvements were achieved in different sectors of the neighbourhood. This demonstrates that legal conflicts can also have an indirect ripple effect that extends beyond the immediate rulings and legislation.

Stage 2: From law to implementation (2009–2015)

By 2009, the Board for Urbanization had already pulled off a series of high-profile actions that garnered considerable social and media attention. The November 2008 blockade of the Illia highway prompted a city prosecutor to criminally charge five neighbourhood leaders from the Board. However, the leaders' resounding acquittal by the presiding judge reaffirmed both the direction in which the neighbourhood struggle was heading and the judiciary's potential as an ally. Concurrently, at least nine lawsuits and precautionary measures regarding Villa 31–31 bis were pending in local administrative courts. These legal challenges targeted diverse objectives, such as public service provision,[23] opposing evictions[24] and electing neighbourhood representatives.[25] This recurrent turn to the judiciary signaled the intense incorporation of legal tactics into the *villa*'s fight. It also underscored the widespread nature of multiple community demands. These were locally rooted yet risked segmentation despite collectively providing evidence of discriminatory government treatment and structural rights violations. The demand for urbanization then emerged as a systemic response unifying these distinct but converging neighbourhood demands. To institutionally address them, the chair of the city legislature's Housing Commission crafted a proposed urbanization law for the *villa*, based on a preliminary draft by a team from University of Buenos Aires (UBA) Faculty of Architecture and Urban Design.

Villa *elections*

While community organization for urbanization was intensifying, a process to legalize the system of elections in the *villas* was also taking place. Its end goal was to ensure a democratic election of those who would represent the collective voice of the neighbourhood in institutional processes. A legislator and several neighbours filed a lawsuit requesting legal recognition of these neighbourhood representatives. In deciding the case, the judges resorted to legal creativity, appealing to activists and actors who were already working on behalf of the community to support implementation of a wide-reaching judgment, which could not be overseen directly by the court. In Villa 31, architect Fernández Castro from the UBA and promoter of the *villa*'s development project was appointed as "judicial auditor" and subsequently brought members of ACIJ onto the team. He was tasked with defining an interim system of community representation and coordination with local government that would serve until the election of delegates and neighbourhood councilors was called. This entire process converged with the discussion on the neighbourhood urbanization law (described in the following section): it took place during the same period and was driven by the same institutional, technical and community factors.

The judicial intervention resulted in a complex system that responded to the population's diverse needs for representation. To this end, delegates were elected, who then chose one councilor per sector, forming a neighbourhood council that has since become the highest political body in the community.

In Villa 31, the process of discussing the representation system was dynamically connected with debates on the urbanization law and its ruling. However, the legalization of elections in the *villas* proved an obstacle to territorial representation insofar as it became yet another bureaucratic hurdle to establishing spaces for state negotiation.

The urbanization law

Throughout 2009, the Board for Urbanization focused on promoting the urbanization law, mobilizing and lobbying the legislature for its approval. Finally, at year's end, Law 3343: Urbanization of Villas 31 and 31 Bis was unanimously passed. It proposes the regularization and urban integration of Villa 31, largely respecting the existing structure built by its residents.

The Law establishes that the "Multidisciplinary and Participative Management and Planning Board for the Urbanization of Villas 31–31 bis"[26] is responsible for providing specific implementation guidelines. This Board would include participation from national and local government agencies, public advocacy and technical bodies, as well as community representatives through delegates and neighbours.[27] The final 2011 ruling represented the culmination of intense coordination between the different levels of local state and neighbourhood stakeholders. Community participation shaped the content of the ruling, which recognized the role of the *villa*'s collective organization and established legal standards to follow.

Despite efforts at collective deliberation, the City's Legislature failed to approve the preliminary draft and it lost its parliamentary status, leaving Law 3343 as a generic reference. This gave the government a pretext for ignoring its obligation to comprehensively urbanize the *villa*, limiting itself to only minor works. Between 2011 and 2015, the state's performance in relation to the *villa* continued to be characterized by a lack of intervention and failure to fulfil its constitutional and legal duties, although it did develop a program of infrastructure improvements. Nonetheless, for residents, the threatening landscape of just a couple of years prior had drastically changed; the last attempt to evict Villa 31 was fading into memory, and a path for the city's other *villas* was being charted.

Reflections on the community's struggles, progress and setbacks

Law 3343 represented a significant achievement for the Villa 31 community, thanks to the efforts of its leaders and their technical and political allies. Despite the ongoing neglect by the state in providing a comprehensive response to the rights violations experienced by neighbourhood residents, the policies implemented by the local government marked a significant shift. They effectively halted previous eviction threats while also spurring at least some modest neighbourhood improvement works. These actions reflect a recurring pattern seen in similar cases: the government fails to meet formal commitments and comply with laws and court rulings, but does take steps to provide some level of service. The Villa 31 improvement plan, despite its limitations, would not have been conceivable without the impetus provided by Law 3343 and judicial rulings against the local government. Nor would it have been possible without the local government's rhetorical shift towards socio-urban integration, spurred by the conflicts and community mobilization of residents.

In this sense, the role of law was pivotal in Villa 31, serving as both a bulwark against eviction attempts and a tool to expose the government's discriminatory service provision practices. It also played a crucial role in legitimizing community demands and legally shaping the neighbourhood's urbanization as a systemic response to structural rights violations. These legal actions had tangible effects, even if not explicitly formalized, and laid the groundwork for future disputes, as evidenced from late 2015 onwards.

Stage 3: Urbanization (2015 to the present)

In December 2015, Horacio Rodríguez Larreta assumed office as Chief of Government of Buenos Aires, having served as Chief of Cabinet under the previous administration. His tenure ushered in several new developments, notably the initiation of urbanization processes in four *villas*, starting with Villa 31. To spearhead this effort, the Department of Social and Urban Integration (SISU) was established specifically for the urbanization of Villa 31. As of 2016, the Housing Institute took on the responsibility of executing urbanization processes in three other *villas*.

Faced with this new landscape, communities were challenged by having to anticipate the terms under which these processes would be developed, both procedurally and substantively. In addition to intense legal collaboration, initiatives emerged that reflected the evolving dynamics of territorial disputes. One such initiative was the Agreement for the Urbanization of Villas, which involved nearly a hundred social organizations, NGOs, public and academic institutions, referents and neighbours and laid the groundwork for a broad "consensus on the need for *villa* urbanization and the conditions under which it should occur, ensuring equitable rights for residents compared to the rest of the city" (Acuerdo por la Urbanizacion, n.d.-a).[28]

In line with these efforts (albeit under tensions that will be discussed below), SISU was tasked with the exclusive mission of *transforming Villa 31 into a neighbourhood* through a comprehensive urban plan. This plan encompasses basic infrastructure provision, urban connectivity, public space and housing and business habitability improvements, along with investments in social, educational and economic integration measures to align the neighbourhood with the surrounding city.

Tensions in the urbanization process

The initial financing for the urbanization process largely came from debt the local government took on with the Inter-American Development Bank (IDB) and the World Bank. Several significant works were planned, drawing inspiration from international models. For instance, initiatives such as relocating the city's Ministry of Education, constructing the new María Elena Walsh Education Hub and establishing a government headquarters within the *villa* were modeled after projects in cities like Medellín in the hope that urban-scale infrastructure would attract people from the rest of the city to the *villa*. Additionally, plans were made for an elevated park on the Illia highway, inspired by the New York High Line. However, the implementation of these projects faced challenges, including forced relocations to a housing complex that was developed without community participation and the subsequent community rejection of the project once it was allocated. This ultimately resulted in the entire project being shelved, despite substantial investment.

Furthermore, initiatives such as the proposed gourmet market La Boquería de Villa 31 (another failed project, in this case inspired by Barcelona's famous market) were also announced, and a McDonald's restaurant was opened in the neighbourhood. The IDB called in Pritzker Prize-winning architect Alejandro Aravena to design the offices it planned to install in the *villa*, and initiatives were announced such as the construction of a headquarters for the Museum of Latin American Art of Buenos Aires, owned by one of the country's largest real estate investors (no progress has been made to date). These initiatives reflect the international scope with which the process was approached and the role it played in the local government's urban marketing policy. None of the aforementioned projects involved neighbourhood participation, despite the provisions of Law 3343; nor was the community invited to participate in defining measures to improve existing housing and build new homes, or the basic infrastructure projects that were also being developed.

While the urbanization process marked a significant departure from previous policies towards Villa 31, the motivations behind this paradigm shift were mixed. In part, the shift reflected a recognition of the impracticality of eradicating the *villa*, whether due to political or urban planning realities or because of territorial conflict. In addition, efforts to bolster and urbanize the neighbourhood aimed to enhance real estate opportunities by increasing the value of the surrounding areas and facilitating the expansion of the port zone as an extension of Puerto Madero (see note 10).

The urbanization process also implies incorporating this area into the formal property market, which could become a major draw for investment. In this sense, it raises concerns in the medium to long term about the potential displacement of current residents due to increased costs and pressure from real estate developers to incorporate the neighbourhood into the formal market. Market forces could thereby achieve what the state was unable to do: drive residents from the area.[29]

These contradictory motivations behind urbanization, pitting the recognition of urban rights against making the area more lucrative for the real estate market, underscore the critical need to challenge the terms of the process. A significant share of neighbourhood leaders have expressed concerns that the original objective of eradication may persist through alternative means. They openly express fears of gentrification or a local form of market-driven displacement.

Despite representing a notable step forward, championed by the very government that once threatened the *villa*'s eviction in 2007, it is now feared that the urbanization process may potentially lead to forced eviction for economic reasons, as an offshoot of urban development.

New urbanization law

Despite pre-existing legal commitments, the urbanization of Villa 31 and Villa 31 bis was launched under the new government without clear planning and regulatory instruments for decision-making. It took until 2018, after a prolonged and contentious process, for a law to guide implementation to be enacted. Unlike previous urbanization laws, Law 6129 was not passed unanimously in the legislature due to concerns from the community, civil society organizations and advocacy groups.[30]

The law establishes guiding principles and specific components of the process, including housing improvements, construction of new housing, provision of infrastructure and basic services, regularization of property ownership and support for productive business activities. It also creates the "Participatory Management Council for the Urbanization Process of Barrio Padre Carlos Mugica" (CGP), which is tasked with supervising compliance with the law (Ley N.° 6129 [Law N.° 6129], 2018, art.vi).[31] However, the CGP has faced challenges in accessing updated, timely, and complete public information, hindering its ability to make decisions and effectively oversee the works executed by the government. Moreover, ensuring the meaningful participation of local residents in the design and execution stages of the interventions has proved difficult.

Near-final thoughts: Achievements and challenges

To paraphrase a classic 1960s activist film, it is difficult to demand urban development, it is even more difficult to turn it into law. But it's only afterwards, when we have won and the urbanization process starts, that the real difficulties begin.[32]

Enforcing rights involves different challenges than defensive or contentious moments at the community and legal levels. In the latter, simple statements appealing to basic rights suffice, even when building complex cases: avoiding evictions, claiming the right to equivalent services, denouncing risks from poor water or health services. But implementing a project of social and urban integration based on the decision of a previously neglectful and hostile executive branch raised the stakes exponentially due to the number of issues and experts involved (covering health, electricity, regulations, social/productive/commercial management, etc.), the lack of precedents at the local level, and tensions between neighbourhood, economic and political interests.

In this context, regulatory and judicial advances served to set state limits, provide enhanced security and establish general principles. But implementation is where seemingly subtle differences have a drastic impact on outcomes, as when regularization leads to market-driven evictions, miscalculated health services become substandard, or a lack of community participation leads to mass rejection of housing solutions — to cite just a handful of observed examples.

The judiciary usually offers few or unsatisfactory answers to these "subtleties", so former allies may now take counterproductive positions, hindering actions or supporting poor public decisions and undermining progress.

As of 2024, the process has made significant headway but is also experiencing tremendous delays in the completion of fundamental works. It faces serious risks from a change in local authority (despite being from the same party, the city's new leaders, elected in 2023, are more averse to investing in the *villas*) especially given the country's economic crisis.

Conclusions

This analysis of the conflicts and judicial processes that unfolded over the past decade and a half in Villa 31 has entailed reconstructing the many facets of a period when state intervention in this neighbourhood and other *villas* radically shifted. Recognizing the aspirations of communities living in these areas, first at the regulatory and judicial levels, then through public policies for urbanization, was the result of urban disputes, legal strategies and broad intersectorial connections. The process's distinctive richness lies in how *villa* organizations and leaders leveraged the law to influence state policies, though not without facing tensions, risks and challenges.

To summarize, this chapter has traced the ascending chain of differentiated but interrelated contentious stages related to (1) the provision of public services, infrastructure and living conditions; (2) residents' representation in decision-making; and (3) the dispute over urban land and Villa 31's urbanization.

These three key issues were subject to conflict and negotiation, involving diverse forms of collaboration and confrontation between state entities and local organizations. Residents' demands can be conceptualized on a gradient ranging from more defensive, urgent claims — such as access to basic services — to demands for fundamental, lasting solutions that will align living conditions with the rest of the city. Throughout, the organization and representation of the *villa*'s residents served as a form of mediation. However, this analytical distinction between stages dynamically manifests in collective action processes and interaction with state entities.

What initially appears a very specific claim can quickly evolve into a broader challenge to public power and demand for urban integration. Conversely, general demands for compliance with urbanization laws can have targeted effects, such as improving certain infrastructures and services.

When it comes to Villa 31's journey, several factors contributed to the enormous social and legal productivity of the process.[33] A diverse array of actors and alliances managed to sustain momentum while adaptively reinventing themselves as circumstances changed — redefining roles, adjusting terms of collaboration, etc. Additionally, the strong territorial presence of organizations and allied professionals provided access to legal and technical tools, while also involving community members and representatives in key decisions and facilitating a cross-pollination of neighbourhood knowledge and professional expertise.

Likewise, collaborative and co-productive relations with the state unfolded throughout, as both governmental and local stances shifted over time. Community actions were not limited to a single institutional pressure point, but rather applied strategically across the local state's three branches (legislative, executive and judicial) as each proved more or less permeable, reticent or hostile to popular demands.

Ultimately, as an effect of the legal empowerment processes developed during this period, there was intense community participation in drafting standards, deploying actions to demand compliance, executing policies and determining guiding criteria and the subsequent monitoring of implementation.

As a final reflection, over the analysed period, the framework of law and rights for the community transformed from a threat ("the *villa* is illegal and must be removed") into recognition, albeit unfulfilled ("it is illegal for the government to violate urbanization rights and laws and must enforce them"). This impressive achievement does not negate the immense expectations the law creates within the community, nor the risk that such expectations may prove unrealistic given the gap between legal victories and the changes enacted, the concessions made in translating neighbourhood demands into legal frameworks, and the potential for legal actors to overshadow local leadership.[34] The Villa 31 process overcame these tensions through diverse community empowerment strategies.

Presently, the law serves as an implementation guide, which proves particularly complex in light of all the "subtleties" that come with implementing urbanization processes. In this role, the law may prove less productive than when used to defend the rights of the *villa* and its residents. The current challenges of the urbanization process were not contemplated by the formal, prescriptive definitions of the law which, until recently, were effective and fit for purpose.

What seems unavoidable, despite the aforementioned tensions, is that the law remains fundamentally an ally, a collective tool and window of possibility for Villa 31's community in its struggle to substantively improve living conditions through its urban integration.

Notes

1 This chapter builds upon insights from previous published and unpublished research. The author is indebted to Luciana Bercovich for her meticulous review and guidance in adapting these reflections to make them easier to understand, although I bear sole responsibility for any excessive detail or challenges in succinctly explaining the complexity of the process.

2 This chapter refers alternately to "Villa 31", "Villa 31–31 bis" and "Barrio Padre Carlos Mugica", all of which denote the same neighbourhood, as defined in Law No. 6129 which addresses its social and urban integration. In Buenos Aires, informal settlements, currently home to approximately 10 percent of the city's population, are colloquially known as *villas*. In other Latin American countries, these types of settlements are called *favela, barriada, callampa*, or *cantegrill*. Popularized in the mid-20th century as *villa miseria* or *villa de emergencia* (informal terms for slums or shantytowns), the nationally adopted term today is *barrio popular* (low-income neighbourhood), based on Law 27,694, which was enacted in 2018 as a product of a broad political consensus driven by local and partner organizations.

3 This period has been discussed in previous articles, most recently by Mesel and Vitale (2019).

4 For an extensive and exhaustively documented history of Villa 31, see Snitcofsky (2022). On *villas* in general, see the various publications by María Cristina Cravino (2006, 2008, 2009).

5 Villa 31 is subdivided into the Güemes (which has the highest density in the *villa*), YPF, Comunicaciones/Correo, Inmigrantes and Autopista neighbourhoods. The latter had partially relocated as of 2019.

6 Villa 31 bis is subdivided into the Playón Este and Oeste, Virgen de Luján, Ferroviario and San Martín sectors.

7 Two sections of public housing were added in 2016 as part of the urbanization process: Containera and YPF.

8 These are a community self-management method for providing meals; a core group of residents collects food to prepare meals shared with the community.

9 Various development plans for the area were announced during the 1990s and 2000s. These provided continuity to the neighbourhood of Puerto Madero, adjacent to Villa 31, which was developed as a large-scale urban intervention in the mid-1990s. One of its hallmarks is the construction of high-income housing.

10 These include the Universal Declaration of Human Rights (Art. 25.1), American Declaration on the Rights and Duties of Man (Art. XI), Convention on the Rights of the Child (Art. 27), Convention on the Elimination of All Forms of Racial Discrimination (Art. 5), Convention on the Elimination of All Forms of Discrimination against Women (Art. 14), American Convention on Human Rights (Art. 26), Convention 169 of the International Labour Organization, and General Comments 4 and 7 of the United Nations Committee on Economic, Social and Cultural Rights.

11 "The City recognizes the right to decent housing and adequate habitat. To this end: (1) It progressively resolves the housing, infrastructure and services deficit, giving priority to people in the sectors of critical poverty and with special needs of scarce resources. (2) It sponsors the incorporation of vacant properties and promotes self-managed plans, urban and social integration of marginalized inhabitants, recovery of precarious housing, and regularization of ownership and land registry, with criteria of permanent settlement" (CCABA, 1996, art. XXXI).

12 In the article we will speak indistinctly of urbanization, reurbanization or urban integration, but the nomination of neighbourhood improvement processes is part of the discussion given in these processes. In the case of Villa 31, the demand was

stated as "urbanization". But the organizations of other villas, such as Villa 20, consider that the neighbourhood is already urbanized and that the intervention should repair the deficit caused by the state's omissions in the provision of services, so the demand is for "reurbanization". Meanwhile, the more precise concept, incorporated into National Law No. 27.453, sanctioned in 2018, is "socio-urban integration".

13 Civil society organizations like ACIJ and COHRE, alongside public defenders from the General Guardianship Office and the Public Defender's Office of the City of Buenos Aires, played instrumental roles. The city's litigation, administrative, and tax courts were also involved.

14 Since the *villas* are not officially registered, there is no cadastral nomenclature as there is elsewhere in the city, and the lots are identified by block number and house number.

15 In December 2001, a political, social and economic crisis broke out in Argentina, leading to the resignation of President De La Rua, and a complex presidential succession that included the transfer of power between five presidents in two weeks. Also, during those months, high unemployment and poverty rates led to episodes of looting of supermarkets, as well as recurrent street protests.

16 See ACIJ (2012): https://acij.org.ar/compromiso-del-gcba-para-paliar-el-riesgo-sanitario-de-villa-31-y-31-bis/

17 For example, a relationship with the National Land Commission for Social Habitat was forged that would last for several years. In mid-2007, an election year, negotiations were opened with the National Agency for the Administration of State Property (ONABE), which had authority over most of the land on which Villa 31–31 bis is located. Several meetings were held between territorial representatives and ONABE authorities, and it seemed that progress was being made towards a settlement and neighbourhood improvement project. This negotiation process came as a surprise to neighbours and those who were following the alternatives for the neighbourhood dispute, since the head of ONABE had declared his willingness to evict recent settlers from the land under his jurisdiction, and later expanded on his position to the press by affirming that Villa 31 bis "is a space where marginal business is conducted by small economic groups and their political point men who charge those who live there between 200 and 300 pesos" (Vitale, 2013).

18 The same day that the first framework agreement was signed between local residents and ONABE, the official responsible was absent and failed to reopen dialogue (see Videla, 2008).

19 A timeline of the process can be found here: https://acij.org.ar/wp-content/uploads/2014/08/L%C3%ADnea-tiempo-causa-ACIJ-por-urbanizaci%C3%B3n-de-Villa-31-y-31-bis.pdf (Asociación Civil por la Igualdad y la Justicia, 2014)

20 The city government even took the protest to court by bringing charges against the neighbourhood leaders who led the blockade of the highway as noted in the next section.

21 The Management and Social Intervention Unit was created, while the powers of the City Housing Institute (IVC) over *villas* and settlements were almost completely removed (Ricciardi & Sehtman, 2008). Likewise, the 2009 budget of the Government of Buenos Aires slashed allocations for the implementation of housing policies in *villas* by more than half compared to 2008. For Villa 31–31 bis, ACIJ (2009) states: "no specific allocations for construction work have been made (2005–2008), and there is no budget for 2009 either. This is despite the fact that local courts have ordered the city government to implement a construction plan to resolve the sanitary risk in Villa 31 bis. According to the case, in April 2008, the IVC presented a construction plan, approved and budgeted for by the board of directors. These works have not started, and there are no budget allocations scheduled for 2009, which casts doubt on the effective compliance with the court ruling".

22 The proposed law was rooted in a preliminary draft prepared by a team from the UBA's Faculty of Architecture and Urban Design, led by architect Javier Fernández Castro. This project was based on the efforts of the technical team and the promotion of participatory spaces with local residents, using several of the actions taken in the *favelas* of Rio de Janeiro as a model (Vitale, 2013).

23 Lawsuits include: Health risk, File Nos. 20898/0 and 24045/1; water supply, File Nos. 20898 and 31796/0; school transport, File No. 32839/0.

24 The lawsuits against the evictions are: For block 107, File No. 30514/0; for the entire Villa district, File No. 31699/0.

25 The lawsuits against the evictions are: For block 107, File No. 30514/0; for the entire Villa district, File No. 31699/0.

26 The Management and Planning Board includes representatives from the Ministries of Environment and Public Space, Urban Development and Social Development; the City's Housing Institute; the City Public Defender's Office; the president and vice president of the Housing Commission of the Legislature of Buenos Aires; the president and vice president of the Urban Planning Commission of the Legislature of Buenos Aires; and the president and vice president of the Budget Commission of the Legislature of Buenos Aires. These permanent members will invite national and railway company representatives, members of the Housing Commission of the National Congress, the technical team that developed the urbanization project, and professionals from the University of Buenos Aires to participate. Likewise, "neighbourhood delegates and residents will be called to participate, who will be able to express their voice within the scope of the same, and who will be able to participate in any decision that specifically affects them" (Ley 3343: Urbanización de Las Villas 31 y 31 Bis [Law 3343: Urbanization of Villas 31 and 31 Bis], 2009).

27 However, at the time the law was passed, judicial intervention to legalize neighbourhood representation had not yet been completed, which weakened the wording regarding community participation in the regulations, at least from the perspective of certain neighbourhood organizations. For a more detailed analysis of the law, see Cravino et al. (2016).

28 The "Agreement for the Urbanization of the Villas" includes ten points/proposals for the socio-urban integration of the settlements and was signed by more than 100 social organizations, NGOs, public and academic institutions, referents and neighbors, with the aim of achieving a broad consensus on the need to integrate the villas, and improve the conditions in which the urbanization processes should be carried out, so that the inhabitants of the villas see their rights guaranteed on equal terms with those of the rest of the city.

See *Acuerdo por la Urbanización de Villas [Agreement for the Urbanization of Villas]*, available at https://acuerdoporlaurbanizacion.org/

29 In this regard, measures and policies were discussed with organizations promoting the Agreement for the Urbanization of Villas, considering community expectations and perspectives, in order to prevent market-driven displacement. These were published in a "Documento complentario" (Complementary document) to "Acuerdo por la urbanization des las villas" entitled "Políticas de gestión de suelo en procesos de reurbanización de villas" (Land management policies in villa reurbanization processes) (Acuerdo por la Urbanizacion, n.d.-b).

30 See the letter signed by 10 of the 11 neighbourhood councilors demanding changes to the draft law (ACIJ, 2018): https://acij.org.ar/villa-31-la-ley-precisa-de-cambios-significativos/

31 The CGP includes neighbourhood representatives, the city's Public Defender's Office, the Public Guardianship Office, the Public Defender's Ministry, the Housing and Urban Planning Commissions of the Legislature, the community boards and SISU, with the participation of national government agencies and civil society organizations, including ACIJ.

32 "It is difficult to start a revolution. It is even more difficult to continue it. And the hardest thing is to win it. But it is afterwards, when we have won, that the real difficulties begin". Former Algerian independence fighter Saadi Yacef wrote these words for the character of Larbi Ben M'hidi in Gillo Pontecorvo's film *The Battle of Algiers* (1966).

33 Here we return to the conclusions of Vitale et al. (2019).

34 Some of these tensions can be found in O'Donnell, 2002.

References

Acuerdo por la Urbanizacion. (n.d.-a). *El acuerdo por la urbanización de villas* [*Agreement for the urbanization of villas*].https://acuerdoporlaurbanizacion.org/.

Acuerdo por la Urbanizacion. (n.d.-b). *Documento complementario: Políticas de gestión de suelo en procesos de reurbanización de villas* [*Complementary document: Land management policies in villa reurbanization processes*]. https://acuerdoporlaurbanizacion.org/wp-content/uploads/2017/12/DOC-SUELO-%C3%BAltima-versi%C3%B3n-AUV.pdf.

Asociación Civil por la Igualdad y la Justicia. (2009). *Presupuesto 2009: Un análisis sobre el grado de avance en la promoción del derecho a la educación, a la igualdad y a la vivienda digna* [*Budget 2009: An analysis of progress in promoting the right to education, equality and adequate housing*] [Unpublished document].

Asociación Civil por la Igualdad y la Justicia. (2012, July 11). *Compromiso del GCBA para paliar el riesgo sanitario de Villa 31 y 31 bis* [*Commitment of the GCBA to alleviate the sanitary risk in Villa 31 and 31 bis*]. https://acij.org.ar/compromiso-del-gcba-para-paliar-el-riesgo-sanitario-de-villa-31-y-31-bis/.

Asociación Civil por la Igualdad y la Justicia. (2014). *Case of urbanization of Villa 31 and Villa 31 bis (Padre Mugica neighborhood)*. https://acij.org.ar/wp-content/uploads/2014/08/L%C3%ADnea-tiempo-causa-ACIJ-por-urbanizaci%C3%B3n-de-Villa-31-y-31-bis.pdf.

Asociación Civil por la Igualdad y la Justicia. (2018, November 10). *Villa 31: La ley precisa de cambios significativos* [*Villa 31: The law requires significant changes*]. https://acij.org.ar/villa-31-la-ley-precisa-de-cambios-significativos/.

Blaustein, E. (2001). *Prohibido vivir aquí. Una historia de los planes de erradicación de las villas de la última dictadura* [*Forbidden to live here. A history of the slum eradication plans of the last dictatorship*]. Comisión Municipal de la Vivienda.

Centre on Housing Rights and Evictions (COHRE) & La Asociación Civil por la Igualdad y la Justicia (ACIJ). (2008, January 2). *El IVC frente a las villas de la Ciudad: Poco derecho y mucha discrecionalidad* [*The IVC vs. The slums of the City: Little right and a lot of discretion*]. Author.

Constitución de la Ciudad Autónoma de Buenos Aires del 1 de octubre de 1996 (CCABA). [*Constitution of the Autonomous City of Buens Airies*] (1996). Government of the Autonomous City of Buenos Aires. www.eleccionesciudad.gob.ar/leyesynormas/ccba.pdf.

Cravino, C., Pilo, S., & Vitale, P. (2016). Villa 31 y 31 bis: La lucha por la urbanización, la sanción de la Ley 3.343 y el rol de la Justicia [Villa 31 and 31 bis: The struggle for urbanization, the enactment of Law 3.343 and the role of the Justice System]. *Revista Institucional de La Defensa Pública de La Ciudad Autónoma de Buenos Aires*, 6(10), 300–313.

Cravino, M. C. (2006). *Las villas de la ciudad. Mercado e informalidad urbana* [*The slums of the city. Market and urban informality*]. Universidad Nacional de General Sarmiento.

Cravino, M. C. (2008). *Vivir en la villa. Relatos, trayectorias y estrategias habitacionales* [*Living in the slum. Stories, trajectories and housing strategies*]. Universidad Nacional de General Sarmiento.

Cravino, M. C. (2009). *Entre el arraigo y el desalojo. La Villa 31 de Retiro. Derecho a la ciudad, capital inmobiliario y gestión urbana* [*Between rooting and eviction. Villa 31 de Retiro. Right to the city, real estate capital and urban management*]. Universidad Nacional de General Sarmiento.

Decreto No 206/Gcaba/01 (2001). Government of the Autonomous City of Buenos Aires.

Law 148. (1998). *De Atención Prioritaria a La Problemática Social y Habitacional En Las Villas y Núcleos Habitacionales Transitorios* [*Law 148 1998: Priority Attention to Social and Housing Problems in Shantytowns and Transitional Housing Centers*]. La Legislatura De La Ciudad Autonoma De Buenos Aires. https://boletinoficial.buenosaires.gob.ar/normativaba/norma/1280.

Law 3343. (2009). *Urbanización de Las Villas 31 y 31 Bis* [*Law 3343: Urbanization of Villas 31 and 31 Bis*]. https://defensoria.org.ar/normativas-cdh/ley-3343-urbanizacion-de-las-villas-31-y-31-bis/.

Law 6129. (2018). Gobierno de la Ciudad Autónoma de Buenos Aires.

Mesel, F., Valentini, M., & Vitale, P. (2018). El derecho y sus usos en el hábitat informal de la ciudad de Buenos Aires. In A. Rincón Patiño & A. Correa Cárdenas (Eds.), *Desarrollo territorial, reasentamiento y desplazamiento de población: Realidad, política pública y derechos en la ciudad latinoamericana del siglo XXI* (pp. 246–285). Universidad Nacional de Colombia, Personería de Medellín.

Mesel, F., & Vitale, P. (2019). La Villa 31: La larga lucha por la reurbanización [La Villa 31: The long struggle for redevelopment]. In N. Echegoyemberry, S. Pilo, L. Bercovich, & M. Almela (Eds.), *Empoderamiento Jurídico y Abogacía Comunitaria en Latinoamérica* (pp. 50–60). Asociación Civil por la Igualdad y la Justicia.

O'Donnell, G. (2002). Las poliarquías y la (in)efectividad de la ley en América Latina [Polyarchies and the (in)effectiveness of the law in Latin America]. In J. E. Méndez, G. O'Donnell, & P. S. Pinheiro (Eds.), *La (in)efectividad de la ley y la exclusión en América Latina* (pp. 305–336). Paidós.

Oszlak, O. (1991). *Merecer la ciudad: Los pobres y el derecho al espacio urbano* [*Deserving the city: The poor and the right to urban space*]. Centro de Estudios de Estado y Sociedad. http://repositorio.cedes.org/handle/123456789/3942.

Pontecorvo, G. (Director). (1966). *The Battle of Algiers* [Film]. Igor Film and Casbah Film.

Ricciardi, V., & Sehtman, A. (2008). *Fragmentación e ineficiencia. Breve descripción y análisis preliminar de las recientes transformaciones en la política de villas del Gobierno de la Ciudad [Fragmentation and inefficiency. Brief description and preliminary analysis of recent transformations in the City Government's slum policy]* [Conference presentation]. Seminario Ciudad y programas de hábitat [City and Habitat Programs Seminar], Universiad Nacional de General Sarmiento (UNGS), Los Polvorines, Argentina, December 4–5.

Snitcofsky, V. (2022). *Historia de las Villas en la Ciudad de Buenos Aires. De los orígenes hasta nuestros días* [*History of the Villas in the City of Buenos Aires. From the origins to the present day*]. Tejido Urbano — Bisman Ediciones.

Videla, E. (2008, November 21). Tras el corte, la Villa 31 tiene un proyecto [After the blockade, the Villa 31 has a project]. *Página 12*. www.pagina12.com.ar/diario/sociedad/3-115361-2008-11-21.html.

Vitale, P. (2013). Entre hechos y derechos. Políticas públicas y normativa hacia las villas de Buenos Aires [Between facts and rights. Public policies and regulations towards the slums of Buenos Aires]. In T. Bolívar & J. Erazo Espinosa (Eds.), *Los lugares del hábitat y la inclusión* (pp. 369–390). FLACSO/CLACSO/Ministerio de Desarrollo Urbano y Vivienda.

Vitale, P. (2016). De la protesta a la propuesta. Acción colectiva territorial y gestión de políticas en villas de Buenos Aires [From protest to proposal. Territorial collective action and policy management in Buenos Aires slums]. In P. Abramo, M. Rodríguez, & J. Erazo (Eds.), *Ciudades populares en disputa: ¿Acceso a suelo urbano para todos?* (pp. 237–264). Ediciones Abya-Yala/CLACSO/Universidad Federal de Río de Janeiro/Universidad Politécnica Salesiana. https://dspace.ups.edu.ec/handle/123456789/12829.

Vitale, P., Echegoyemberry, M. N., Mesel, F., & Valentini, M. (2019). Prácticas de empoderamiento jurídico y abogacía comunitaria en latinoamérica: Asentamiento y pobreza urbana [Legal Empowerment Practices and Community Advocacy in Latin America: Settlement and Urban Poverty]. In N. Echegoyemberry, S. Pilo, L. Bercovich, & M. Almela (Eds.), *Empoderamiento Jurídico y Abogacía Comunitaria en Latinoamérica*. Asociación Civil por la Igualdad y la Justicia.

9 Here to stay

Using legal strategies to claim rights in informal settlements in South Africa

Lauren Royston, Thato Masiangoako and Nerishka Singh[1]

Introduction

The transformative nature of South Africa's Constitution lies in the justiciability of both civil and political and socio-economic rights. This provides an enabling legal framework for the use of litigation to protect and advance the rights of poor and marginalized groups. The shack dwellers movement Abahlali baseMjondolo (Abahlali), which is regarded as South Africa's largest movement of the organized poor, has used the law to advance the rights of informal settlement residents. Those efforts have given rise to a rich housing jurisprudence that has shifted the power dynamics between the propertied and the landless in post-1994[2] South Africa and improved the balance between the right to property and the right to housing.

This chapter draws on the authors' experiences at the Socio-Economic Rights Institute of South Africa (SERI) in informal settlement research and advocacy, especially with Abahlali. We also reflect more broadly on the use of legal empowerment in informal settlements in South Africa.

SERI uses litigation, research and advocacy in mutually reinforcing ways to realize socio-economic rights. It works with groups and individuals, other non-governmental organizations (NGOs), community-based organizations (CBOs) and social movements like Abahlali baseMjondolo. SERI's approach is client-led, and explicit about amplifying the voices of partners — not speaking for them, and not speaking at all when they are best placed to voice their own issues. SERI has developed partnerships with clients across a range of sectors, including informal settlement occupiers, farm workers, domestic workers, waste reclaimers and informal traders. Longstanding relationships with these partners are important for successful legal empowerment.

Abahlali is a non-partisan shack dwellers' social movement that is democratic and membership-based. Its work focuses primarily on the interests of informal settlement residents but also includes housing and land issues beyond informal settlements to address tenure insecurity, basic services and confronting corruption in the allocation of housing subsidies. As of 2024, Abahlali's membership exceeded 120,000 of which at least 60 percent were

DOI: 10.4324/9781003538806-9

women. Abahlali enjoys wide national reach with representation in five of South Africa's nine provinces.

The movement was established in 2005 following a series of protests and road blockades organized by informal settlement dwellers to denounce the lack of service delivery and housing. The residents of the Kennedy Road informal settlement in eThekwini — a metropolitan municipality that encompasses the metropolitan area of Durban — discovered that a vacant site promised to their community for housing development was being cleared for the construction of a brickyard (Socio-Economic Rights Institute of South Africa [SERI], 2022a). The protests came during a period of wider national unrest by poor communities described by some as the "rebellion of the poor" (Alexander, 2010). These protests expressed the discontent of poor communities with their social, economic and political exclusion under South Africa's neoliberal economic policies (Dugard et al., 2014, p. 27).

Abahlali embraces socialist principles and grounds its struggle in its philosophy of "living politics" — the daily experiences, needs and challenges of ordinary people (SERI, 2022a, p. 66). The movement confronts these challenges with a range of interwoven strategies and tactics, including engagement and dialogue with the state, defending land occupations, direct action such as appropriating basic services through unauthorised self-supply of water and electricity, protests, litigation and meticulous documentation and broadcasting of abuses (such as unlawful evictions, intimidation and harassment and, in extreme cases, assassination). Since its establishment, Abahlali has used the law alongside these measures to expand the rights of informal settlement residents to housing, land and basic services such as water, sanitation, electricity and their right to the city. Abahlali's use of the law is augmented by community organizing and political education that involves cultivating rights awareness or legal consciousness.

SERI's relationship with Abahlali dates to the establishment of SERI in 2009. Some of its first cases focused on defending members of the movement against unlawful eviction; later cases expanded to arguing criminal defence cases brought against individual members of Abahlali as a means of repression. SERI became increasingly involved in defending civil and political rights as other client or partner organizations suffered similar repercussions after staging political protests against ineffective municipalities for their poor service delivery.

This chapter analyses two litigation cases — a challenge of the KwaZulu-Natal Slums Act and the linked *Mzimela* and *Zulu* cases — and a case study of the eKhenana settlement to demonstrate how Abahlali uses the law as an approach to legal empowerment in informal settlements, specifically to resist evictions. The authors reflect on how Abahlali's use of litigation and its insistence on independent and oppositional organizing — outside the dominant parameters of party politics — have made the movement effective, yet also the target of political violence and repression, including the assassination of its leaders and members. These experiences demonstrate how socio-economic rights and civil and political rights are indivisible and inseparable from fundamental rights, especially to equality and dignity. This chapter explores Abahlali's unequivocal position, in navigating this difficult terrain in pursuit of structural change, that people must hold onto their own power in using legal empowerment strategies, and litigation must work hand-in-hand with organization, mobilization, popular education and political conscientization. This mix of mutually reinforcing methods (as opposed to public interest litigation alone) to realize rights is imbued with a deeply held sense of the Constitution's transformative values and its historical origins.

The chapter begins by describing the informal settlement context in South Africa, and how the injustices that characterize these settlements are shaped by historical and current exclusionary attitudes of the state and by legal frameworks shaping tenure arrangements and access to basic services. It then analyses how Abahlali has used legal empowerment strategies to overcome such injustices. Finally, the conclusion summarizes how the experiences presented in this chapter contribute to the notion of legal empowerment in the wider context of informal settlements.

Informal settlements in South Africa

Informal settlements in South Africa today have been shaped by both historical and contemporary exclusions in land tenure and property ownership. Today, this exclusion is driven by current patterns of migration, rapid urbanization and persistently high levels of poverty, inequality and unemployment. But it also has roots in the country's colonial past, and the decades of apartheid that imposed strict racial segregation in work, marriage, housing and overall settlement patterns.

In terms of scale, a lack of accurate data on informal settlements makes it difficult to provide anything but a population range. In 2011, conservative estimates held that between 1.1 and 1.4 million households (2.9 to 3.6 million people) lived in informal settlements in South Africa (SERI, 2018). However, according to the United Nations Human Settlements Programme (UN-Habitat, 2020), in 2018, South Africa's "urban population living in slums" was approximately 10 million (p. 319). Another estimate is that 60 percent of people living in South Africa are "off-register", living in backyard accommodation, government-subsidized houses which have not received title deeds, customary areas and informal settlements (Hornby et al., 2017). Because the data is not gender-disaggregated, the proportion of women living in informal settlements cannot be firmly estimated.

While informal settlements emerged in the 1990s as a significant phenomenon (Klug & Charlton, 2016, p. 56), they have formed part of South Africa's urban terrain for decades, dating back to the 1940s. They are the result of industrialization driven by South Africa's mining industry and the historically segregated nature of land ownership (Huchzermeyer, 2002, p. 88). Black people were not permitted to reside in urban areas unless they were employed and had the evidence to prove it. Only in 1986 did some Black South Africans obtain the right to settle permanently in urban areas (Durand-Lasserve & Royston, 2002). As described by Stuart Wilson (2021), "the exclusion of the majority of South Africans from access to land and adequate housing is the result of patterns of property ownership and land ownership developed under colonialism and apartheid" (p. 17). Laws like the Natives Land Act of 1913, the Native Trust and Land Act of 1936, the Group Areas Act of 1950, and the Prevention of Illegal Squatting Act of 1951 curtailed Black individual property ownership and formalized segregation through forced evictions. This legal framework made it possible to dispossess 80 percent of the population and confine them to 13 percent of the land (SERI, 2018, p. 14). These laws protected the "most attractive portions of the urban areas as enclaves for the development of an exclusive white property market and white business" (Huchzermeyer, 2002, p. 88). From 1994, the incoming post-apartheid government committed to an ambitious program of reconstruction and development (African National Congress, 1994). Critical to the approach was capital state subsidy for housing, as encapsulated in the Reconstruction and Development Programme (RDP), which was intended to address the legacy of exclusion while also expanding the construction sector (Cirolia et al., 2016, p. 6). What began as a political promise on the eve of democracy became, over the years, an avenue of political patronage. The government has delivered over one million state-subsidised housing units since 1994, a significant achievement by most measures. But this has not kept up with the need for access to affordable housing as the population has grown and as more people move to urban areas for economic opportunities (Dugard et al., 2016, p. 209). An austerity framework in place since 2021 makes it less and less likely that the subsidy program will catch up with the backlog.[3]

Eviction and tenure

Until recently, defending unlawful evictions in court has been hard to lose because the law is unequivocal. Section 26(3) of the Constitution and the Prevention of Unlawful Eviction and Occupation of Land Act (PIE Act) — and case law under them — provide clear legal principles to protect against eviction, including procedural requirements for a lawful eviction, finding alternative accommodation in the case of homelessness and for meaningful engagement between affected parties, the municipality and residents. This approach gives life to the constitutional promise of transformation and its spirit of redress. For a while, the democratic legal regime looked like it was set to balance the right to housing with the right to property. However, this balance has proven elusive.

For one thing, access to the legal system is highly contingent. Many residents do not get to court, and if they do, they may not have adequate representation. Further complicating matters, under South African law, informal settlement residents are formally considered unlawful "occupiers" but are entitled to statutory protection. With the PIE Act, unlawful occupiers can claim the right to lawful procedure, but a court can still grant an eviction if it is deemed just and equitable, after all relevant circumstances have been considered. State actors use the status of occupation to unlawfully evict occupiers from land on which they reside, despite the procedural protections. Illegal evictions are those executed without a court order, or which render occupiers homeless. They take place through forced evictions, demolitions and other forms of constructive eviction under the guise of preventing what the state refers to as "land invasion" or jumping the housing subsidy queue.[4] For a long time, the state's position on informal settlements was to eradicate them (Huchzermeyer, 2011, p. 114) and only recently has a policy shift towards *in situ* upgrading been discernible. However, the shift has yet to materialize at sufficient scale nationally to call it an implementation shift. Despite the policy change, significant resistance to occupations, which become informal settlements, persists in the local government sphere.

Tenure in informal settlements, finally, is characterized by a variety of local tenure arrangements. These can be seen as another layer, sitting atop the underlying land ownership and statutory protections. "Off-register" in nature (Hornby et al., 2017), these local tenure arrangements are socially determined, and rely on negotiation and local procedures for property access, holding and transfer. Residents, thus, face threats to both local and statutory tenure security from the state and private actors, and (within an informal settlement, for instance) from leadership structures, less visible forms of authority and even the family. These threats can affect an entire settlement — as when the state or private owners execute evictions — but can also be individualized and gendered in nature. Women face insecurities related to the processual nature of the tenure arrangements. A woman living with a male partner, whether or not she occupied the property first, faces the threat of dispossession if the relationship dissolves; widows can also be dispossessed by the relatives of a deceased spouse. Authority is often male-dominated and the resources for negotiation are unevenly held (Peters, 2002).

Basic services

In addition to self-organizing around land access and holding, informal settlement residents must make alternative arrangements for access to services, where the state is absent or only partially present. The condition of basic services varies across settlements and provinces: water may be available through communal taps, which are usually located along servitudes and on the outskirts of settlements; through water tankers filled irregularly with water of questionable quality; or through self-provision, with water pumped from boreholes. Sanitation services come in the form of chemical toilets, usually located on the peripheries of settlements, self-dug pit latrines, and communal ablution blocks (SERI, 2018).[5] These facilities are shared among large numbers of households and are often very poorly maintained. This can lead to limited water access at certain times of the day or perpetually low water pressure due to high demand. Refuse removal is irregular, if provided at all, leading to heaps of uncollected waste in and around informal settlements.

Residents use various strategies and tactics, over and above self-supply, to demand recognition and claim their rights to housing, electricity and water-based services. A first set of strategies uses established state-based processes, such as meeting with local ward councillors, writing letters, submitting petitions and participating in various community forums. When these strategies fail and residents are ignored, they turn to strategies such as protest, litigation and self-supply, to assert their socio-economic rights and compel local government to take the necessary steps to recognize them, their claim to land, and by extension, their dignity (SERI, 2019, pp. 66–67). These alternative strategies use "invented" spaces of participation — to evoke Faranak Miraftab's (2004) distinction — in contrast to "invited spaces" and forms of state-led participation, such as public meetings hosted by a local politician, municipal steering committees or task teams, or participatory budgeting. We extend the notion of invented spaces beyond participation here to the innovative forms of self-organization mentioned above, such as self-supply of services, local tenure arrangements and community-led forms of democratic participation.

Informal settlements are no longer just a legacy of apartheid and colonial-era land dispossession and economic exclusion, but an expression of democratic-era state- and market-led failures in supply and legal recognition. Urban land reform has yet to occur, despite the centrality of confronting land dispossession in the post-apartheid vision of South Africa. Inequality persists in land ownership patterns, with precarious and working-class Black residents the most excluded. Black women are particularly precarious as the "invented spaces" do not recognize everyone equally. The impact of local solutions is socially differentiated, with women negatively affected because of their sex.

Against this backdrop, the efforts of Abahlali baseMjondolo offer a compelling example of invention in opening spaces for informal settlement residents to confront this legacy of inequality and exclusion.

Abahlali baseMjondolo and legal empowerment

> There's something that I've learnt about the power of organizing and the law. That if you are not organised, when you lose in court you will actually have lost everything. But when you organise and lose in court it doesn't matter. The power remains with the people… The courts have done their part, the law has done its part. Yes, we are aware of instances where the state is in contempt of court, but I think as far as it is concerned, does [the law] work? … We have the duty as well not to use the law and expect the law to do miracles.
>
> S'bu Zikode, President of Abahlali baseMjondolo (personal communication, 2021)

Abahlali's first experiences using the law came in its formative stage, in February 2006. The eThekwini municipality had imposed prohibitions on

Abahlali marches, which it successfully overturned in the High Court, with the support of the Foundation for Human Rights and pro bono legal services (SERI, 2022a, p. 15). As the movement's president, S'bu Zikode, has highlighted, the impact of evictions cases for Abahlali extends beyond the result of a court case. The movement's approach to legal empowerment is systemic, in that it is "oriented towards systemic change, and links efforts to addressing structural injustices, socio-economic barriers, and shifting power dynamics" (Di Giovanni & Bercovich, 2021, p. 103). This approach recognizes the structural challenges shack dwellers confront: the law has a part to play but it cannot perform miracles. Real power lies with the people, and when it comes to systemic change, organization is what matters most. Similarly, as SERI has argued elsewhere, the impact of eviction cases can be significant even when unsuccessful in court — for instance, by contributing to policy change, mobilization and changes in public discourse, or by deepening democracy and strengthening the public interest sector (SERI, 2015). Framing impact in this way has implications for how lawyers use the law, engage with clients and position a case in relation to community organization and mobilization. It takes lawyers off the professional pedestal, where they are often found in commercial practice, and shifts the balance of power towards a more equal client relationship, premised on partnership.

This dynamic is demonstrated by Abahlali's successful challenge of the KwaZulu-Natal Elimination and Prevention of Re-emergence of Slums Act (Slums Act), which was found to be unconstitutional in a landmark judgment (*Abahlali BaseMjondolo Movement SA and Another v Premier of the Province of Kwazulu-Natal and Others*, 2009).

Constitutional challenge to the Slums Act

The KwaZulu-Natal provincial legislature tabled the proposed Slums Act Bill in 2006. Abahlali responded by establishing a reading group and holding frequent meetings in various settlement branches to engage with the legislative process (Dugard et al., 2014, p. 32). These gatherings were for Abahlali members to study the Bill and determine the movement's position at a community level. Abahlali also participated in the public hearings on the Bill, made a submission to the provincial legislature and encouraged allies to do the same.[6] In its submission, Abahlali submitted that:

> We do not need this Bill. The first thing we need is for government (local, provincial and national) to begin to follow the existing laws and policies that protect against evictions, forced relocations and which recommend in situ upgrades instead of relocations. After that we need laws that break the power that the very rich have over land in the cities and we need laws to compel municipalities to provide services to shack settlements while people wait for houses to be built.
>
> (Abahlali baseMjondolo, 2007, as cited in Huchzermeyer, 2011, p. 208)

The submission noted that, if implemented, the legislation would provide a legal mechanism to trigger mass evictions. The fear at the time was that eThekwini municipality would use the Act to eradicate shack settlements ahead of the 2010 FIFA World Cup, which was to be hosted in South Africa.[7] Abahlali took issue with eThekwini's interpretation of the Slums Act, which the municipality saw as advancing the national Breaking New Ground housing policy[8] and the Millennium Development Goals (MDGs). Abahlali, in contrast, asserted that the Act departed from the state's obligations under the Constitution, notably, the progressive realization of access to adequate housing.

Despite Abahlali's efforts, the Slums Act was enacted in June 2007. Abahlali then took its challenge to the High Court — represented by the Centre for Applied Legal Studies at the time — and to the streets, to prevent the municipality from driving poor and landless people out of the city (SERI, 2022a, p. 71). Abahlali's prior work in political education and community organizing helped raise awareness about informal settlement residents' concerns with the law and was critical to building and sustaining a grassroots coalition of support for the subsequent litigation process to challenge the Slums Act.

The High Court dismissed Abahlali's application to have the Act declared unconstitutional. Abahlali then successfully appealed the case to the Constitutional Court (SERI, 2022a) which, in October 2009, declared Section 16 of the Slums Act invalid and unconstitutional, that is, "seriously invasive of the protections against arbitrary evictions" in the PIE Act, the National Housing Act, the National Housing Code and Section 26(2) of the Constitution (Chenwi, 2015, pp. 85–86). Section 16 compelled landowners to institute eviction proceedings against unlawful occupiers but made it criminal to oppose an eviction. The Constitutional Court similarly found that Section 16 contradicted the "dignified framework" established by housing jurisprudence, which embeds within it requirements for meaningful engagement when instituting eviction proceedings, and the principle that evictions should be instituted as measures of last resort when implementing housing projects (Wilson, 2021, p. 80).

The Constitutional Court victory was a vital step towards protecting informal settlement residents and other poor people at risk of evictions across the country. KwaZulu-Natal province scrapped the Slums Act and could no longer present it as an example for other provinces to emulate. As the movement's president, S'bu Zikode, put it:

> [T]he KwaZulu-Natal provincial government wanted to be seen as smart and leading the way in carrying the mandate of the MDGs by introducing the then "Slums Act" which would have led to mass evictions… This judgment has a lot to say about transforming the understanding of shack settlements so that we can all see them as communities to be integrated in our urban centres.
>
> (S'bu Zikode, 2012, as cited in Dugard et al., 2014, p. 33)

On top of its legal and policy impact, the victory cemented Abahlali's place as the foremost dissident social movement in post-1994 South Africa. It raised Abahlali's profile and attracted more informal settlement residents to join the movement. As a result, the movement also faced the repressive consequences of challenging entrenched political authority (SERI, 2022a, p. 21). Two weeks before the Constitutional Court handed down its judgment, police violently raided the Kennedy Road settlement, home to one of Abahlali's founding branches and a significant number of its leaders. Two Abahlali members died as a result, several people were injured, over a dozen members were arrested and the leadership fled into hiding.

Challenging evictions in the Mzimela and Zulu cases

Following the Slums Act victory, Abahlali successfully challenged additional attempts by the eThekwini municipality to conduct mass evictions, this time through the use of interdicts (a type of court order), which effectively circumvented the PIE Act. These two cases involved residents of Cato Crest and Madlala Village, two informal settlements on the outskirts of Durban, the largest city in KwaZulu-Natal.

In March 2013, the KwaZulu-Natal provincial government obtained an interim court order from the High Court requiring eThekwini and South Africa's Minister of Police to "prevent any persons from invading and/or occupying and/or undertaking the construction of any structures" on 1,568 properties in the municipality and to "remove any materials placed by any persons upon" that land (SERI, 2022a, p. 48). The municipality used this order between 2013 and 2015 to carry out numerous unlawful evictions by its Anti-Land Invasion Unit (ALIU) in the settlement of Cato Crest. Abahlali challenged those practices, and in September 2013, the High Court granted an urgent interdict in *Mzimela and Others v eThekwini Municipality and Others*, which ordered the municipality to provide "temporary habitable dwellings that afford shelter, privacy and amenities at least equal to those destroyed" (SERI, 2022a, p. 48).

In a separate case, *Zulu and 389 Others v eThekwini Municipality and Others*, a community of 390 residents of Madlala Village (represented by the Legal Resources Centre) challenged the constitutionality of the standing court order granted to eThekwini. The municipality had used the order to evict the residents 25 times. Abahlali and 30 Cato Crest residents intervened as *amicus curiae* (friends of the court), based on their experiences in *Mzimela*, in support of the *Zulu* occupiers. The municipality submitted that the High Court order only authorized the prevention of land occupations which meant the municipality's actions did not constitute the eviction of people from their homes. In June 2014, however, the Constitutional Court ruled against them, and found that the High Court order amounted to an eviction order — which the municipality was using to evict people. The municipality's submissions were further found to be dishonest and unacceptable. The Constitutional Court remitted the *Zulu* and *Mzimela* matters back to the High Court which, in August 2015, set aside the interim order. As a matter of law, municipalities across the country could no longer use interim interdicts to circumvent the PIE Act, which gives effect to s. 26(3) of the Constitution.

Abahlali's victory in these cases is significant both for thwarting the municipality's practice of unlawful evictions and for affirming fundamental protections under the PIE Act, namely, that prior to any eviction, occupiers must be afforded the dignity of being engaged by the party seeking the eviction, and of being allowed to present their circumstances before a court of law.

Fighting unlawful evictions in eKhenana

The eKhenana informal settlement,[9] also known as the eKhenana Commune, began as an occupation in 2018 by backyard tenants who were excluded from the upgrading of Durban's Cato Manor informal settlement (SERI, 2022a, p. 9). More residents moved to the settlement when they were evicted elsewhere, or the costs of backyard rental became unaffordable. The residents organized the occupation into a commune and adopted socialist principles in their division of labour and duties across communal initiatives. These included a subsistence vegetable garden, a poultry farm and a community hall — each named after an assassinated Abahlali leader — among other shared assets. For Abahlali, eKhenana soon represented a vision of what occupations can aspire to, a model of land reform from below, self-sufficiency and community organizing and building that embodied gender equality.

During 2018, eKhenana endured several evictions — none of which were ever carried out with a court order. This rendered them unlawful in terms of the PIE Act. These evictions often involved the eThekwini municipality's ALIU and metro police descending on the settlement, demolishing residents' shacks and burning their belongings (*Nokuthula Mabaso and Others v eThekwini Municipality and Others*, 2018). In some evictions, ALIU used tear-gas and rubber bullets to disperse residents, injuring and arresting many. After each eviction, residents rebuilt their homes, only to be attacked again. Residents described these evictions as follows:

> "They kick us out like dogs. They don't even recognize us as humans. They even destroy the food we cook and throw sand everywhere. Without even engaging with us they demolish and burn our homes and leave. We are only good for votes, nothing more. We have no jobs and no land". — Wiseman Buthelezi
>
> (Xolo, 2018)

> "It's been painful before but today it's unbearable. We have children who will come back to ashes. Just yesterday we were picking up the pieces of what the security officers destroyed but today everything is gone. All of my son's school books have been burnt, books that I had bought with my last cents. What will I tell him? Where will he even sleep?" — Yongama Myeni
>
> (Xolo, 2019)

In December 2018, the eKhenana settlement joined the Abahlali movement and, with its support (and SERI's legal assistance), obtained an urgent, interim interdict prohibiting the municipality from carrying out further evictions. The order also restricted residents from erecting any new structures in eKhenana. Despite the interdict, the municipality carried out another seven evictions (*eThekwini v Nokuthula Mabaso and Others [Answering Affidavit]*, 2019). In response, in February 2019, the Durban High Court granted another order prohibiting the municipality from conducting evictions. The order went farther and effectively legitimized the settlement. It recognized the 109 families living in eKhenana at the time and ordered both sides to carry out a joint inspection of the settlement, to reach an agreement on the settlement's demarcation and enumerate the households. Significantly, the order gave the occupiers a sense of security following a period of turbulence, no matter how short-lived.

The municipality then brought an eviction application under the PIE Act, offering alternative accommodation at a site more than 50 kilometres away from eKhenana. Residents opposed the eviction, submitting that the alternative accommodation was unreasonable, unjust and inequitable. The relocation would drastically increase transportation costs, jeopardize the employment of those with jobs, and curtail their access to key amenities like health care and schools. Currently, this eviction application remains open but is yet to proceed due to inaction by the municipality (*eThekwini v Nokuthula Mabaso and Others [Answering Affidavit]*, 2019).

By February 2020, at least five eKhenana residents had been killed in the settlement. The municipality then resumed the unlawful evictions during the national COVID-19 lockdown. By April 2020, another 14 had been carried out, despite the 2019 interdict and a standing national moratorium on evictions. The residents approached the Court on an urgent basis to seek another interdict and compensation for property damage, and to institute contempt proceedings. Of the 15 applicants, 14 had had their homes demolished. Nine of the applicants were women, and four of them were heads of their households with children in their care (*Thabethe & others v eThekwini Municipality [Founding Affidavit]*, 2020).[10] The matter was settled with a signed undertaking that the municipality would refrain from "demolishing, burning and removing or disposing of the applicants' informal housing structures in the informal settlement or from causing this to take place" (SERI, 2022a, p. 54). And yet, the municipality's ALIU attacked the settlement on the very day the agreement was reached, firing live ammunition and leaving one resident with a gunshot wound.

Although the evictions ceased later in 2020, eKhenana residents faced new kinds of harassment in 2021 and 2022. Some were arrested (up to three times) on charges ranging from assault to conspiracy to commit murder, spending months in prison each time awaiting trial. As of early 2024, no charge had resulted in a successful conviction. Then, in 2022, groups of men allegedly associated with the ruling party, the African National Congress, attacked the settlement (Duma, 2023). Tragically, three eKhenana leaders were assassinated: Ayanda Ngila, deputy chairperson of the Abahlali's eKhenana branch, Nokuthula Mabaso, a mother of four and a prominent leader in eKhenana and Abahlali's Women's League, and Lindokuhle Mnguni, chairperson of the eKhenana Branch (SERI, 2022a). The settlement has since shrunk to about half its population as some households have fled in fear.

Although eKhenana is relatively young, compared to other informal settlements with Abahlali representation, its experience illustrates the high costs of defending an occupation in the face of unrelenting evictions. eKhenana is just the latest example in Abahlali's history of a settlement first encountering unlawful evictions, followed by the local government seeking lawful evictions, and then suffering a combination of harassment, violent attacks and targeted assassinations. Its experience demonstrates the extent to which national and local political authorities resort to brute force to suppress grassroots formations and land occupations that disrupt vested interests. It is unclear why eKhenana has been the target of such high levels of repression, though the defiant nature of its occupiers represents a threat to political figures who rely on a zero-sum form of politics operated along local networks of patronage. Abahlali has argued that, in this form of politics, informal settlements are seen as voting banks during elections instead of valued constituents with whom politicians engage to meaningfully address concerns (SERI, 2022a).

eKhenana's litigation was primarily about restraining the municipality's unlawful conduct by invoking the right to housing and protections under the PIE Act. Its success in court, however, did not protect the settlement from further unlawful evictions. Here is where community organizing and political education play a vital role as part of a broader legal empowerment strategy. Litigation is insufficient on its own, particularly in an environment hostile to informal settlements. eKhenana's survival has been largely due to its occupants' resilience, and their practical efforts to hold on to the land in the face of brutal demolitions, threats and violence. While the occupiers rebuilt their demolished homes repeatedly because they felt they had nowhere else to go (*eThekwini v Nokuthula Mabaso and Others [Answering Affidavit]*, 2019, paras. 24 & 35), this rebuilding was also a way to assert their humanity, dignity and right to the city.

Lessons on legal empowerment in informal settlements

A number of important lessons can be drawn from Abahlali's movement building among informal settlements and its work with SERI to pursue legal empowerment strategies. These include the importance of political realities on the ground, which in the case of South Africa effectively defy the purported state intentions to address historic injustices in land and property ownership. This can be seen in state attempts to circumvent the PIE Act and Section 26 (3) of the Constitution.

As both the success and limitations of Abahlali's use of litigation show, other measures are essential, if the residents of informal settlements are ever to enjoy tenure security. These include an urgent need for reform of South Africa's property system, and the ongoing use of community mobilization strategies that complement and strengthen legal empowerment.

The role of politics

Very few would have anticipated the South African democratic state to evolve as it is revealed in the experiences of the Abahlali-affiliated settlements, that is, anti-poor and even opposed to the transformative values espoused in its Constitution and Bill of Rights. Persistent state failures and corruption have given rise to high levels of disillusionment about the state. Many in the social justice sector in South Africa are torn between holding the state accountable through the courts and the recognition that political, economic and administrative realities make it unlikely that the state will deliver. This is due to a combination of state incapacity and unwillingness.

The cases discussed in this chapter show Abahlali's astute use of litigation to protect informal settlement residents from the risks of insecure tenure, in contrast with the government's use of legislative, legal and extra-legal methods to carry out evictions. The state often justifies evictions in terms of its housing policy priorities and preference for greenfield housing development, while painting informal settlement residents as land invaders who unlawfully occupy land to jump the queue to benefit from such policies.

The use of violence in the Kennedy Road settlement in 2009, and in eKhenana more recently, shows the extreme lengths local authorities go to protect and advance vested interests that may be financial or political in nature. Abahlali leaders have had to go into hiding, always reluctantly, because it affects the movement's mobilizing strategies. They live and work with daily insecurity and always take measures for the personal safety of targeted leaders. As a result, SERI and Abahlali have had to devise legal empowerment strategies that take into account political dynamics on the ground and the intended and unintended risks these dynamics create for litigation and other tactics. Since 2009, Abahlali has lost 24 of its members, 18 of whom were killed in politically motivated attacks, including three leaders from eKhenana murdered in 2022 (Masiangoako, 2022).[11]

More than ever, the role of social movements and community-based organizations is critical for realizing systemic change, despite the costs. Politics matter for a significant social movement like Abahlali: whether the smaller "p" of its political vision of an alternative, socialist future, its political education and conscientizing strategies or the formal process of electoral politics.

Abahlali's litigation strategy: Impacts and state responses

Abahlali's use of litigation has had strategic and jurisprudential impacts. In the Slums Act case, Abahlali stopped provincial government efforts to legislate mass evictions, while the consolidated *Mzimela* and *Zulu* cases introduced the prospect of holding municipal officials to account in situations of non-compliance. The movement's numerous successes in court to halt evictions, as in the eKhenana case, also provided direct material gains for member communities. Abahlali litigates preventatively, as seen with the Slums Act, but also defensively, as seen in *Mzimela/Zulu* and eKhenana, where unlawful evictions had already been conducted repeatedly.

Since the Slums Act was declared unconstitutional, the state has made numerous attempts to circumvent the PIE Act, most recently through efforts to amend the Act itself.[12] In the trajectory of state responses to Section 26(3) of the Constitution, the state's ahistoric position on land is puzzling. The origins of both Section 26 and the PIE Act lie in redressing apartheid's history of forced removal and land dispossession — which the state arguably perpetuates through individual cases and its attempts to change the law.

Informality and the shortcomings of the property system

In South African law, the PIE Act is a defensive law, providing due process protections against arbitrary eviction to unlawful occupiers. This approach should ideally resolve the tensions between law and informality. However, the discussion above on the trajectory of the state's responses shows how far we have to go in representing groups like Abahlali that face multilayered challenges, ranging from the deeply vested private interests in the current property system (such as banks and property developers) to the interests of political actors and their patronage networks.

Beyond the significant challenges of unlawful eviction, little progress has been made on long-term tenure security for informal settlement residents. This lack of secure tenure is a key obstacle to upgrading settlements. While official instruments such as housing policies and grants for settlement upgrading imagine a range of tenure options, these do not exist in practice. The only option is ownership via a registered title deed, or some little-used collective ownership options. Access to housing delivery is limited and slow, from application to approval and eventual upgrading, and does not always lead to the registration of a title deed, as identified earlier. Other options are needed, such as the introduction of land records, which have the potential to bridge the gap between a formal property system and its laws, and the reality on the ground which, while characterized as informal, often consists of highly organized processes which constitute the social production of habitat. In truth, reform of the property system itself is needed so that it can recognize the range of land holding arrangements that exist in informal settlements, such as land records legislation.

Other legal empowerment and social change strategies

Despite their positive impacts, Abahlali's litigation strategies also demonstrated the limited progress that the law and litigation alone have made in achieving the transformation envisaged by our constitutional democracy. Abahlali's use of litigation alongside other strategies discussed in the three cases above is thus instructive. Being the largest social movement in the country, Abahlali's strength lies in its membership base and its ability to grow this membership, mobilize its branches and organize around specific issues.

Training and raising awareness among residents about their housing rights and the need to resist eviction efforts are central to Abahlali's mode of organization and mobilization. Its successful use of litigation has made the movement attractive to other informal settlements. In the eKhenana case, the settlement joined the movement because of the support Abahlali could offer against the state. Other settlements have since been inspired by the efforts of eKhenana residents to establish an Abahlali branch, then organize themselves to physically defend the settlement from evictions, rebuild, and later mobilize around litigation. These efforts have had a nationwide impact: Abahlali's success in the Slums Act case in overturning the provincial Bill reverberated nationally, dissuading many other provinces[13] from enacting similar laws and foreclosing the potential eviction of millions of people. Similarly, the impact of *Zulu* and *Mzimela* in putting an end to the use of blanket interdicts in one municipality prevented further incursions into people's housing rights across the country. The Constitution prevailed in these instances.

However, court victories alone are not sufficient in Abahlali's experience: without the power of organizing, the power of the law counts for little when the state is willing to brazenly act unlawfully. The eKhenana Commune narrative shows this: while Abahlali succeeded in the courts with strategic impact litigation, the government initially responded by directly defying the court rulings and continuing its violent incursions into the settlement. It has taken the commune's subsequent pushback and persistence to prevail where litigation alone was ineffective. Finally, Abahlali uses political education, including on socialist principles, and international exchanges to advance education, livelihoods and liberation for settlement residents. Beyond using legal strategies, Abahlali is engaged in the material struggles of its members while exposing them to an inspiring vision of an alternative future.

Conclusion

This chapter has shown how solutions to deep, structural problems affecting informal settlements require a combination of legal empowerment approaches, of which litigation is one. Partnerships between lawyers and client organizations that seek to complement one another are critical. In the cases discussed here, the strengths and abilities of Abahlali and SERI have been well matched: Abahlali brings the critical strength of committed, grassroots organizing and builds communities that understand their socio-political circumstances and objectives. SERI brings its abilities to litigate, research and advocate in the public interest and in support of communities. For both parties, popular education is another vital component of legal empowerment. And as Abahlali seeks to develop its capacity to represent itself in court, SERI is adding a court navigation and guidance dimension to the partnership, including by drafting a practical guide on self-representation.

Since litigation is often protracted, such partnerships are needed to sustain community advocacy efforts — especially where the empowerment of communities can be perceived as a threat to political or commercial interests. We have seen how political forces work against Abahlali in brutal and systematic ways. More recently, SERI and other public interest legal service organizations have faced their own attacks, accused of having agendas driven by foreign funders or agents of the CIA (Nyathi, 2023).

Abahlali's experience and SERI's work with the movement over the years show how success can pose a threat to local political elites, with devastating results. We are facing the sobering conclusion that democratic political space and the tolerance for dissent have shrunk beyond what could ever have been imagined at the outset of South Africa's democratic era. However, Abahlali's history of struggle adds to experiences the world over, which show that grassroots social movements and community-based organizations are critical for realizing systemic change. Legal empowerment strategies are most effective when they are movement-led and combined with strong community organization. In this way, they inspire a vision of a more dignified future and sustain the efforts of informal settlement residents to hold their own power.

Notes

1 The authors are currently employed at the Socio-Economic Rights Institute of South Africa (SERI) which has worked with the shack-dwellers movement Abahlali baseMjondolo to advance rights in informal settlements. SERI is a human rights-focused public interest law clinic that uses litigation, research and advocacy to advance socio-economic rights. The authors write here in their personal capacity, drawing on SERI publications, some of which they have written.

2 In 1994, the country's first majority-rule government was elected, replacing the exclusionary pro-apartheid National Party that had ruled South Africa since 1948, to the advantage of the country's white minority.

3 See for example, Mboweni, Tito. 2021 Budget Speech. Available at: www.gov.za/news/speeches/minister-tito-mboweni-2021-budget-speech-24-feb-2021

4 The terms "queue jumping" and "land invasion" are pejorative terms used to describe unlawful occupiers "as 'opportunists' who attempt to gain preference over those who have followed the prescribed legal procedures and patiently await state-subsidised housing". See SERI (2016, p. 47).

5 See also SERI (2019).

6 See Huchzermeyer (2011, p. 206).

7 The Bill was identified as "a blueprint for other provinces to follow" by the African National Congress, South Africa's ruling political party since 1994. See Huchzermeyer (2011, p. 14).

8 Introduced in 2004, Breaking New Ground, the Comprehensive Plan for the Development of Sustainable Human Settlements, was an update of the 1994 white paper, A New Housing Policy and Strategy for South Africa. It was significant for recognizing that the previous emphasis on rapid greenfield housing development projects to meet the housing needs of the poor was inadequate and replicated apartheid-era spatial planning. See e.g. Huchzermeyer (2011).

9 eKhenana is the isiZulu name for the biblical land of Canaan, the promised land of the Israelites. The settlement was named that by the occupiers because of its symbolic value. As described in *eThekwini v Mabaso* (Answering Affidavit), 2019, para 18.

10 The other applicants were five men and Abahlali itself.

11 See SERI (2022a).

12 See SERI's (2022b) submission here: www.seri-sa.org/index.php/more-news/1252-submission-seri-makes-a-submission-on-the-prevention-of-illegal-eviction-from-and-unlawful-occupation-of-land-amendment-bill-10-october-2022

13 South Africa is made up of nine provinces.

References

Abahlali BaseMjondolo Movement SA and Another v Premier of the Province of Kwa-zulu-Natal and Others (2009) BCLR 99, CC.

African National Congress. (1994). *The reconstruction and development programme: A policy framework*. Umanyano Publications.

Alexander, P. (2010). Rebellion of the poor: South Africa's service delivery protests — a preliminary analysis. *Review of African Political Economy*, 37(123), 25–40.

Chenwi, L. (2015). Implementation of housing rights in South Africa: Approaches and strategies. *Journal of Law and Social Policy*, 24(1), 68–87.

Cirolia, L. R., Görgens, T., van Donk, M., Smit, W., & Drimie, S. (2016). Upgrading informal settlements in South Africa: An introduction. In L. R. Cirolia, T. Görgens, M. van Donk, W. Smit, & S. Drimie (Eds.), *Upgrading informal settlements in South Africa: A partnership-based approach*. UCT Press.

Di Giovanni, A., & Bercovich, L. (2021). Legal empowerment in informal settlements: Lessons on using the law to overcome urban exclusion and poverty in the Global South. *New York University Journal of International Law and Politics*, 54(1), 93–151.

Dugard, J., Clark, M., Tissington, K., & Wilson, S. (2016). The right to housing in South Africa. In *Socio-economic Rights: Progressive Realisation?* (pp. 155–262). Foundation for Human Rights. www.saferspaces.org.za/uploads/files/Socio_Economic_Rights_-_Progressive_Realisation.pdf.

Dugard, J., Madlingozi, T., & Tissington, K. (2014). Rights-compromised or rights-savvy? The use of rights-based strategies to advance socio-economic struggles by Abahlali baseMjondolo, the South African shack-dwellers' movement. In H. A. García, L. A. Williams, & K. Klare (Eds.), *Social and economic rights in theory and practice* (1st ed., pp. 23–42). Routledge.

Duma, N. (2023). Abahlali baseMjondolo activist's killer handed a 15-year jail term. *News24*. www.news24.com/news24/southafrica/news/abahlali-basemjondolo-activists-killer-handed-a-15-year-jail-term-20230724.

Durand-Lasserve, A., & Royston, L. (Eds.). (2002). *Holding their ground: Secure land tenure for the urban poor in developing countries* (1st ed.). Routledge. doi:10.4324/9781849771566.

eThekwini v Nokuthula Mabaso and Others (Answering Affidavit) (2019) KwaZulu-Natal Local Division of the High Court of South Africa.

Hornby, D., Kingwill, R., Cousins, B., & Royston, L. (Eds.). (2017). *Untitled: Securing land tenure in urban and rural South Africa*. University of KwaZulu-Natal Press.

Huchzermeyer, M. (2002). Informal settlements: Production and intervention in twentieth-century Brazil and South Africa. *Latin American Perspectives*, 29(1), 83–105.

Huchzermeyer, M. (2011). *Cities with "slums": From informal settlement eradication to a right to the city in Africa*. UCT Press.

Klug, N., & Charlton, S. (2016). Pressures on practice: How RDP housing and other factors have shaped informal settlement upgrading in eThekwini Municipality. In L. R. Cirolia, T. Görgens, M. van Donk, W. Smit & S. Drimie (Eds.), *Upgrading informal settlements in South Africa: A partnership-based approach*. UCT Press.

Masiangoako, T. (2022, October 18). The Abahlali baseMjondolo experience exposes South Africa's shrinking democratic space. *Daily Maverick*. www.dailymaverick.co.za/article/2022-10-18-the-abahlali-basemjondolo-experience-exposes-south-africas-shrinking-democratic-space/.

Miraftab, F. (2004). Invited and invented spaces of participation: Neoliberal citizenship and feminists' expanded notion of politics. *Wagadu*, 1(1), 3.

Nokuthula Mabaso and Others v eThekwini Municipality and Others (2018) KwaZulu-Natal Local Division of the High Court of South Africa.

Nyathi, M. (2023, September 14). Mantashe accuses NGOs of being CIA funded. *The Mail & Guardian*. https://mg.co.za/the-green-guardian/2023-09-14-mantashe-accuses-environmental-activists-of-being-cia-funded/.

Peters, P. E. (2002). The limits of negotiability: Security, equity and class formation in Africa's land systems. In K. Juul & C. Lund (Eds.), *Negotiating property in Africa* (pp. 45–66). Heinemann.

Socio-Economic Rights Institute of South Africa. (2015). *Public interest legal services in South Africa: Project report*. https://seri-sa.org/images/Seri_Pils_report_Final.pdf.

Socio-Economic Rights Institute of South Africa. (2016). *Evictions and alternative accommodation in South Africa 2000–2016: An analysis of the jurisprudence and implications for local government*. www.seri-sa.org/images/Jurisprudence__Revised_2016_Final_to_print.pdf.

Socio-Economic Rights Institute of South Africa. (2018). *Informal settlements and human rights in South Africa: Submission to the United Nations Special Rapporteur on adequate housing as a component of the right to an adequate standard of living*. https://docslib.org/doc/8238251/informal-settlements-and-human-rights-in-south-africa.

Socio-Economic Rights Institute of South Africa. (2019). *Here to stay: A synthesis of findings and implications from Ratanang, Marikana and Siyanda* (Informal Settlement in South Africa: Norms, Practices and Agency). www.seri-sa.org/images/SERI_Synthesis_FINAL_WEB_READY.pdf.

Socio-Economic Rights Institute of South Africa. (2022a). *Abahlali baseMjondolo: Living politics* (Community Practice Notes: Social Movements Series). Author.

Socio-Economic Rights Institute of South Africa. (2022b). *SERI makes a submission on the Prevention of Illegal Eviction from and Unlawful Occupation of Land Amendment Bill*. www.seri-sa.org/index.php/more-news/1252-submission-seri-makes-a-submission-on-the-prevention-of-illegal-eviction-from-and-unlawful-occupation-of-land-amendment-bill-10-october-2022.

Thabethe & others v eThekwini Municipality (Founding Affidavit) (2020) High Court of South Africa.

UN-Habitat. (2020). *World cities report 2020: The value of sustainable urbanization*. https://unhabitat.org/sites/default/files/2020/10/wcr_2020_report.pdf.

Wilson, S. (2021). *Human rights and the transformation of property* (1st ed.). Juta.

Xolo, N. (2018, November 6). "We are only good for votes" say Cato Crest families. *GroundUp*. https://groundup.org.za/article/we-are-only-good-votes-say-cato-crest-families/.

Xolo, N. (2019, January 18). Cato Crest residents battle continuous demolitions. *GroundUp*. https://groundup.org.za/article/cato-crest-residents-battle-continuous-demolitions/.

10 And our voice opened up the pathway

Four women's fight to provide water to their community

Maria Silvia Emanuelli

Introduction

This chapter recounts the complex legal pathway undertaken to confront the violation of the human right to water and sanitation in a low-income neighbourhood (*colonia*) located within a municipality in the state of Morelos, Mexico. It aims to contribute to the debate on what can be achieved by using positive law and legal strategies within social struggles to advance the economic, social and cultural rights of vulnerable populations.

The background section below describes the evolution of Mexican housing policy in the relevant period and its impacts on the people and communities in the state of Morelos; the next section describes the legal case in the Ampliación Tres de Mayo neighbourhood, highlighting the human rights violations that prompted it. The third section outlines the community legal strategy that was followed and the outcomes obtained, while the fourth section explores some of the dilemmas that the case revealed in relation to the human right to water in Mexico. Finally, the chapter concludes with some general observations on the connection between certain theoretical reflections on the effects of human rights litigation in the region and the specific results of this case.

Background

As analysed by various authors (Rodríguez & Sugranyes, 2005; Sepúlveda Ocampo & Fernández Wagner, 2006, among others), starting in the 1990s, the implementation of neoliberal housing policies that assigned fundamental weight to the macroeconomic role of housing's commercial production had catastrophic effects on territorial, urban and housing areas throughout Latin America and on the populations that inhabit them.

In the case of Mexico, this situation intensified especially during the six-year term of President Felipe Calderón Hinojosa (2006–2012), with a very significant increase in housing production aimed at those in the formal sector earning more than five times the minimum wage who could acquire these homes by assuming a long-term mortgage. This entailed the construction of

DOI: 10.4324/9781003538806-10

more than 500,000 new homes per year, predominantly located in rural or semi-rural areas very far from work, education and recreation centres. In most cases, these developments involved land usage authorizations that violated the corresponding planning instruments, without updating the information on water availability, a topic of special relevance to this chapter. The result of these policies was a proliferation of homes that were inadequate in size (around 40 m^2) and location, with limited access to services and the urban grid (Eibenschutz Hartman & Goya Escobedo, 2009, p. 26). These effectively became dormitory "cities" in which many types of violence are concentrated.[2]

The failure of these policies to satisfy the demand of the target population was reflected for years in the census, which reported thousands of empty homes — not all of them new — reaching 6.1 million in 2020 (INEGI, 2020). This demonstrated a serious waste of both public funds and the resources of the working-class residents who had bought homes by taking on mortgage debts of over 30 years. In addition, and less visibly, the original residents of these semi-rural areas that had developed as mega-projects continue to suffer the consequences of the massive influx of new residents without adequate planning. This is the case in Morelos, a state of just 4,958 km^2 that borders Mexico City, which in just a few years became the third most densely populated state in the country (INEGI, 2020).

A confrontation between at least three different groups, with different relationships with the territory — each living within metres of each other — can be seen in this accelerated housing growth: (1) those with indigenous-peasant roots; (2) wealthy urban families; and (3) the urban population of salaried individuals. Among the pre-existing groups with indigenous-peasant roots, people have a direct relationship with the commons. It is often managed directly by communities, without commercial interest,[3] and continues to be largely organized collectively. The absence of rural aid policies and the modification of article 27 of the Constitution, which has permitted the sale of socially owned land since 1992,[4] has favoured urban and housing growth in rural and semi-rural areas. The hoarding of agricultural land and water by the real estate sector, supported by state policies, has enabled the arrival in these areas of mostly urban residents who, despite differing income levels, are destined to occupy spaces following a hegemonic model that does not favour the building of networks or respect for the environment. Wealthy families from the capital city, who have resided in the state of Morelos for several decades, have a second way of relating to the territory. They have long chosen the area to build vacation homes in luxury, walled subdivisions fully equipped with services, golf courses and swimming pools. The third group is comprised of the salaried population that has arrived more recently — people who continue to work in the nation's capital. They have bought housing here or in surrounding areas, using credit that they enjoy as one of their social benefits. Due to the distance from their places of work, these residents use their homes mainly as dorms, which makes it difficult to create relationships and alliances with the local indigenous population — even though they can suffer from the same absence of services and scarcity of water, which neither the construction companies nor the municipalities provide.

As a reaction, in the first years of this century, a large movement emerged in Morelos representing 40 indigenous groups within the pre-existing population — several of which had already led socio-territorial struggles. They organized to oppose the invasion of previously agricultural lands, the construction of housing units that mostly lacked water treatment, and other mega-projects identified as deepening the country's environmental crisis. With regards to water, concern focused mainly on the overexploitation of underground sources, the contamination of surface waters and discrimination in water distribution. The problem was not a minor one. According to official data, Morelos "is among the states with the smallest water supply in the country, which is around 3,120 cubic metres per inhabitant per year" (Bolongaro et al., 2006, p. 25).

This is how the Morelos Council of Peoples first appeared in defence of water, air and land.[5] The original collective of indigenous groups was soon joined by poor residents, academics and networks, and organizations and social movements of various kinds that ended up forming a socio-environmental movement (Svampa, 2012, p. 10).[6] When analyzing the different positions that the Council made public or shared in its meetings, there is a lot of similarity with what Svampa considers common characteristics of different struggles throughout Latin America. Conflicts are "linked to access and control of natural resources and the territory, which suppose, on the part of the opposing actors, divergent interests and values around them in a context of great asymmetry of power". In this framework, "different concepts of territory, nature and the environment are expressed" and "a dispute is established about what is understood by development and, more generally, by democracy" (Svampa, 2012, p. 19).

Among other strategies, the Council of Peoples considered resorting to legal means to stop the construction of new mega-housing developments, as well as garbage dumps and mines on its territory. Some networks, organizations and groups that collaborated with them proposed following this path — at that time, a new one due to the limited number of cases on social rights that had been won in the courts — in pursuit of justice. The intention was to accompany the political-social strategies already promoted by the movement with a legal one that could be reinforced by the former.

To identify the case that was finally litigated, in coordination with the Council of Peoples, a detailed analysis of the different state-level issues of concern to them was developed and five cases were prioritized. Considering the near-total lack of legal precedents that existed on social rights in the country,[7] and the limited human and economic resources available for the litigation — which were focused on promoting the human right to water — a diagnosis of each of the possible cases was proposed, in order to select the one that would have the greatest chance of success in court. The task was assigned to a team of lawyers coordinated by the Latin American office of the International Habitat Coalition (HIC-AL), which presented the results in 2008. Based on the analysis shared, and considering the limitations, the Council and its supporters decided to litigate the case of Ampliación Tres de Mayo, a neighbourhood in the town of Alpuyeca, which lies in the municipality of Xochitepec. The locale is described in official documents as an area of priority due to its high degree of marginalization.

There were three main water-related problems in Alpuyeca that were pertinent to this case: (1) the contamination of the Colotepec River, which the low-income population uses when water is scarce in the pipeline, due to the runoff of leachate from a nearby garbage dump that also contaminates the wells that supply the community; (2) the shortage of water, since it is only distributed once or twice a week to those who have access to a water network; and (3) the total absence of a network in some neighbourhoods, such as Ampliación Tres de Mayo, even when they are located near subdivisions with golf courses, swimming pools and water 24 hours a day.

Ampliación Tres de Mayo was finally chosen due to contextual and procedural considerations.[8] Although the litigation was considered relevant by the Council of Peoples, as it sought to ensure the right to water to a very low-income population that participated in the movement, it was also clear from the beginning that its outcome would have a very low possibility of directly confronting the mega-projects that were proliferating in the state.

Ampliación Tres de Mayo: A marginalized and thirsty neighbourhood

Approximately 100 families live in Ampliación Tres de Mayo. Most residents are employed in the informal sector and have certificates of ownership of *ejido* lots, parcels of communal land over which they have usufruct rights. The first family to settle the area by building their own home did so in the 1980s. The other families arrived about 20 years later. Their establishment in the area occurred almost in parallel with the construction of a luxurious subdivision of vacation homes. These communities are separated only by a bridge, which many women from the neighbourhood cross every day to reach the wealthy homes where they work.

Seeking services for their area, the residents of Ampliación Tres de Mayo have, over the years, addressed a series of requests to the authorities. Questions regarding water were never answered, so they had no option but the Colotepec River, which is very difficult to access during the rainy season, or buying water from private tanker trucks at prices much higher than those paid for public distribution. Women — as is usually the case — were the main people in charge of ensuring water supplies for their families and were the most active in requesting them.[9] Planning of the litigation began with four of these women — Lidia, Carlota, Gloria and Martha[10] — through long conversations in the shade of the avocados that grow in their patios.

Since there was no possibility of collective litigation at that time, four individual injunctions had to be implemented. Each one asserted violation of the right to life (article 1 of the Constitution), the right to health and housing (article 4), and the right to an adequate standard of living (article 11.1 of the International Covenant on Economic, Social and Cultural Rights [ICESCR] in relation to article 25, first paragraph, of the Universal Declaration for Human Rights). To assert violation of the human right to water, reference was made to General Comment (GC) No. 15 of the Committee on Economic, Social and Cultural Rights; article 14, paragraph 2 of the Convention on the Elimination of All Forms of Discrimination against Women; and article 24 paragraph 2 of the Convention on the Rights of the Child.

Of the four cases, two were not admitted from the beginning due to procedural issues. The other two were successful. Although both were put forward prior to the 2012 constitutional reform — which included explicit recognition of the human right to water and sanitation in article 4 — one received a first decision prior to the reform and the other only afterwards. An earlier constitutional reform on human rights, in 2011, had already come into force. This was a fundamental turning point for Mexico because it gave constitutional status to treaties on human rights.

The court that heard the first of the trials did not hesitate to resort to international legal instruments on the matter to recognize the human right to water as an integral part of the Mexican legal system (*Amparo en Revisión* 381/2011). Even so, the court considered that, since ownership of the homes for which water was requested had not been demonstrated, a decision on the violation of the corresponding right could not be made. Despite this, it demanded that the municipal authority justify its decision not to provide water to the homes. The ruling implied a partial success since, for the first time, it was recognized that the human right to water was enforceable in Mexico. In practice, however, the decision did not force the authority to provide water to the complainant, thus making a social right conditional on private property ownership.

The court (Fourth District Court of the Eighteenth Circuit) that heard the second complaint — the one brought forward by Lidia — determined not to go into the substance of the matter or establish any obligation on the part of the authority, since the plaintiff had not demonstrated ownership of the property for which access to water was requested. The legal team filed an appeal against this ruling in which it maintained that the right to water cannot be subordinated to private property ownership.

This appeal obtained a favourable ruling, which is analysed in the following section. In parallel, the four women started a complaint process before the Human Rights Commission of the State of Morelos. Informal interviews with the relevant authorities revealed that this complaint, together with the ongoing litigation, generated the necessary pressure for the municipal authority to install the water pipes, taking advantage of works being carried out at the entrance to the settlement.

Litigation outcomes

The appeal of the second case was decided in 2012 in favour of Lidia, who was thereby granted recourse. The Collegiate Court ruled on the underlying issue, thus establishing the first precedent and interpretation of article 4 of the Constitution.

The Collegiate Court then referred to the constitutional recognition of the human right to water and sanitation, but for the interpretation of its scope and principles (availability, quality, physical and economic accessibility, non-discrimination, and equality) it referred to the ICESCR and GC 15. It also recognized that the authority responsible for providing water and sanitation had given ambiguous responses to deny access to the requested drinking water and drainage, even though the service is available 24 hours a day at nearby locations.

The Collegiate Court, analyzing the reasons put forward by the authority for the alleged impossibility of providing the service due to a lack of the necessary infrastructure, stated:

> (It is not admissible that) public authorities can allege unjustified reasons to fail to comply with their constitutional obligations. In this specific case, it is not an isolated matter in which the petitioner requests access to water on a whim, but rather the complainant asserts that there is infrastructure in subdivisions surrounding or adjoining the settlement… where she reported having her place of residence and, therefore, the person responsible cannot deny that right to water, based on the existing equal conditions.
>
> (*Amparo en Revisión* 381/2011)

The Collegiate Court then determined that the Drinking Water and Sanitation System of the Municipality of Xochitepec (SAPXO) had to take the measures necessary to ensure that the project or program focused on expanding water distribution in Alpuyeca would be reviewed and the corresponding procedures completed to provide sufficient, healthy, acceptable and affordable access, disposal and sanitation of water for personal and domestic consumption in the complainant's home. Meanwhile, it established that the authority had to supply water to the complainant through tanker trucks free of charge.

The analysis by the Collegiate Court was the first favourable interpretation at a national level of the newly reformed constitutional articles and their joint application with international treaties. Furthermore, the ruling established specific obligations for the authorities, warning that excuses such as those related to a lack of resources cannot be used to avoid compliance.

As anticipated, before the ruling was issued, the responsible authorities had begun to provide the entire settlement with pipes, which is relevant considering that an individual trial ended up having some beneficial effects for the 100 families living in the area. Even so, the network receives water only once a week (sometimes less) for an average of four hours, which does not meet international standards for water availability. This aspect unfortunately could not continue to be litigated solely in favour of the person whose injunction was successful.

Despite the insufficient availability of water, the authority maintained that it had complied with the ruling by allowing the complainant to connect to the water network. The Fourth District Court of the Eighteenth Circuit agreed with this argument and considered the ruling fulfilled.

On consideration of this decision, the team of lawyers filed a non-conformity action arguing that the human right to water cannot be satisfied by receiving it for an average of just four hours per week.

The First Chamber of the Supreme Court of Justice of the Nation (SCJN) was aware of the disagreement and for the first time in its history, it was called to analyse an issue related to the human right to water and sanitation. In its resolution of November 2014, it considered that:

> to have fulfilled the protective ruling, it is not enough to prove that there is a water connection in the complainant's home, since this would imply going to the extreme of considering people's right to water fulfilled by providing only one minute of the vital liquid per week.
>
> (Inconformidad, 2014, p. 26)

It further noted that,

> in the contested agreement, the records should have been analyzed with a sufficient degree of exhaustiveness… to determine whether the distribution of the vital liquid was actually done equitably and in accordance with the guidelines of the World Health Organization and, thus, determine whether the protective ruling was fulfilled or not.
>
> (p. 28)[11]

The Supreme Court also stressed that there was no evidence in the file to prove that the complainant had been provided with the vital liquid by tanker truck until water was provided to her under the terms established in the injunction application, as it had been determined therein. The SCJN also recognized, for the first time in the country, that sanitation should be understood as a system for "the collection, transportation, treatment and disposal or reuse of human excrement and the corresponding promotion of hygiene" (p. 10). It therefore revoked the decision of the Fourth District Court establishing that the authority must fully comply with the specifications indicated in the injunction ruling and certify that the vital liquid is provided to the complainant under the established standards.

The case returned to the Fourth District Court of the State of Morelos where it remained for four years largely due to multiple extensions requested by the municipality, but also due to the non-proactive attitude of the responsible judge. During this time, the authority tried to demonstrate, without success, that it had complied with the ruling in relation to the availability of water.[12] It likewise failed to demonstrate compliance in relation to the provision of sanitation. Finally, on January 21, 2018, the presiding judge sent the file to the Collegiate Court for non-execution. At this point, having previously threatened the plaintiff and her lawyers in order to get them to withdraw from the lawsuit, the director of SAPXO committed to sending the complainant free water by tanker to complement her piped water supply. As of 2024, this supply continues, although every time the person in charge of the network changes, the threats and pressure return.

Challenges and dilemmas in the justiciability of the human right to water and sanitation in Mexico

This case allows us to reflect on at least three challenges faced during the litigation to realize the human right to water and sanitation. First, there was the difficulty of responding to an urgent demand from the settlement in question, so it could enjoy water and sanitation, while at the same time responding to a structural claim regarding the unequal and discriminatory distribution of water. Second, there were the consequences of not being able to fully satisfy this right through the trial process. And finally, there were the difficulties of having to sustain litigation for more than 10 years without obtaining completely satisfactory results in relation to the right claimed.

Regarding the first point, the Special Rapporteur on the Human Right to Drinking Water — in her 2014 report to the Human Rights Council — states the following:

> Violations of the human rights to water and sanitation are often complex and interrelated. For instance, victims of violations of the obligations to respect rights, such as those living in informal settlements, are often in precarious situations caused by violations of the obligation to fulfil rights. Many violations can be traced to unequal power relationships and systemically entrenched patterns of discrimination. Given this context, the notion of restorative remedies for violations, whereby the status quo ante is restored, may fall short of addressing the underlying violations at the structural or systemic level. Consequently, transformative remedies, which aim not only to correct direct violations but also the underlying structural conditions, are required in order to provide comprehensive remedies to structural and systemic violations. Examples of such transformative remedies are participatory structural injunctions that require the State to adopt a plan to correct a structural violation with the meaningful participation of beneficiaries and report back to the court on progress made. This allows courts to supervise progress and make ancillary orders to ensure that both the process and outcomes are consistent with the rights to water and sanitation.
>
> (UN Human Rights Council, 2014, paras. 77 & 78)

In the case analysed, there were neither advanced remedies nor the necessary political will to confront the discrimination in terms of water availability that Ampliación Tres de Mayo was suffering and which it shared with all the other neighbourhoods of the municipality, including the original population and even the new social housing units. This situation, in addition to being explained by administrative issues, derives from a clientelistic water management system that is not focused on satisfying the human right to water and therefore does not prioritize it over other uses.

The second challenge is due to the fact that, even though the lack of water and sanitation was a problem for the entire neighbourhood, it was impossible to solve it from a collective perspective because at that time there was no such protective mechanism.[13] Therefore, while providing the network benefited the entire community, they did not equally benefit in terms of the amount of water or the access to sanitation services that each family received. The individualization of the litigation through four different *amparos*, the different decisions reached in each and the fact that only one was successful led to the demand for sufficient water to meet basic needs and the construction of a septic tank only for one complainant, Lidia.[14] This has caused some tensions in the community.

In addition, the challenges of temporal and financial sustainability of the case were enormous. The slow pace of the processes discourages the use of judicial tools to advance the justiciability of rights and it is very complex to count on such long-term financial support. In this specific case, funding was interrupted after eight years and the team subsequently worked entirely pro bono. In the final balance, it is also necessary to acknowledge that the development of this case involved long-term work, with moments of wear-and-tear for all parties, which might be difficult to sustain in similar cases. The long legal timelines also explain the low number of funders interested in supporting this type of litigation. This is worrying, considering the near absence of popular lawyers and the very small number of public defenders in the country. Moreover, the result obtained is precarious. If the municipal authority fails to comply with the judgment by stopping the delivery of water trucks to Lidia, there is no other option but to file a new injunction.

Conclusions

Contrary to what has been observed and theorized over the years, in this case it can't be argued that the success achieved in court depended on the presence of a strong organized social movement (Sousa Santos & Rodríguez Garavito, 2007, pp. 18–21) since, given the characteristics of the litigation, the Peoples' Council remained an observer of the trial.

It is more likely that the 2012 ruling was mainly due to those factors:

1 There was a very clear case of a violation of the human right to water and sanitation and discrimination, which helped establish the central requirement of the litigation even if not necessarily the route to resolution.

2 It involved a small number of state actors, did not involve large economic interests and did not directly involve the real estate sector with its strong political links, which could have made the success of the case more complicated.
3 The lawsuit was constructed by a group of lawyers knowledgeable in social rights administrative and *amparo* matters and who faced the legal team of a small municipality that almost always demonstrated weakness in constructing evidence and arguments in the matter.
4 Litigation was promoted in the context of the constitutional reform on human rights — and subsequent reform of article 4 — which implied a relevant change in the Mexican legal system and justified the development of training for the judiciary to enable its correct implementation.

We could argue that this case lies halfway between an ordinary litigation and a strategic one capable of influencing public policies and promoting the effectiveness of rights that are not guaranteed. By achieving a favourable ruling on the human right to water and sanitation it has set an important precedent for the whole country and also helped to understand that access to water and sanitation is a right that can be claimed. The litigation has also contributed to the public debate on the human right to water, as it has provoked much interest among national and international civil society organizations and academia. It has subsequently even had an impact on advocacy related to the drafting of the General Water Law that should implement it as a consequence of the constitutional reform regarding the human right to water and sanitation. However, it may also have had a counterproductive effect. According to some informal conversations that have been held with representatives of the National Water Commission, one of the most controversial articles of the first draft of this new legislation released in 2015, which limited the enjoyment of the public water service to formal settlements, was based on the concern that the decision on Ampliación Tres de Mayo had generated in the governmental sphere. Fortunately, this proposed law did not pass.

Finally, it is important to note that the Council of Peoples has achieved some victories, especially in terms of articulating and giving visibility to the issues they wanted to address. But the Council has also suffered from criminalization and even the murder of some of its members, which unfortunately is not surprising in a country that for several years has been considered the deadliest for environmentalists.

Notes

1 This chapter is an update to a previous article (Emanuelli, 2019).
2 For more information on the topic see Francisco et al. (2016).
3 Community or social water management, for example, is carried out in some indigenous towns of Morelos (Guzmán Ramírez, 2009), several of which participated in the Council of Peoples.

4 The agrarian reform, which began after the Mexican revolution of 1917, provided land to the peasant and indigenous population through the modality of social property (*ejido* lands or communal property, depending on the case), establishing certain policies to ensure that they fulfilled their social function. The law thus ensured that they were inalienable, non-transmissible, imprescriptible, non-seizable and indivisible.

5 For more information about the Council, refer to its blog (Consejo de Pueblos, 2007) and one of its founding documents, the Manifesto of the Peoples of Morelos (Pueblos de Morelos, 2007).

6 According to Svampa, socio-environmental movements are characterized by territoriality, the combination of direct action with institutional action, assembly democracy and a tendency towards autonomy.

7 Even though Mexico is one of the first countries to have elevated social rights to constitutional status, for many years their enforceability has faced a series of obstacles that have been widely analysed by different authors (Gutiérrez Rivas, 2005).

8 At that time, to submit a case to the attention of a judge, it was necessary to demonstrate that there had been a direct impact on a human right of the person requesting to be defended, by proving the causal link between an event and the violation itself. This was impossible to do in the cases submitted for consideration by the Council of Peoples, which maintained that the construction of housing units was responsible for affecting the availability of water in certain populations, which depended on the same underground sources from which the new population would also be supplied.

9 This situation is evident from accompanying territorial struggles in the region and even finds support in theoretical reflection. For example, according to Federici (2013), women, being the main people in charge of reproductive work, have depended more than men on access to common resources and have been more committed to their protection (p. 15).

10 Only the women's first names are used here to protect their privacy.

11 The World Health Organization (WHO) considers an average of 20 litres per day per person as basic access to drinking water, 50 litres per day as intermediate access and 100 litres per day as optimal access (WHO, 2003, p. 22).

12 As part of this strategy, it equipped Lidia's home with a meter and, for two weeks, sent her more water than usual, trying to prove the supply of water was in accordance with WHO guidelines. This was done for completely instrumental purposes without making any changes to the management system. After evidence was provided, the amount of water returned to what she had been receiving since 2012. Lidia's lawyers demonstrated through factual evidence the discrimination that the complainant suffered compared with other areas of the same municipality — most residents also receive staggered water, but the frequency is greater — requesting that her situation be immediately matched to that of others. The explanations provided by the municipality refer to the proximity that other areas of the town have to the supply wells.

13 In 2013, Mexico's new Amparo Law came into force, which provides for the possibility of filing collective *amparos* to defend rights that a group has in common when those rights are harmed by the same act. Had this regulation been in place with authority, the legal strategy would have been different and surely the results would also have been different.

14 Faced with these limitations, HIC-AL has promoted training workshops to build cisterns to collect rainwater for all the families who have wanted to join the proposal and who have been able to assume the costs of the necessary materials. This has been possible thanks to the articulation with other communities led by women who have passed on their constructive knowledge. The efforts have served to reduce dependence on other sources of water, but have not solved the problem in the long months of drought.

References

Amparo en Revisión [Protection in Review] 381/2011 (2011) Segundo Tribunal Colegiado del Decimoctavo Circuito [Second Collegiate Court of the Eighteenth Circuit], (Mex.).

Bolongaro, C. R. A., Sierra, O. R., Torres, R. V., Márquez, G. A. Z., Ramírez, V. J. D., Uribe, N. S., & Monsalvo, J. C. B. (2006). *Análisis de la vulnerabilidad y capacidad de adaptación al cambio climático en los sectores más relevantes del Estado de Morelos* [*Analysis of vulnerability and adaptive capacity to climate change in the most relevant sectors in the State of Morelos*]. Universidad Autónoma del Estado de Morelos. Instituto Nacional de Ecología.

Consejo de Pueblos. (2007). *En defensa del aire y la tierra* [*In defense of air and earth*]. http://13pueblos.blogspot.com/.

Eibenschutz Hartman, R., & Goya Escobedo, C. (2009). *Estudio de la integración urbana y social en la expansión reciente de las ciudades en México 1996–2006* [*Study of urban and social integration in the recent expansion of Mexico's cities 1996–2006*]. Secretaría de Desarrollo Social, Universidad Autónoma Metropolitana. http://biblioteca.diputados.gob.mx/janium/bv/ce/scpd/LX/estud_urb.pdf.

Emanuelli, M. S. (2019). Ampliación Tres de Mayo: Un barrio construido por sus pobladores/as abre camino a la justiciabilidad del derecho humano al agua y al saneamiento [Ampliación Tres de Mayo: A neighborhood built by its residents opens the way to the justiciability of the human right to water and sanitation]. In E. del Pozo & J. C. Martínez (Eds.), *In Caminos desde abajo. Organización social y los usos del Derecho en la defensa del territorio en Mexico* (pp. 305–329). Fundar, Gedisa.

Federici, S. (2013). *La revolución Feminista Inacabada. Mujeres, reproducción social y lucha por lo común* [*Unfinished Feminist. Women, social reproduction and the struggle for the common good*]. Taller Editorial Escuela Calpulli.

Francisco, C. J., Carreón, I. G., Jusidman de Bialostozky, C., & Osiris, M. E. (2016). *El crecimiento urbano y las violencias en México* [*Urban growth and violence in Mexico*]. Naciones Unidas Comisión Económica para América Latina y el Caribe (CEPAL). https://hdl.handle.net/11362/39899.

Gutiérrez Rivas, R. (2005). Jueces y derechos sociales en México: Apenas un eco para los más pobres [Judges and social rights in Mexico: Barely an echo for the poorest]. *Revista Mexicana de Justicia*, 1(6). doi:10.22201/iij.24487929e.2005.6.8636.

Guzmán Ramírez, N. (2009). La gestión social del agua potable en los altos de Morelos [Social management of drinking water in the highlands of Morelos]. In S. Vargas, D. Soares, O. Pérez-Peña, & A. I. Ramírez (Eds.), *La gestión de los recursos hídricos: Realidades y perspectivas* (Vol. 2). IMTA, Universidad de Guadalajara.

Inconformidad [Non-compliance] 49/2014 (2014). Primera Sala de la Suprema Corte de Justicia de la Nación [First Chamber of the Supreme Court of Justice of the Nation], (Mex.). https://desc.scjn.gob.mx/inconformidad-492014.

Instituto Nacional de Estadística y Geografía (INEGI). (2020). *Censo de población y vivienda 2020* [*Population and housing census 2020*] [Dataset]. INEGI. www.inegi.org.mx/programas/ccpv/2020/.

Pueblos de Morelos. (2007). *Manifiesto de los pueblos de Morelos* [*Manifesto of the peoples of Morelos*]. Author.

Rodríguez, A., & Sugranyes, A. (Eds.). (2005). *Los con techo. Un desafío para la política de vivienda social* [*Those with roofs. A challenge for social housing policy*]. Ediciones SUR.

Sepúlveda Ocampo, R., & Fernández Wagner, R. (2006). *Un análisis crítico de las políticas de vivienda en América Latina* [*A critical analysis of housing policies in Latin America*]. Centro Cooperativo Sueco. https://repositorio.uchile.cl/handle/2250/118190.

Sousa Santos, B. de, & Rodríguez Garavito, C. (2007). El derecho, la política y lo subalterno en la globalización contrahegemónica [Law, politics and the subaltern in counterhegemonic globalization]. In B. de Sousa Santos & C. Rodríguez Garavito (Eds.), *El derecho y la globalización desde abajo: Hacia una legalidad cosmopolita* (pp. 7–28). Anthropos.

Svampa, M. (2012). Consenso de los commodities, giro ecoterritorial y pensamiento crítico en América Latina [Commodity consensus, the eco-territorial turn and critical thinking in Latin America]. *Observatorio Social de América Latina*, XIII(32), 15–35.

UN Human Rights Council. (2014). *A/HRC/27/55: Report of the Special Rapporteur on the human right to safe drinking water and sanitation — Common violations of the human rights to water and sanitation*. www.ohchr.org/en/documents/tools-and-resources/ahrc2755-report-special-rapporteur-human-right-safe-drinking-water.

World Health Organization (WHO). (2003). *Domestic water quantity, service level and health*. www.who.int/water_sanitation_health/diseases/WSH03.02.pdf.

11 Winning the battle, losing the war

Land displacement and the limits of legal empowerment in urban Pakistan

Muhammad Arsam, Soha Macktoom, Kanza Rizvi and Nausheen H. Anwar[1]

Introduction

In 2020, amid fieldwork in Ghareebabad, a low-income informal settlement threatened with eviction, a respondent commented on the limits of law:

> There is also a finality attached to the Supreme Court. You can't do anything. In [the city court and high court] you have the option of losing, but you have no option here. Even God cannot appeal here.
>
> (Male, lawyer and resident)

This quote illustrates the two-faced nature of Pakistan's legal institutions, as they swing from benevolent and empowering to draconian and heavy-handed in adjudicating citizens' claims to land, housing and livelihoods in the urban context. As a team of lawyers, planners, social scientists and researchers looking at recent cases of development-related eviction and resettlement in Karachi, the authors have observed the law, as implemented by these institutions, disempower marginalized residents in low-income informal settlements by criminalizing their sources of income and weakening tenure and ownership of land.

This chapter examines this process by reviewing laws, legal practices and debates around land acquisition, displacement and compensation as stated in documents, legal judgments and acts of violence imposed on affected communities. It addresses not only the law's violent imposition of state power, but also the constitutional provisions that seek to enforce individuals' fundamental rights and hold state governing bodies accountable.

The law as a field of practice in Pakistan offers individual citizens, civil society organizations (CSOs) and other groups various legal means and avenues to defend their rights to land. However, spaces for contestation — where state and non-state actors battle over the regulation and appropriation of land and seek compensation — narrow considerably as one climbs the judicial ladder from lower to higher courts, and ultimately the Supreme Court. Here, one enters a non-negotiable and increasingly authoritarian legal terrain. Currently, the power of the courts makes law a space of violence for the residents

DOI: 10.4324/9781003538806-11

of informal settlements as they struggle for the right to land and housing in megacities such as Karachi. This violence takes different shapes throughout the process of displacement, including epistemic (Taussig, 1984), discursive (MacKinnon, 1996), symbolic (Bourdieu & Wacquant, 1992) and structural violence (Galtung, 1969). This chapter investigates violence within Karachi's urban planning landscape that engenders social and political norms deleterious to the city's marginalized and low-income settlements.

Karachi — the country's largest city and the capital of Sindh province (Figure 11.1) — serves as a useful lens to explore the complexities of land displacement in Pakistan. These complexities intertwine with histories of colonial and postcolonial governance, especially in the case of urban infrastructural development. This dynamic can be seen in specific projects in Karachi, such as the Lyari Expressway (LEW) and Karachi Circular Railway (KCR), which are explored as case studies in this chapter. The construction of the Lyari Expressway started in 2000 and displaced over 77,000 families living along the banks of the Lyari River. Between 2018 and 2020, the revival of the Karachi Circular Railway project resulted in large-scale anti-encroachment drives across the city that displaced 3,200 families even before the project was officially commenced (Anwar et al., 2021).

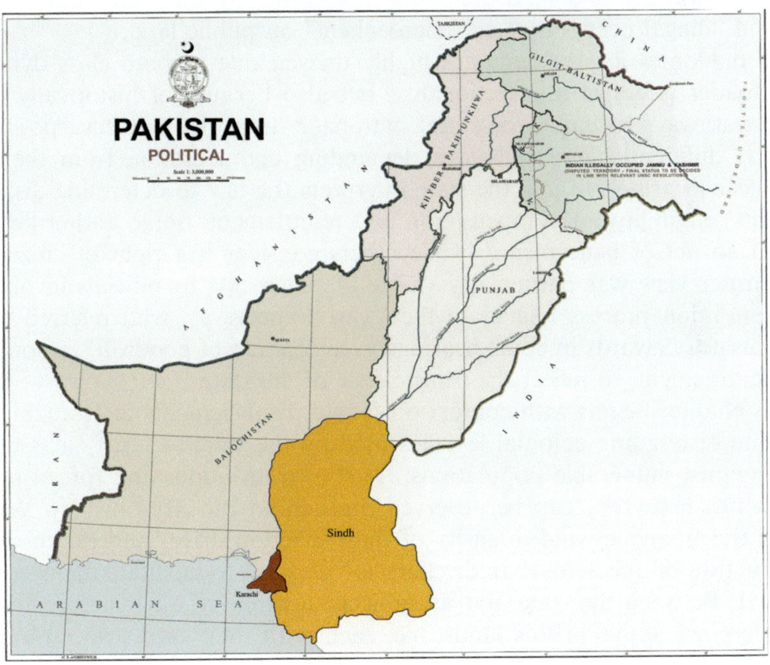

Figure 11.1 Map showing location of Karachi, in the southern province of Sindh
Source: Original map by Government of Pakistan; annotation by Karachi Urban Lab.

The research for this chapter draws on field work conducted between 2018 and 2021, when demolitions linked to the KCR project were underway and over 4,653 households were under threat of displacement (Japan International Cooperation Agency [JICA], 2011). The field work sought to observe the state-sponsored efforts and legal processes that give way to evictions and displacements in Karachi. The research team also used historic precedents from the Lyari Expressway Project to make a case for compensation and adequate resettlement for those displaced, and a wider involvement by stakeholders in the entire process. In addition to conducting over 670 surveys with residents of affected neighbourhoods and over 30 in-depth interviews with residents, activists and state officials, the team also took part in several meetings with community activists and CSOs and attended court proceedings and ongoing protests within and beyond these neighbourhoods.

This chapter considers the ways in which the Pakistani state has deployed notions of "public purpose" and "national importance" to facilitate development projects and justify forced displacements. Currently, this language dovetails with state discourse on climate risk mitigation that has driven large-scale demolitions and evictions of communities living in riparian regions such as the Kausar Niazi colony along the Gujjar Nullah stormwater drain. For residents who premise their sense of security on factors other than property titles, the process of seeking redress and accountability is onerous. Their claims to housing and land are often discredited by the state, and they are declared "illegal occupants" or "encroachers" on public land.

The outcomes for residents are highly uneven due to both class dynamics and broader issues of intersectionality, but also because of historically determined pathways to land access and patronage networks that have positioned them as differentiated populations demanding compensation from the state. This has a bearing on how the state interprets the law to determine displaced residents' eligibility for compensation and resettlement. Some authorities consider it an act of benevolence, while others consider it a right of citizenship. The former view was particularly visible in statements by officials involved in the demolition process related to the Lyari Expressway, who referred to the compensatory awards in court hearings as a "gesture of goodwill", as opposed to an entitlement, to reflect the benevolence of the state.

This chapter begins with context on forced displacements in Karachi as an outcome of ongoing colonial legacies used by the state to justify acts of violence against vulnerable populations. As shown, evictions and forced removals are not new: they can be observed throughout the city's history. What is new is the frequency and intensity of these eviction drives and the discursive construction of affected urban dwellers as "illegals" to facilitate the process of removal. Between the state and its subjects, a range of other actors and stakeholders are active in this landscape, each with their own associations and entanglements with various legal institutions. This chapter discusses the role these varied participants play in strategizing resistance and empowerment for those affected by displacement, and how legal avenues and more active methods of mobilization have led to both successes and failures within this landscape. As demonstrated, the narrative of legal empowerment is complicated, in that the law not only reinforces existing power dynamics but further perpetuates them.

Contextualizing forced displacement in Karachi

Since independence, postcolonial Pakistan's heavy reliance on colonial legacies and the state's violent histories and modes of articulating power (Alavi, 1991) have given way to different kinds of conflict and contestation (Ansari, 2011; Mustafa et al., 2013). This is all the more pertinent in a city like Karachi, with an official population of 16 million, where over 62 percent of the population lives in informal settlements (*katchi abadis*) (Hasan et al., 2015), occupying less than 9 percent of urbanized land (Anwar et al., 2021). These residents live in a continuous state of uncertainty, without tenure security or other official documents of land ownership, thus living through *de-facto* tenure (Hasan & Arif, 2018).

This section traces the violence associated with major displacements and eviction drives in Karachi as located within broader historical, political and legal trends. Karachi's case is unique given its specific history of land and housing shortage as the first capital of the newly formed state. Its present policies of land displacement can be traced to the early 1950s (Ansari, 2005; Anwar et al., 2021). Rooted in the history of post-independence urban planning and development, the desire to relocate refugee-migrants squatting on city land to peripheral refugee colonies resulted in large-scale removal of people from their land in inner city neighbourhoods. Figure 11.2 traces key moments in the city's history, where evictions and rare instances of relocation are observed as part of its socio-spatial transformation.

Many of these displacements have taken place under the guise of urban renewal and infrastructure projects, such as the LEW and KCR project, among several others, and more recently urban flood risk mitigation, as with the widening of Gujjar Nullah. This change in the city's socio-spatial geography was particularly intense in the early 2000s, when land acquisition for mega-infrastructure development to "clean" the city and achieve "world class" status led to widespread displacements and evictions. An estimated 67,562 household units were demolished between 1997 and 2020, displacing 400,000 to 600,000 people, as a conservative estimate, across Karachi (Anwar et al., 2021). Of these forcibly displaced households 33 percent received some form of compensation. But most of these demolitions happened before 2010: since then, compensations have become the exception rather than the rule. An examination of diverse cases of forced removal reveals how evictions facilitate accumulation by differentiated displacement (Doshi, 2013), and engender a process where race and class interlock to produce different categories of urban citizens: this process results in different outcomes in terms of rights and entitlements to land and housing.

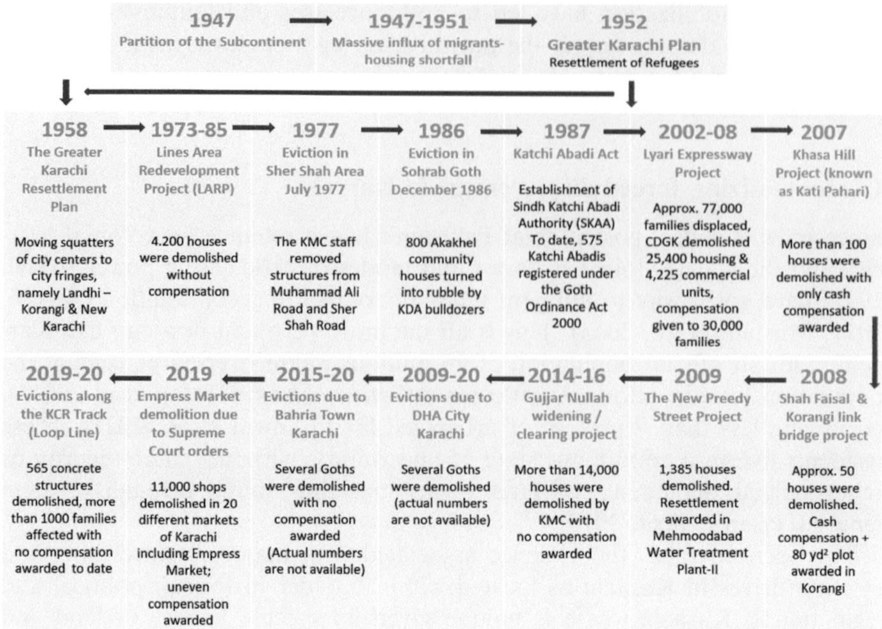

Figure 11.2 Historic timeline of land displacements in Karachi's post-partition context
Source: Anwar et al. (2021).

Furthermore, all tiers of state authority — federal, provincial and local — have deliberately avoided efforts to document, survey or map the ensuing demolitions and displacements. This omission stems not only from the complexities of multiple landowners claiming the same parcel of land (Hasan et al., 2015), but also deliberate attempts to avoid paying compensation claims from subjects discursively constructed as illegals and encroachers or conferring any degree of legitimacy to their tenancy. Systems of governance thus work to disempower citizens by "obscuring the locus of power and creating confusion when communities make claims on the state" (Castro, 2023). In this way, they impede resistance and social mobilization against eviction drives by displaced residents who are forced to self-document.

It is important to note that certain fundamental rights, including the right to property and protection of property, are afforded to every Pakistani citizen under the Constitution. However, property rights have been provided as negative rights (Baig et al., 2020), subject to "any reasonable restrictions imposed by law in the public interest" as stated in Article 23 of the Constitution. This article renders the state the sole arbiter of the "reasonableness" of any restrictions, thus lending constitutional legitimacy to state actions. It grants the state another avenue through which to disempower and limit citizens' control over the acquisition and disposal of their properties. Furthermore, Articles 24(1) and (2) state that, "No person shall be deprived of their property save in accordance with law" and:

> No property shall be compulsorily acquired or taken possession of save for a public purpose, and save by the authority of law which provides for compensation therefore and either fixes the amount of compensation or specifies the principles on and the manner in which compensation is to be determined and given.

The restricted control over property leads to the restricted right to property protection under Article 24. Of particular relevance to this chapter is the limitation of property rights protection in Article 24(3)(e)(ii) (Constitution of Pakistan) concerning infrastructure development, along with the complete exclusion from justiciability regarding the "adequacy or otherwise of any compensation provided" as stated in Article 24(4). These constitutional limitations, coupled with the precarious tenure security of informal settlement residents, provide only weak protection. These limitations restrict residents' ability to seek redress in court or demand that the state uphold the constitutional provisions.

The rights granted under Article 24(1) are not unfettered, particularly where the state requires the property of a Pakistani citizen for "public purpose". In such a case, the state is granted the power of eminent domain, which allows it to appropriate land for "public purpose" while depriving the affected persons of their constitutional right to housing and prevention of compulsory acquisition. In invoking its power of eminent domain in the absence of a clear-cut definition of "public purpose", the state inflicts violence. Hence, the constitutional right to housing does not fetter the acquisition of land in the name of public purpose, perpetuating existing cycles of violence and anti-poor bias towards already marginalized urban populations. As Anwar et al. (2021) observe, "when it comes to infrastructural development in Pakistan, the 'public' whose interests, mobility and aspirations are privileged, generally comprises people who shape policy-making agendas, such as real estate developers, the military, and the urban middle and upper class" (p. 83). This contradiction in the Constitution favours the state over affected persons. The courts lend additional support by interpreting the term "public purpose" as synonymous with national interest, which directly interferes with the ordinary right of private owners regarding disposal of their property (Maqsood & Sajjad, 2021).

This is further complicated by the fact that the principles of policy enshrined in Articles 23 and 24 of the Constitution are not actually justiciable and thus binding on government policy. As seen in the case studies examined below, when faced with a potential clash between state property rights and the collective interests of the poor and vulnerable majority of people in Karachi, the courts and government have ignored or even contradicted principles in the

Constitution that are supposed to provide guidance where law and policy might fall short. On the contrary, when it comes to informal settlement residents' rights, policymakers and courts appear time and again to negate some of these larger aspirations in the Constitution related to social and economic equality.

Informal settlement residents are further restricted in their ability to contest forced evictions, unfair compensation or improper resettlement and rehabilitation because the law enforced for this purpose is a colonial law, the Land Acquisition Act, 1894 (LAA). It does not take into account on-the-ground realities of land ownership in urban Karachi in the post-colonial age. While the LAA outlines the process for acquisition by the state, including the compensation mechanism, it fails to recognize non-titleholders as beneficiaries of compensation. Nor does it take into account the patriarchal power that restricts women's control over formal and informal land.

In the survey conducted among those affected by the KCR project, individuals were asked the gender of the person designated as proprietor on their formal or informal land ownership documents. Only 8 percent were identified as women, while 92 percent of designated proprietors were men. Qualitative interviews further revealed that even these few women held possession due to extenuating circumstances that had removed their male household heads, leaving them *de facto* owners only by chance. Sometimes far-removed male family members with tenuous claim to the property, such as siblings, nephews or even cousins once removed, were called in to occupy that patriarchal place of power. This issue first came to the fore when the project funder, the Japan International Cooperation Agency (JICA), identified individual KCR affectees to be compensated, and the tabulated list was almost entirely male.

Additionally, the LAA neither accounts for the changes imposed by development on the social, cultural, economic, political or environmental landscape nor addresses the resettlement and rehabilitation needs of those affected. With the loopholes in the statutory law that governs land acquisition in Pakistan, Ananya Roy asserts that the degree of legitimacy enjoyed by different forms of informality is a direct outcome of the state's actions through its planning and legal apparatuses. Consequently, the state is the holder of the power "to determine what is informal and what is not, and to determine which forms of informality will thrive and which will disappear" (Roy, 2007). Thus, (in)formality emerges through the process by which the state draws the line between what is inside and outside the rule of law. In the context of the study sites, these spaces exist at the boundaries of "illegal" and "informal" practices or even in a liminal gray space (Yiftachel, 2009) between legality and illegality where people's tenure status remains in constant limbo. Such ambiguous tenure arrangements place residents' lives in a continuous state of uncertainty, whereby their status can change from "landowners" to "illegals" and "encroachers" overnight. Hence, rights to shelter in Karachi are not necessarily rights to propertied citizenship. These complicated, contested and fragmented dynamics are further compounded by competition among political parties that only marginally protect the housing rights of the urban poor (Bhan, 2009; Hasan, 2019; Weinstein & Ren, 2009).

Against these limitations and complexities, the strategies employed by affected residents vary in accordance with factors such as the settlement location, its access to political patronage, ties with social activists, its economic capital and other such variables discussed in the next section.

Strategies for resistance and self-determination

Several authors have shown how residents of informal settlements in the urban Global South premise their sense of tenure security on factors other than those dictated by legal identities or property titles (De Souza, 1999; Garr, 1996; Gilbert, 2002; Mahadevia, 2011; Van Gelder, 2010). The authors' research in informal and low-income settlements in Karachi revealed that people rely on their length of residency at a certain location, inclusion in the area's voting list, absence of any legal action in response to their occupation of land, access to public utilities, and the residential addresses written on their national identification cards as proof of their tenure. The award of land ownership documents such as leases, ownership certificates and offer letters that form the basis of negotiations between politicians or bureaucrats and ordinary citizens are also important, thus making the right to land and property a politically driven affair.

The loopholes and limitations imposed by the Land Acquisition Act have resulted in several instances of unfair compensation and rejection of resettlement for residents facing eviction, particularly within informal and low-income settlements. In response, residents deploy various forms of resistance

Figure 11.3 The rubble of a house in Quaid-e-Azam colony, demolished in 2019 to make way for the Karachi Circular Railway project
Source: KUL photo archives.

to defend their right to housing, land and fair compensation or resettlement. To further explore these dynamics of negotiation, coalition-building and on-the-ground protest in the face of evictions, two large-scale infrastructure projects in Karachi serve as valuable case studies: construction of the Lyari Expressway and the revival of the Karachi Circular Railway project. As the authors observed in following the legal battles, contestations and mobilization of affected residents across both projects through primary and secondary research, many strategies of resistance and self-determination were deployed to substantiate communities' claims over the contested land.

Case 1: Lyari Expressway project

The LEW project — planned as a highway extension aimed at alleviating traffic congestion in downtown Karachi —took over 16 years to complete, from 2000 to 2016. To make way for the project, 15,000 housing units were demolished, displacing over 24,400 families (Dawn News, 2003). This huge human toll meant the process was ensnared in court cases, stay orders, affidavits and public interest litigation (PIL) filed by residents' lawyers to stave off evictions and negotiate fair compensation (Dawn News, 2003). This PKR23 billion (USD81.5 million) project was a joint venture of the federal, provincial and local governments, and was deemed a project of national interest that would benefit the people of Karachi. In 2002, affected residents filed petitions in the Sindh High Court (SHC) contesting the demolition of their homes. The outcome of these petitions depended largely on whether or not residents possessed land ownership documents, disregarding the realities of land ownership in Pakistan. Residents who were non-title holders, mostly from informal settlements, found themselves in a double bind where violent governmental practices intersected with legal edifices to construct them as "encroachers" and "illegal occupants".

Civil society organizations, urban planners, human rights advocates and international organizations such as the Asian Coalition of Human Rights and the United Nations Human Settlements Programme voiced opposition before the project commenced. This criticism proved effective in mobilizing affected residents to seek redress from the courts. In their letters to the editor of the daily English national newspaper *Dawn*, well-established NGOs highlighted that far from resolving the city's traffic problems, the LEW would instead trigger a social and environmental disaster. One such organization, the Urban Resource Centre (URC) (2006), called on government agencies "to hold a public discussion on the Lyari Expressway, followed by public hearings. Only after such a process should the Lyari Expressway [either] be constructed or be shelved". International agencies and different local organizations also wrote letters appealing to then-President General Pervaiz Musharraf to stop the evictions and demolitions along the Lyari River.

Legal avenues and support from the court of law were also pursued, including the filing of a Constitution Petition (2003) by political parties and civil society organizations. Similarly, an appeal was filed in the Sindh High

Court by a collective of community representatives under the Action Committee for Civil Problems coalition. The appeal asked the Chief Justice to take *suo moto* notice on various irregularities in the project, including its side-stepping of required procedures and documentation (such as a compulsory environmental impact assessment), and its lack of demarcation plans and notifications for land acquisition. While no specific action was taken in response, various other strategies for resistance and self-determination were successful when accompanied by social mobilization, through alliances formed with different NGOs, CSOs and other activists.

On-the-ground community mobilization remained one of the most popular and effective mechanisms against demolition crews. Repeated acts of protest in Hasan Auliya Village — a settlement along the Lyari River affected by the eviction drive — garnered city-wide and even international attention. The village's successful resistance was showcased in articles, magazines and even a documentary film (Cabannes et al., 2010; Centre on Housing Rights and Evictions, 2006; Syed Ali, 2002). Eventually, the civil society letters, combined with community protests, forced the state to formulate a compensation package for affected residents — including those who did not possess valid land tenure documents such as leases.

Given the many different land-owning agencies in Karachi, each awarding its distinctive lease to residents, these protracted court cases highlighted the differentiated nature of leasing arrangements and the irregular, non-transparent and arbitrary manner of land valuations conducted by the state. These arbitrary measures were observed in compensation packages for the 39 settlements with official documents of ownership. For example, residents from Angara Goth and Area A Liaquatabad, where average plot sizes were between 80 and 120 square yards, had filed dozens of petitions in the Sindh High Court to contest the land evaluation process. During the state's land evaluation process, plots leased under the Karachi Metropolitan Corporation (KMC) in Area A Liaquatabad were valued at twice as much as plots leased under the Sindh Katchi Abadi Authority (SKAA) in Angara Goth, even though both were formal settlements (Anwar et al., 2021). After litigating for over a decade, the residents of Angara Goth and Area A Liaquatabad and other similar settlements finally received a compensation package that included damages or consequences of acquisition and an additional 15 percent on the market value of land (Table 11.1).

Table 11.1 Compensation packages for Angara Goth and Area A Liaquatabad

Settlement name	*Type of lease*	*Compensation offered before court intervention*	*Compensation offered after court intervention in accordance with LAA provisions*
Angara Goth	SKAA Lease	PKR6,000 per yd^2	PKR24,000 per yd^2
Area A Liaquatabad	KMC Lease	PKR13,000 per yd^2	PKR38,000 per yd^2

Source: Anwar et al. (2021); figures borrowed from Case Reference No.1/2016.

It is important to note that these residents were able to obtain stays over their property because they possessed official land tenure documents, something the vast majority did not possess. Hence, 30,000 families who had no official documents were provided only PKR50,000 (approximately USD180) and an 80 square yard plot on the city's rural–urban margins as compensation. As the Advocate General of Sindh province stated, this meagre compensation was offered as a "gesture of goodwill and in order to provide better facilities of life [to people] who were residing in subhuman conditions" (*Taj Haider & Ors v. Government of Pakistan & Ors*). The stark contrasts in compensation reflect the non-inclusive manner of the compensation process, which has had long-term harmful effects on these families.

Even further down the hierarchy, there were still tens of thousands who were never acknowledged as affected by the LEW, or simply fell through cracks in the compensation process and received nothing. A similar story emerges in the case of the KCR project, where most affected residents had no official tenure documents, restricting their avenues for legal redress and compensation.

Figure 11.4 The Lyari Basti neighbourhood, where some of those affected by the LEW were resettled on plots of 80 square yards, given as a "gesture of goodwill"

Source: KUL photo archives, 2020.

Case 2: The Karachi Circular Railway revival project

To address Karachi's traffic congestion and mobility issues, the revival of the defunct Karachi Circular Railway project was announced in 2003. As a result, over 28 informal settlements across Karachi would be affected, with 4,653 households under direct threat of displacement. What is particularly unique about this case study is that the Supreme Court actively encouraged violent evictions of settlements across the railway track, with the affected residents addressed as "encroachers" on state land in court proceedings. This wording was echoed in media reports and by other state officials. This afforded court-sanctioned impunity to state authorities, giving residents no recourse to accountability. Most importantly, this justified circumvention of the land acquisition process enshrined in the LAA, as the 2010 Removal of Encroachment Act became the relevant law to be invoked. For municipal agencies and the provincial bureaucracy, evictions for the construction of KCR were in compliance with the Supreme Court order.

The evictions for the KCR project find their roots in a public interest litigation petition filed in the Supreme Court by Karachi's ex-mayor Naimatullah Khan (2001–2005) to resolve alleged problems with "land grabs" and "encroachers" (*Naimatullah Khan v. Federation of Pakistan*). Historically in Pakistan, the primary objective of PIL was to facilitate social justice for poor and underprivileged individuals and groups, and classes of people who suffered from state oppression or were unable to pursue claims through the formal justice system because of various physical, economic and social constraints (Khan, 2014). The enmeshment of land governance in legality and violence was seen when the Supreme Court took a *suo moto* action in the case brought by Naimatullah Khan. This petition by Karachi's ex-mayor asking the Supreme Court to intervene in the city's governance was simultaneously an attempt to defend existing land-use laws and also a strategic move to discipline other government officials for their "corruption" and "incompetence" in this regard.

The residents living along the KCR track explored different legal avenues to build their case against forceful evictions. This started with a request filed in 2013 in the Ombudsman's office by the KCR community representatives, with support from the URC, an NGO that works to better inform and support communities affected by land displacements, to gather information on the details of the KCR project. The request was based on the Sindh Freedom of Information Act 2006 and Article 19-A of the Constitution, which enshrines citizens' right to information. Among other details, URC requested access to a list of people affected by the project, which had been compiled by JICA — a key funder of the KCR project. After two years of continuous follow-up through letters and visits to the Ombudsman's office, the community, through URC, gained access to the list and was able to identify discrepancies through rigorous cross-checking. This process unearthed several fake entries and affectees left off the list. To substantiate these claims, community representatives distributed these lists to all 28 affected settlements,

Figure 11.5 Houses demolished in Moosa Colony, located along the KCR track
Source: KUL photo archives, 2019.

asking residents to confirm their names in the list. Over 20 households in Ghareebabad colony — another settlement located in District South and threatened by evictions for the KCR project — had been overlooked, among the gaps identified.

The residents of Ghareebabad then filed a case in 2017 seeking an injunction against evictions without proper compensation in the Karachi Civil Court. Generally, the pathway for redress through courts is mired in delays and the proceedings stretch over several years, only for the case to be later disposed of by a ruling of the Superior Court. The case filed by Ghareebabad residents met a similar fate, experiencing back-to-back adjournments: it was disposed of by the Civil Court pursuant to orders issued by the Supreme Court to dispose of all lower court cases that were causing "hindrances" in the KCR land acquisition process.

In efforts to exhaust all possible avenues, the residents of the 28 affected settlements approached the National Commission for Human Rights (NCHR), and filed a petition in 2017 seeking proper compensation if the land was to be acquired for the project. The NCHR was established as an impartial state body for the protection and promotion of human rights in Pakistan, and reports directly to Parliament. Upon reviewing the facts, NCHR took notice of the human rights violation resulting from forced evictions and concluded that affected persons did not fall within the definition of "encroachers" and therefore could not be evicted without proper compensation. However, as the NCHR had no legal standing with the Supreme Court, its dissension did

Figure 11.6 Forum organized by URC in April 2019 for those affected by the Karachi Circular Railway to strategize anti-eviction protests and plan a way forward
Source: KUL photo archives, 2019.

not impact the Court's judgment on the matter. This is one of many instances where the courts have failed to independently adjudge the brutal impacts of developmental projects.

The only remaining pathway was to approach the Supreme Court, which for ordinary citizens is only possible with civil society support, which presents an additional barrier to access. In 2018, the KCR affectees filed an intervener application in the Supreme Court through a prominent social activist, Jibran Nasir, urging the court to acknowledge that residents' fundamental rights were being violated by the eviction drives. As a veteran Supreme Court lawyer observed, the presiding Justice was hardly impartial:

> Chief Justice Gulzar Ahmed, in my opinion, is adamant on the revival of Karachi Circular Railway to show his legal authoritarianism, which was also evident from Justice Saqib Nisar's efforts. The Supreme Court judges feel they do not have enough time, hence they issue orders/judgments based on their instincts without giving any rational thought to it.[2]

Once the petition was filed, the Supreme Court took a strict stance in favour of the revival of the defunct railway, rejecting any arguments that opposed the project. Seeing the court's adamancy, arguments were modified in the intervener petition. Instead of arguing that KCR was a non-viable project, it asked the Court to constitute a committee to decide on the resettlement and rehabilitation of affected persons. As the lawyer representing the affectees said,

"The court has made its decision [to revive the KCR] which leaves us with two choices, ... between a worse outcome and an absolute disaster".[3]

When residents started losing hope in pursuing legal avenues, they started to use mobilization as an effective tactic for resisting the demolitions. This was the case in Ghareebabad, where they held sit-in protests in their neighbourhood as news spread that eviction teams might be visiting. Social media, WhatsApp groups and announcements made through loudspeakers at local mosques were all used to mobilize residents for the moment when bulldozers would arrive at the settlement. As a result, residents of Ghareebabad successfully warded off the first of many attempts to demolish their settlement. Other acts of resistance included gathering large crowds to make themselves visible outside the court on the day of their hearings. This, as one resident pointed out, was a tactic "to intercept the car of the Chief Justice as he enters the Supreme Court on the day of the hearing and make him see the number of people affected by his decision". While these tactics proved somewhat effective at a moment when various tiers of government were themselves fragmented over project implementation, which has stalled its commencement, residents of these neighbourhoods continue to live under the looming threat of evictions.

Resettlement and rehabilitation policies, past and present

The Land Acquisition Act of 1894 remains the primary legislation dealing with all matters of acquiring land, for government and private projects, and any decisions related to compensation for affected persons. While it does not cover resettlement, the Act has been cited in other laws for sector-specific land

Figure 11.7 Ghareebabad residents protesting outside the Karachi Press Club after notices for demolition were placed in their neighbourhood

Source: KUL photo archive, 2019.

acquisition, including the Railway Act of 1890 and the Karachi Development Authority Order of 1957, to name a few.

There have been subsequent attempts at legal reform to address the exclusionary loopholes in the LAA, but with limited success and at an excruciatingly slow pace when compared with progress in neighbouring countries. In 2013, India, which inherited the same colonial-era laws, replaced the LAA with the Right to Fair Compensation and Transparency in Land Acquisition, Rehabilitation, Resettlement Act. Among other clauses, it requires the government to conduct surveys of affected families, and pushes for improvement in their social and economic status. Similar protections for affectees are awarded in the National Involuntary Resettlement Policy approved by the Sri Lankan Cabinet in 2001 (Sajjad, 2022).

In Pakistan, two documents that identified and addressed the limitations of the LAA were drafted by the Pakistan Environmental Protection Agency: the Resettlement Ordinance, 2001 and the National Resettlement Policy, 2002. These measures outlined mechanisms for fair resettlement and rehabilitation and for social assessments, and emphasized the need to integrate public participation and consultations on resettlement. However, neither has been implemented. The Supreme Court itself has stressed the need to amend the LAA in a full bench judgment, directing that "such overhaul becomes necessary in light of the shortcomings of the current scheme of land acquisition with respect to compensation and matters incidental thereto" (Civil Appeals No.1476 to 1485 of 2018, SC 2018). Yet between 2018 and 2022, while large-scale demolition exercises continued to be executed across Karachi, no progress was made on this front.

Figure 11.8 Demolitions in Kausar Niazi colony, a settlement located along the Gujjar Nullah, to make way for storm water drainage
Source: KUL photo archives, 2021.

As of 2024, a new wave of evictions is underway. These latest evictions are linked to installation of stormwater drains in the Orangi, Gujjar and Mehmoodabad *nullahs*; road-widening projects near Mujahid Colony and Moosa Colony; and construction of the Malir Expressway. As a response, mobilizations against forced evictions in Karachi have re-emerged, led by organizations such as the Urban Resource Centre, Karachi Bachao Tehreek, Awami Workers Party and a host of independent activists and journalists.

Consequently, the Government of Sindh has expedited work on drafting a Sindh Rehabilitation and Resettlement Policy 2022. The primary goal of this policy is to:

> [A]void and/or minimize displacement and resettlement... Where displacement and/or social and economic impacts are unavoidable, to provide adequate compensation, resettlement and rehabilitation assistance and support to affected and/or displaced populations, so that affected people and communities can at least maintain their pre-displacement socio-economic status.
>
> (Draft Sindh Resettlement & Rehabilitation Policy, 2022, Government of Sindh, 2023, p. 6)

The document goes further, to also address displacement caused by climate-related or other natural disasters. However, it has been subject to critique in various consultations arranged by provincial representatives and meetings organized by stakeholders, such as the National Commission for Human Rights and The Knowledge Forum. Critics highlight a need to amend the LAA 1894 before new policy can be formulated, and to gain consent of affected parties. Some also view the current attempt as a mere gesture of appeasement to international funding organizations such as the World Bank. It is important to mention that the draft policy has no legal cover obligating practical implementation. As one of its clauses states, "the proposed measures are in harmony with existing laws, acting as additions to the LAA (1894) and other relevant laws. The LAA (1894) will continue to apply in full force to all the situations envisaged in the law" (p. 7).

A glaring omission in the aforementioned policy efforts has been their failure to involve Karachi's most vulnerable communities in the decision-making process, or ensure the prevention of future cycles of displacement. Low-income residents are especially vulnerable to cycles of displacement. Residents displaced by the KCR demolitions, for example, were initially promised a new plot in Jumma Goth in 2011 in the first resettlement plan proposed by JICA. However, in early 2023, Jumma Goth faced a new round of displacement linked to the Malir Expressway, another approved project that overrides several laws and regulations. An active petition has been lodged against it in the Sindh High Court. Hence, even if residents displaced by KCR had been able to claim the plots they were legally entitled to, they would have been displaced again by this new project. The latest draft of the state's resettlement and rehabilitation policy was in part informed by these histories, in particular the Karachi Circular Railway case; yet it still fails to acknowledge such on-the-ground realities, and most importantly, the sheer opaqueness of land title rights for citizens of Karachi. As such, the policy remains incomplete.

Conclusion

This chapter has illustrated how Pakistani law regarding the right to housing, as currently formulated and enacted, is still riddled with gaps and loopholes, and skewed in favour of powerful state institutions with a well-documented anti-poor bias. This enables courts to interpret and implement these laws in ways that disempower populations seeking recourse, especially those living in low-income informal settlements who lack tenure security. In the present context, law is not just concerned with what is "legal" or "just": it also attempts to impose certain sensibilities, as when a Supreme Court judge wanted to "restore Karachi to its former glory" (Kureshi, 2002). This has little to do with the writ of law and is instead derived from a personal sense of aesthetic norms — what Ghertner (2015) terms "Rule by Aesthetics". Moreover, this tendency has become intertwined with larger narratives of development and nationalistic ideals, adding new intensity to Karachi's decades-long, violent and hegemonic process of eviction and displacement. While, the court's interjection through *suo moto* actions has been legitimized in the Constitution, it does not define the limits under which such powers can be exercised. Hence, individual's ideals of what the city should look like dominate interpretations of law and consequent decisions in Pakistan's higher courts.

Karachi's informal settlements, buffeted by land speculation and climate risk mitigation strategies, are frontiers of novel legal struggles. Their populations have limited room, however, to negotiate and mobilize against the lack of resettlement and compensation mechanisms, and the increasingly arbitrary determination of compensation and resettlement plans in the few instances when they exist. Drafting laws that will secure the proposed policy interventions is a pressing need, particularly when the recently proposed Karachi Comprehensive Coastal Development Zone is bound to result in a new wave of large-scale demolitions in coastal communities.

This is not to imply that legal mechanisms for empowerment do not exist. Affected populations and NGOs have used public interest litigation and right-to-information requests, in addition to filing appeals and constitutional petitions, in their legal battles against forced evictions. Yet without other grass-root, activist-led approaches and on-the-ground mobilization and resistance, even laws that were conceived to be emancipatory will fall short. Thus, legal empowerment does not simply derive from smarter legislation or an excess of judicial intervention; it comes from creating structures that allow common citizens and those affected by these laws to participate in this process as much as possible.

Notes

1 The authors were part of a three- year project funded by the International Development Research Center (IDRC). The objectives of the research were to observe how the process of development-bound land is governed and acquired for infrastructure projects in Karachi and the ways in which people negotiate compensation for their homes, respond to their marginalization and how they organize and demand redress. While our initial role was restricted to that of researchers, several sites received eviction notices during our fieldwork, making us rethink our positionality, agency and ethical responsibility towards the communities being researched. Consequently, our role extended to that of activists, journalists and providing data to the legal team representing the evictees in court.
2 Notes from informal conversations with the lawyer.
3 Authors' notes.

References

Alavi, H. (1991). Nationhood and the nationalities in Pakistan. In H. Donnan & P. Werbner (Eds.), *Economy and Culture in Pakistan* (pp. 163–187). Palgrave Macmillan UK. doi:10.1007/978-1-349-11401-6_8.

Ansari, S. (2005). *Life after partition: Migration, community and strife in Sindh, 1947–1962*. Oxford University Press.

Ansari, S. (2011). Everyday expectations of the State during Pakistan's early years: Letters to the editor, Dawn (Karachi), 1950–1953. *Modern Asian Studies*, 45(1), 159–178. doi:10.1017/S0026749X10000296.

Anwar, N., Anjum, G., Abdullah, A., Toheed, M., Macktoom, S., Kanza, R., Qureshi, F., Maheen, A., & Saleem, A. (2021). *Land, governance and the gendered politics of displacement in urban Pakistan*. doi:10.17605/OSF.IO/YSM28.

Baig, M. R., Idrees, R. Q., & Nawaz, H. U. (2020). An analytical study of the laws relating to housing industry in Pakistan. *Pakistan Social Sciences Review*, 4(1), 1014–1025. doi:10.35484/pssr.2020(4-I)77.

Bhan, G. (2009). "This is no longer the city I once knew". Evictions, the urban poor and the right to the city in millennial Delhi. *Environment and Urbanization*, 21(1), 127–142. doi:10.1177/0956247809103009.

Bourdieu, P., & Wacquant, L. (Eds.). (1992). *An invitation to reflexive sociology*. University of Chicago Press.

Cabannes, Y., Yafai, S. G., & Johnson, C. (Eds.). (2010). *How people face evictions*. Development Planning Unit/University College London.

Castro, B. (2023). Between a rock and a hard place: Heterogeneous governance, claims making and forced eviction in a megacity. *International Journal of Urban and Regional Research*, 47(1). doi:10.1111/1468-2427.13152.

Centre on Housing Rights and Evictions. (2006). *Lyari-highway of tears*. https://cinemata.org/view?m=LLCzt8MvV.

Constitution of Pakistan, art. VIII–XXVIII, §2. www.pakistani.org/pakistan/constitution/part2.ch1.html.

Dawn News. (2003, March 7). Karachi: Court sees flaws in LEW land ownership. *Dawn News*. www.dawn.com/news/86151.

De Souza, F. A. M. (1999). Land tenure security and housing improvements in Recife, Brazil. *Habitat International*, 23(1), 19–33. doi:10.1016/S0197-3975(98)00033–00032.

Doshi, S. (2013). The politics of the evicted: Redevelopment, subjectivity, and difference in Mumbai's slum frontier. *Antipode*, 45(4), 844–865. doi:10.1111/j.1467-8330.2012.01023.x.

Draft Sindh Resettlement & Rehabilitation Policy, 2022, Government of Sindh (2023). https://cm.sindh.gov.pk/storage/resourcePage/v2WDTRFBoXUJqB2E50thFoaWrtOnhBiyMPN9l1MX.pdf.

Galtung, J. (1969). Violence, peace, and peace research. *Journal of Peace Research*, 6(3), 167–191. doi:10.1177/002234336900600301.

Garr, D. J. (1996). Expectative land rights, house consolidation and cemetery squatting: Some perspectives from Central Java. *World Development*, 24(12), 1925–1933. doi:10.1016/S0305-750X(96)00077–0.

Ghertner, A. (2015). *Rule by aesthetics: World-class city making in Delhi*. Oxford Academic. doi:10.1093/acprof:oso/9780199385560.001.0001.

Gilbert, A. (2002). On the mystery of capital and the myths of Hernando de Soto: What difference does legal title make? *International Development Planning Review*, 24(1), 1–19. doi:10.3828/idpr.24.1.1.

Hasan, A. (2019). Residential segregation in Mithi and Karachi, Pakistan. *Environment and Urbanization*, 31(2), 635–638. doi:10.1177/0956247818812331.

Hasan, A., Ahmed, N., Raza, M., Sadiq, A., Ahmed, S. U., & Sarwar, M. B. (2015). *Karachi: The land issue*. Oxford University Press.

Hasan, A., & Arif, H. (2018). Pakistan: The causes and repercussions of the housing crisis. *International Institute for Environment and Development*. http://hdl.handle.net/2451/44207.

Japan International Cooperation Agency, Karachi. (2011). *Resettlement action plan — Revival of KCR, Karachi Urban Transportation Corporation (KUTC)*. Author.

Khan, M. (2014). Genesis and evolution of public interest litigation in the supreme court of Pakistan: Toward a dynamic theory of judicialization. *Temple International and Comparative Law Journal*, 28(2), 285–359.

Kureshi, Y. (2002). Chief Justice Gulzar Ahmed: Master planner or yet another populist judge? *Dawn News*. www.dawn.com/news/1673274.

MacKinnon, C. A. (1996). *Only words*. Harvard University Press.

Mahadevia, D. (2011). *Tenure security and urban social protection in India*. Centre for Social Protection Research.

Maqsood, A., & Sajjad, F. (2021). Victim, broker, activist, fixer: Surviving dispossession in working class Lahore. *Environment and Planning D: Society and Space*, 39(6), 994–1008. doi:10.1177/02637758211029290.

Mustafa, D., Brown, K. E., & Tillotson, M. (2013). Antipode to terror: Spaces of performative politics. *Antipode*, 45(5), 1110–1127. doi:10.1111/anti.12014.

Naimatullah Khan v. Federation of Pakistan (2011) Constitutional Petition No. 09 of 2010 (Pak.). www.supremecourt.gov.pk/downloads_judgements/const.p._9_2010.pdf

Roy, A. (2007). Urban informality: Toward an epistemology of planning. *Journal of the American Planning Association*, 71(2), 147–158. doi:10.1080/01944360508976689.

Sajjad, F. (2022). *Land acquisition, resettlement and rehabilitation policies — The need for a new approach*. Mahbub Ul Haq Research Centre at LUMS. https://mhrc.lums.edu.pk/land-acquisition-resettlement-and-rehabilitation-policies-the-need-for-a-new-approach/.

Syed Ali, N. (2002). Highway to hell. *Newsline*. https://newslinemagazine.com/magazine/highway-to-hell/.

Taj Haider & Ors v. Government of Pakistan & Ors (2003) Constitutional Petition No. D 1437 of 2003 (Pak.).

Taussig, M. (1984). Culture of terror — Space of death: Roger Casement's Putumayo report and the explanation of torture. *Comparative Studies in Society and History*, 26(3), 467–497. doi:10.1017/S0010417500011105.

Urban Resource Centre. (2006). *Lyari Expressway in Pakistan: Violence and eviction*. Author.

Van Gelder, J.-L. (2010). What tenure security? The case for a tripartite view. *Land Use Policy*, 27(2), 449–456. doi:10.1016/j.landusepol.2009.06.008.

Weinstein, L., & Ren, X. (2009). The changing right to the city: Urban renewal and housing rights in globalizing Shanghai and Mumbai. *City & Community*, 8(4), 407–432. doi:10.1111/j.1540-6040.2009.01300.x.

Yiftachel, O. (2009). Theoretical notes on "gray cities": The coming of urban apartheid? *Planning Theory*, 8(1), 88–100. doi:10.1177/1473095208099300.

12 Building coalitions and cases

Towards climate and housing justice in Bangladesh's informal settlements

Sara Hossain, Efadul Huq and Priya Ahsan Chowdhury

Introduction

Some 50 percent of Bangladesh's 1,736,302 slum dwellers are located in the megacity of Dhaka according to the Population and Housing Census, 2022 (Bangladesh Bureau of Statistics, 2023). The 2022 census also found that 51.7 percent of slum dwellers were male, 48.3 percent female and 0.03 percent *hijra* (gender diverse). However, these numbers are conservative estimates: in 2022, the Special Rapporteur on the promotion and protection of human rights in the context of climate change estimated that the slum population of Dhaka alone was approximately 4 million (United Nations Human Rights Special Procedures, 2022). A 2014 census that focused specifically on slum and "floating" residents in Bangladesh — with gender- and occupation-disaggregated data on residents of each slum — identified that the vast majority of those living in slums and settlements were employed in the informal sector (Bangladesh Bureau of Statistics, 2014, p. 34). In contexts where statistical datasets are unreliable, community-led and NGO-supported local enumeration (as discussed later in this chapter) plays a crucial role in highlighting the existence of slum dwellers, thus enabling legal professionals to advocate effectively on their behalf.

The slum census indicates that slums typically develop on various types of land, including government or semi-government land, private vacant land, abandoned buildings, hill slopes, railway lines and roadsides. The informal settlements in Dhaka are also arrival cities for climate-impacted people from all over Bangladesh. Located in the Ganges-Brahmaputra Delta and facing an increased risk of natural disasters, Bangladesh is one of the most climate-vulnerable countries in the world. According to multiple reports, millions of Bangladeshis have been and will continue to be displaced due to climate-related hazards (Huq & Shafique, 2023). Climate injustice in Bangladesh manifests as both the displacement of climate migrants from their places of origin and the increased vulnerability to flooding, heatwaves and other extremes in the urban destinations where low-income migrants make their homes.

DOI: 10.4324/9781003538806-12

Legal interventions on behalf of slum dwellers in Bangladesh

From the late 1980s, public interest litigation has been initiated (Siddiqi, 2006) to seek emergency intervention from the High Court Division of the Supreme Court of Bangladesh to stall threatened evictions of informal settlement dwellers in Dhaka and other rapidly urbanizing areas of Bangladesh.[1] In many of these cases, the High Court's interim orders have effectively prevented the police or bulldozers from demolishing shanties and huts (Ain O Salish Kendra, 2012). Over the years, these orders have been largely respected by the state and relevant public authorities.[2] Many such cases have remained pending for long years, with interim orders of stay continuing to provide legal protection for settlement dwellers. A few cases have concluded in final decisions, with significant judicial observations, contributing to a nascent housing jurisprudence. These have rejected public authorities' characterization of settlement dwellers as "trespassers", "encroachers" or "criminals". Instead, the courts have recognized through their observations the critical role these communities play in the city as hawkers, street vendors, rickshaw pullers or as workers in homes, public institutions or private companies and factories. Such re-characterization by the courts has been accompanied by consistent observations that evicting bodies must comply with minimal procedural safeguards and ensure prior resettlement or rehabilitation.

While public interest litigation (PIL) did not result in direct recognition of housing rights, the courts' innovative interpretations of constitutional rights and sustained observations on the need for protection for slum and settlement dwellers living on public land did have an effect in shaping public discourse, and arguably, public policy. Over the next two decades, the language used in at least some court cases shifted to claims that the authorities had already taken action for rehabilitation and resettlement, while relevant policies spoke to prioritizing housing for vulnerable communities and individuals.[3] Anti-eviction advocacy thus became part and parcel of a broader agenda and struggles for housing justice. The courts' orders enabled settlement dwellers to remain in their homes,[4] and to raise broader demands for recognition of their rights to the city. These demands gradually won a response in political commitments, more progressive national policies on housing and climate adaptation, and housing programs for low-income and marginalized communities.

Climate change and informal settlements

Millions of Bangladeshis have been and will continue to be displaced due to climate-related hazards, including more frequent and severe cyclones; heavier and more erratic rainfall, which is accelerating riverbank erosion; droughts; and increased salinity in groundwater and coastal rivers (Huq & Shafique, 2023). Predominantly, people move from coastal districts and mainland areas along major rivers where flooding, storms and erosion risks are higher. Although comprehensive statistics are lacking, the spatial trend of rural-to-urban migration clearly exceeds any other movement pattern in Bangladesh and underpins the country's accelerated urbanization. National-level climate adaptation plans in Bangladesh — such as Bangladesh Delta Plan 2100, the National Strategy on the Management of Disaster and Climate Induced Internal Displacement 2015, and the Bangladesh Climate Change Strategy and Action Plan 2009 — recognize that climate migrants will move to urban areas and concentrate in informal settlements, the only places they can find affordable housing and work. Furthermore, the National Strategy on the Management of Disaster and Climate Induced Internal Displacement 2015 recommends *in situ* upgrading for informal settlements, along with promoting collective tenure rights.

About this chapter

This chapter draws on advocacy work, field experiences and research undertaken by the Bangladesh Legal Aid and Services Trust (BLAST). It analyses three ongoing cases related to *bostis* (slums) in Dhaka, one of which led to a flagship public–private partnership focused on slum rehabilitation. As discussed below, the legal empowerment approach used in these cases demonstrates three key dynamics:

- First, settlement dwellers mobilized against eviction.
- Second, NGOs facilitated legal interventions and strengthened support and survival networks within the settlements.
- Third, NGOs and housing advocates creatively manoeuvred within a shrinking democratic sphere to create participatory spaces where settlement dwellers could present their concerns to city and national authorities.

BLAST was established by leading lawyers to institutionalize legal aid in 1993, and now works across the country. To date, BLAST has litigated about 20 cases filed in the public interest (Huq et al., 2022), challenging forced evictions and seeking alternative land allocations and rehabilitation. It has also conducted related advocacy outside the courts for recognition of a legal right to housing. These cases and campaigns have involved slum and settlement dwellers and a range of experts and other development and rights organizations, such as Ain o Salish Kendra (ASK), BRAC, Dustho Shastho Kendra (DSK) and the Coalition for the Urban Poor (CUP), among others.

This chapter begins with a discussion of housing laws, policies and programs relevant to poor people's self-built settlements in Bangladesh and the contributions of PIL in forestalling evictions and advancing slum dwellers' rights. It then presents case studies of community resistance in three self-built settlements within metropolitan Dhaka: Korail, Bhashantek and Kallyanpur. In Korail, residents have used PIL to resist forced evictions on multiple occasions. In Bhashantek, residents have been caught in limbo by a stalled rehabilitation project that was developed as a flagship public–private partnership, intended to deliver housing for low-income groups and landless *bosti* dwellers. In Kallyanpur, community organizing supported by Dushtha Shasthya Kendra has helped residents resist eviction and increasingly advocate on their own behalf.

The chapter then offers some reflections on the role of civil society in supporting a multipronged approach to empowerment in Bangladesh's informal settlements. Going beyond litigation, this approach combines legal education and advocacy, community organizing and the design of participatory processes for community engagement. Finally, the chapter concludes with a series of recommendations focused on emerging directions (such as the intersection of climate and housing justice) and possible strategies to advance just housing for all.

Housing laws, policies and programs and the emerging use of public interest litigation

While the Constitution of Bangladesh (1972) — which was promulgated following a nine-month war of independence — contains no express recognition of the right to housing, it guarantees the right to life (art. 32) and the right to be treated in accordance with the law (art. 31). It also provides for fundamental principles requiring the state to ensure the basic conditions of life for all citizens (art. 15), including to a livelihood and shelter. These principles are significantly complemented by commitments made in the earlier Proclamation of Independence to ensure all citizens "equality, human dignity and social justice".

With regard to international obligations, Bangladesh is party to the core international human rights treaties, all of which contain provisions which provide for the right to adequate housing. These include the International Covenant on Civil and Political Rights (ICCPR), the International Covenant on Economic, Social and Cultural Rights (ICESCR), the Convention on the Elimination of All Forms of Discrimination Against Women, the Convention on the Rights of the Child (CRC) and the Convention on the Rights of Persons with Disabilities. Bangladesh has also committed to achieving the Sustainable Development Goals, of which Goal 11 focuses on creating inclusive, safe, resilient and sustainable cities and human settlements.

In general, forced evictions will be incompatible with the ICESCR and can only be justified in exceptional circumstances and in line with international law principles (Committee on Economic, Social and Cultural Rights [CESCR], 1991, para. 18). The Basic Principles and Guidelines on Development-Based Evictions and Displacement also note that forced evictions involve severe violations of internationally recognized human rights, including adequate housing, food, water, health, education, work, personal security, security of the home and freedom from cruel, inhuman and degrading treatment (United Nations Human Rights Council, 2007, para. 6, Annex 1).

Under Article 11(1) of the ICESCR (1966), the state is bound by international human rights law treaty obligations to ensure adequate housing for all. This obligation includes putting safeguards in place for any forced evictions, including the need for substantial justification (CESCR, 1997, paras. 11 & 14), exploration of alternatives in consultation with affected individuals (para. 13), and procedural protections such as adequate notice before eviction (para. 15). The state must also ensure that evictions do not lead to homelessness or violation of other human rights, and provide appropriate measures, within its available resources, to ensure access to alternative housing, resettlement or productive land for those affected (para. 16). In addition, the state is required to guarantee that individuals are not subjected to arbitrary or unlawful intrusions into their privacy and family life (International Covenant on Civil and Political Rights; UN, 1966, art. 17). Given that a very significant portion of Bangladesh's population are children, the obligations in Article 27 of the CRC (1989) to provide children with material assistance and support programs, specifically in relation to housing, are particularly relevant.

Many of the above provisions have been cited before the Bangladesh High Court in pending cases (Writ Petition No. 567, 2003), and it remains to be seen whether the Court will invoke them when interpreting the scope of fundamental right to life and whether it encompasses a right to housing.

Notwithstanding Bangladesh's international commitments, there are no express laws in place that recognize a right to housing or establish obligations on any authority to ensure housing for the homeless or destitute. However, the Town Improvement Act 1953 empowers the City Development Authority (RAJUK) to establish re-housing initiatives for displaced individuals, and in particular to offer residences and commercial spaces to those from lower-income and working-class backgrounds impacted by improvement projects. It also empowers RAJUK to compensate individuals for losses incurred as a result of the implementation of its provisions (ss. 3, 4, 42, & 174), and to improve any area by creating new housing, water supply, drainage systems or other amenities for public benefit, if they notice that buildings in an area are not suitable for living or pose health risks (s. 38).

While limited, there are some safeguards against eviction for those living in slums and informal settlements on government land. Prior written notice of 30 days must be given for any eviction pursuant to the Government and Local Authority Lands and Buildings (Recovery of Possession Order) Ordinance 1970, a pre-constitutional law. The relevant executive authority (the district Deputy Commissioner) is required to conduct a prior inquiry and may only issue an eviction notice on being satisfied following such an inquiry (para. 5).

The country's current legal framework also notably fails to recognize climate-induced migration in Korail and other urban slums across Bangladesh. Across the country, millions have been displaced from their villages by the loss of homes or livelihoods due to flooding and erosion. In 2019 alone, more than 4 million people were displaced by catastrophically intense cyclones (International Displacement Monitoring Centre, 2019). As Sinthia (2020) highlights, legal frameworks should consider environmental degradation and climate migration. This is particularly important for ensuring legal protections for those who move to urban slums like Korail due to the impacts of climate change.

In contrast to the law, policy on housing has evolved incrementally over the past 30 years. The first National Housing Policy, adopted in 1993, recognized the need for government involvement in inclusive city-making with regards to housing for the urban poor (Ministry of Housing and Public Works, 1993). The more recent National Housing Policy 2016, which came into effect in 2017, expressly recognizes the need for informal settlements to be upgraded. It proposes "incremental construction/transformation and gradual up-gradation of all prevailing slums towards progressive improvement of infrastructure" (National Housing Authority, 2016, para. 4.7.4).

The 2016 Housing Policy was adopted to address the challenges stemming from rural-to-urban migration, including, among others, increased slum growth, and housing shortages. This framework necessitates a shift in societal perceptions of slum residents, adherence to UN settlement guidelines, and the execution of rehabilitation programs through government efforts. Key components of this policy involve local authorities creating detailed resettlement plans for slum dwellers, supporting gradual improvements in existing slum areas, exploring funding options for housing projects, and offering social housing for vulnerable groups such as women-led households, elderly citizens and the poor. The Policy commits to inclusivity and social welfare by emphasizing targeted programs to address the housing needs of "distressed women" (paras. 4.10.1–4.10.3), along with provisions for widows, unmarried women, female-headed households and individuals with disabilities facing poverty.

The Policy (2016) also aims to strengthen housing initiatives through evaluation and revision of urban planning and building regulations, enacting new laws as necessary. It underscores the need for government oversight of developer activities in the land and construction sectors, subjecting them to regulatory frameworks. Moreover, it suggests potential amendments to land reform legislation to streamline the rehabilitation of disaster-affected and displaced individuals while upholding land users' rights. Most critically, the Policy prioritizes housing provision for low-income groups, incorporating strategies for cost recovery and income generation within housing schemes. Acting as a facilitator and overseer, the government is tasked with ensuring that private sector entities adhere to prescribed standards. Furthermore, the Policy advocates for decentralized housing projects, with client involvement in planning, execution and resource mobilization across rural and urban settings (paras. 4.11.3, 4.11.6, 4.11.11, 4.11.14, 4.11.17).

In recent years, some significant housing schemes have been initiated for low-income communities, including in municipal areas. High level pledges had been made to ensure a home for every citizen (Dhaka Tribune, 2023) and rehabilitation in cases of eviction. These pronouncements, combined with the rollout of housing programs such as Asrayon — a large-scale rehabilitation project for homeless and displaced people started in 1997 — created opportunities for expanding advocacy by slum dwellers to press for legal recognition of their rights to housing. However, such housing programs are largely in rural areas rather than metropolitan areas where real estate values are at a premium. Bhashantek, which is further discussed below, is a rare exception. This in itself, combined with the lack of legal and policy reforms, is a strong indicator of the countervailing power of developers and other vested interest groups. As identified in a study by the Research Initiatives Bangladesh (2007), one resettlement program faced several challenges, including failure to allocate land, unauthorised construction on the land by external parties, and conflicts among residents, with political divisions hindering development efforts.

The private housing market largely determines the supply of housing in Bangladesh's urban areas. In general, developers ignore low-income communities (and have no legal requirement to address their needs) and instead focus on the supply of residential and commercial buildings for middle- and high-income groups. Impoverished urban communities — many of which are climate-impacted — are compelled therefore to construct housing on unused public lands or in marginal and hazardous areas, such as beside railway lines or close to landfills and water bodies. A recent study by Rahman et al. (2022) examined the key drivers of climate mobility into Bangladesh's urban slums. It found that 86 percent of participants cited food insecurity and 12 percent cited riverbank erosions from climate processes, as well as 40 percent cited a climate event (i.e., flood) as a reason for migrating into an urban slum in Rajshahi City. Other reasons that were cited included a lack of alternative livelihood and the aspiration to improve their living standards.

City corporations and other urban authorities do not generally provide essential services in these informal settlements. However, the Dhaka Water Supply and Sewage Authority (WASA) — after collaboration with, or advocacy by, NGOs — had committed to providing legal pipeline water services to all of Dhaka's slums by 2015. It has done so in many, but not yet in all.

In this context of expanding housing injustice, PIL has been effective in stalling evictions in urbanizing Bangladesh. In the absence of clearly defined housing rights, communities facing eviction have sought legal protections by invoking the constitutionally guaranteed right to life and arguing that it includes the right to shelter. In public interest cases challenging forced evictions, they have also relied on the fundamental right to be treated in accordance with the law, to argue that their rights to natural justice have been denied, as they were given no opportunity of a hearing before having their homes demolished and their lives uprooted. In doing so, they have relied on the denial of procedural safeguards in the 1970 Ordinance, asserting that the relevant authorities failed to issue written notices, making instead only public announcements in their locality. They also assert that community leaders and organizers faced intimidation and threats or arrest, before police and bulldozers were deployed to clear the area.

In reported judgments, the Supreme Court recognized slum dwellers as citizens on whom many essential services depend (*Kalam and others v.*

Bangladesh and others, 2001, para. 6), and proposed alternative approaches to immediate eviction, highlighting measures for prior "rehabilitation" (*Ain O Salish Kendra (ASK) v. Government of Bangladesh and others*, 1999, para. 10). In the landmark judgment of *ASK v. Bangladesh* delivered in 1999, the Court suggested that this would mean an alternative to being located within the area on which the slum stood,

> for a peaceful growth of City life for a country like ours *they has* [have] *to be taken away from their slums and should be rehabilitated as far as possible in the spirits of our constitutional commitments* [emphasis added] attaining democracy, socialism, realizing through democratic process a socialistic society from exploitation honoring the Rule of Law, fundamental human rights and freedom securing equality and justice.
>
> (para. 10)

In this judgment, the Court specifically directed the government to rehabilitate slum dwellers and provide them with a reasonable timeframe prior to any eviction proceedings. It also set out guidelines for phased rehabilitation, emphasizing that a comprehensive master plan or rehabilitation scheme should be developed (Byrne & Hossain, 2009). This scheme would allow slum dwellers to choose either to return to their villages or remain in the city.

In later rulings, the Court continued to underscore the critical importance of providing alternative rehabilitation for slum dwellers as equal citizens (*Modhumala v. Director, Housing and Building Research Institute*, 2001; *Aleya Begum and others v. Bangladesh*, 2001; *BLAST v. Bangladesh and others*, 2008). Notably, in *Modhumala v. Director* (2001), the Court endorsed the guidelines given for phased rehabilitation in the 1999 judgment passed in *ASK v. Bangladesh* (mentioned above). It also emphasized the need to prioritize rehabilitation of slum dwellers, and to create a dedicated unit within the relevant ministry for acknowledging the substantial contributions of slum dwellers to urban development and city amenities. In 2001, in *Aleya Begum and others v. Bangladesh*, the Court asserted that justice necessitates that slum dwellers should not be evicted without ensuring appropriate alternative arrangements for their rehabilitation.

Despite some progressive judgments recognizing limited rights for slum dwellers, the current legal framework for protection against forced eviction and the right to shelter is insufficient — particularly in addressing the pressing reality of climate-induced migration in Korail and other urban slums. As the following case studies illustrate, this inadequacy arises in part from competing interests of the government and the private sector.

Korail community goes to court

The largest informal settlement in Bangladesh — Korail, in Dhaka — offers living testimony to how anti-eviction advocacy is part and parcel of broader struggles for housing justice in the country. Korail's roughly 200,000 residents are almost all migrants from rural areas (Huq & Shafique, 2023). They face critical challenges regarding access to land, housing, infrastructure and amenities, along with worsening environmental degradation within the slum and significant flood risk and heat stress due to inadequate implementation of government policies and poor management of available resources (Sinthia, 2020).

Over the years, Korail's residents have negotiated or secured access to limited services such as water and waste collection from relevant government agencies, through sustained advocacy in collaboration with NGOs. However, there have been few improvements to the housing structures and the area has faced multiple eviction threats. Part of the settlement had been slated for a high tech park development.

The Korail case illustrates the experience of settlement dwellers, involving a cycle of evictions, anti-eviction organizing, ongoing housing struggles and the importance of their engaging with legal arguments to frame their demands. Supported by several NGOs, Korail's residents first went to court in 2008, when the government issued a notice upon several of them, ordering the immediate removal of all structures. Informed by residents about the threatened eviction, ASK, BLAST and CUP filed a writ petition in the public interest. In response, the High Court ordered the eviction to be halted.

In 2012, Korail residents again faced eviction. Even though protective stay orders were in place, a separate High Court bench, referencing media reports about alleged encroachments into Gulshan Lake (adjoining Korail), issued a *suo motu* order for evicting people living "beside the lake", framing this as an environmental issue. Fatema, a Korail resident and activist with the settlement dwellers' organization Nagar Doridra Bostibasheer Unnoyon Shongstha (NDBUS), described how this led to homes being pulled down, including those of people who lived far inside the settlement and not beside the lake; meanwhile, none of the "premium" apartments beside the lake were touched. After lawyers from ASK and BLAST highlighted this, the Court appointed another NGO, the Bangladesh Environmental Lawyers Association, to carry out an onsite assessment. On reviewing its report, which confirmed Fatema's findings, the Court halted further evictions. Disturbingly, however, it gave no direction to compensate those whose homes had been destroyed following its earlier order.

Again, in 2013, the Korail community was compelled to return to the High Court after the land was acquired by a new entity for the purpose of developing a high tech park. ASK and five other organizations (BLAST, BRAC, CUP, DSK and Nijera Kori) filed a fresh writ petition[5] before the Court, along with five Korail residents, challenging the renewed threat of eviction without notice. The High Court this time asked the government to explain why steps should not be taken for alternative resettlement of the residents. The petitioner organizations drew the Court's attention to a feasibility study for the high tech park, which set out options for the population in the event of eviction, ranging from cash payments to providing alternative land for community resettlement. The Court directed the government to set up a commission to examine the situation of the slum dwellers and make recommendations for alternative resettlement. The commission, however, included no independent housing experts; it also conducted its site visit in a single day, with no consultations held with local residents (Writ Petition No. 3814, 2012).

In the meantime, the high-tech park owners that had acquired the land (Mahmud, 2017) sought to explore an out-of-court settlement of the case, but with the petitioners rather than residents. The petitioners made clear that they could not make decisions on behalf of the community and the issue remained unresolved at the time of writing.

As this case illustrates, the rights of Korail residents to housing and the possibilities of developing inclusive solutions have been subordinated to powerful commercial interests. Needed reforms to the legal framework have been inhibited by the interests of the private sector, which has resisted taking any responsibility for providing social housing. Sinthia (2020) analyses how construction companies prioritize investments for middle-income and affluent communities, offering little to no support for affordable housing for those living in urban slums like Korail. In the face of inadequate government support and neglect by the private sector, NGOs have played a crucial role in providing health, education and essential services in these areas, while framing, in however limited a fashion, demands around housing rights. Rahman et al. (2022) also emphasize the crucial role of NGOs in addressing the plight of urban slum residents migrating from climate-displaced settings, highlighting their need for safe drinking water, toilet facilities and shelter. They note that while NGOs play a limited role in improving access to these essentials, their willingness to act is a key factor.

Existing legal frameworks that fail to address the state's obligation to extend rights and protection to those displaced by climate change in Korail and other urban slums of Dhaka stem not only from a lack of coordination between policymakers and NGO management but also from increasing political pressures, public sentiments and perceptions of climate migrants within Bangladesh. A survey conducted by Castellano et al. (2021) revealed significantly lower public support for assisting climate migrants in Korail than other categories of migrants. The authors attribute this to several factors, including polarizing opinions on the impacts of climate change, a belief that the Global North should be responsible for assisting climate migrants, a perceived economic threat from climate migrants in urban areas, and increasing distrust of NGOs, especially those funded by foreign organizations.

Absent express recognition of the right to shelter, political commitments and programs have had more influence than legislation in shaping actions to address the needs of climate migrants residing in Korail and other urban slums. To strengthen legal frameworks for those displaced by climate change in urban shelters, a rights-based approach must be advocated more effectively. This approach will need to identify the duties of public authorities for improving living conditions and ensuring that housing is recognized as a constitutional right for individuals displaced by climate change.

Bhashantek rehabilitation project

In the early 1970s, the Bhashantek *bosti* was established on the outskirts of what would grow into the megacity of Dhaka.[6] By 2014, it had almost 20,000 residents.[7] Over the years, the residents of Bhashantek resisted repeated efforts at eviction, and received promises of rehabilitation and alternative housing. In 1998, following an attempted eviction successfully resisted by the community, the government initiated a flagship low-cost housing project expressly for "rehabilitation of slum dwellers and low-income groups".[8] However, many residents, including those who had moved there in the 1970s and their descendants, have not been rehabilitated to this day due to bureaucratic complications, as discussed below.

In the mid-1990s, the Ministry of Housing and Public Works allocated the land on which Bhashantek was located (Section 17, Mirpur) to the Bangladesh Handloom Board[9] for Sari Village, a project for artisan weavers of traditional *benaroshi* silk sarees. After acquiring the *bosti* land for this project, the Handloom Board began eviction efforts in 1997 to clear the area. The *bosti* dwellers held immediate protests, pointing out that they had been settled in that area by the government led by Prime Minister Sheikh Mujibur Rahman in the early 1970s. In a highly unusual step, the housing minister resigned, and the prime minister declared that the slum dwellers would remain until they could be rehabilitated (The Daily Ittefaq, 1997; Daily Janakantha, 1997; Hasan, 1997), and within a year, in 1998, the Ministry of Land launched a project titled "Rehabilitation for slum dwellers and low-income groups in Dhaka".[10] It identified and acquired a site close to the *bosti*, in Mirpur Section 15, for the purpose of rehabilitation, and marked this as a flagship public–private partnership.

The project languished for some years while private parties litigated over issuance of the tender for construction. Once this was resolved, the Ministry of Land awarded a contract for construction of a total of 111 buildings, including 54 A-type buildings with 7,776 flats for "slum dwellers" and 57 B-type buildings with 5,472 flats for "low-income groups".

Notably, it extended the category of priority beneficiaries of this scheme beyond the initial group of slum dwellers to "low-income groups including 3rd and 4th class government employees". This appeared to have been done through negotiation with the private partner, and as a precondition for their investment (Writ Petition No. 567, 2003). At one stage, in 1999, the Housing and Settlement Authority conducted a survey in the *bosti* enlisting over 3,000 slum dwellers for potential resettlement in the flats. In 2004, however, following media reports about the company's arbitrary distribution of application forms for the sale of flats on the private market, the contract was revoked in 2010.

The Bhashantek Rehabilitation Project (BRP) progressed fitfully for several years (until it ground to a halt). Since the flats were not ready, the slum dwellers remained in the *bosti* area, and the Sari Village Project in turn remained at a standstill. In 2002, at an inter-ministerial meeting, the government took a decision to evict the slum dwellers. The meeting minutes noted that the eviction could be conducted by "creating terror", "picking people up"[11] and "disconnecting utility services" (Writ Petition No. 567, 2003).[12]

On learning of this decision, several *bosti* residents immediately filed a writ. The High Court dismissed this initial petition, noting that the residents were "illegal occupants" and directed the authorities to issue written notices of eviction after conducting a local inquiry (pursuant to the 1970 Ordinance). In 2003, three slum dwellers filed another petition in the public interest, challenging forced eviction without service of notice, not only on their own behalf but for an estimated 3,260 families, roughly 12,000 residents, of the *bosti*. [13] This time the High Court admitted the petition, halting the threatened eviction. Although the petitioners in the writ had received no written notice from any authority, the government's lawyers had argued before the Court that extensive litigation over two decades should be sufficient notice for slum residents. As noted above, the law requires a written notice to be issued following a detailed inquiry held at least 30 days prior to eviction (which may be reduced to seven days in public interest).

As of the time of writing, the BRP remains halted, with only 18 buildings — six for settlement dwellers and 12 for low-income groups — constructed.[14] Much of the site remains vacant, dotted with a mosque, a school and a graveyard, along with pillars or foundations of partially built structures. The area has poor sanitation and is scattered with foul-smelling rubbish (Writ Petition No. 567, 2003). Notably, there has been no development progress since at least 2016, although a BRP office is located there with a project officer in daily attendance.

Some *bosti* dwellers flagged that the payment structure for securing a flat was prohibitive for many of them. It was initially BDT55,000 for a 215-square-foot flat valued at BDT200,000, in addition to the fee for buying application forms which was later increased to BDT70,000. A number of slum dwellers made applications requesting the Ministry to allot flats at the price fixed earlier and appealed to the prime minister to resume the BRP and allot them flats (Writ Petition No. 567, 2003).

The BRP Implementation Action Association, which includes remaining residents of the *bosti*, continues today to advocate for full implementation of the Project and resettlement in the flats. However, they remain in limbo, facing ongoing threats of eviction without rehabilitation and the lack of progress on building construction: only one of the three writ petitioners in the PIL secured a flat.

In Mirpur, the two rehabilitation projects (the BRP for slumdwellers, and Sari Village, for artisans), if completed, will have very different potential impacts on the affected communities. The *bosti* dwellers, already marginalized, face a dire situation pending relocation by the Ministry of Land to section 15 (the BRP). The sari weavers' project, while aiming to improve living and working conditions for artisans, places slum dwellers at risk of losing their shelter if implemented without coordination with the BRP. While they also need state support, the artisans are not at risk of losing their homes and livelihoods as the slum dwellers are. This situation has arisen from the lack of coordination between relevant public authorities, exacerbated by the lack of participation and voice of affected communities, and the absence of democratic accountability.

Mobilizing to resist displacement in Kallyanpur

The case of Kallyanpur, another long established *bosti* in Dhaka, illustrates both the power of community-led organization and mobilization, and the critical role that civil society organizations have played in strengthening communities' ability to resist displacement.

The informal settlement of Kallyanpur expanded after the 1988 floods, and several eviction attempts have been made since then. Over the years, residents have worked closely with Dushtha Shasthya Kendra — an NGO that provides development services for informal settlement dwellers, particularly poor women — in resisting eviction (DSK project manager, personal communication, 16 September 2023). DSK has worked to support community organizing in its service areas, first working on water and sewerage projects with World Bank support, and later working with the international NGO Water Aid to construct drains, footpaths, sanitation facilities and water points, and assist the local community in creating its own resource centre.

When an eviction was threatened in Kallyanpur in 2003, local residents successfully filed a petition in the High Court, halting the eviction. DSK had directed Kallyanpur dwellers to secure pro bono legal services from ASK; it also collaborated with Coalition for the Urban Poor to mobilize the dwellers. When another eviction was attempted in 2016, residents mobilized, using their collective and physical presence to prevent their removal. As DSK's project manager recalled in his interview, "slum dwellers lay down in front of the bulldozer to prevent eviction… They also created a human chain at the time" (personal communication, n.d.).

DSK has adopted an expansive understanding of its role in informal settlements. As its project manager explained,

> many NGOs think on the basis of their projects, why should I discuss housing when I have come to work on water and sewage facilities? However, we believe housing is a fundamental human right and, in this situation, we must stand by their side.
>
> (personal communication, 16 September 2023)

Advocating for informal settlement dwellers during evictions required addressing complex situations and feelings of fear, helplessness and panic. For example, to counter predatory local leaders who were extorting money from communities in the name of fighting court cases on their behalf, DSK provided accurate information to allay community fears and confusion, clarifying that ASK's legal team were providing pro bono services. Providing residents with both confidence and information, it helped informal settlement dwellers to mobilize and advocate for themselves with their representatives in local government.

DSK also worked with informal settlement dwellers in participatory data collection for use in advocacy in court and policy engagement. Dweller-generated accurate data on settlement conditions helped in pushing back against unfounded claims in the public sphere. For example, during one of the hearings in 2003, there were claims from the government that the population in the Kallyanpur slum was much lower than claimed by the petitioners. Afterwards, to counter claims that the population was too small to warrant court protection, DSK and Kallyanpur community members who had been mobilized by CUP ran a survey that identified at least 2,600 households in the settlement. Community leaders went door-to-door and spoke to residents about their basic information, employment and length of stay in the settlement. DSK later verified the survey.

The residents of Kallyanpur are not the only ones to have pursued collective organization to resist evictions. In Korail too, during the 2012 eviction described above, slum dwellers at one point declared a day-long strike, with vegetable sellers, drivers, garments workers, rickshaw pullers, domestic workers and others withholding their labour (Hackenbroch & Hossain, 2012). As a result, many houses in surrounding affluent neighbourhoods reportedly did not have cooked food that day, there were few rickshaws for transport and garment production shut down. Although the strike did not halt the eviction, it made visible the reality that poor people run much of the city. Strikes also draw painful attention to informal settlement dwellers' plight compared to those in more affluent parts of the city.

NGO contributions to settlement advocacy, support and survival

Beyond litigation, NGOs have been instrumental in working to empower informal settlements and their residents, working with public authorities on service provision, advocating for housing rights, helping communities organize and advocate for themselves, and gain voice in decision-making processes that affect them.

CUP, a broad network, has played a prominent role, including in supporting residents in Korail, Kallyanpur and Bhashantek. CUP's efforts involve empowering settlement dwellers to foster community unity. As Executive Director Rebeka Sanyat explains, "slum dwellers as petitioners are often under threat of coercion or made to withdraw their cases through intimidation tactics. To prevent this, we engage in organizing the communities" (personal communication, July 11, 2024).

CUP also conducts research and helps communities seek legal recourse through referrals for legal advice and assistance. It collaborates closely with community-based organizations (CBOs) that are directly engaged in organizing among slum residents, including by setting up decision-making processes, and disseminating information. Such CBOs include the slum dwellers' organization NDBUS, Nogor Bostibashir Unnoyon Shongstha, and Bostibashir Odhikar Shurokkha Committee, whose representatives are involved in community engagement. In some earlier instances, CUP also worked with the NGOs Activity for Reformation of Basic Needs and Proshika in educating community members on land rights, which led to clarification of land ownership in some instances. CUP has held stakeholder consultations with its members, including BRAC, ASK, and others, and engaged closely with relevant ministries and authorities. It also has held public and media campaigns to highlight threats of eviction, coordinated emergency responses and supported sustained advocacy for legal and policy reforms.

NGOs have also helped facilitate and strengthen support and survival networks within the settlements. Many NGOs provide education, health, sanitation and other services to settlement areas across Dhaka and elsewhere. These services are often funded through grants, with prior approval of government authorities. NGOs and networks frequently collaborate with city corporations and municipalities for provision of essential services in slums. However, they have faced challenges building meaningful partnerships with these entities or with RAJUK and the Real Estate and Housing Association of Bangladesh (REHAB) on housing rights solutions.[15]

CUP was also involved in developing the city's Detailed Area Plan in 2016, which contributed to the provision of housing, growth centres, shops and income sources for 40,000 families. However, the organizations involved raised concerns regarding transparency and participation in decision-making due to their exclusion from the process of preparing the latest detailed area plan.

CUP has also advocated with government authorities for housing solutions and climate justice for the urban poor. However, while the city corporations have provided essential services in informal settlements, they have not yet secured or disbursed climate funds for climate refugees who make up the bulk of these communities (R. Sunyat, personal communication, 11 July 2024).

Focusing on legal rights, BLAST has organized legal empowerment programs in many of these communities, with paralegals engaging in community education with women and men, informing them on their legal rights, remedies and available services, particularly regarding issues that affect their everyday lives (such as their rights at work, or protection against domestic violence). As well as building legal knowledge, these initiatives have enabled members of the community, particularly young people, to build their communication skills, confidence and resilience. For example, through a community hub established by BLAST, young residents of Korail organized street theatre and karate clubs, and trained as community paramedics and paralegals, providing services otherwise absent within the area and building linkages to public bodies such as the local law enforcement agencies, health clinics or marriage and divorce registration offices.

Alongside other housing advocates, NGOs have also formed coalitions to push for wider systemic change, offering a seat at the table for residents to proactively advocate for their rights. They have created participatory spaces where settlement dwellers can present their concerns to urban and national authorities. Such efforts have mainstreamed the notion of "no eviction without resettlement" and created a foundation for government efforts to provide apartment housing for urban low-income dwellers. For instance, DSK has worked with other NGOs to develop common platforms and a shared vision, aiming to move beyond issue-specific engagement to build a broader consensus around housing rights, and to engage public authorities. It has organized conferences with settlement dwellers and facilitated their access to organizations such as ASK, BLAST and CUP. As DSK's representative reflected on mobilizing settlement dwellers:

> Because of these meetings, slum dwellers understood that the civil society organizations we have in our country are there beside them. The slum dwellers get a lot of courage from this. We are doing this work with all the NGOs that were working at the time. Even if something happens now in that slum, we all sit together, have meetings, and decide how we will proceed to address it. We work according to that decision.
>
> (A. C. Das, personal communication, September 16, 2023)

BLAST has also undertaken efforts to refine and focus its advocacy on housing rights beyond the courts by collaborating with experts from other disciplines. Together with an informal housing rights platform, Nyajjo Abashon Moncho (Just Housing Platform), it convened its in-house lawyers alongside academics to examine the scope for ensuring legal protection for slum and settlement dwellers. These discussions generated ideas for developing law reform proposals, incorporating duties on developers to build social housing alongside their "premium" projects, ensuring *in situ* development of slums, or allocating alternative land for resettlement initiatives. To make relevant data more easily and publicly accessible, BLAST has documented and archived pending and disposed PILs on forced evictions in an online data base and website[16] and has used right-to-information requests to glean information on the status of slum rehabilitation initiatives and policy commitments, with the results supporting arguments in strategic litigation cases discussed above.

Earlier and long-running efforts at advocacy for legal reform were undertaken by Ain O Salish Kendra, which worked closely with urban planning experts at the Centre for Urban Studies.[17]

Conclusion

In the absence of any legal recognition of a right to housing, informal settlement dwellers face severe housing and climate injustices in Bangladesh. Although judicial interventions and community organizing have been effective in providing emergency protection and may seed a broader urban housing and climate justice movement, they need to be bolstered. Direct action and engagement with city authorities and political actors, ensuring the participation of affected communities and addressing the intersection of climate and housing justice are all essential. To that end, we offer seven insights for advancing housing and climate justice movements in Bangladesh.

First, impelled by market forces, and with no countervailing legal duties, private developers do not invest in low-income housing. Housing rights advocacy will need to focus on strengthening private sector obligations to increase housing for the poor (workers in particular). Advocates will need to develop inclusive policies and programs that can be incorporated into legally binding instruments. It is critical for the private and public sectors to collaborate with civil society in creating community-based platforms for housing development projects. The private sector should also offer low-interest loans or micro-credit for housing for the urban poor to increase affordability. Furthermore, the private sector should provide climate-resilient housing with consideration for low-cost and locally sourced building materials and labour.

Second, the lack of effective communication and coordination among rights advocates, development organizations and affected communities impedes the progress of anti-eviction advocacy in Bangladesh and the development of long-term housing solutions. There is a need for more easily accessible material on housing rights struggles to foster broader conversations and develop response strategies. Moreover, by creating or collaborating with neighbourhood councils, local governments can ensure participatory planning and decision-making processes in urban governance. Governments should also partner with NGOs and advocates to oversee the implementation of court directives related to slum areas.

Third, to increase the climate resilience of informal settlements, a survey is needed to identify climate impacts among the urban poor (both migrants and long-term dwellers). There is also a need to ensure transparency in climate change funding; advocate for greater funding from developed countries for climate-impacted communities through housing and climate justice organizations; and address the issue of compensation not reaching informal settlement dwellers but instead benefiting landowners. Local governments also need to identify and support climate-impacted slum dwellers through specific projects.

As climate injustices deepen, with more climate-impacted migrants moving to Bangladeshi cities and existing residents facing urban climate impacts such as excessive flooding and heat waves, housing rights and climate justice advocates and community groups will need overlapping strategies. Research has shown that Bangladesh's national climate adaptation policies contain equitable and inclusionary approaches for housing urban informal settlement dwellers that are ignored in urban plans (Huq & Shafique, 2023). Settlement upgrading can connect effectively with urban climate adaptation and resilience, aligning national proposals with local plans. For instance, urban authorities can support green infrastructures developed by communities like Korail as cost-effective adaptation solutions for urban climate challenges (Huq, 2024). Bridging national and urban divides in policy formulation and implementation can be a generative arena for advocates, NGOs and community partners. Civil society organizations can play a pivotal role by investing in and collaborating with government agencies and the private sector to ensure housing projects for poor and marginalized communities. They can further strengthen legal empowerment initiatives for informal settlement residents, ensuring their participation in decision-making processes and advocating multidisciplinary approaches for comprehensive housing solutions.

Fourth, comprehensive legal and policy reforms are crucial for the government to enhance urban land allocation and ensure equitable housing solutions. These would include:

- Establishing a land ceiling system to limit the size of land parcels in urban areas, and reforming outdated, discriminatory land laws to strengthen fair land distribution and address allocation challenges faced by the urban poor
- Ensuring transport equity for informal settlement residents, prioritizing access to high-speed rail networks
- Integrating environmental and climate justice considerations into urban development plans, emphasizing the needs of the urban poor and necessitating legislation with a clear definition of slums or settlements for better planning and resource allocation
- Introducing social housing legislation aligned with the National Housing Policy that requires public and private entities to allocate 20 percent of flats to low-income individuals, creating a legal framework for social housing construction
- Amending the Local Government Act of 2009 to establish housing provisions for low-income populations as a core local government responsibility
- Making government lands accessible to developers at reduced costs, incentivizing affordable housing unit construction for marginalized communities
- Ensuring the National Housing Authority remains focused on improving housing conditions for the urban poor

Fifth, it is essential for government programs to strategically identify and utilize lands owned by the government within and near Dhaka to establish affordable housing schemes. These schemes could incorporate instalment-based payment options and improved funding terms to ensure financial accessibility for the urban poor. Engaging Bangladesh Bank in financing mechanisms specifically designed to support this demographic would further enhance affordability. At the same time, projects should be aligned with RAJUK's Detailed Area Plan, which designates 56 areas to accommodate low-income groups.

Sixth, the government should empower city corporations and municipalities to effectively address the housing, infrastructure and basic service needs of slum dwellers. Concurrently, the prioritization of land tenure security for residents of informal settlements could be incorporated into RAJUK's land development projects. Establishing local-level commissions is needed to develop policy recommendations related to housing and land, negotiate the approval of these recommendations and then monitor their implementation. Furthermore, there should be greater transparency regarding land owned by government entities. The challenge of identifying land ownership could be mitigated through a streamlined verification process at the district Deputy Commissioner's office.

Finally, to enhance community welfare, local and municipal governments could expand provisions for basic amenities such as clean water, sanitation and waste management. Upgrading infrastructure in informal settlements — specifically roads, drainage systems and housing — to meet safety and structural standards is crucial, particularly in areas prone to flood and fire disasters. Local governments should also support alternative and green livelihoods, such as urban agriculture and aquaculture, to provide viable economic opportunities for residents of informal settlements.

The insights from combined strategies of legal empowerment, community organizing and coalition building explored in this chapter highlight already existing convergences between housing and climate justice that could be deepened to address the structural inequalities and climate challenges facing Bangladeshi cities, and ensure inclusive development and urban planning for those living in informal settlements across the country.

Notes

1 These settlements are usually described as "bosti" in Bangla, closer to the more pejorative "slum".

2 In one case, when bulldozers were sent into Kallyanpur Bosti at the behest of the Housing Building Research Institute, even with a stay order in place, the High Court issued an injunction, which was later upheld by the Supreme Court (see the Kallyanpur case discussed below). While court orders have not often been directly flouted in this way, there have been many instances of slums or their dwellers being compelled to relocate following the outbreak of fires.

3 Arguably this has had some impact: in the Bhashantek case, the Ministry of Textiles termed slum dwellers as "unauthorized occupants" (see court records in Writ Petition No. 567 of 2003, on file with authors), while by 2024, the Bangladesh Handloom Board claimed they had rehabilitated the slum dwellers.

4 Albeit in precarious circumstances, with limited access to utilities (water, gas, electricity) or basic services (health, education, justice) and vulnerable to fires and sporadic intimidation by local *mastaans* (strongmen).

5 Available at: https://bdpil.org/2012/01/17/145/

6 The residents claimed to have been brought there in 1974–75 after being evicted from areas in central Dhaka, including Karwan Bazar and Nilkhet, to which they had migrated after losing their village homes to river erosion. See Writ Petition No. 567 of 2003 (on file with authors). See also Huq (2020).

7 The Government's Census of Slum Areas and Floating Population 2014 identified some 5,482 households and 19,446 slum dwellers in the Bhashantek Bosti, including 9,681 women or girls and 9,760 men or boys; five were identified as third gender (Sl No. 4553, p. 312).

8 In a separate project in 1976, the Ministry of Planning planned to relocate about 2,600 squatter families from slums of Bhashantek and Mirpur to Section 11 of Mirpur ("Section 11 Rehabilitation Project"). The Housing and Settlement Directorate, under the Ministry of Works, developed this project profile, with government approval obtained in 1977. In 1986, ten years after its conception, the project received financial aid from the UN Capital Development Fund and other sources. The same year, the Ministry of Works appointed CONCERN, an international NGO, to execute the project. It also prepared a policy proposal stating that only families holding CONCERN cards from 1978–1984 were prioritized for resettlement under this project. Accordingly, in 1994, CONCERN identified and issued cards to 218 families living in Bhashantek Bosti. However, this count missed many residents, excluding them from the Section 11 Rehabilitation Project. See Writ Petition No. 567 of 2003 (on file with authors).

9 Twenty-three acres were allocated in 1995, with a further 17 acres allocated in 2004. See Writ Petition No. 567 of 2003 (on file with authors).

10 *Dhaka Mohanogorir Chinnomul Bostibashi ebong Nimmobittoderke Dhakai Shorkari Jomitey Bohutol Bishishtho Bhoboney Punorbashon Prokolpo.* See Writ Petition No. 567 of 2003 (on file with authors).

11 In January 2003, some 38 slum dwellers were reportedly arrested under charges related to a criminal case. The allegations included membership in an unlawful assembly, assault on public servants in the line of duty, intentional obstruction of public servants and theft.

12 "এলাকায় ভীতি সঞ্চার এবং প্রয়োজনে ধরপাকড় করা যেতে পারে; উচ্ছেদ অভিযানের এক সপ্তাহ পূর্ব হতে উক্ত এলাকায় গ্যাস, পানি, বিদ্যু□ সরবরাহ… হ্রাস বা বন্ধ করা যেতে পারে" [*Elakai bhiti shonchar ebong proyojone dhorpakor kora jetey pare; uchhed obhijaner ek shaptaho purbo hote ukto elakai gas, pani, biddut shorborah… hrash ba bondho kora jete parey*] ["Terror may be created in the area and if necessary arrests may be made; from one week before the eviction process, the supply of gas, water and electricity to the area may be reduced or stopped".] From proceedings of inter-ministerial meeting dated 11.12.2002, in files of Writ Petition No. 567 of 2003.

13 Two of the three original petitioners, Hasina Begum and Intaj Uddin, died during the course of the hearing. In 2024, their daughters were added as parties substituting for their deceased parents, as they had been resident in the *bosti* throughout and were otherwise landless. Notably, on March 6, 2024, the hearing of the petition concluded more than 21 years after it was filed, with the judgment still pending.

14 In response to an application under the Right to Information Act 2009, seeking information on the progress of the BRP. Right-to-information applications and responses on file with BLAST.

15 See interview with Rebeka Sunyat of Centre for the Urban Poor, on file with the authors. Sanyat said, "Our aim is to provide essential services, necessitating a strong partnership with the City Corporation through regular meetings and open communication. Despite lobbying and advocacy, RAJUK disavows any association with us. REHAB is reluctant to grant access and shows no willingness to collaborate on affordable housing initiatives either. The lack of funding and support from these authorities, particularly RAJUK, poses a significant challenge. We

proposed research on informal settlements and strategies for formalization, but RAJUK indicated they are not focused on housing for the poor unless delegated by the government. City corporations said that our involvement in their housing plans is not required, as it falls outside their jurisdiction. They requested assistance in socio-economic development of slum dwellers, emphasizing that housing of slum dwellers 'is not our job'" (Personal communication, n.d.).

16 Accessible at: https://bdpil.org. BaSHA website: https://bashadotblog.wordpress.com/

17 Such as Prof. Nazrul Islam and Architect Salma Shafi.

References

Ain O Salish Kendra. (2012). *Right to shelter*. www.askbd.org/ask/wp-content/uploads/2013/12/Right-to-Shelter.pdf.

Ain O Salish Kendra (ASK) v. Government of Bangladesh and Others (1999) 19 BLD 488.

Aleya Begum and Others v. Bangladesh (2001) 53 DLR 63.

Bangladesh Bureau of Statistics. (2014). *Census of slum areas and floating population*. http://203.112.218.65:8008/WebTestApplication/userfiles/Image/Slum/FloatingPopulation2014.pdf.

Bangladesh Bureau of Statistics. (2023). *Population and housing census 2022: National report*. https://bbs.portal.gov.bd/sites/default/files/files/bbs.portal.gov.bd/page/b343a8b4_956b_45ca_872f_4cf9b2f1a6e0/2024-01-31-15-51-b53c55dd692233ae401ba013060b9cbb.pdf.

BLAST v. Bangladesh and Others (2008) 13 BLC 384.

Byrne, I., & Hossain, S. (2009). South Asia: Economic and social rights case law of Bangladesh, Nepal, Pakistan and Sri Lanka. In M. Langford (Ed.), *Social rights jurisprudence: Emerging trends in international and comparative law* (pp. 125–143). Cambridge University Press.

Castellano, R., Dolšak, N., & Prakash, A. (2021). Willingness to help climate migrants: A survey experiment in the Korail slum of Dhaka, Bangladesh. *PloS ONE*, 16(4), e0249315.

Committee on Economic, Social and Cultural Rights. (1991). General Comment No. 4: The Right to Adequate Housing, Sixth Sess, U.N. Doc. E/1992/23.

Committee on Economic, Social and Cultural Rights. (1997). General Comment No. 7: The Right to Adequate Housing, Sixteenth Sess, U.N. Doc. E/1998/22, Annex IV.

The Daily Ittefaq. (1997, February 19). Bikolpo Babostha Na Howa Porjonto Apnara Jekhane Chilen Shekhanei Thakben [You will remain where you are until alternative arrangements are made]. *The Daily Ittefaq*.

Daily Janakantha. (1997, February 18). Purto Protimontri Borkhasto [Minister of State for Works dismissed]. *Daily Janakantha*.

Dhaka Tribune. (2023, March 22). PM Hasina: Working to ensure houses for all homeless people. *Dhaka Tribune*. www.dhakatribune.com/bangladesh/307340/pm-hasina-working-to-ensure-houses-for-all.

Hackenbroch, K., & Hossain, S. (2012, May 18). The voice of Korail on inhabitants' sufferings and aspirations. *BDNews24.com*. https://bdnews24.com/opinion/comment/the-voice-of-korail-on-inhabitants%E2%80%99-sufferings-and-aspirations.

Hasan, N. (1997, February 19). Bhashantek Bostir 2 Sohosradhik Poribarer Upor Diya Jeno Proloy Bohiya Giyache [A deluge seems to have swept over 2,000 families in Bhashantek Bosti]. *The Daily Ittefaq*.

Huq, E. (2020, February 16). What really happened in Bhashantek? *The Daily Star*. www.thedailystar.net/opinion/human-rights/news/what-really-happened-bhashantek-1868377.

Huq, E. (2024). Green informalities as socially just ecological infrastructure: Enduring with dignity at the edges of resilient development in Dhaka. *International Journal of Urban and Regional Research*, 48(4), 560–583.

Huq, E., Hossain, S., & Akhter, A. (2022, February 11). *Tackling climate displacement in the city: Legal interventions to ensure life and livelihood in informal settlements.* Bangladesh Paribesh Andolon/Bangladesh Environment Network Conference: "Energy, Climate Change, and Sustainable Development", Dhaka. https://blast.org.bd/content/report/Climate-Displacement-In-The-City.pdf.

Huq, E., & Shafique, T. (2023). People move, policies don't: Discursive partition against climate-impacted dwellers in urbanizing Bangladesh. *Environment and Urbanization*, 35(1), 91–100. doi:10.1177/09562478221149863.

International Displacement Monitoring Centre. (2019). *Bangladesh: Summary of internal displacement in 2019*. https://api.internal-displacement.org/sites/default/files/inline-files/GRID-2019-Disasters-Figure-Analysis-Bangladesh.pdf.

Kalam and Others v. Bangladesh and Others (2001) 21 BLD (HCD).

Mahmud, A. H. (2017, July 18). Korail slum residents look to courts for respite. *Dhaka Tribune*. www.dhakatribune.com/bangladesh/dhaka/29960/korail-slum-residents-look-to-courts-for-respite.

Ministry of Housing and Public Works. (1993). *National housing policy*. Author.

Modhumala v. Director, Housing and Building Research Institute (2001) 53 DLR, 540.

National Housing Authority. (2016). *National housing policy*. https://nha.gov.bd/sites/default/files/files/nha.portal.gov.bd/law/76f125dc_8e5e_4095_b03d_7d9ac29f842d/National%20Housing%20Policy%202016_English%20Version.pdf.

Rahman, S. M., Mamoon, M., Islam, M. S., Hossain, S., Haque, R., & Zubair, A. B. M. (2022). Post-displacement status of climate migrants in Rajshahi City, Bangladesh. *Regional Sustainability*, 3(3), 183–187.

Research Initiatives Bangladesh. (2007, May). *Shelter & infrastructure upgrading programme at Chator Noyapara Resettlement Area (ATI)*. Gazipur.

Siddiqi, D. M. (2006). *Ain O Salish Kendra: Twenty years on the frontline, ASK 20 anniversary commemorative report*. Ain o Salish Kendra. www.askbd.org/ask/wp-content/uploads/2006/12/20_Years.pdf.

Sinthia, S. A. (2020). Analysis of urban slum: case study of Korail slum, Dhaka. *International Journal of Urban and Civil Engineering*, 14(11), 416–430.

United Nations. (1966). *International covenant on civil and political rights* (opened for signature Dec. 16, 1966, 999 U.N.T.S. 171). www.ohchr.org/en/instruments-mechanisms/instruments/international-covenant-civil-and-political-rights.

United Nations Human Rights Council. (2007, February 5). *Report of the Special Rapporteur on adequate housing as a component of the right to an adequate standard of living*. Miloon Kothari. A/HRC/4/18.

United Nations Human Rights Special Procedures. (2022). *Statement at the conclusion of the country visit to Bangladesh by the Special Rapporteur on the promotion and protection of human rights to human rights in the context of climate change, Mr. Ian Fry*. www.ohchr.org/sites/default/files/documents/issues/climatechange/2022-09-14/SR-ClimateChange-EOM-Statement-Bangladesh-20220915.pdf.

Writ Petition No. 567. (2003). https://bdpil.org/2003/01/11/37/.

Writ Petition No. 3814. (2012). https://bdpil.org/2012/01/17/145/.

Index

For Product Safety Concerns and Information please contact our EU representative GPSR@taylorandfrancis.com Taylor & Francis Verlag GmbH, Kaufingerstraße 24, 80331 München, Germany